BTEC
Level 3

edexcel
advancing learning, changing lives

PUBLIC SERVICES LEVEL 3

BTEC National

Book 2

Charlotte Baker | Debra Gray | Lizzie Toms | John Vause

A PEARSON COMPANY

Published by Pearson Education Limited, a company incorporated in England and Wales, having its registered office at Edinburgh Gate, Harlow, Essex, CM20 2JE. Registered company number: 872828

www.pearsonschoolsandfecolleges.co.uk

Edexcel is a registered trademark of Edexcel Limited

Text © Pearson Education Ltd 2010

First published 2010

13 12 11
10 9 8 7 6 5 4 3 2

British Library Cataloguing in Publication Data
A catalogue record for this book is available from the British Library.

ISBN 978 1 846907 20 3

Designed by Wooden Ark
Typeset by Tek-Art
Original illustrations © Pearson Education Limited 2010
Cover design by Visual Philosophy, created by eMC design
Front cover photo © Alamy Images: Jack Sullivan
Back cover photos (clockwise from top) © Thinkstock: Bananastock; www.imagesource.com; iStockphoto: Yin Yang;
Printed in the UK by Scotprint

Websites
The websites used in this book were correct and up to date at the time of publication. It is essential for tutors to preview each website before using it in class so as to ensure that the URL is still accurate, relevant and appropriate. We suggest that tutors bookmark useful websites and consider enabling students to access them through the school/college intranet.

Disclaimer
This material has been published on behalf of Edexcel and offers high-quality support for the delivery of Edexcel qualifications.

This does not mean that the material is essential to achieve any Edexcel qualification, nor does it mean that it is the only suitable material available to support any Edexcel qualification. Edexcel material will not be used verbatim in setting any Edexcel examination or assessment. Any resource lists produced by Edexcel shall include this and other appropriate resources.

Copies of official specifications for all Edexcel qualifications may be found on the Edexcel website: www.edexcel.com

Contents

About your **BTEC Level 3 National Public Services** book   vii

Credits

Debra Gray would like to thank the following:

From Pearson Education: Amanda Hamilton, Lewis Birchon, Kathy Peltan and Caroline Low whose editing, patience and support have been invaluable.

From Dearne Valley College: A big thank you to the entire public services team for their humour, patience and resilience in the face of the challenging FE section and having me as a boss, John Vause, Barry Pinches, Paul Meares, Charlotte Baker, Boris Lockyer, Kelly Ellery, Nick Lawton, Mick Blythe, Jean Tinnion and Debbie. Thanks also to my boss Julie – you are one in a million.

From the Services: Lance Corporal Kelly Stevens 38 Signals, South Yorkshire Police, South Yorkshire Fire and Rescue Service, South Yorkshire Ambulance Service.

My family: Ben, India, Sam and Genevieve who make every day brighter. And to Jin who started me on this path

The publisher would like to thank the following for permission to reproduce photographs:

(Key: b-bottom; c-centre; l-left; r-right; t-top)

1 Press Association Images: Bengt af Geijerstam / Scanpix. **3** Shutterstock: Monkey Business Images. **11** Press Association Images: Bengt af Geijerstam / Scanpix. **15** Pearson Education Ltd: Jules Selmes. **25** Shutterstock: Monkey Business Images. **27** Alamy Images: Gianni Muratore. **29** Thinkstock: Photodisc. **32** Rex Features: Phanie Agency. **43** Reuters: Dan Chung. **44** Stefan Hamilton. **53** PhotoDisc: Photolink / D. Falconer. **59** Alamy Images: Mark Bassett. **61** Getty Images. **63** Thinkstock: Bananastock. **69** Rex Features: Kirk O'Rourke. **90** Press Association Images: Haydn West / PA Archive. **92** PhotoDisc: Photolink / D Falconer. **95** Alamy Images: Janine Wiedel. **97** Getty Images: AFP. **99** Thinkstock: Digital Vision. **103** Getty Images: AFP. **106** Getty Images: Jeffrey Coolidge. **110** Rex Features: Sipa Press. **117** Thinkstock: Photos.com. **119** Getty Images. **121** Thinkstock: Polka Dot. **130** Illustrated London News Picture Library. **131** Getty Images. **132** Corbis: (b). www.imagesource.com: (t). **143** Thinkstock: Comstock. **145** PhotoDisc: Photolink. **147** Thinkstock: Digital Vision. **149** Rex Features: Phanie Agency. **160** Pearson Education Ltd: Gareth Boden. **169** www.imagesource.com. **171** Thinkstock: Comstock. **173** Getty Images: Stephen Marks. **175** Thinkstock: Photos.com. **184** Rex Features: Martin McCullough. **197** Thinkstock: Comstock. **199** Corbis: Toby Melville / Reuters. **201** Thinkstock: iStockphoto. **212** Press Association Images: Gareth Fuller / PA Archive. **235** Thinkstock: Comstock. **237** Rex Features. **239** Thinkstock: iStockphoto. **242** PhotoDisc. **247** Rex Features: Sipa Press. **267** Thinkstock: Polka Dot. **269** Digital Vision. **271** Thinkstock: Polka Dot. **273 PhotoDisc:** Photolink / C Sherburne. **277** PhotoDisc: Photolink / Tracy Montana. **280** Corbis: Geoff Caddick / epa. **299** Digital Vision. **301** Construction Photography: BuildPix. **307** Alamy Images: Nick Hanna. **309** Thinkstock: Bananastock. All other images © Pearson Education

Picture Research by Alison Prior

Crown Copyright data and information is reproduced under the terms of the Click-Use Licence.

Every effort has been made to contact the copyright holders of material reproduced in this book. Any omissions will be rectified in subsequent printings if notice is given to the publishers.

About the authors

Charlotte Baker has worked with the BTEC qualifications in Public Services since 2003 and has taught from academic levels 2–4. She has a degree in Social and Cultural Studies with Business Management and a PGCE. Charlotte is currently the programme tutor for the BTEC National Diploma Public Services, and has been for 3 years. She completed her MA in Education, Leadership and Management in June 2010, and has recently written a published activity for the 14–19 diplomas in public services, with a particular focus on functional skills.

Debra Gray has taught public services in the Further Education sector for 13 years. She has a degree in Criminology and masters degrees in Criminal Justice and Education Management. She has written numerous publications for both learners and tutors on public services and other issues, such as the new diplomas. Debra also served as an External Verifier for three years.

Lizzie Toms is the Principal Standards Verifier for Public and Security Services and has been a Senior Verifier since 2002. She is also a Principal Examiner and Moderator for Public Service Diplomas. Lizzie has masters degrees in both Education and Organisational Consultancy and is an experienced tutor covering levels 1 to 7. She has worked closely with the Magistrates' Courts, the Probation Service and HM Prison Service. Lizzie has also written a range of Public Services materials including BTEC publications and delivers a range of training events.

John Vause has taught public services for the past 10 years. He studied Philosophy after his career in the West Yorkshire and then the South Yorkshire Police. During this period he was involved in planning, organising and taking part in numerous outdoor activities and expeditions while training Police Cadets. He has also attended several major incidents, including multiple-vehicle road traffic collisions and fire incidents. As a detective in the Criminal Investigation Department, John investigated hundreds of crimes, including murder.

About BTEC Level 3 National Public Services

There are many different optional units in your BTEC Level 3 Public Services qualification, which you may use to focus on specific services or to build a broader programme of learning. This student book covers additional units for the Edexcel BTEC Level 3 Subsidiary Diploma, Diploma or Extended Diploma in Public Services

Written in the same accessible style with the same useful features to support you through your learning and assessment, **BTEC Level 3 National Public Services Student Book 1** (ISBN: 978 1 846907 197) covers the following units:

Unit number	Credit value	Unit name
1	10	Government, policies and the public services
2	15	Leadership and teamwork in the public services
3	15	Citizenship, diversity and the public services
4	10	Understanding discipline in the uniformed public services
5	10	Physical preparation, health and lifestyle for the public services
6	10	Fitness training and testing for the uniformed public services
7	5	International institutions and human rights
8	5	Understand the impact of war, conflict and terrorism on public services
12	10	Crime and its effects on society
13	10	Command and control in the uniformed public services
25	10	Public service data interpretation

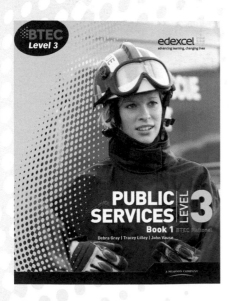

Available direct from www.pearsonfe.co.uk/btec2010 and can be ordered from all good bookshops.

About your BTEC Level 3 National Public Services books

BTEC Level 3 National Public Services will give you an insight into the different uniformed and non-uniformed public services, from fire fighters, the army and the police to mountain rescue, teaching and custodial care. Your qualification will help you to understand the importance of team work and effective communication within the public services as well as the entry requirements and working environment for the services you are most interested in.

Your BTEC Level 3 National in Public Services is a **vocational** or **work-related** qualification. This doesn't mean that it will give you all the skills you need to do a job, but it does mean that you'll have the opportunity to gain specific knowledge, understanding and skills that are relevant to your chosen subject or area of work.

What will you be doing?

The qualification is structured into **mandatory units** (ones that you must do) and your choice of **optional units**. How many units you do and which ones you cover depend on the type of qualification you are working towards.

Qualifications	Credits from mandatory units	Credits from optional units	Total credits
Edexcel BTEC Level 3 Certificate	10	20	30
Edexcel BTEC Level 3 Subsidiary Diploma	40	20	60
Edexcel BTEC Level 3 Diploma	50	70	120
Edexcel BTEC Level 3 Extended Diploma	60	120	180

How the books cover the qualifications

The table below shows how the units covered by the books in this series cover the different types of BTEC qualification.

Unit	Credit value		Cert.	Sub. Dip.	Uniformed pathway		Non-uniformed pathway	
					Dip.	Ex. Dip.	Dip.	Ex. Dip.*
1	10	Government, policies and the public services	M	M	M	M	M	M
2	15	Leadership and teamwork in the public services	O	M	M	M	M	M
3	15	Citizenship, diversity and the public services	O	M	M	M	M	M
4	10	Understanding discipline in the uniformed public services	O	O	M	M		
5	10	Physical preparation, health and lifestyle for the public services	O	O	O	O	O	O
6	10	Fitness testing and training for the uniformed public services			O	M		
7	5	International institutions and human rights	O	O	O	O	O	O
8	5	Understand the impact of war, conflict and terrorism on public services	O	O	O	O	O	O
9	10	Outdoor and adventurous expeditions	O	O	O	O	O	O
12	10	Crime and its effects on society	O	O	O	O	O	O
13	10	Command and control in the uniformed public services	O	O	O	O		
14	10	Responding to emergency service incidents			O	O		
15	10	Planning and management of major incidents	O	O	O	O	O	O
17	5	Police powers in the public services	O	O	O	O	O	O
18	5	Behaviour in public sector employment	O	O	O	O	O	O
20	10	Communication and technology in the uniformed public services			O	O		
21	10	Custodial care services			O	O	O	O
22	10	Aspects of the legal system and the law making process			O	O	O	O
24	10	Current and media affairs in public services			O	O	O	O
25	10	Public service data interpretation					M	M
34	10	Environmental policies and practices	O	O	O	O	O	O

* The Non-uniformed Extended Diploma also requires Unit 26: Enhancing public service delivery through the use of ICT, which is not covered here.

Units in yellow are covered in this book. Units in green are covered in BTEC Level 3 National Public Services Student Book 1 (ISBN: 978 1 846907 19 7)

How to use this book•

This book is designed to help you through your BTEC Level 3 National Public Services course.

It contains many features that will help you develop and apply your skills and knowledge in work-related situations and assist you in getting the most from your course.

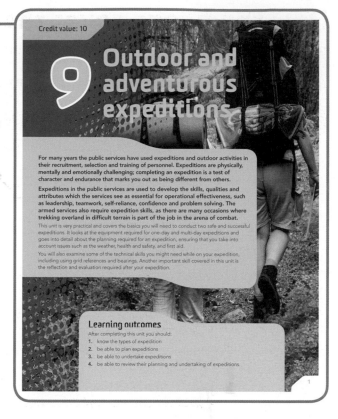

Introduction

These introductions give you a snapshot of what to expect from each unit – and what you should be aiming for by the time you finish it!

Assessment and grading criteria

This table explains what you must do to achieve each of the assessment criteria for each of the mandatory and optional units. For each assessment criterion, shown by the grade button **P1**, there is an assessment activity.

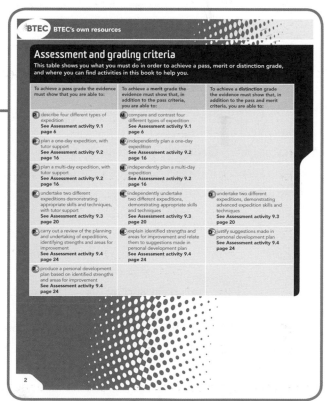

Assessment

Your tutor will set **assignments** throughout your course for you to complete. These may take a variety of forms including simulations, presentations, case studies. The important thing is that you evidence your skills and knowledge to date.

Learner experience

Stuck for ideas? Daunted by your first assignment? These learners have all been through it before…

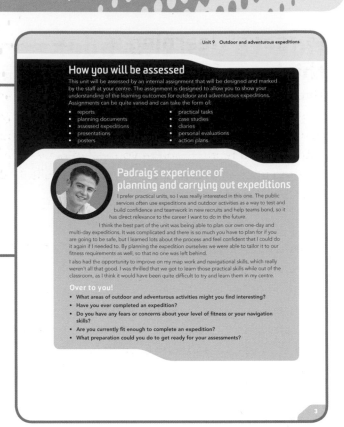

Unit 9 Outdoor and adventurous expeditions

How you will be assessed

This unit will be assessed by an internal assignment that will be designed and marked by the staff at your centre. The assignment is designed to allow you to show your understanding of the learning outcomes for outdoor and adventurous expeditions. Assignments can be quite varied and can take the form of:

- reports
- planning documents
- assessed expeditions
- presentations
- posters
- practical tasks
- case studies
- diaries
- personal evaluations
- action plans.

Padraig's experience of planning and carrying out expeditions

I prefer practical units, so I was really interested in this one. The public services often use expeditions and outdoor activities as a way to test and build confidence and teamwork in new recruits and help teams bond, so it has direct relevance to the career I want to do in the future.

I think the best part of the unit was being able to plan our own one-day and multi-day expeditions. It was complicated and there is so much you have to plan for if you are going to be safe, but I learned lots about the process and feel confident that I could do it again if I needed to. By planning the expedition ourselves we were able to tailor it to our fitness requirements as well, so that no one was left behind.

I also had the opportunity to improve on my map work and navigational skills, which really weren't all that good. I was thrilled that we got to learn those practical skills while out of the classroom, as I think it would have been quite difficult to try and learn them in my centre.

Over to you!

- What areas of outdoor and adventurous activities might you find interesting?
- Have you ever completed an expedition?
- Do you have any fears or concerns about your level of fitness or your navigation skills?
- Are you currently fit enough to complete an expedition?
- What preparation could you do to get ready for your assessments?

Activities

There are different types of activities for you to do. **Assessment activities** are suggestions for tasks that you might do as part of your assignment and will help you develop your knowledge, skills and understanding. **Grading tips** clearly explain what you need to do in order to achieve a pass, merit or distinction grade.

Assessment activity 9.1 **P1** **M1** :BTEC

Knowing about the types and descriptions of expeditions is essential before you begin the planning process for your own two expeditions. As group leader for your expeditions, it is your responsibility to ensure all your team members know about the different types of expedition so that you can make informed choices about which type you will complete.

Produce a written report which:

1 describes four different types of expedition **P1**
2 compares and contrasts four different types of expedition. **M1**

Grading tips

For **P1** you should choose four of the seven types of expedition outlined in Table 9.1 above, providing a full description and an example of each type. You can draw on your own experience or study past expeditions.

For **M1** you should look at the similarities and differences between the four types of expedition you have chosen in terms of their aims, objectives, area, duration and form.

There are also suggestions for activities that will give you an insight into the individual services, stretch your understanding and develop your skills.

Activity: Expedition food

A typical 24-hour army ration pack might contain the following items:

- corned beef hash (boil in the bag)
- chicken and pasta (boil in the bag)
- vegetable stock drink mix, 1 x sachet
- cheese, processed, or meat paté
- chocolate pudding (instant)
- an oatmeal block
- chocolate bars or a bar of Kendal Mint Cake
- biscuits, brown (malted and hard, pack of six)
- biscuits, fruit-filled (malted, hard, garibaldi-like, pack of six)
- sweets, boiled, 1 pack assorted flavours
- instant soup (varying flavours), 2 x sachets
- tea, instant, white, 4 x sachets
- coffee, instant, 2 x 5 grams sachets
- drinking chocolate mix, 1 sachet
- sugar, quick dissolving, 8 x 10 grams sachets
- beverage whitener (non-dairy creamer), 2 x sachets
- fruit drink mix, either orange or lemon (enough for 1 litre of drink)
- gum, chewing, 5 sticks
- sweets, boiled, 1 pack assorted flavours
- tissues, paper (individual pack)
- waterproof matches (10) and striker (1)
- water purification tablets (6).

1 Why do you think so much food is needed for a soldier in a 24-hour period?
2 Would you be happy to eat this menu?
3 What kinds of things would improve the menu for you?

Personal, learning and thinking skills

Throughout your BTEC Level 3 National Public Services course there are lots of opportunities to develop your personal, learning and thinking skills. These will help you work in a team, manage yourself effectively and develop your all-important interpersonal skills. Look out for these as you progress.

PLTS

This activity will help you develop your skills as an **independent enquirer**.

Functional skills

It's important that you have good English, Mathematics and ICT skills – they're important for communicating information effectively and accurately, which could be the difference between life and death. Use these activities to help develop and stretch your skills.

Functional skills

Researching the types of expedition will help you to develop your functional skills in **ICT**.

Key terms

Technical words and phrases are easy to spot. The terms and definitions are also in the glossary at the back of the book.

Key terms

Aims – why you are going on the expedition.
Objectives – what you are hoping to get out of the expedition by the end.

WorkSpace

WorkSpace provides snapshots of life in the public services and shows you how the knowledge and skills you are developing through your course can be applied in your future career.

WorkSpace **Geoff**
Walking Group Leader

I work as a Walking Group Leader at an outdoor residential centre in the Lake District. The centre does all kinds of outdoor activities, such as canoeing, kayaking, abseiling, caving and hiking. We see many different groups from small schoolchildren to pensioners and everything in between, so we need to be able to adjust what we do to match the groups we are responsible for.

It's my job to ensure that walking groups are properly prepared, well equipped and safe on their journey. I do this by spending the day before they set off on an expedition with the group going through all the basics and ensuring everyone has everything they need and is comfortable with the route.

A typical day

A typical day out on the hills involves an early start. We aim to get walking straight after breakfast because if the route is a long one we may need the full day to complete it. Once we are away from the centre and into the countryside, I nominate one person to navigate for each of the legs of the journey. Then I'll monitor them and check their understanding of the map or correct their compass work if they are not doing it right. It doesn't help people to learn if I always do the navigating – they need to learn and practise those skills themselves.

I'm responsible for safety throughout the trip and the group always gets a health and safety briefing before we set off, which I reinforce all the way around the route if any hazards crop up.

The best thing about the job

It's great to go out into the countryside several times a week. I'm not one to sit in an office, so being able to teach people practical skills in the fantastic Cumbrian countryside is the perfect job for me.

Think about it!

- What topics have you covered in this unit that might give you the background to be a good walking group leader?
- What knowledge and skills do you think you need to develop further if you want to be a walking group leader or outdoor specialist in the future?

25

Just checking

When you see this sort of activity, take stock! These quick activities and questions are there to check your knowledge. You can use them to see how much progress you've made and to identify any areas where you need to refresh your knowledge.

Edexcel's assignment tips

At the end of each unit, you'll find hints and tips to help you get the best mark you can, such as the best websites to go to, checklists to help you remember processes and useful reminders to avoid common mistakes. You might want to read this information before starting your assignment…

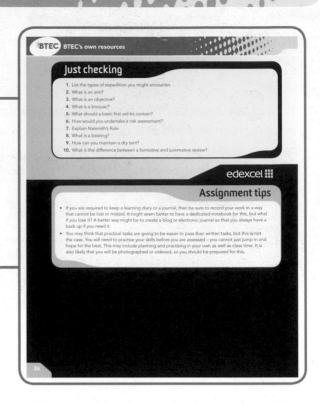

Link

In the margin, alongside a topic in the main text, you will find cross references that guide you to other parts of the book where the topic is covered in more detail or where you will be able to find relevant information.

Don't miss out on these resources to help you!

Link

You can see the response times for these incidents in Table 14.4 on page 34.

Have you read your **BTEC Level 3 National Study Skills Guide?** It's full of advice on study skills, putting your assignments together and making the most of being a BTEC Public Services student.

Your book is just part of the exciting resources from Edexcel to help you succeed in your BTEC course.
Visit

- www.edexcel.com/BTEC or
- www.pearsonfe.co.uk/BTEC 2010

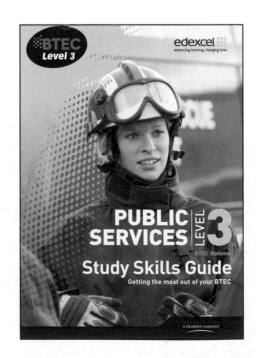

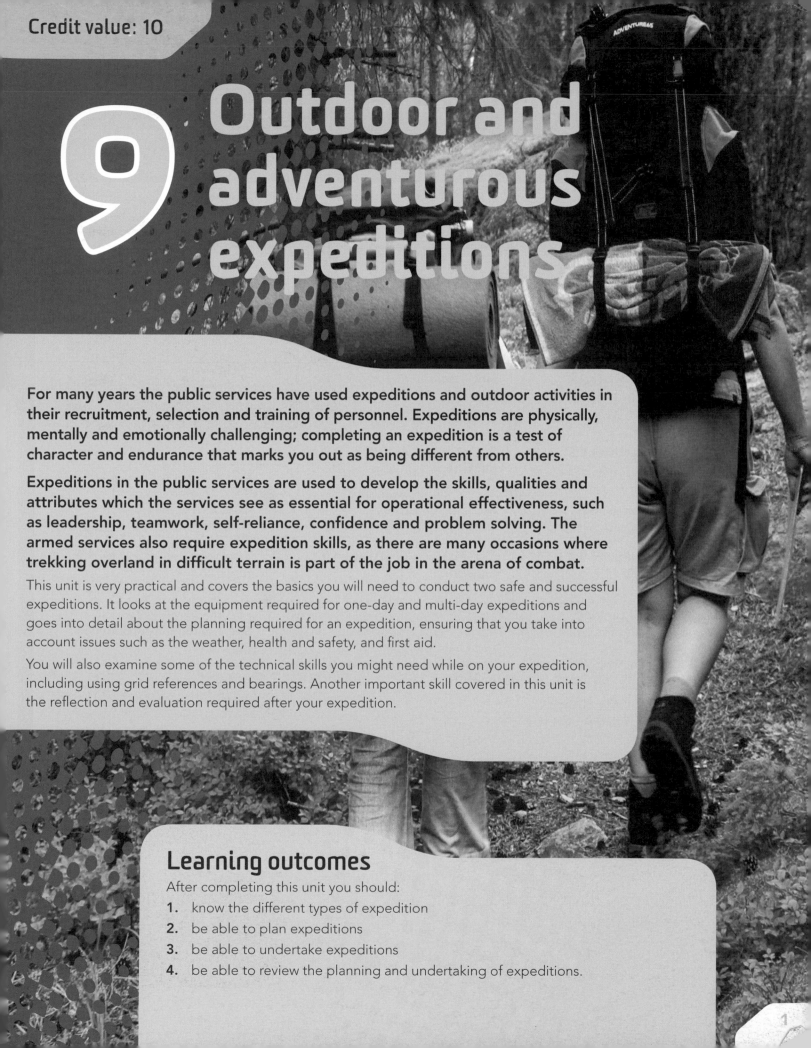

9 Outdoor and adventurous expeditions

For many years the public services have used expeditions and outdoor activities in their recruitment, selection and training of personnel. Expeditions are physically, mentally and emotionally challenging; completing an expedition is a test of character and endurance that marks you out as being different from others.

Expeditions in the public services are used to develop the skills, qualities and attributes which the services see as essential for operational effectiveness, such as leadership, teamwork, self-reliance, confidence and problem solving. The armed services also require expedition skills, as there are many occasions where trekking overland in difficult terrain is part of the job in the arena of combat.

This unit is very practical and covers the basics you will need to conduct two safe and successful expeditions. It looks at the equipment required for one-day and multi-day expeditions and goes into detail about the planning required for an expedition, ensuring that you take into account issues such as the weather, health and safety, and first aid.

You will also examine some of the technical skills you might need while on your expedition, including using grid references and bearings. Another important skill covered in this unit is the reflection and evaluation required after your expedition.

Learning outcomes

After completing this unit you should:

1. know the different types of expedition
2. be able to plan expeditions
3. be able to undertake expeditions
4. be able to review the planning and undertaking of expeditions.

Assessment and grading criteria

This table shows you what you must do in order to achieve a pass, merit or distinction grade, and where you can find activities in this book to help you.

To achieve a **pass** grade the evidence must show that you are able to:	To achieve a **merit** grade the evidence must show that, in addition to the pass criteria, you are able to:	To achieve a **distinction** grade the evidence must show that, in addition to the pass and merit criteria, you are able to:
P1 describe four different types of expedition **See Assessment activity 9.1 page 6**	**M1** compare and contrast four different types of expedition **See Assessment activity 9.1 page 6**	
P2 plan a one-day expedition, with tutor support **See Assessment activity 9.2 page 16**	**M2** independently plan a one-day expedition **See Assessment activity 9.2 page 16**	
P3 plan a multi-day expedition, with tutor support **See Assessment activity 9.2 page 16**	**M3** independently plan a multi-day expedition **See Assessment activity 9.2 page 16**	
P4 undertake two different expeditions demonstrating appropriate skills and techniques, with tutor support **See Assessment activity 9.3 page 20**	**M4** independently undertake two different expeditions, demonstrating appropriate skills and techniques **See Assessment activity 9.3 page 20**	**D1** undertake two different expeditions, demonstrating advanced expedition skills and techniques **See Assessment activity 9.3 page 20**
P5 carry out a review of the planning and undertaking of expeditions, identifying strengths and areas for improvement **See Assessment activity 9.4 page 24**	**M5** explain identified strengths and areas for improvement and relate them to suggestions made in your personal development plan **See Assessment activity 9.4 page 24**	**D2** justify suggestions made in your personal development plan **See Assessment activity 9.4 page 24**
P6 produce a personal development plan based on identified strengths and areas for improvement **See Assessment activity 9.4 page 24**		

How you will be assessed

This unit will be assessed by an internal assignment that will be designed and marked by the staff at your centre. The assignment is designed to allow you to show your understanding of the learning outcomes for outdoor and adventurous expeditions. Assignments can be quite varied and can take the form of:

- reports
- planning documents
- assessed expeditions
- presentations
- posters
- practical tasks
- case studies
- diaries
- personal evaluations
- action plans.

Padraig's experience of planning and carrying out expeditions

I prefer practical units, so I was really interested in this one. The public services often use expeditions and outdoor activities as a way to test and build confidence and teamwork in new recruits and help teams bond, so it has direct relevance to the career I want to do in the future.

I think the best part of the unit was being able to plan our own one-day and multi-day expeditions. It was complicated and there is so much you have to plan for if you are going to be safe, but I learned lots about the process and feel confident that I could do it again if I needed to. By planning the expedition ourselves we were able to tailor it to our fitness requirements as well, so that no one was left behind.

I also had the opportunity to improve on my map work and navigational skills, which really weren't all that good. I was thrilled that we got to learn those practical skills while out of the classroom, as I think it would have been quite difficult to try and learn them in my centre.

Over to you!

- **What areas of outdoor and adventurous activities might you find interesting?**
- **Have you ever completed an expedition?**
- **Do you have any fears or concerns about your level of fitness or your navigation skills?**
- **Are you currently fit enough to complete an expedition?**
- **What preparation could you do to get ready for your assessments?**

1. Types of expedition

Where would you like to go on an expedition?

What about costs, transport and equipment? How much planning do you think you will need?

Share your chosen destinations with your class. Do most of you want to go to the same place, or do you all have different destinations in mind?

Plot your possible destinations on a map of the UK and pin it up for reference when you get to the point in the course where you have to choose a final destination.

Many people think about walking the first time they hear the term 'expedition'. However, expeditions are not just about walking; they can also involve cycling, boats, 4 x 4 vehicles or any other method of transport. An expedition is simply any journey that has a clear and defined purpose. The kind of expeditions you may be required to do by your tutor in this unit could include any or all of these methods of transport, but by far the simplest, and most common, is the walking expedition.

Key term

Expedition – any journey that has a clear and defined purpose.

1.1 Expedition types

There are many different types of expedition that you could be involved in and may need to be aware of, as described in Table 9.1.

Table 9.1: Types of expedition

Type of expedition	Description
Individual or solo	Undertaken by one person, even if they have a large support team to assist them, e.g. round-the-world sailing, treks to the Poles and solo mountain climbs. For example, yachtswoman Dame Ellen MacArthur made the fastest solo circumnavigation of the globe in 2005. The term also covers any trip you might make alone, such as a walk through the Lake District.
Group or team	Undertaken by two or more people, working as a team to complete the challenge of reaching a destination. Has the benefit of being able to draw upon a wide range of expertise among the participants, but can be more costly and more complex to organise than a solo expedition.
Corporate	Run by businesses that are paid to provide the expedition experience to a group of people and to make all the arrangements. Although the individuals complete the trek, they are not normally involved in any of the planning and organising. Popular destinations for organised treks include Mount Everest base camp and Mount Kilimanjaro.
Student	Some learners take a gap year, either between college and university or between university and employment, when they undertake some independent travel. This may include travelling and working their way around the world for up to a year. It can improve language skills, develop confidence and resilience and improve job prospects.
Educational	Designed to teach the participants something, e.g. soft skills such as teamwork and leadership or technical skills such as navigation and camp-craft. The expeditions you will undertake for this unit are educational; you may already be familiar with or have completed Duke of Edinburgh expeditions.

Type of expedition	Description
Military	Used by the armed services as a way of training their employees in a variety of skills. Expeditions in terrain such as jungle or snow are essential if the service men and women are going to learn effective combat in those locations. Expeditions also foster teamwork, resilience, leadership and initiative in the face of adversity and act as a test of character for service personnel. The armed services are often involved in mountaineering expeditions all over the world.
Club	There are many different clubs you can join which conduct expeditions of one sort or another, for example Scouts, Guides, Cadets and ramblers' groups.

Case study: Laura Dekker

In 2009 a Dutch court placed 13-year-old Laura Dekker in the care of the state after she had planned to sail solo around the world with her parents' approval. Laura had her own yacht when she was 6 years old, was sailing solo by the age of 10 and wanted to be the youngest person to circumnavigate the globe. The current record is held by British 17-year-old, Mike Perham.

The court expressed serious concerns about the ability of a 13-year-old to manage the emotional and physical challenges involved in the 45,060-kilometre (28,000-mile) journey. They were also concerned about the impact on Laura of being isolated and out of education for the two-year trip. Laura was placed in the care of the state so that her parents would lose the right to give her permission to go.

1 Do you think it is appropriate for a 13-year-old to make a solo expedition such as this? Explain your reasons.
2 In your opinion, was the court correct to place Laura in state care?
3 What are the potential difficulties in making a 45,060-kilomete (28,000-mile) solo sailing expedition?
4 What is your view on the fact that her parents are supportive of Laura's decision?

1.2 Expedition descriptions

When describing an expedition you should consider the following factors:

- **Duration.** This is the length of time you will be on your expedition. You could do a one-day, multi-day or extended expedition that may take several weeks or months to complete.

- **Form.** Expeditions can take many forms, such as mountaineering, trekking, canoeing/kayaking, sailing, caving, pony trekking, multi-activity or cycling. The form you choose will be a key factor in determining your location and your equipment.

- **Area and location.** You can choose to do an expedition locally, regionally, nationally or internationally. The area you choose will affect your planning and organisation considerably.

- **Aims.** The **aims** of an expedition can be very varied and depend largely on the individual, group or company organising it. Some expeditions might be military in nature and focus on territorial acquisition and conquest. Others might be scientific and focus on exploration or information gathering. Some are filmed for documentaries or educational purposes. Other expeditions are aimed at the entertainment industry or to make money for expedition companies. Still others are designed for personal development or teambuilding.

- **Objectives.** What you might get out of an expedition is as varied as why you might go on one in the first place. Some key **objectives** include fundraising for charity, an extended holiday, improving technical expedition skills such as navigation or mountaineering, and improving employment opportunities in the future. For example, a gap-year expedition can be used to show prospective employers how your personal and organisational skills have improved by seeing new places and experiencing new cultures.

Key terms

Aims – why you are going on the expedition.

Objectives – what you are hoping to get out of the expedition by the end.

Assessment activity 9.1

Knowing about the types and descriptions of expeditions is essential before you begin the planning process for your own two expeditions. As group leader for your expeditions, it is your responsibility to ensure all your team members know about the different types of expedition so that you can make informed choices about which type you will complete.

Produce a written report which:

1 describes four different types of expedition **P1**
2 compares and contrasts four different types of expedition. **M1**

Grading tips

For **P1** you should choose four of the seven types of expedition outlined in Table 9.1 (pages 4–5), providing a full description and an example of each type. You can draw on your own experience or study past expeditions.

For **M1** you should look at the similarities and differences between the four types of expedition you have chosen in terms of their aims, objectives, area, duration and form.

PLTS

This activity will help you develop your skills as an **independent enquirer**.

Functional skills

Researching the types of expedition will help you to develop your functional skills in **ICT**.

2. Plan expeditions

Planning is essential if your expedition is going to be safe and successful. You need to think very carefully about a whole range of different issues in order to achieve what you set out to do, including possible routes, your group and individual abilities and strengths, and the weather.

Did you know?

The main reasons expeditions fail are because of poor planning and poor communication.

2.1 Planning essentials

There are several key issues you must consider when planning your expedition, as shown in Figure 9.1.

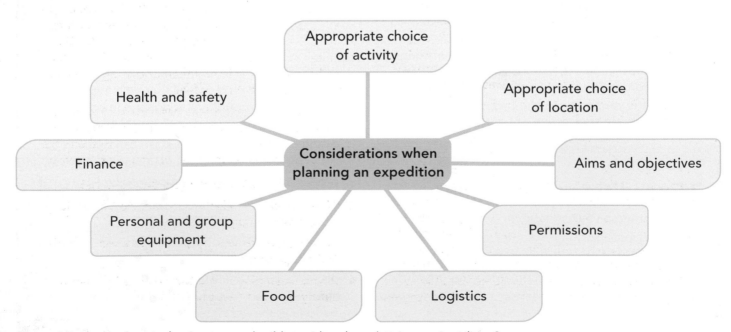

Figure 9.1: Are there any other issues you should consider when planning an expedition?

Appropriate choice of activity

Knowing your own abilities and those of your party is essential if you are going to choose a route that is challenging but not impossible. This includes issues such as navigational skills, fitness levels, disabilities or illnesses. If each member of the group has to complete the expedition, but some party members have low fitness levels, then choosing a route that is very strenuous means that some members are bound to fail. The experience of your team is also a key factor. If you have all completed several expeditions in the past, this would influence your choice of route and the length of the journey. If some party members have never been on an expedition before, it might be best to choose an easier route for them to begin with.

Appropriate choice of location

Your destination depends on a number of factors, such as:

* How much money do you have?
* How large is your group?
* How fit is your group?
* How experienced is your group?
* How well equipped is your group?

A walking expedition to Kilimanjaro in Tanzania may sound wonderful, but if your party cannot afford several thousand pounds each for the costs of the expedition, then you may have to set your sights a bit lower. The destination you choose should be a compromise between all these factors, ensuring a safe and achievable destination, suitable for the abilities and wallets of all party members.

Case study: Low's Gully

Low's Gully is a 1.6-kilometre-deep (one mile) canyon in the side of Mount Kinabalu in Borneo. In 1994, a British Army expedition sought to be the first to explore it. They planned to travel light, so did not take radios or flares, and they had just ten days' rations. The team consisted of seven British soldiers and three Chinese soldiers, some of whom knew each other and some of whom did not. It was reported that the Chinese soldiers had only learned to abseil a few days prior to the expedition and were not physically fit enough for the challenges ahead. The team had estimated that climbing Mount Kinabalu, making the descent and **traversing** the 9.6-kilometre-long (6 miles) gully back to civilisation would only take six days, so they assumed ten days' rations would be sufficient. This was based on an assessment of the maps of the area, which showed the gully as **navigable**.

Due to the differences in the fitness of the team members, the team divided into two groups, with the fittest soldiers going ahead and the older, slower soldiers to follow. The fitter group of soldiers made the first descent and were instructed to set up fixed abseil points to make it easier for the rear party to climb down. However, there was insufficient rope to set up fixed abseil points for the rear party. It was clear to the advance party members that, without sufficient rope, both parties would not be able to climb back out after they had descended, leaving the 9.6-kilometre-long gully as the only way out for everyone. The advance party made it to the bottom and waited for the rear party to catch up, but the rear group became hemmed in by jungle and fast-moving water and never rejoined the advance party.

Although the **terrain** in the gully had looked navigable on the map, it was appalling. The advance party had to descend waterfalls of up to 80 metres (262 feet) in extremely poor weather. They finally exited the gully in poor health and raised the alarm on day 17 of what should have been a 10-day expedition. The Malaysian military mobilised search helicopters and the Ministry of Defence organised an elite RAF mountain rescue team. The rear party was found on day 31, having lost a fifth of their bodyweight. All ten members survived their ordeal.

The expedition team had underestimated the brutal conditions in the gully and overestimated their own abilities to deal with the conditions, leaving them in a life-or-death situation that they were lucky to survive.

1   **What is the value of military expeditions?**

2   **How could the failed expedition to Low's Gully have been managed differently?**

3   **What errors do you think the team made during their expedition?**

4   **If you were planning a trip such as this, what safety measures would you take?**

Key terms

Traverse – to travel or cross terrain.

Navigable – to navigate. In Low's Gully, the team thought the expedition looked straightforward to navigate – therefore they thought it was navigable.

Terrain – the territory you are travelling over, such as a hill, mountain or path. It can also refer to the conditions underfoot. For example, if the terrain is rough there may be lots of loose rocks around; if the terrain is boggy then it will be wet and muddy.

Logistics – the detailed coordination of a large and complex operation.

Aims and objectives

An aim is a reason why you are going on the expedition and an objective is what you hope to achieve by completing it. For example:

- aim – to practice my map work and navigation skills
- objective – by the end of the expedition I will be able to set a map and take compass bearings.

Once you know why you are going on an expedition (aim) and what you are hoping to get out of it (objective), it will be easier to decide where and when to go. If you are inexperienced, then aiming to complete a Scottish mountain range in winter would be very foolish, and a summer expedition to the Peak District or North Yorkshire Moors would be a more suitable destination. So you can see that having clear aims and objectives are an essential part of the planning process.

Permissions

Depending on the type of expedition you are undertaking, and factors such as the age of your party members, there may be a series of permissions you need to obtain before you can start your journey. These permissions are an important part of the planning process and may include agreement from:

- parents
- participants
- line manager
- organisations
- appropriate administrative bodies
- governing body
- local authority
- landowners.

Remember!

Make sure that you have consent from the landowner if you are planning to cross any private land. If you do not, then you and your party could be prosecuted for trespass.

It is very important that you obtain consent from your party members to go on the expedition. For under-18's, this consent must come from a parent or guardian. The consent form should give enough detail about what you are planning to do and where you are planning to go so that the person signing the form understands what is involved. Consent forms normally also include consent for medical treatment if the need arises.

Remember!

If you don't receive the appropriate permissions you could be subject to legal action if anything goes wrong while on expedition.

Logistics

Group size and ratios

You need to take into account the size of the group on an expedition and what the ratio of staff should be for each participant. The risks and **logistics** involved in each activity will determine the staff to group ratio. For some activities a ratio of 1:6 might be suitable, but for less risky activities 1:10 might be acceptable. The governing body for each activity normally sets out the ratios that should be followed.

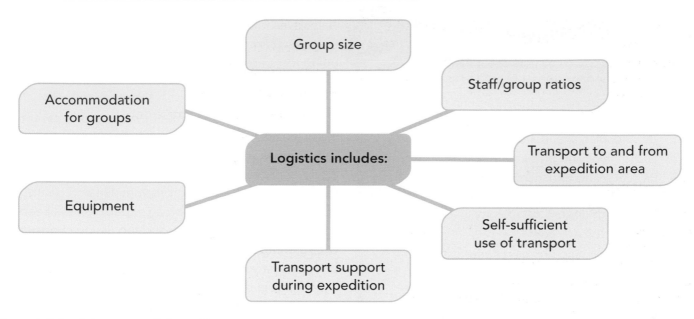

Figure 9.2: Logistics covers all these things

Activity: Ratios

Find the governing body guidelines for the following activities and note the staff to participant ratio for each:

- abseiling
- low-level hill walking
- sea kayaking.

Why do you think the ratios are set at those levels? What might happen if they were raised?

Transport

Transport for your expedition needs to be booked well in advance. You may need a coach to take you to the start point of your journey and to pick you up again at the end. For other types of expedition your transport may include cycles or boats. You cannot leave booking transport to the last minute, particularly with larger groups, or you may be stranded. As well as transport to get to and from your expedition start and end points, you may also require a support vehicle with you during the journey. Support vehicles can be used to carry heavy equipment from one location to another or to ferry injured members of the party back to base.

Accommodation for groups

Planning your accommodation in advance is very important. If you are camping you need to be aware that some campsites do not take groups of young people, and some refuse bookings from single-sex parties. Campsites can also be fully booked, especially at peak times, so if you don't plan ahead you may be left without accommodation. For multi-day expeditions you will need to book suitable accommodation for each night; this could be a campsite, youth hostel or hotel. You need to check the prices, reputation and cleanliness of the accommodation. It makes sense to go and check it in person if you can; that way there are no unpleasant surprises when you arrive.

If you are camping overnight, you may well be sharing a tent with others. This is sensible for several reasons. Firstly you can share the weight of the tent between the group while you are walking. Secondly, when you arrive exhausted at the campsite there will be lots of willing hands to help you set up, and to take it down when you leave. Thirdly, if it is particularly cold, the tent will be full of bodies to share warmth.

If you have the option to choose your own tent group, make sure you choose people who you get along with. Sharing a very small space with someone you don't like can be a challenge.

Activity: The countryside code

The countryside code is based around five key points:

1 Be safe. Plan ahead and follow any signs.
2 Leave gates and property as you find them.
3 Protect plants and animals and take your litter home.
4 Keep dogs under close control.
5 Consider other people.

During the planning process of your expedition you should ensure all your party members are familiar with the code and are able to follow it when you arrive.

Produce a leaflet which explains the countryside code to all of your party members.

Food

On an expedition, you need to carry food that is high in energy, such as carbohydrates. Good things to carry are sandwiches, cereal bars, biscuits, fruit and nuts. You can also buy pre-prepared camping food in bags that just require heating in boiling water. You must take plenty of water to drink, particularly if you are wild camping – there may not be a source of fresh water available. You should also consider taking more than you think you will need to cover emergencies like being lost or stranded.

Equipment

Having the correct equipment for any task is essential if you are going to be successful. This is especially true of expeditions, where not having the right equipment could not only be the difference between success or failure, but also between life and death. The equipment you take on an expedition will keep you warm, dry, comfortable and fed. If you choose the wrong equipment, at best you will be uncomfortable and at worst you will be placing yourself and your colleagues in danger.

Depending on the size and type of expedition, some equipment (e.g. tents, cooking equipment, ropes, etc.) may belong to or be supplied to the group. Other equipment, such as clothing, footwear and toiletries, will be personal and belong to the individual participants.

Remember!

Make sure group members know exactly what they need to bring and how much they will have to carry. Are tents being shared or do they need their own? What is happening about food and cooking equipment?

Activity: Expedition food

A typical 24-hour army ration pack might contain the following items:

- corned beef hash (boil in the bag)
- chicken and pasta (boil in the bag)
- vegetable stock drink mix, 1 x sachet
- cheese, processed, or meat paté
- chocolate pudding (instant)
- an oatmeal block
- chocolate bars or a bar of Kendal Mint Cake
- biscuits, brown (malted and hard, pack of six)
- biscuits, fruit-filled (malted, hard, garibaldi-like, pack of six)
- sweets, boiled, 1 x pack assorted flavours
- instant soup (varying flavours), 2 x sachets
- tea, instant, white, 4 x sachets
- coffee, instant, 2 x 5 grams sachets

- drinking chocolate mix, 1 x sachet
- sugar, quick dissolving, 8 x 10 grams sachets
- beverage whitener (non-dairy creamer), 2 x sachets
- fruit drink mix, either orange or lemon (enough for 1 litre of drink)
- gum, chewing, 5 x sticks
- sweets, boiled, 1 x pack assorted flavours
- tissues, paper (individual pack)
- waterproof matches (10) and striker (1)
- water purification tablets (6).

1 **Why do you think so much food is needed for a soldier in a 24-hour period?**
2 **Would you be happy to eat this menu?**
3 **What kinds of things would improve the menu for you?**

Choosing tents

The type of tent you take on an expedition will depend on where you will be camping and whether you have to carry your tent with you. If your tent is being carried to a campsite or base by a support vehicle, then weight will not really matter and you can choose something with plenty of space. If you are carrying your tent to a remote or mountainous area then the tent will have to be lightweight and designed specifically for those conditions.

The size of your tent depends entirely on how many people are planning to share it. Remember that in wet weather your rucksacks and gear will have to be accommodated inside the tent as well. If you are part of a large expedition with vehicle support you may also have access to a cooking tent where meals are prepared. This is important as it can be very dangerous to cook inside a small tent.

Bivouacs

A bivouac is an individual sleeping shelter which can be used to bed down in at night, as a temporary shelter in severe weather, or when awaiting rescue in case of injury. Bivouacs, or 'bivvys', can be as simple as a piece of plastic sheet or tarpaulin draped over a branch, or they can be more complex structures built with materials such as fallen branches, moss and foliage. You are unlikely to need to build a bivouac or 'bivvy' on your expeditions, but the armed services use them on their expeditions.

If you need an emergency bivvy while out on expedition, you are most likely to use a survival bag. The most common type of survival bag used for learner groups is a bright orange plastic bag which covers you from feet to head and is used if you have to unexpectedly spend the night outdoors without your camping gear. Each member of the group should carry one for emergencies and they are normally very cheap to buy. You should ensure that you have ventilation at the top of your survival bag so you don't suffocate.

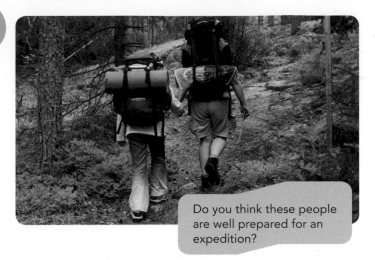

Do you think these people are well prepared for an expedition?

Cooking equipment

You will need to cook or warm the food you take on expedition, and for this you will need a stove. A good stove should be stable on the ground, have protection from the wind and have an adjustable flame so food can be cooked correctly. Stoves come in many different varieties and use different sorts of fuel. The most common type used by school or scout groups is the meths-burning trangia because it is stable and very simple to use. Cooking should be done outdoors where possible. Tents are often made from material that burns easily. *Do not take risks.*

Personal equipment

The choice of what to take with you is often based on experience of previous expeditions, the time of year, the predicted weather and the country you are conducting your expedition in. For example, an expedition to the north of Europe in winter may require thermals, whereas for a safari expedition in Central Africa you would need protection from the sun.

In order to decide what to take with you, you need to know:

- where you are going
- the time of year you are going
- how long you are going for
- the equipment carried by other people in the expedition
- the abilities and skills of your colleagues.

There are some things you need to take on every expedition, such as suitable footwear, clothing, food and water, whereas other items will be optional, based on the information above. Table 9.2 shows some personal equipment you might need.

Table 9.2: Personal equipment

Personal equipment	Description	Types and sizes
Rucksack/backpack	The best way of carrying equipment and supplies while walking, as it is designed to sit comfortably on the back and leave the hands and arms free for other tasks. Most rucksacks are made from very lightweight material so they are easier to carry over long distances. They should also be shower-proof.	**Day sacks** have shoulder straps but don't have a metal frame, so are more flexible than larger rucksacks. Perfect for carrying waterproofs and some lunch, but not much else. **Larger rucksacks** have rigid frames and shoulder straps; they usually have a hip belt and often a chest strap as well. Often come in specialised shapes for women and children. **Pack sizes:** (pack sizes are measured in litres) • Small day sack: around 20 litres • Short day expedition pack: 35–55 litres • Longer camping expeditions: 60–80 litres probably required.
Sleeping bags	Even in the height of summer in the UK you will still need a sleeping bag. The type will vary depending on the time of year, where you will be sleeping (higher altitudes require warmer sleeping bags as it gets colder the higher you go) and what you are sleeping on.	Different grades are based on 'seasons' to match different weather conditions. There are two main types. **Caravan bags:** rectangular, quilted bags with long zips down one or two sides. **Mummy bags:** shaped to fit the body. Lighter and more easily packed into a rucksack for expeditions and backpacking.
Sleeping mat	Sleeping directly on the ground is not a pleasant experience. The ground is often cold, damp and uneven, and if you sleep directly on it you can lose a lot of your body heat very quickly. Using a sleeping mat is important to provide a layer of insulation between you and the ground.	There are several types of sleeping mat with different advantages and disadvantages. **Roll mat:** one of the most common types, often used on expeditions. It is a rectangular piece of foam to put under a sleeping bag which is waterproof, rolls up tightly and can be strapped onto a rucksack. You can usually buy a basic one for about £5.
Clothing: layering system	Being prepared for outdoor expeditions means having enough clothing to suit the weather conditions. Make sure that you have enough to layer up or down several times during the day as the weather and/or your activity levels change. This is called 'layering'. For example, you may need several layers when it is cooler in the morning and evening or just a t-shirt and trousers or shorts in the middle of the day. Spare layers will be useful if you are caught in a downpour. Fewer layers are needed when you get hot and sweaty going up hill.	Layers must be lightweight so you can carry them for many miles and fast-drying, in case you are caught in rain showers. They should also have '**wicking**' properties. You need the following layers: • **base layer** sits next to the skin • **insulating or thermal layers** provide more or less warmth according to how many layers you need • **protective layer** is the outermost layer that protects you against wind and moisture.
Waterproofs	In the UK we have a lot of rain, so good quality waterproofs are an essential part of your expedition kit.	Waterproofs consist of a breathable jacket and over-trousers, designed to fit comfortably over your other layers, with taped seams to prevent water leaking in.

Personal equipment	Description	Types and sizes
Footwear	There are several types of footwear you could choose depending on the terrain you will be covering. The wrong footwear can cause blisters, making walking difficult and painful. **Figure 9.3:** Which kind of footwear will you choose for your expedition?	**Walking boots** – designed specifically for walking. Tough, moulded soles give solid grip in most terrain; provide ankle support to avoid injuries on steep slopes. There are different types of walking boot available, depending on where you are walking and the time of year. Manufacturers describe their boots in terms of seasons. *One-season boots:* flexible, for use on easy path walking or long stretches of road; not suitable for difficult terrain or very wet weather. *Two-season boots:* can be made of soft leather, suede or gortex. Useful on a variety of different terrains, but not so good on very rocky or uneven surfaces because they provide only minimal ankle support *Three-season boots:* have a stiffer sole for more uneven ground and better ankle support. Can also be used for easy winter walking. *Four-season boots:* for the most challenging terrain and winter walking and climbing. Can be very rigid and quite uncomfortable for summer walking. **Walking shoes:** a much lighter alternative to boots. Can be used in good weather on easy terrain. **Trainers:** useful for urban walking on paths and pavements. Can also be used in dry conditions for low-level countryside walks on clear paths. Not suitable for most expeditions, as not waterproof and do not offer the foot the protection of boots. Can be very slippery in wet conditions, leading to injuries. **Walking sandals:** specially-designed sandals for summer walking. Have solid soles and a reasonable grip, but are not waterproof and provide no protection from sharp stones or brambles. Many walkers use these as camp shoes only and do not use them for expeditions

Figure illustrations labelled: Boot, Shoe, Trainer, Sandal

Key terms

Layering – having enough clothing so that you can mix and match items and add or remove clothing, depending on the weather conditions.

Wicking – the movement of moisture away from the body to the outside of a fabric, which helps keep you warmer and dryer. Not all materials wick so it makes sense to choose expedition or sports clothes that do.

Remember!

- Your footwear is arguably the most important part of your expedition equipment, as it keeps your feet comfortable, safe and dry.
- Everything you need will have to go in your rucksack and be carried by you.
- Packing too much in your rucksack can be as foolish as packing too little.

Did you know?

A blister is a bubble of fluid underneath the top layer of skin. The fluid is called serum. Blisters are normally caused through friction or extreme temperatures. They can vary in size and be excruciatingly painful. The skin over the top of a blister acts as a natural barrier to prevent infection, and most blisters will heal naturally if left alone.

Other equipment

You should also think about whether you need any of the following items, based on the location of your expedition and the probable weather conditions:

- hat
- gloves
- mobile phone
- whistle
- torch
- flares
- sun cream
- insect repellent
- good quality socks to prevent blisters.

Activity: Which shoe for you?

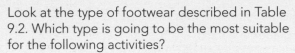

Look at the type of footwear described in Table 9.2. Which type is going to be the most suitable for the following activities?

- Walking to school or college.
- Climbing a hill in snowy conditions.
- Walking through a valley after a rainstorm.
- Relaxing at your campsite.

Remember!

You will need to take a whistle with you in case you get lost and have to be found. The emergency signal is six blasts on your whistle or six flashes on your torch. A mobile phone will not always alert people if you need help as coverage in remote areas can be poor and signals can be blocked by hills and mountains.

Activity: Sample kit list

A sample kit list for a day expedition might look like this:

- rucksack
- survival bag
- waterproofs
- map and compass
- boots
- torch
- food and drink
- whistle
- hat and gloves
- spare clothing
- first aid kit/sanitary supplies
- sunglasses and sun cream.

1 **Can you think of anything else you might want to take?**

2 **What kit would you add if you were staying overnight?**

3 **If you were on a multi-day expedition, what kit could be shared among your group?**

Finance

An expedition might seem like a very cheap way of travelling. After all, you are supplying your own food and accommodation and using your own legs for transport. However, once you have factored in campsite costs, transport costs and payment for specialist walking leaders, the costs can add up. You need to plan carefully to ensure that all of your party members can afford the expedition and make adjustments if they cannot.

Calculating the cost of an expedition can be a challenge as there are often unexpected costs. It is therefore important to budget your income and expenditure carefully and identify the major cost areas such as food, transport and accommodation. A sensible group leader will also ensure there is money left over for emergencies, such as overseas emergency medical treatment. Don't forget to have proper systems in place to record all payments and receipts, and to keep the groups' funds safe.

Health and safety

The health and safety of your expedition group is not just the responsibility of the walking group leader – it is the responsibility of *every* party member. You will be relying on each other when you are on an expedition and you must behave sensibly and responsibly. Even the best walking leader can do very little to protect you if you choose to behave like a fool. The health and safety of the party can be jeopardised by:

- not paying attention to instructions
- not obeying instructions
- use of alcohol or drugs
- failure to disclose medical conditions, such as asthma
- horseplay
- not bringing the right equipment.

Health and safety is managed through **risk** assessments. Risk assessments estimate the risks of certain activities and describe the **control measures** that can be put into place to minimise the risks. All of your planned activities will require a full risk assessment which all party members should be familiar with. Anything that is not planned should either be avoided or a dynamic risk assessment made at the time. A dynamic risk assessment is an on-the-spot consideration of the risk factors of the activity. If the risk is too high and you cannot put control measures in place, then you should not do the activity.

Activity: Risk assessment

The Health and Safety Executive (HSE) is the government department responsible for making sure health and safety legislation and risk assessments are followed and that businesses and organisations take all reasonable steps to protect people. They recommend five steps to risk assessment.

Step 1: Identify the **hazards**.
Step 2: Decide who might be harmed and how.
Step 3: Evaluate the risks and decide on precautions.
Step 4: Record your findings and implement them.
Step 5: Review your assessment and update if necessary.
Part of your expedition route requires you and your party to cross a river. Produce a risk assessment based on the five steps above.

Key terms

Risk – the chance that someone might be harmed from a hazard.

Control measures – the preventative measures you put into place to try and make sure that the hazard doesn't cause a high risk. For example, a control measure on a busy road is a zebra crossing; control measures when abseiling are a safety harness and a helmet.

Hazards – anything that may cause harm, such as chemicals, working at height, river crossings or fire.

When you are planning an expedition you should ensure you have a complete list of the participants' medical conditions that might affect their health and safety, such as asthma or pregnancy. This list can be easily compiled by having participants complete a medical questionnaire. It is also essential to have up-to-date emergency contact details for all of your group in case a problem arises. A sensible group leader will also check that the party is covered by adequate insurance and will make sure that a copy of the route card is left with a responsible person who can raise the alarm if the party doesn't return by a set date or time.

First aid

Minor injuries such as small cuts, bruises, aches and strains can easily happen on an expedition and it is your responsibility to plan for your own safety. Taking a personal first aid kit is essential, but if you are responsible for a group you may need to take a walking leader's first aid kit as well. It is also sensible to plan for several of your group to have a first aid qualification. These are offered by most local ambulance services and some charities for a small cost.

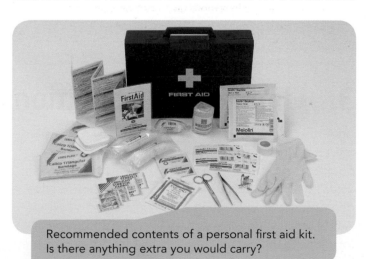

Recommended contents of a personal first aid kit. Is there anything extra you would carry?

You should carry a small personal first aid kit for yourself. This would normally contain the following items:

- plasters
- scissors and tape
- blister kit
- sterile wipes.
- tweezers
- bandages and small wound dressings

You should also bring any personal medication you need, such as asthma inhalers or antihistamines for allergies.

Remember!

Your tutor or group leader will not be able to give you painkillers or paracetamol, so if you know you are prone to aches and pains, it makes sense to take your own as long as you are not allergic to them.

Weather forecasts

If you are going on an expedition, your plan might be weather-dependent. This means the weather may dictate some of your choices, such as your route and your footwear. Make sure you know where to find reliable weather information. You can get weather forecasts from the following places:

- telephone/fax
- television
- Internet
- newspapers
- posted bulletins
- radio.

Good planning allows you to deal with whichever type of weather you are faced with during your expedition.

Assessment activity 9.2

Planning for your two expeditions is essential if you are going to be able to conduct them safely and complete them successfully.

1 Plan a one-day expedition. **P2 M2**

2 Plan a multi-day expedition. **P3 M3**

Grading tips

For **P2** and **P3** you should plan your expeditions with support from your tutor, making sure you can show that you understand the equipment and other resources needed.

For **M2** and **M3** you need to show that you can plan single-day and multi-day expeditions independently.

PLTS

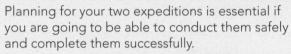

Planning your one-day expedition will help you develop your skills as a **creative thinker** and **team worker**.

Planning your multi-day expedition will help you develop your skills as a **self manager**.

Functional skills

Estimating distance travelled and time required when you create your route card will help you develop your functional skills in **Maths**.

3. Undertake expeditions

Undertaking an expedition is a practical activity that must be done by you in person. The information in this book is no substitute for spending time in the outdoors actually learning and practising the skills you will need to demonstrate on expedition. Experienced and qualified staff at your centre will supervise planning and preparation for your expedition. You may start by making short journeys that eventually build into longer, overnight expeditions.

3.1 Skills

The skills in this section of the course need to be taught to you by your tutor in a practical setting. This could be classroom-based, but is more likely to occur in the field, as it is difficult to learn or demonstrate these skills without the right physical setting.

You should expect your tutor to cover some or all of the following skills:

- **Navigation skills** – orientation of map, direction finding, interpretation, grid references, scale and distance, handrail features, use of key, compass skills.

- **Camp craft skills** – erecting tents, striking tents, selecting campsites, use of terrain for shelter, cooking, bivouac building.

- **Travelling skills** – pace and rhythm, energy conservation, control skills, traversing difficult ground, avoidance of hazards.

- **Weather-related skills** – weather forecasts, predicting conditions, assessing conditions.

- **Advanced skills** – navigation using interpretive features, aiming off using compass bearings, identification of position by methods of relocation, navigation in poor visibility/darkness, navigation with speed and accuracy in all conditions, elementary interpretation of weather.

3.2 Techniques

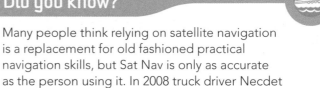

Did you know?

Many people think relying on satellite navigation is a replacement for old fashioned practical navigation skills, but Sat Nav is only as accurate as the person using it. In 2008 truck driver Necdet Bakimci needed to get a lorry load of luxury cars from Turkey to Gibraltar – he ended up 2574 kilometres off target in Skegness in Lincolnshire.

Navigation techniques

Table 9.3: Navigation techniques are strategies you use to ensure you can navigate accurately

Navigation technique or tool	Uses
Route card	Essential – puts all your planning on one document. Enables you to measure your progress against the card several times a day, so you can make adjustments if you are going slower or faster than anticipated. Can contain grid references and bearings.
Calculating time	Calculating each section of the route means you can plan to cover an achievable distance each day. Enables you to see when you would arrive at a specific point for transport pick up, or at accommodation. Two types of estimates: • *General* – working in chunks of time (e.g. half hours), then working out how long the route should take, bearing in mind group ability, weather conditions, etc. • *Detailed* – planning each section or 'leg' of the expedition in minutes – aiming to be within 10 per cent of set time.
Calculating distance	Very straightforward method based on measuring between points on a map. Maps use specific scales (e.g. 1:50,000 or 1:25,000). On a 1:25,000 scale map, 4 centimetres on the map = 1 kilometre distance; 1 centimetre = 250 metres; 1 millimetre equals 25 metres. Can be measured with a ruler, but most compasses come with a **roamer** – a small ruler, **calibrated** for measuring distances.
Map care and folding	Your map is essential equipment – you need to look after it. Paper Ordnance Survey maps are very large when opened and get easily damaged. Avoid unfolding maps in wet and windy weather as this could cause permanent damage. Fold the map into a small square that shows the part of the route you are on. Then put the map into a jacket pocket or waterproof map pouch. Laminated maps are stronger, but more difficult to fold to show specific places and are heavier to carry.
Counting off features	Features, such as buildings, fences or hills, occurring at conveniently-spaced points on a route, which you tick off on a list or map as you pass them. (They are also called 'tick off' features.) Not a good technique in featureless terrain.

Destination: Bleaklow Stones   Date: 21/6/10

Party members: I M Lost, H Elp, May Day, 0 Ops

Speed: 4 km/hr, + 1 min/10 m climbed   Emergency contact number: 0123 456 789

From	To	Distance	Rests	Time taken (a)	Height climbed	Time taken (b)	Height lost	Direction	Time (a+b)	Description	Escape routes
Cairn, Nether Moor 147873	Druid's Stone 134874	1300 m	0	19.5	140 m	14	0	278	33.5	From flat head uphill to stone on 2nd footpath	Lady Booth Brook to YHA
Druid's Stone 134874	Spot height, Hartshorn 115877	2400 m	0	36	60 m	6	30 m	W	42	Carry on along footpath, at Upper Tor head up to high ground	Ollerbrook Clough to Vale of Edale
Spot height, Hartshorn 115877	Ford, Blackden Rind 115883	650 m	0	9.75	10 m	1	30 m	012	10.75	Follow bearing across plateau to footpath	Golden Clough to Grindsbrook Booth

Figure 9.4: Look at this example of a route card. What will the route card for your expedition look like?

Key terms

Roamer – a small ruler on the side of a compass, calibrated for measuring distances.

Calibrated – marked into smaller divisions, such as millimetres or degrees.

As you can see, a good route card contains information such as:

- destination – where you are intending to go
- date – when you are intending to go
- times – the times it will take you to complete specific legs of your journey and the total time of your journey overall
- leg – your journey broken down into easily manageable sections called legs
- distances – the distance overall and the distances of each leg, usually measured in metres or kilometres
- height gained or lost – so you can look at whether you will be going up or downhill

- rest stops – you may want to break after a long uphill climb or for lunch
- escape routes – this is a quick way down from the hill or back where you came from in case of emergency or poor weather.

Did you know?

A traditional way of estimating time when going up hill is Naismith's Rule. This states that you can use the formula 5 kph + 30 mins for each 300 metres climbed (or 3 mph + 30 mins for each 1000 feet). This rule should be adjusted to account for factors such as the fitness of the party, the weight carried and very poor weather conditions such as strong winds or deep snow.

Remember!

You can also estimate distance using pacings. This is a method of counting every double step (i.e. every time a particular foot, either left or right, touches the ground). An average adult will take about 64 double steps every 100 metres.

Activity: Pacings

Using a long measuring tape or a **measuring wheel**, measure out 100 metres on flat ground and mark the start and end points clearly. Walking with a normal stride, count how many double steps it takes for you to reach the end. This is your pacing figure. If you need to measure distance travelled, you can count this number of double paces and know you have moved 100 metres.

Practice this by walking random short distances and calculating how far you have gone. Confirm your distances with the measuring wheel.

Camp craft techniques

Good camp craft is about ensuring you maintain a safe and hygienic campsite while causing minimal disruption and damage to the environment.

Maintaining a dry tent

If the weather is poor, there is nothing you can do to maintain a dry tent on the outside, but you can ensure the interior of your tent is kept clean and dry. This is crucial if you are going to be comfortable inside the tent, and it will also help maintain your equipment to prolong its life. Most modern basic camping tents are double-skinned. This means they have an outer shell and an inner shell. If the outer tent is wet then make sure your inner is packed to protect it from the dampness. Basic housekeeping is also important. Check the seams on your tent to ensure they are not torn or frayed, as this might lead to rain leaking into the inner tent. Avoid cooking in a tent as the condensation can collect, making the inner tent very damp and leading to a cold uncomfortable night for you.

Cooking

How much cooking and the type of cooking you do while on expedition will vary considerably. If you are on a one-day expedition it is unlikely you will do any cooking at all since you will be able to take a packed lunch and a thermos with you. On a multi-day expedition many people bring food that does not need much preparation and cooking, such as ration packs or expedition boil-in-the-bag meals. There are even self-heating meals which require no cooking. This is not to say that you can't or shouldn't cook full meals while you are camping, but remember that lots of different ingredients will increase the weight of your pack and you may only have one pan and one stove to work with. It is also likely that after a hard day on the trail you will be exhausted, and cooking a complex meal in those circumstances is not a great deal of fun.

Waste disposal

All your waste should be picked up and taken with you if you are **wild camping**. If you are using a campsite then you should follow the site's rules on waste disposal and recycling. Do not leave your rubbish and waste out in the countryside as it poses a hazard for wildlife, damages the environment and spoils the beauty of the countryside for others.

Key terms

Measuring wheel – a special wheel-shaped device which allows you to measure long distances on the ground by pushing it along.

Wild camping – camping in the countryside, not at a campsite. This needs to be done carefully so that you do not cause problems for livestock or farmers.

Personal hygiene

If you are going on an expedition where you don't expect to encounter many toilets, then a small plastic trowel can be useful, as can a toilet roll or toilet wipes, wrapped in a plastic bag to keep them dry. For women, having a period while you are on an expedition can be a nuisance, as it may not be easy or convenient to change your sanitary protection without access to a toilet. It is not recommended that you keep tampons in for extended periods of time, but products such as menstrual cups can be suitable for backpacking. Taking some wet wipes and antibacterial hand gel can help if you have limited access to hand-washing facilities. Tissues are also a useful item to have handy.

Pack, use and store equipment

Before you go on your day or multi-day expeditions, your tutor should ensure you know how to pack, use and store your equipment. This may mean that they give you ample opportunity to practise these skills at school or college before you go. They may also provide expert guidance on how to develop these skills.

Advanced techniques

Advanced techniques will be demonstrated to you by your tutor in class time and also out in the field. These are practical techniques that are best learned in a small group setting where you will have the opportunity to practise your skills and ask for guidance if necessary. Advanced skills include:

- pacing
- calculating distance travelled through time
- good route choice, with alterations appropriate to conditions

- walking on **bearing**
- camping in high wilderness terrain
- camping comfortably in difficult weather.

Key term

Bearing – a measurement of direction between two points. Bearing is usually given either a direction such as 'The hikers proceeded on a north-easterly bearing' or as a number based on the degrees of a compass, e.g. 'The ship travelled on a bearing of 36 degrees'.

Activity: Compass bearings

There are some excellent web-based compass exercises that allow you to work out compass bearings such as: http://geographyfieldwork.com/Compass/randomMap.html.

Use this site, or another like it, to practise your skills if you don't have access to a map and compass at home.

Assessment activity 9.3

 **BTEC**

1 Undertake two different expeditions, demonstrating appropriate skills and techniques, with tutor support. **P4**

2 Independently undertake two different expeditions, demonstrating appropriate skills and techniques. This assessment must be done practically and will be assessed by your tutor in situ, for example via witness statements, observations, etc. **M4**

3 Undertake two different expeditions, demonstrating advanced expedition skills and techniques. **D1**

Grading tips

For **P4** you need to be able to demonstrate practical skills and techniques. The expeditions could include a day spent kayaking, or a day-long wilderness hike.

For **M4** you must carry out the two expeditions independently. Although these don't have to be multi-day expeditions, it is strongly recommended that you take part in at least one multi-day expedition so that you really understand what is involved.

D1 brings together all the work you have done in P2, P3, P4, M2, M3 and M4. You must show advanced navigation skills and techniques while on your expeditions and produce an observation record to confirm what you have achieved.

PLTS

Working with others when completing your expedition will help develop your skills as a **team leader** and **effective participator**.

4. Review planning and undertaking of expeditions

Once you have completed your expeditions, you need to be able to review them to see what went right and what you could have done better. This enables you to continually improve, as the things you learn can be applied to the next expedition, and the things that didn't go so well can be worked on. The public services routinely evaluate their expeditions since they are often designed with a specific mission in mind. If the mission fails, the services need to know why so they can avoid those mistakes in the future.

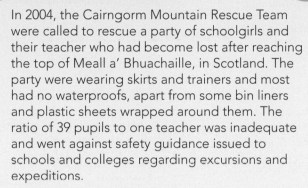

Case study: Cairngorm mountain rescue

In 2004, the Cairngorm Mountain Rescue Team were called to rescue a party of schoolgirls and their teacher who had become lost after reaching the top of Meall a' Bhuachaille, in Scotland. The party were wearing skirts and trainers and most had no waterproofs, apart from some bin liners and plastic sheets wrapped around them. The ratio of 39 pupils to one teacher was inadequate and went against safety guidance issued to schools and colleges regarding excursions and expeditions.

Rescue leader John Allen said that, in all his experience, he had never seen a group of people so unprepared for a mountain expedition.

1 **If the group had not been rescued from the mountain, what would have happened to them?**

2 **What planning should they have done to ensure their safety?**

3 **Who is responsible for the safety of school pupils on expeditions?**

Remember!

If you want to know more about the work of Mountain Rescue or make a donation to this public service then you can find out more at http://www.mountain.rescue.org.uk.

4.1 Review of planning and undertaking

Formative and summative reviews

Reviewing your planning and undertaking of an expedition is very important because if something does go wrong with your expedition you will have to identify where responsibility for the problem lies. A **formative review** of your planning and undertaking enables your team members and tutor to continually comment and evaluate the process of the expedition. It is very useful because it allows changes to be made to improve the expedition on an ongoing basis. It can also lead to any major errors or omissions being picked up before you actually go on the expedition, and they can be corrected if they occur while you are in situ. A **summative review** of the planning and undertaking processes of an expedition can also be helpful, as it provides an overall look at the expedition organisation and execution, from start to finish, allowing areas for development to be improved for next time.

Key terms

Formative review – the process of reviewing the effectiveness of an action while the action is ongoing. An example would be gathering feedback from your expedition team members during your planning and execution so that the expedition can be improved on a continuous basis.

Summative review – the process of reviewing an action and making judgements about its effectiveness when the action is complete. An example of this would be gathering feedback from the expedition participants at the end of the expedition.

Feedback

Feedback is the process of gathering views on an issue from a range of relevant people in order to improve an aspect of performance. In the case of your expedition, you might ask for feedback from observers, such as your tutor and class peers or those on your course. These people should provide constructive comments on your strengths and areas for improvement in terms of your planning and undertaking of the expedition. You might also want to ask for feedback on more specific aspects of your performance, such as your communication, leadership and decision-making skills.

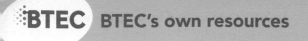

Activity: Appropriateness of the expedition

After you have completed your expedition, you should review some key aspects of its planning and undertaking. Write a 250-word review which looks at the following points:

- suitability of area
- choice of expedition
- matching of expedition to participants
- health and safety.

Expedition Evaluation

Name (of learner) ....

Expedition/event ....

Date(s) expedition took place ....

Brief summary of expedition (including objectives, location, group size, etc.)

....

....

Feedback from group ....

....

Feedback from tutor ....

....

Date(s) expedition took place ....

Brief summary of expedition (including objectives, location, group size, etc.)

....

....

What went well ....

What didn't go well ....

What I learned ....

What I will do differently next time ....

....

Figure 9.5: Can you think of anything else you should consider before you prepare your personal development plan (PDP)?

Case study: Charlotte's expedition review

We had to do a full review of our BTEC National in Public Services expedition last year. It had been a really poor expedition for my group, our planning had gone quite badly because none of us would give up the time to meet and discuss things properly, so we just ended up doing whatever was easiest – which turned out to be a 8-kilometre walk to a nearby campsite.

The walk was really boring. It was all flat and with clear paths so we didn't get a chance to try out many of the navigation skills we had practised. We arrived at the campsite mid afternoon and had nothing to do for the rest of the day. We ended up messing about on the campsite and being told off by the owners and some of the other campers. Worse than that, they told our tutor when she came to assess us.

We ended up failing the expedition and having to redo it. I was so angry with myself and the group for the time we wasted and I made sure that I sorted the group out so we got it right the second time. It meant I had to be a bit bossy and some of my team mates didn't like it, but I didn't care – I wasn't going to fail a second time just because we couldn't get our act together.

1   **What went wrong in the initial planning process for this expedition?**

2   **What went wrong during the first expedition?**

3   **What do you think Charlotte did to improve the expedition for the second attempt?**

One of the key aspects of an evaluation is making clear recommendations about what can be improved for next time. These recommendations are not just so you and your group can improve, but also so that following groups, such as the next year's BTEC National group, can learn from your mistakes.

4.2 Development plan

A personal development plan (or PDP) looks at how a particular activity or undertaking can be improved upon in the future. In terms of developing your expedition planning and execution, you might consider using a template that clearly shows aims, objectives, monitoring milestones and possible obstacles to overcome. These templates are often used in school or college for your tutorial sessions and can be adapted easily to fit the needs of developing your expedition and outdoor skills. Alternatively, you can find many different development and action plan templates on the Internet. You could use the headings on the document in the case study above and the review you wrote about your expedition to help you think about what you should include in your PDP.

Activity: Development plan

Once you have completed your expedition and formative and summative reviews, create a development plan to improve your performance for next time. Your PDP should include:

- aims (your overall goals)
- objectives (what targets you are hoping to achieve; remember to make your targets SMART)
- milestones (when you will achieve your set targets)
- potential obstacles to development (such as resources, human, physical and financial).

Remember!

SMART targets are:

- Specific
- Measurable
- Achievable
- Realistic
- Time-related.

Assessment activity 9.4

P5 P6 M5 D2 BTEC

After completing your expedition you will need to conduct a review of it and produce a development plan for improvement. Ensure you cover the following tasks:

1 Carry out a review of the planning and undertaking of expeditions, identifying strengths and areas for improvement. **P5**

2 Produce a personal development plan based on identified strengths and areas for improvement. **P6**

3 Explain identified strengths and areas for improvement and relate them to suggestions made in your personal development plan. **M5**

4 Justify suggestions made in your personal development plan. **D2**

Grading tips

For **P5** you could review your expeditions by asking participants to evaluate their own and your roles in the expedition. You could also ask your tutor for feedback. Make sure you are honest when you identify your strengths and weaknesses; remember that reviewing your performance properly will help you improve next time. If done properly, your development plan will become an action plan showing how you can build on your strengths and overcome your weaknesses.

For **P6** your tutor can help you assess your skills and techniques for your PDP form.

For **M5** you need to explain and highlight your strengths and weaknesses and tie them back to your PDP. Make sure it is clear what skills you need to obtain and how to achieve this.

For **D2** you need to give reasons or evidence to support your PDP suggestions. Make sure that the actions on the development plan are well thought out and considered.

PLTS

Reviewing your expedition and producing a development plan will develop your skills as a **reflective learner** and **self-manager**.

Functional skills

Presenting the information in your PDP will help you develop your functional **English** skills in writing.

Geoff
Walking Group Leader

I work as a Walking Group Leader at an outdoor residential centre in the Lake District. The centre does all kinds of outdoor activities, such as canoeing, kayaking, abseiling, caving and hiking. We see many different groups from small schoolchildren to pensioners and everything in between, so we need to be able to adjust what we do to match the groups we are responsible for.

It's my job to ensure that walking groups are properly prepared, well equipped and safe on their journey. I do this by spending the day before they set off on an expedition with the group going through all the basics and ensuring everyone has everything they need and is comfortable with the route.

A typical day

A typical day out on the hills involves an early start. We aim to get walking straight after breakfast because if the route is a long one we may need the full day to complete it. Once we are away from the centre and into the countryside, I nominate one person to navigate for each of the legs of the journey. Then I'll monitor them and check their understanding of the map or correct their compass work if they are not doing it right. It doesn't help people to learn if I always do the navigating – they need to learn and practise those skills themselves.

I'm responsible for safety throughout the trip and the group always gets a health and safety briefing before we set off, which I reinforce all the way around the route if any hazards crop up.

The best thing about the job

It's great to go out into the countryside several times a week. I'm not one to sit in an office, so being able to teach people practical skills in the fantastic Cumbrian countryside is the perfect job for me.

Think about it!

- What topics have you covered in this unit that might give you the background to be a good walking group leader?
- What knowledge and skills do you think you need to develop further if you want to be a walking group leader or outdoor specialist in the future?

Just checking

1. List the types of expedition you might encounter.
2. What is an aim?
3. What is an objective?
4. What is a bivouac?
5. What should a basic first aid kit contain?
6. How would you undertake a risk assessment?
7. Explain Naismith's Rule.
8. What is a bearing?
9. How can you maintain a dry tent?
10. What is the difference between a formative and summative review?

edexcel

Assignment tips

- If you are required to keep a learning diary or a journal, then be sure to record your work in a way that cannot be lost or mislaid. It might seem better to have a dedicated notebook for this, but what if you lose it? A better way might be to create a blog or electronic journal so that you always have a back up if you need it.

- You may think that practical tasks are going to be easier to pass than written tasks, but this is not the case. You will need to practise your skills before you are assessed – you cannot just jump in and hope for the best. This may include planning and practising in your own as well as class time. It is also likely that you will be photographed or videoed, so you should be prepared for this.

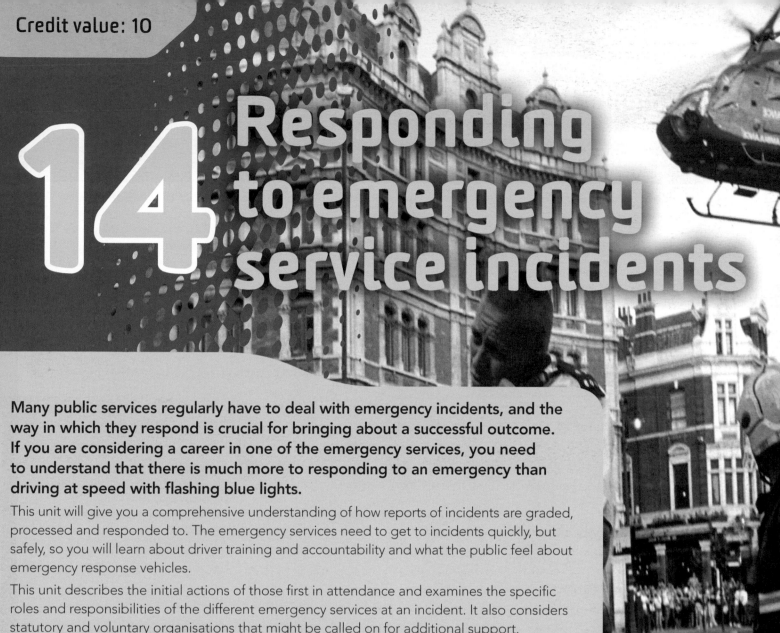

14 Responding to emergency service incidents

Many public services regularly have to deal with emergency incidents, and the way in which they respond is crucial for bringing about a successful outcome. If you are considering a career in one of the emergency services, you need to understand that there is much more to responding to an emergency than driving at speed with flashing blue lights.

This unit will give you a comprehensive understanding of how reports of incidents are graded, processed and responded to. The emergency services need to get to incidents quickly, but safely, so you will learn about driver training and accountability and what the public feel about emergency response vehicles.

This unit describes the initial actions of those first in attendance and examines the specific roles and responsibilities of the different emergency services at an incident. It also considers statutory and voluntary organisations that might be called on for additional support.

This unit also highlights the necessity for incident scene preservation. It looks at the need for accident investigation by different organisations and the various methods of gathering evidence for use in court. Finally, the unit will take you through the health and safety considerations when dealing with a variety of emergency incidents, as well as the safety measures emergency personnel take to protect themselves. It also covers relevant health and safety legislation and regulations that govern how emergency response situations are dealt with.

Learning outcomes

After completing this unit you should:

1. know the importance of responding to emergency incidents safely in response vehicles
2. understand the roles and responsibilities of public services when attending the scene of an emergency response incident
3. understand the necessity for scene preservation at emergency incidents
4. be able to review health and safety considerations during an emergency response incident scenario.

Assessment and grading criteria

This table shows you what you must do in order to achieve a pass, merit or distinction grade, and where you can find activities in this book to help you.

To achieve a **pass** grade the evidence must show that you are able to:	To achieve a **merit** grade the evidence must show that, in addition to the pass criteria, you are able to:	To achieve a **distinction** grade the evidence must show that, in addition to the pass and merit criteria, you are able to:
P1 describe how emergency incidents are graded by a selected public service call centre **See Assessment activity 14.1 page 40**		
P2 describe the importance of responding safely to emergency incidents as an emergency response driver **See Assessment activity 14.1 page 40**		
P3 identify the statutory and voluntary agencies who may work together at the scene of an emergency incident **See Assessment activity 14.2 page 48**	**M1** assess the roles and responsibilities of the key services attending an emergency incident **See Assessment activity 14.2 page 48**	**D1** evaluate the inter-agency cooperation of the emergency response services **See Assessment activity 14.2 page 48**
P4 explain the roles and responsibilities of the public services when attending the scene of an emergency incident **See Assessment activity 14.2 page 48**		
P5 describe the necessity for scene preservation units at emergency incidents as part of an incident investigation **See Assessment activity 14.3 page 52**	**M2** explain how scene preservation contributes to an accident/incident investigation **See Assessment activity 14.3 page 52**	
P6 assess the health and safety measures to be taken to ensure personal safety and that of others when attending an emergency incident scenario, with reference to the relevant health and safety legislation **See Assessment activity 14.4 page 58**	**M3** review the need for measures to be taken to ensure personal safety and that of others when attending an emergency incident scenario, with reference to relevant health and safety legislation **See Assessment activity 14.4 page 58**	**D2** evaluate the impact of health and safety measures on services responding to an emergency incident scenario with reference to relevant health and safety legislation **See Assessment activity 14.4 page 58**

How you will be assessed

This unit will be assessed by an internal assignment that will be designed and marked by the staff at your centre. The assignment is designed to allow you to show your understanding of the learning outcomes for responding to emergency service incidents. Assignments can be quite varied and can take the form of:

- portfolio of evidence
- wall display
- learning journal
- video diary
- role play
- presentation
- leaflet
- report.

Chloe learns more about the emergency services

There was a lot more to this unit than I thought there would be. I had no idea that emergencies were graded differently by each emergency service, and I was interested to learn about the types of driver training in each service too.

I enjoyed looking at various emergency situations and how different services deal with them. A lot of their work is very dangerous, but the training is excellent and they always seem to know what to do. I'm not sure I'd want to be the first at the scene of an emergency, though. The more I learn about the work the uniformed public services do, the more I want to join. However, I'm still not sure which service I want to work for yet.

For a few years now I've wanted to be a police officer and to train as a traffic officer, but I also like the idea of joining the Highways Agency and getting involved in emergencies on the motorways. Then, when we did the section on evidence and scene preservation, it crossed my mind to think about becoming a Scenes of Crime Officer, as I'd never really thought about that before.

The health and safety legislation was surprisingly interesting. I really don't know how the services manage to think about their own and others' safety when they are dealing with an emergency. I can see why it's necessary, but I think some of the rules and regulations are a bit restricting.

Over to you!

- What area of the emergency services appeals to you?
- Do you think you could remain calm in an emergency?
- What sort of qualities do you think are needed to cope with emergency situations?
- What preparation could you do to get ready for your assessments?

1. The importance of responding to emergency incidents safely in response vehicles

Talk up

All emergency incidents require an emergency response, but what is meant by an 'emergency incident'?

What would your priority be if you were called to the scene of a serious road traffic collision? Can you deal with difficult situations like this?

By studying this unit you will be able to give reasoned answers to these questions, as well as having a comprehensive understanding of the concept of emergency incidents.

1.1 Emergency incidents

Some emergencies, such as natural disasters, are more serious and visible than others. Large-scale emergency incidents are known as major incidents, but even smaller incidents, such as someone falling from a ladder, may still be classed as emergencies. Through the Civil Contingencies Act (CCA, 2004), the government defines an emergency as:

- an event or situation which threatens serious damage to human welfare, or
- an event or situation which threatens serious damage to the environment, or
- war or terrorism, which threatens serious damage to security.

All emergency incidents are graded by experienced call handlers, and you will see in the following section how the different emergency services grade incidents.

1.2 Incident grading

The emergency services (Police, Fire and Ambulance) are duty-bound to respond to all emergency situations, but because they have different roles and responsibilities, they have different graded response policies. It is important to understand that emergencies are graded by the call handler, according to the information provided by the caller, and not by the way the incident is reported. So if a caller dials 999 in the genuine belief that an incident is an emergency, once the call handler has assessed the information, they may

decide it is not a top priority or that the incident does not even require an emergency response.

How incidents are graded by emergency services

Tables 14.1, 14.2 and 14.3 opposite show how the different emergency services grade incidents.

Link

You can see the response times for these incidents in Table 14.4 on page 34.

Inter-agency approaches and agreements

The emergency services are known as **Category 1 responders** under the Civil Contingencies Act (2004) and they are legally bound to cooperate in an emergency with **Category 2 responders**. Inter-agency approaches and agreements are established at **Local Resilience Forums**, which are located within the boundary of police areas. Emergency service personnel must attend a Forum at least once every six months, where they cooperate with other personnel in both preparing for and responding to emergencies.

Link

See *Unit 15: Planning and management of major incidents*, for more about the Civil Contingencies Act (2004).

Table 14.1: Grading of incidents by the Police (England and Wales). Responses graded in accordance with the *National Call Handling Standards*, published by the Home Office, in conjunction with the Association of Chief Police Officers. Incidents are graded as 'emergency' or 'non-emergency' in four grades, as shown below.

Grade	Type of incident	Risks/criteria for grading level
Grade 1 Emergency	Incident currently taking place, and there is a risk of:	• danger to life • the use or immediate threat of use of violence • serious injury to a person and/or serious damage to property
	Criminal conduct, if:	• it involves a crime which is likely to be serious and in progress • an offender has just been disturbed at the scene • an offender has been detained and poses, or is likely to pose, a risk to other people
	Traffic collision, if:	• it involves, or is likely to involve, serious personal injury • the road is blocked or there is a dangerous or excessive build up of traffic
	Incident can also be Grade 1 if:	the call handler has strong and objective reasons for believing that the incident should be classified as an emergency
Grade 2 Priority	The call handler acknowledges that the incident requires a degree of importance or urgency, but an emergency response is not required.	Includes incidents such as: • a genuine concern for somebody's welfare • an offender has been detained and does not pose, or is unlikely to pose, a risk to others • a road traffic collision that involves injuries or serious obstruction • the likelihood that a witness or evidence might be lost • a person involved is suffering extreme distress or is believed to be vulnerable
Grade 3 Scheduled response	It is believed that the needs of the caller can be best achieved through scheduling because:	• the response time is not critical in apprehending offenders • better quality of initial police action can be given if it is dealt with by a pre-arranged response by a police officer or other appropriate resource, or attendance at a police station
Grade 4 Resolution without deployment		Used where the incident can be resolved through telephone advice, help desk intervention, frequently asked questions or the involvement of other appropriate agencies or services

Table 14.2: Grading of incidents by the Ambulance Service. Three categories. Note that this grading also applies to urgent calls from GPs and other health professionals, as well as to calls from members of the public.

Grade	Risks/criteria for grading level
Category A Priority	Incident is considered to be immediately life-threatening
Category B	Incident is serious, but not immediately life-threatening
Category C	Incident is neither serious nor life-threatening.

Table 14.3: Grading of incidents by the Fire Service: five risk categories

Grade	Risks/criteria for grading level
Risk Category A	Normally refers to large cities and towns and includes shopping areas, business, entertainment or industrial centres
Risk Category B	Normally refers to large cities and towns with multi-storey buildings; includes large areas of residential accommodation, as well as industrial trading estates containing high-risk occupancies
Risk Category C	Normally refers to the suburbs of larger towns and the built-up areas of smaller towns, including terraced and semi-detached dwellings, as well as low-risk industrial and residential areas
Risk Category D	Refers to all areas that do not come within Categories A to C
Rural and remote	A separate category and has no pre-determined response.

Key terms

Category 1 responders – the organisations that are at the centre of planning and responding to an emergency. Category 1 responders are the emergency services (Police, Fire and Ambulance), local authorities and the Health Protection Agency.

Category 2 responders – these include the Highways Agency and the utility companies (gas, water and electricity).

Local Resilience Forum – a meeting of the emergency services and other invited agencies who are brought together to discuss emergency planning issues so that the community is prepared and ready to return to normal in the event of a major incident. (To be resilient means to quickly bounce back to normal after a shock or upheaval.)

Emergencies are graded by the call handler according to certain response policies. Have you called the emergency services in the past? How was your call handled?

Preparing for and responding to emergencies is done by assessing local risks, emergency planning, sharing information and producing multi-agency plans and agreements. Emergency preparation also includes joint training and exercises with the utility companies (gas, water and electricity), local authorities and voluntary agencies that would be involved in emergency incidents.

Local Resilience Forums are the key to emergency preparedness because they bring together all the agencies that have to cooperate at emergency incidents. By training together and taking part in partial or full-scale scenarios, the emergency services and the other agencies know each organisation's roles and responsibilities and can respond to an incident efficiently.

At the Hillsborough Disaster of 1989, for instance, there was little cooperation between the different services. The lack of joint preparation resulted in an inadequate response in dealing with the situation. On the other hand, the 7/7 bombings in London had a better outcome because the agencies involved had prepared for such an incident.

Role of call centres and incident managers

Most emergency call centre staff work in the control room of one of the emergency services and deal with both emergency and non-emergency telephone calls from members of the public. They identify the needs of the caller through careful listening and effective questioning, so they can assess the urgency of the call before deciding upon the most suitable course of action.

Depending upon the nature of the call, the call handler is responsible for the tasks shown in Figure 14.1.

Call handlers work under the supervision of team leaders and incident managers, though all emergency call handlers are involved in incident management to some degree. The incident manager is also responsible for liaising with other organisations such as local authorities, utilities companies, local transport companies, voluntary agencies, the Environment Agency, and any other agency whose services may be required in order to provide an efficient response to the incident.

Policies and procedures for dealing with incidents

When attending emergency incidents, all the emergency services follow their own service policy and procedures. Where a joint response is required at a major incident, the responders would follow the policy and procedures of the joint emergency plan, as decided at the Local Resilience Forum. As a result, each service is aware of the common objectives, as well as their own specific objectives.

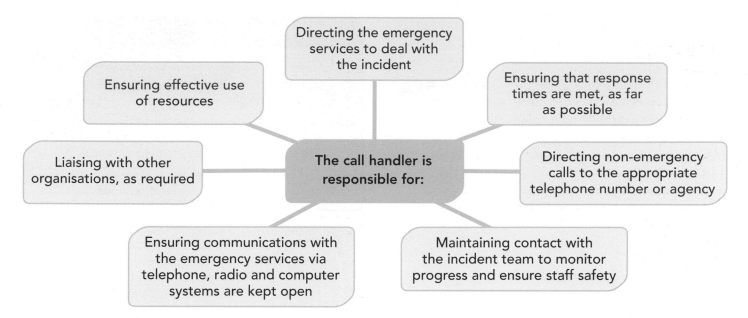

Figure 14.1: A call handler's responsibilities

Common objectives of the emergency services include:

- saving life and alleviating suffering at the scene
- protecting property
- **mitigating** the incident and preventing its escalation
- safeguarding the environment
- restoring normality
- maintaining normal services where possible
- providing resources.

Each of the services is aware of the need to establish command and control of the incident, namely, **Gold, Silver** and **Bronze Command**. The personnel for each level of command will have been decided before the onset of a major incident.

Key terms

Mitigate – to reduce or lessen

Gold Command (also known as strategic command) – where the plans, or strategies, are drawn up by the senior officers to attempt to bring a successful conclusion to an emergency. This command is located away from the scene of the incident – usually at Police headquarters.

Silver Command (also known as tactical command) – the link between Gold and Operational command. It is closer to the scene, usually in an outer cordon.

Bronze Command (also known as Operational command) – located at the scene and involves the rescue operation by the emergency services and other agencies.

Link

See *Unit 15: Planning and management of major incidents*, page 76, for more about Gold, Silver and Bronze Command.

Definitions of emergency response

There are two meanings of the term 'emergency response', as described below.

Firstly, an emergency response is the fourth of five related elements that make up Integrated Emergency Management (IEM) when dealing with major incidents. The five elements are:

1. risk assessment
2. hazard prevention and minimisation
3. preparedness
4. response
5. recovery.

Secondly, an emergency response can refer to the *manner in which an emergency service* (or services) *responds* to an emergency incident. It is the immediate, safe response in accordance with authorised driver grades and may require the use of blue lights and audible siren. This emergency response could be to either a localised or wider-area emergency.

A localised emergency is contained or restricted to a particular area. It can be dealt with by the attendance of the local emergency services without the need for a coordinated response by other agencies, for example the immediate response by a paramedic to a heart attack victim.

A wider-area emergency cannot be dealt with at the local level without the coordinated response of other agencies. For example, an incident involving chemical, biological, radiological and nuclear materials will need the response of specialist agencies to offer scientific and technical advice and support, as well as Health Advisory Teams to give public health advice.

A coordinated response may also be required for such incidents as:

- influenza pandemics
- animal health outbreaks
- terrorist attacks
- structural failures
- transport accidents
- environmental pollution.

Response times

Emergency response times vary from service to service and from area to area. Government guidelines for response times of the different emergency categories are outlined in Table 14.4.

Activity: Grading incidents

Consider the following examples and see if you can grade each incident by the relevant service, as well as giving the response time.

1 A man and wife return home to their house in the countryside and find a broken door lock. They suspect intruders are in their house.

2 The owner of a burger bar in a small shopping centre on the outskirts of a large town dials 999 to report a cooker on fire and out of control.

3 A labourer in a scrap yard, on the outskirts of town, has become trapped when a scrapped car, which was stacked on top of another car, toppled on him and trapped his leg. He is in great pain and his leg is crushed.

4 A man walking his dog late at night notices some youths acting suspiciously near a neighbour's car. The youths run off as he approaches and he notices that a car window has been broken.

5 There is a multi-vehicle collision on the motorway, approximately eight miles out of town; there are serious injuries and people are trapped.

Table 14.4: Emergency response times for the Police, Fire and Ambulance Services

Police	Ambulance	Fire
Grade 1: Emergency Urban response time: 10 minutes. Rural response time: 17 minutes.	**Grade A (life threatening)** Within 8 minutes or less.	**Risk category A** Two appliances should arrive within 5 minutes. A further appliance should arrive within 8 minutes.
Grade 2: Priority Resources to be sent as soon and safely as possible – within 15 minutes.	**Category B** Within 14 minutes in urban areas. Within 19 minutes in rural areas.	**Risk category B** One appliance should arrive within 5 minutes. A further appliance should arrive within 8 minutes.
Grade 3: Scheduled response Incident to be resolved to satisfaction of caller as soon as possible. Must be within 48 hours of initial contact.		**Risk category C** One appliance should arrive within 8 to 10 minutes.
Grade 4: Resolution without deployment Caller advised of agreed call-back time, to be as soon as possible and within 24 hours.		**Risk category D** One appliance should arrive within 20 minutes.

Initial response services

Out of the three emergency services, it is normally the Police who respond first to most incidents. This is because they are constantly on patrol, whereas the Fire and Ambulance Services are on call at stations or strategic locations where they are ready to respond to emergency calls. There are few incidents to which the Police do not respond initially because, even if they attend in a supporting role, say, for an injury that requires the skills of the Ambulance Service, they may still be required in some capacity. For example, they might have to break into a house because the owner has collapsed. If attending a traffic collision where the Fire Service take the lead role in a rescue operation, the Police are needed to control traffic, take witness statements and investigate the cause.

Additional public services offering specialist knowledge

Despite the skills and abilities of the emergency services, some incidents cannot be resolved without the specialist knowledge and expertise of additional public services. For example, the services of the military would be required in the event of a suspicious package that was believed to be an explosive device. Royal Navy divers might be called on for an underwater search and rescue.

> ### Activity: Specialist knowledge
>
> Think of three situations where additional public services offering specialist knowledge might be called to an incident.

Accountability

All emergency service personnel are **accountable** for their actions while performing their duty. They are governed by the rules, regulations and codes of conduct of their services. This is for the good of the service, the safety of the public and their own safety. The fact that emergency personnel have to respond quickly to emergencies does not give them any special **dispensation** while driving at high speeds, even when using flashing lights and sirens.

> ### Key terms
>
> **Accountable** – required or expected to justify actions or decisions.
>
> **Dispensation** – exemption from a rule or usual requirement.

> ### Link
>
> You can read more about driver accountability on page 38 of this unit.

1.3 Driving in response to an emergency

Emergency vehicles and equipment

As well as responding to emergency incidents quickly and safely, the emergency services must also have the necessary equipment so that they can deal efficiently with each incident. Certain emergency equipment is carried as standard in all emergency vehicles, although some vehicles are larger than others and carry more equipment because of the nature of that service. Tables 14.5 and 14.6 overleaf show the standard and additional vehicles and equipment used by the emergency services.

> ### Activity: A visit to your local fire station
>
> Contact your local fire station and explain to them that you are studying this course. Ask them if you can call in at a convenient time to have a look at their rescue equipment.

Table 14.5: Emergency vehicles used by the Police, Fire and Ambulance Services

Police vehicles	Ambulance Service vehicles	Fire Service vehicles
Standard equipment		
• Volvo V70 T5 • Vauxhall Omega • BMW 5 Series • BMW X5 • Vauxhall Vectra • A selection of 4x4 vehicles	• Ambulances with two crew members • Rapid response cars with one crew member • Paramedic motorcycles	• Standard fire engines (or fire tenders)
Additional equipment held by Services in some places		
• Most Police services also use motorcyles and have access to a force helicopter	• Bicycles for paramedics to respond to emergency incidents in busy towns and cities • Air ambulances for responding to really serious incidents or incidents that are not easily accessible by any other means • The South Western Ambulance Service has an ambulance boat for incidents in the Isles of Scilly	• Incident Support Units (ISUs), e.g. Water/Ice Rescue Units that are fully equipped with boats for rescues from deep water • Heavy Rescue Units containing cutting and lifting apparatus for incidents involving building collapse or large-scale road traffic accidents (hydraulic cutters, spreads, rams, high pressure hoses and chains for stabilising vehicles) • Pollution Containment Units for dealing with chemical or hazardous material incidents.

Table 14.6: Emergency equipment carried by the Police, Fire and Ambulance Services

Police	Ambulance	Fire
• traffic cones • lamps • accident signs (slow, diversion, use hard shoulder and rejoin main carriageway) • tow ropes • fire extinguisher • crowbar, hacksaw and axe • industrial gloves • first aid kit, resuscitation kit and infectious diseases kit • space blankets • 'stinger' tyre deflation unit	• electrocardiograph machines • immediate aid response kit (**resuscitation** bag/valve with adult and child masks, hand-held suction, **airways**, burns gel packs, assorted dressings) • portable oxygen sets with a range of face masks • battery-operated suction unit • pulse oximeter • manual sphygmomanometer and stethoscope • defibrillator with accessories • drugs packs, intravenous fluids and cannulae • rigid neck collars • long spinal board, orthopaedic stretcher • vacuum splints and fracture splints • moving and handling equipment, pillows, blankets and carrying chairs • universal precaution equipment including disposable gloves, face masks, aprons, waste bins and sharps boxes • maternity pack and blankets • tissues and incontinence pads	• flat-head and pick-head axe • fire-retardant, pathogen and chemical resistant and water-resistant boots with steel toe and a full-length steel sole • flashlight • self-contained breathing apparatus (SCBA) • helmet, face mask and/or visor • fire-resistant work gloves • PASS (Personal Alert Safety System) device • hand-held radio • hydraulic rescue tools • duck-bill lock breaker • spanner wrench • circular saw ('K-12') • cutters edge • laser heat gun • thermal imaging camera (infrared) • pager/receiver (for fire alerts).

Driver training and driving standards for emergency response vehicles

In 2000, the Driving Standards Agency (DSA) became responsible for assessing the standards and training needs of all drivers who are entitled to drive emergency response vehicles that are fitted with blue lights and sirens. The vehicles included are shown in Figure 14.2.

In consultation with other agencies, the DSA drew up the *Blue Light Users Working Party Expectations Document*. It contained a list of the **core competencies** that drivers should meet before being allowed to drive emergency vehicles in response to emergency calls. This document has been accepted by the three main emergency services (Police, Fire and Ambulance) as the basic standard that has to be met.

The competencies include performance criteria as well as underpinning knowledge. They consist of the following three elements:

- **Element one** – the ability to assess the need for an emergency response
- **Element two** – the ability to drive the vehicle safely to emergencies
- **Element three** – the ability to demonstrate the correct attitude when responding to emergencies.

Police Service drivers

Besides the standards set by the DSA, the Police Services in England and Wales have their own driving

Key terms

Core competencies – basic or key skills.

Resuscitation – action taken to revive a person who is not breathing.

Airway – a plastic tube inserted in an unconscious person's throat via their mouth to ensure a clear airway during resuscitation.

centres. Here police drivers are trained and graded according to National Training Standards, which are approved by the Association of Chief Police Officers (ACPO). The type of driver training given depends on the job role of the police officer. For example, police drivers can be graded as:

- standard response drivers
- advanced drivers
- pursuit drivers.

Advanced drivers and pursuit drivers receive intense training. They use high-powered vehicles and advanced techniques for responding quickly and safely to emergency calls.

Fire Service drivers

The Fire Service has its own driver training centres where drivers are trained to the standards set by their Fire Authority. In order to drive an Emergency Fire Appliance, drivers must hold a Large Goods Vehicle (LGV) licence and have received the appropriate

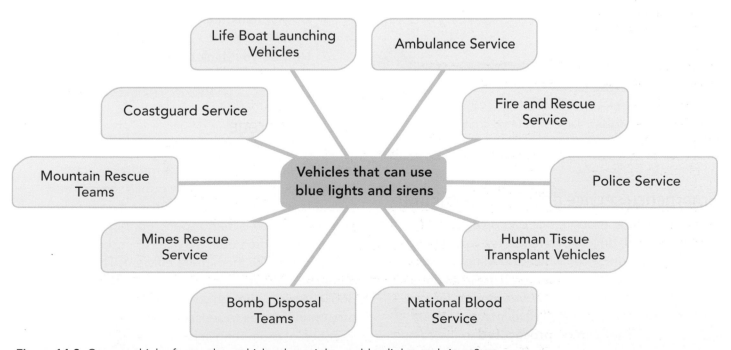

Figure 14.2: Can you think of any other vehicles that might use blue lights and sirens?

training and assessment. They are then allowed to drive when responding to emergency situations, provided the vehicle is fitted with audible/visual warning devices.

Ambulance Service drivers

Ambulance drivers need to hold C1 (medium-sized vehicle) and D1 (minibus) licences and receive the appropriate training, as specified by the DSA. However, some Ambulance Services, for instance in London, specify that drivers must hold a LGV licence.

Ambulance driver training and assessment is usually carried out by independent driver training centres, rather than by the Ambulance Service.

Public perception and reaction to emergency response vehicles

Members of the uniformed public services are often judged harshly by the public, especially as far as their driving goes. You may often hear negative comments about drivers of emergency vehicles, but you will rarely hear them being praised.

When people see emergency vehicles responding to incidents, they have very mixed views and reactions. Some feel that the Police, for instance, abuse their powers and speed through traffic with their lights flashing simply because they do not want to queue like everyone else. Other people believe that pursuing drivers of stolen vehicles causes more danger than not pursuing them. There are even others who believe that there is one law for the emergency services and one law for the public when it comes to speeding or driving dangerously.

Did you know?

There have been instances when drivers have followed emergency vehicles through congested areas to avoid queues. This is against the law.

Emergency service driver accountability

The fact remains, though, that bad driving causes accidents. Also, drivers of emergency vehicles are not above the law, even when attending emergency incidents. If it can be shown that a driver of an emergency service vehicle drove without due care and attention, or that they drove in a dangerous manner, then they can be **prosecuted** in the same way that a member of the public can. Furthermore,

if convicted of a serious traffic offence, they may be disqualified from driving both emergency and privately owned vehicles.

Key term

Prosecute – take legal proceedings against someone for breaking the law.

Case study: PC jailed after death of schoolgirl

At 11.20 pm on 19 May 2008, a 16-year-old schoolgirl, Hayley Adamson, was struck by a police car travelling at 70 mph as she was crossing the road in a residential area in Newcastle, which had a 30 mph speed limit.

Hayley died immediately from the impact of the police car, a Volvo. The police car was being driven in pursuit of an unlawful vehicle that had just registered on the police vehicle's automatic number plate recognition system.

At the time of the accident, the driver of the police car, PC John Dougal, had his headlights on but was not sounding sirens or displaying blue flashing lights because he did not want to alert the unlawful car that it was being pursued. The incident was investigated by the Independent Police Complaints Commission and the following year PC Dougal was sentenced to three years' imprisonment for causing the death of Hayley by dangerous driving.

1 **Do you think the officer was driving dangerously?**

2 **How do you think the public reacted to the verdict?**

Media coverage

When drivers of emergency vehicles are involved in accidents this always attracts media coverage. You should not forget that the public services are accountable to the public, who have a right to know how their money is being spent. Furthermore, public opinion helps the public services to improve their service and make them more efficient. Therefore, the media have a duty to inform us of the behaviour of the public services, though some might think the press often print articles to sensationalise events with the intention of promoting sales. However, this is not the case, as the following activity shows.

Activity: How do you feel about emergency vehicles?

What do you think when you see an emergency vehicle speeding through busy traffic with sirens sounding and blue lights flashing? What do your friends think?

Carry out research on the Internet to find articles reporting on fire engines involved in collisions when responding to emergency calls.

Discuss your findings as a group.

Use of warning systems

To reduce the danger to both the public and themselves, emergency service drivers must use their sirens and blue flashing lights to warn other road users (including pedestrians and cyclists) that the vehicle is responding to an emergency. Flashing blue lights and sirens should only be used when attending emergencies, though police drivers are also instructed to use blue flashing lights when attempting to stop another driver.

Although drivers of emergency response vehicles are subject to the same traffic laws as everyone else, while using blue lights and audible warnings in response to an emergency call they are **exempt** from a number of motoring regulations. This means that they may:

- treat a red traffic light as a give way sign
- pass to the right of a keep left bollard
- drive on a motorway hard shoulder (even against the direction of traffic)
- disobey the speed limit.

Key term

Exempt – free from the same obligations as others.

The impact of the Highway Code on response drivers

The Highway Code is a book of rules and a code of conduct that applies to pedestrians, riders and drivers in England, Scotland and Wales. Many of the rules in the Code are legal requirements and must be adhered to. However, some of the rules are not legally binding

and breaking them may not lead to prosecution, though the Code may be used as evidence to establish a person's liability.

The Code makes no special provision for response drivers, other than a mention in Rule 219 where it advises road users to listen for emergency vehicles and take the appropriate action to let them pass (while still complying with all traffic signs).

Activity: Impact of the core competencies code of practice

What do the case studies and your research imply about the standard of driver training for emergency responders? Are the core competencies sufficient?

You read earlier that the Police Service train their own officers in different standards of emergency response driving. Even though they are trained to a very high standard, you may have seen or read about examples of bad driving, particularly relating to speed. Does the core competency standard mean anything, then, or is it insufficient? How could it be improved?

1   Do you think that Ambulance Service drivers are trained to the same high degree as police emergency responders?

2   Should the Driving Standards Agency examiners play a greater role in testing the competencies, instead of just conducting the standard driving test that all emergency service drivers undertake?

3   What do you think about Fire Service driver training?

4   Have you ever come across any reports of excellent driving by the emergency services?

Remember!

There are thousands of emergency responses every week in the UK. The media reports on only the cases where something bad has happened as a result of a driver responding to an emergency call, but this doesn't give a true reflection. There will be many examples of excellent driving. Remember to keep things in context.

Assessment activity 14.1

As a member of the uniformed public services you will need to understand the concept of emergency incidents, especially if you are called upon to respond to such an incident. You will also need to realise the importance of responding safely.

Give a presentation to the class in which you:

1 Describe how emergency incidents are graded by a selected public service control room. **P1**

2 Describe the importance of responding safely to emergency incidents as an emergency response driver. **P2**

Grading tips

For **P1** you should give a description of how incidents are graded by a specific public service control room. You need to know the grading categories used, as well as the roles of the call handler and the incident manager.

For **P2** you need to say why it is important to respond to emergency incidents safely. You should be able to show you understand driving standards and the accountability of emergency response drivers – how there are no exemptions for drivers of emergency vehicles. You should illustrate your points with examples of what might happen if incidents were not responded to safely.

2. Understand the roles and responsibilities of public services when attending the scene of an emergency response incident

Because of their training in Local Resilience Forums, all of the emergency services know each other's roles and responsibilities as well as those of other organisations including voluntary agencies. As a result, the first member of the emergency services to attend the scene can make an assessment of the situation and request the services of any other organisations as necessary.

Link

See pages 30 and 32 of this unit for more about Local Resilience Forums.

2.1 Initial actions of first in attendance

It is important that emergency responders arrive at the scene safely because the information they relay to their control room is vital for the successful outcome of the incident. This is especially true if an integrated

response by the emergency services is needed. As mentioned earlier, it is normally, but not always, a police officer who first attends the scene, and they follow a routine procedure.

Information updates using CHALET

If the incident is minor and there is no need for further assistance, the first responder will let the control room know. However, if the incident is serious and immediate assistance is required, then this is transmitted to the control room using the **mnemonic** CHALET:

Casualties – number or estimated number

Hazards – present or potential

Access – routes in and out for the emergency and other services

Location – exact location of incident

Emergency services – present and needed

Type of incident – e.g. building collapse, traffic collision, fire, chemical hazard

Key term

Mnenomic – a pattern of letters or words that aids memory.

In serious incidents, the first officer at the scene does not become involved in rescue work because their role is to assess the situation and maintain contact with control in order to coordinate the response. The first officer takes command of the incident until the formal control structure is established. Their vehicle becomes the forward control point and the officer also keeps a record of messages passed and received and decisions taken.

Ambulance Service first responder on scene

In really serious incidents, the Ambulance Service will be coordinated by an Ambulance Incident Officer (AIO). Until their arrival at the scene, the first ambulance or paramedic response unit will:

- report arrival on scene to Ambulance Control
- liaise with other emergency service incident officers
- provide Control with details of the incident
- confirm the type of incident, for example whether it is a major incident
- commence a log of all communications and actions
- ensure that the nearest appropriate receiving hospitals are aware of the incident.

Fire Service first responder on scene

The first Fire Officer to arrive at a fire scene takes the role of Fire Incident Commander. They do not become directly involved with rescue or fire fighting because their role is to:

- complete a dynamic risk assessment
- instigate Incident Command
- assess the size and nature of the incident and communicate this information to Control
- form a plan of action to deal with the developing situation
- continue the risk assessment process and issue instructions
- designate a suitable meeting point
- establish communications and liaise with the other emergency services
- set up a restricted zone and cordons.

2.2 Practical public service work

When dealing with emergency incidents, each of the public services has specific roles. However, they all share the following common objectives:

- saving life and minimising suffering at the scene
- protecting property
- preventing the escalation of a disaster
- protecting the environment

Activity: You are first on the scene!

Consider the following scenario, then answer the questions that follow.

At 3.30 am a fully laden petrol tanker developed a mechanical fault while descending a steep hill on the outskirts of a heavily populated town. The driver struggled in vain to control the vehicle and, after demolishing a set of traffic lights and a lamp-post, it eventually collided into the side of a care home for older people, causing serious structural damage to the building and extensive damage to the tanker.

Petrol from the tanker is spilling onto the floor near the building and some of the residents have been disturbed by the collision. It is not known how many residents live in the home, though it is believed that several are physically disabled and unable to walk.

A member of staff from the home is in shock and distressed, but has the presence of mind to make an emergency telephone call.

The driver of the tanker is breathing, but is unconscious and has a cut on his head.

1. **You are the first emergency responder at the scene. What should your initial response be?**

2. **Using the mnemonic of CHALET, what precise information would you transmit to your control room?**

3. **What other information would you need before a combined response could be effectively mounted?**

4. **Apart from the emergency services, what other agencies would you request and why?**

- sharing information between all agencies involved
- protecting and preserving the scene
- contributing to debriefing and any investigations or enquiries into the incident
- restoring normality
- maintaining normal services where possible
- providing whatever resources are needed.

Table 14.7 lists the specific duties of each of the emergency services when attending emergency incidents.

Police investigations

If police investigations at the incident discover that it was caused by a **negligent** or **malicious** act, then criminal proceedings will have to be brought against the person or persons responsible. If anyone dies as a result of the incident then those responsible may be charged with murder or **manslaughter**.

Table 14.7: Roles of the Police, Fire and Ambulance Services at major incidents

Police	Ambulance	Fire
Provide and update Control Room with clear information	Provide emergency aid and **triage**	Fight fires
Ensure access and exit routes are clear	Resuscitate where necessary	Minimise fire risk by removing combustible materials or using foam
Collect and pass on information	Establish casualty loading area	Advise other services on health and safety at the scene
Control crowds, sightseers and onlookers	Transport casualties to designated hospitals	Search for and rescue casualties using specialist equipment
Safeguard victim's personal property	Give police details of victims taken to designated hospitals so relatives can be informed	Identify hazardous substances
Obtain witness statements	Establish casualty clearing area	Dilute or neutralise harmful chemicals
Preserve the scene and gather evidence	Order medical resources (drugs, blood supplies, personnel) where necessary	Establish decontamination units
Identify the dead on behalf of **HM Coroner**		Assist in salvage operations
Investigate the cause		Provide first aid at the scene
Inform and warn the public via the media		Use pumping apparatus to remove water
		Investigate the cause of the fire

Key terms

Negligent – lack of proper care or attention.

Malicious – intending to do harm.

Manslaughter – killing committed without intent. Manslaughter is considered a less serious crime than murder, which is killing another with intent.

Triage – assessing the condition of casualties and attending to the most serious first.

HM Coroner – the person who holds inquests into deaths that are thought to be of a violent or accidental nature.

If the cause of an emergency incident is suspicious, for example a warehouse fire that was discovered in the early hours of the morning, Scene of Crime Officers (SOCO) will be called to examine the scene and gather evidence to establish the cause. Even charred remains can be **forensically examined** and used in evidence. Scene preservation is therefore an essential task that is the responsibility of the Police.

Key term

Forensic examination – a detailed examination of a crime scene, or of material gathered from a crime scene, using scientific techniques. The results of this investigation may be presented as evidence in a court case.

Link

See Section 3 of this unit for more about scene preservation.

Remember!

The charge would be murder if malicious intent could be proved, but it would be manslaughter if death was the result of negligence.

Activity: Responding to a major incident

Can you think of three other examples where Scene of Crime Officers could be called to investigate the cause of an incident?

What must the Police be aware of when they are dealing with a major incident? Carry out research using the Internet into the Police response to the flooding in Cumbria in 2009.

Navy, Army and Royal Air Force assistance in civil emergencies

The military (Royal Navy, Royal Air Force and Army) are not usually directly involved in planning for major incidents in the civilian community because of their operational commitments. However, military assistance is often provided at emergency incidents, as they can offer expert advice and guidance, highly-skilled personnel and a wide range of vehicles. For example, in the Boscastle Floods of 2004, seven helicopters from the Royal Navy and Royal Air Force were used to evacuate 150 people from the town. Furthermore, following the devastating floods in the Cumbrian town of Workington in December 2009, a footbridge was constructed over the River Derwent by the Royal Engineers, Royal Logistic Corps, Royal Signals and Royal Military Police.

Help from soldiers from the 2nd Signal Regiment was invaluable during the floods at York in November 2000.

Mountain and cave rescue

Mountain and cave rescue organisations consist of highly trained volunteers who can operate efficiently in all weathers on mountainous terrain, rock faces, remote moorland and in underground cave systems. They are often called out by the Police to help with land-based search and rescues, because of their skills and expertise. Mountain rescue teams are particularly skilful in responding to search and rescues in an avalanche situation, but they were also called out to motorists who had been trapped in heavy snow near Middleton in Teesdale in December 2009.

2.3 Practical work of the Fire Service

Fire-fighters are highly trained in all types of rescues, including collapsed buildings, burning buildings, floods and road traffic collisions. They also carry defibrillators and other first-aid equipment in their vehicles for administering emergency first aid. When they attend road traffic collisions, with victims trapped inside vehicles, fire-fighters are expert in the use of hydraulic cutting equipment and other apparatus to free trapped victims from wreckage.

Fire Investigation Units

When the fire has been dealt with, mobile Fire Investigation Units can be driven to the scene to carry out an investigation. The unit is like a mobile office where interviews can be conducted and plans discussed relating to the investigation; CCTV footage can also be viewed. Units are equipped with specialised equipment, lighting and excavation tools, which allow investigation teams to work independently so they do not have to rely on the resources of operational staff.

The Fire Service also becomes involved at incidents involving dangerous chemical spillages or leaks.

> ### Link
> You can read more about chemical spills and PPE in Section 4 of this unit.

The very nature of their work means that fire-fighters have a comprehensive understanding of health and safety, and they continuously assess risks and hazards as they develop at the scene. Because of this, and their vigorous training, fire-fighters act as health and safety advisors to other services at emergency incidents.

Fire-fighting and rescue equipment

Some of the UK's fire services are equipped with Incident Support Units (ISUs) which have been especially designed to deal with certain types of incidents. For example, Water/Ice Rescue Units are fully equipped with boats for rescues from deep water, and Heavy Rescue Units contain vital cutting and lifting apparatus for incidents involving building collapse or large-scale road traffic accidents. Such apparatus consists of hydraulic cutters, spreads, rams, high pressure hoses and chains for stabilising vehicles. Furthermore, the Fire Service has Pollution Containment Units for dealing with chemical or hazardous material incidents.

Can you identify the equipment in this Fire Service vehicle?

Did you know?

A specialist team of 61 fire and rescue workers, from eight different Fire Services, were deployed to Haiti as part of the UK International Search and Rescue response to the earthquake disaster of 2010?

2.4 Roles of other statutory and voluntary agencies

Highways departments

Most emergency incidents, regardless of their cause or nature, are likely to involve serious disruption to major road networks. Even if the incident is not on or near a motorway or major road, long queues of traffic, often involving hundreds of people, can occur as a result of road closures and traffic congestion near the actual scene. Traffic has to be managed effectively so that the congestion does not prolong the emergency incident, or even cause a further incident.

The **Highways Agency** is responsible for maintaining and managing all motorway systems and 'A' class roads throughout England, while local authorities are responsible for other roads. The Highways Agency monitors and manages congestion through Regional and National Traffic Control Centres, and makes detailed information readily available to the public through the agency's Traffic Radio and illuminated signs on motorways (and updates on the Internet). The agency also has the technical capability to close roads and lanes, and divert traffic quickly through the **matrix system** on motorways and other major roads.

Key terms

Highways Agency – branch of the Department of Transport responsible for managing traffic and dealing with congestion and traffic problems on the motorways and other main roads in England.

Matrix system – a system of digital instructions and directions on motorways that inform motorists of hazards and diversions.

Local radio

Local radio stations provide information and regular updates of incidents that are in the public interest. They can be used to warn of dangers, school closures and any disruptions to services as a result of an emergency incident. Local radio stations can also advise the community of any urgent action they need to take and give out emergency telephone numbers. For example, in the case of a chemical leak, local radio can let people know whether they need to evacuate or stay indoors and await further information.

Activity: Public information

What sort of public information have you learned from your local radio in the last month? See if you can list three things.

Bomb disposal

Since the London bombings in July 2005, members of the public have become increasingly aware of suspicious packages. The Police Service receives many calls claiming that suspicious packages have been found. Although the Police realise that not all of these packages present a threat to the public, they cannot take any risks and have to treat such reports seriously. They assess each situation and take the necessary immediate action, such as evacuating the area.

Where there is good reason to believe that a suspicious package poses a threat to the public, bomb disposal experts will be requested. Bomb disposal (or explosive ordnance disposal) is normally carried out by Bomb Disposal Engineers of the British Army's Royal Engineers. They will clear any suspicious areas before allowing members of the public to return. Suspicious packages may be cleared by a controlled explosion if there is any doubt as to the content.

Case study: Explosive device found in Doncaster

In the early hours of 22 April 2009, CCTV operators noticed suspicious activity outside a council building in Doncaster town centre. Police officers were called to the scene and noticed a bag containing a number of canisters leading up to the back door of the building. The building was immediately sealed off, a cordon was put in place and guests from a nearby hotel were evacuated while fire-fighters remained at the scene.

Bomb disposal experts from Catterick were summoned; they arrived at the scene at 4.00 am and disarmed the explosive device. A South Yorkshire Police spokeswoman said: 'A suspicious device was found adjacent to council premises in Doncaster town centre. Officers cordoned off the area after finding an improvised explosive device which was intended to cause damage.'

A spokesman for Doncaster Metropolitan Borough Council said: 'The device has now been made safe and the Police are investigating the circumstances around this incident. Our other buildings are being checked and managers have been issued with advice on what to do if they become aware of anything suspicious.'

If you were a member of the public services dealing with the above incident, would you have the presence of mind to evacuate the surrounding area?

1 How would you organise the evacuation in terms of transportation?

2 Where would you accommodate the evacuees until the area was safe?

3 Would you evacuate from the immediate area only? If not, then how would you decide on the extent of the evacuation?

4 Now carry out some research into the following incidents:
- controlled explosion of a suspicious package in Frodsham by army bomb disposal experts in April 2009
- removal of a suspicious package in Glasgow by bomb disposal experts, May 2009.

a) How do the two cases differ?

b) Had you been the officer in charge at both incidents, would you have alerted the bomb disposal team?

2.5 Voluntary agencies

Other agencies that can offer assistance in the event of an emergency incident include:

- St John Ambulance (first aid)
- British Red Cross (first aid)
- Victim Support Scheme (welfare and emotional support)
- WRVS – formerly Women's Royal Voluntary Service (welfare assistance, provision of food and shelter).

St John Ambulance

St John Ambulance is a charitable organisation staffed by trained volunteers. The organisation responds to hundreds of emergency incidents (including major incidents) such as floods, fires, road traffic collisions and train crashes. The service supports and assists those in need, and is an excellent resource in terms of trained staff, medical aid and emergency vehicles. It can also provide evacuation centres.

Did you know?

During the London bombings of 2005, St John Ambulance provided 120 volunteers, 37 ambulances and 20 mobile treatment centres to support the London Ambulance Service. What is more, the service was present at the three affected underground stations for five days, offering support and assistance.

British Red Cross

The British Red Cross is a voluntary humanitarian organisation that provides an emergency response to help individuals and communities recover from emergencies, such as floods, fires and evacuations. It also provides health and social care to reduce difficulty and suffering that may follow an emergency incident.

In times of major emergency, the British Red Cross may be called upon to staff reception centres, support the Ambulance Service, assist in the process of tracing missing persons at the incident, and many other tasks. The British Red Cross can provide emergency response volunteers as well as ambulances and equipment. In the aftermath of an incident, the organisation can offer a range of support including:

- emotional support
- support with the care of children and pets
- use of shower and toilet facilities
- provision of toiletries
- clothing
- light refreshments
- use of a telephone
- first aid.

Did you know?

The British Red Cross is part of the International Red Cross and Red Crescent Movement.

Activity: The British Red Cross

Visit the following website and write a brief account of the work of the British Red Cross in the flooding in Cumbria of November 2009: www.redcross.org.uk/news

Your account should mention the type of work they did, the number of volunteers and the equipment they used.

How vital was British Red Cross assistance in Cumbria?

Victim Support Scheme

Major incidents can affect countries, communities and individuals in many ways. Apart from the obvious economic upheaval, many individuals suffer psychological trauma at the loss of a family member or even a whole family. Therefore, emergency planning not only involves dealing with the immediate incident, it takes into account the long-term care of those in need of emotional and welfare support.

In addition to the welfare and emotional support provided to victims of major incidents by local authorities, charitable organisations such as the Salvation Army and WRVS (see below) also play a significant role. There is also the need to provide emotional support to UK citizens with relatives from other countries affected by disaster. For example, the UK's Sri Lankan communities were severely affected after the tsunami of 2004 by the loss of communities and family members. In other words, it is not only major incidents in this country that can affect the public and cause them to need emotional and social welfare.

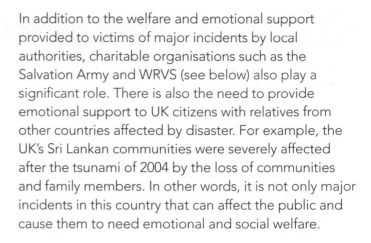

Activity: Salvation Army

Carry out research using the Internet into the work of the Salvation Army when dealing with emergency incidents.

Make some notes so that they can be included in your assignment.

WRVS (formerly Women's Royal Voluntary Service)

The WRVS is a charitable organisation that consists of volunteers with a variety of skills and talents, particularly in the event of an emergency situation. The WRVS has an emergency response team which can support the emergency services by:

- helping with evacuation and providing rest centres
- establishing helplines and casualty bureaus
- providing crisis support
- providing emergency feeding stations (which the WRVS can do on a large scale for extended periods of time).

Did you know?

In August 2009 both the British Red Cross and the WRVS were included in a government emergency planning scenario involving a nuclear incident at Sellafield in Cumbria.

Assessment activity 14.2

As an emergency responder in the public services, your initial actions will have a large bearing on how the incident is dealt with. An effective response and knowledge of the roles and responsibilities of other agencies is required so that the relevant agencies can be called to deal efficiently with the incident.

Address the following tasks in the form of a leaflet:

1   Identify the statutory and voluntary agencies that may work together at the scene of an emergency incident. **P3**

2   Explain the roles and responsibilities of the public services when attending the scene of an emergency incident. **P4**

3   Assess the roles and responsibilities of the key services attending an emergency incident. **M1**

4   Evaluate the inter-agency cooperation of the emergency response services. **D1**

Grading tips

For **P3** you should say which agencies are likely to work together at an emergency incident (although not all agencies are likely to attend the same incident). Give a few examples of emergency incidents so you can include all the relevant agencies. You should say which the statutory and voluntary agencies are.

For **P4** you should explain what the different roles and responsibilities of the emergency services are when attending the scene, including the roles and responsibilities of the first service on the scene. It would be a good idea to include the mnemonic CHALET here.

M1 is an extension of **P3** and **P4**, so you will need to explain the roles of the key emergency services in detail, beyond the initial stages.

For **D1** you should weigh up what is good (or not so good) about the inter-agency cooperation of the emergency services. You could use a case study or research a recent emergency incident to illustrate your point. Say what the emergency services should do when they cooperate and what they actually did at particular incidents. You could research the Hillsborough Disaster to aid your evaluation.

PLTS

Carrying out research on the roles and responsibilities of the public services when attending incidents will develop your skills as an **independent enquirer**.

Functional skills

Writing documents, including extended writing pieces, communicating information, ideas and opinions effectively and persuasively will help you to develop your functional **English** skills in writing.

3.   Understand the necessity for scene preservation at emergency incidents

3.1 Scene preservation for scene investigation

All incident scenes are potential crime scenes. Scene preservation is therefore essential so that any vital evidence can be collected. This is often difficult at large incidents because the first priority of the emergency services is to save lives and take care of casualties. Inevitably, rescuing and treating casualties, establishing control posts and taking steps to prevent escalation of the incident, disturbs the ground at the immediate site of the incident. This is why the incident must be coordinated and the scene protected as far as is practical from the outset.

Need for road traffic accident investigation

All serious and fatal accidents are thoroughly investigated by the Police and other agencies so that the exact cause can be known. By far the most common cause of death in the UK is road traffic collision. It is essential that investigations are conducted meticulously and that evidence is gathered accurately and objectively, since the evidence will be required for a **Coroner's Court (inquest)**.

> ### Did you know?
>
>
> In 2008, 2538 people were fatally injured and 26,034 people were seriously injured on the roads of the UK. *Source*: Department for Transport, 2008.

If the driver of a vehicle involved says the car had a mechanical failure, or if there is a possibility that the vehicle is faulty, it will be examined by an officer of the Accident Investigation Branch. This examination will help to determine if there was any mechanical failure and whether the car was roadworthy or not.

Investigations into accidents include:

- the condition of component parts of vehicles (e.g. are the brakes faulty or the tyres worn?)
- any contributory factors (e.g. weather or road conditions)
- the length of any brake or skid marks
- type of road and speed limits
- witness statements
- evidence of reckless or dangerous driving
- evidence of driving while under the influence of drink and/or drugs.

When the investigation is complete, and the cause has been determined, anyone found to be guilty of causing the accident can be prosecuted. However, accident investigations do not only apportion blame, they can also highlight instances where road safety needs to be improved to help prevent accidents.

> ### Key term
>
> **Coroner's Court (inquest)** – an enquiry into sudden, unnatural and suspicious deaths.

Need for fire investigation

Fires need to be investigated to determine whether they were started maliciously or accidentally. Unlike road traffic collisions, fires tend to destroy any evidence or clues as to the cause. However, specialist Fire Investigation Officers (FIO) can discover what the likely causes of fires are, as well as where the fire started.

FIOs have to complete a fire data report on all fires they attend. This report asks the officer for the most likely cause of the fire. Although this level of report is not conclusive and is not intended to serve as evidence for a prosecution, experienced Fire Investigation Officers may be able to say with some certainty what the cause of a fire is. The Home Office also recommends the use of forensic scientists and Scene of Crime Officers to examine the causes of some fires.

Role of Health and Safety Executive

The Health and Safety Executive (HSE) is a public body sponsored by the Works and Pensions Department. It is an enforcing authority that ensures health and safety in the workplace is adhered to, so it can bring about prosecutions if employers, employees and contractors break health and safety regulations while at work. In addition, the HSE is responsible for:

- conducting and sponsoring research
- promoting training
- providing an information and advisory service
- submitting proposals for new or revised regulations and approved codes of practice.

It is the duty of the HSE to look after many aspects of health and safety, including:

- nuclear installations
- mines and factories
- farms
- hospitals and schools
- offshore gas and oil installations
- the gas grid
- the movement of dangerous goods and substances.

> ### Link
>
> See pages 56–58 of this unit for more on health and safety legislation.

British Transport Police

The British Transport Police (BTP) is a national Police Service that is funded by train operating companies and the London Underground. It is responsible for providing a service to rail operators, staff and passengers throughout England, Wales and Scotland. The BTP also have jurisdiction over:

- Docklands Light Railway
- Glasgow Subway
- Midland Metro tram system
- Croydon Tramlink.

Prior to 2005, railway accidents were investigated by Her Majesty's Rail Inspectorate and the BTP, but following the recommendations of the Cullen Report into the Ladbroke Grove rail crash in 1999, a new investigation agency was established. The Railways and Transport Safety Act 2003 created the Rail Accident Investigation Branch (RAIB), which is an independent body responsible for establishing the objective facts of rail accidents and dangerous occurrences resulting in:

- the death of at least one person
- serious injury to five or more people
- extensive damage to rolling stock, the infrastructure or the environment.

As with road traffic accidents, examining the scene might reveal the cause of the incident and help in the prevention of further accidents. For example, if an investigation suggests that metal fatigue in railway lines was the cause of a derailment, immediate repair elsewhere on the network could prevent the occurrence of a similar incident.

Security for scene preservation

Incident scenes can vary greatly, not only because of the type of incident but also because of where and when it occurred. However, whether the incident is a train crash or a major traffic collision, the scene must be preserved for investigation. This is because, as mentioned at the beginning of this section, all incident scenes are potential crime scenes and any vital evidence must be collected.

Some scenes may be easier to secure than others and police tape might be sufficient. Other scenes, however, may be difficult to secure and cordons, road closures, public rights of way and the use of extra police officers may be required.

Use of cordons

A cordon is a barrier used to surround the scene of an incident in order to restrict access, thereby preserving the scene. A cordon could be formed using plastic tape, rope, barriers, vehicles or people. It should be large enough to contain the scene of the incident and to allow for emergency personnel to enter.

Cordons must be sufficiently guarded along the perimeter, as well as at entry and exit points, to ensure that only authorised personnel are admitted. A rendezvous point for emergency services attending the incident is normally set up near the entrance of the cordon, along with an officer designated to keep a log of personnel entering and leaving the cordon.

Activity: Securing the scene of an incident

Look at the four scenarios below and then answer the questions which follow.

- A major traffic collision on the M25 at 4.30 pm on a Friday evening
- A train derailment on the London to Scotland line at 5.30 am in a remote area of Derbyshire
- A fire at a busy shopping complex in Birmingham city centre on a Saturday afternoon
- A moorland fire high on the Pennines between Yorkshire and Lancashire, with raging winds blowing the flames towards the M62.

1. How would you secure the scenes of each of these incidents?
2. Which other agencies would you require to attend if you were the first officer at the scene?
3. Would you inform the public of any of the emergencies? If so, how would you do this?

3.2 Scene preservation for evidence collection

Need for scene preservation

Scene preservation for evidence collection is needed to:

- ensure any evidence is not contaminated
- help in establishing the cause of an incident
- gather information to prevent further incidents occurring
- accurately identify and assess the damage attributable to the incident.

Crime scene investigation

The objectives of investigating crime scenes are similar to those for other incidents, but there are some differences:

- preserve and recover evidence and information
- minimise contamination
- discover the truth about the incident
- bring the offenders to justice
- **vindicate** the innocent.

> **Key term**
>
> **Vindicate** – clear of blame or suspicion.

The tools used for investigating crime scenes are photography, video, forensics and witness testimony.

Photography

The nature of some incidents makes it very difficult to preserve and produce evidence in court such as brake marks on the road, damaged rail carriages and rail tracks and damaged vehicles. In cases like these, photographic evidence is both necessary and acceptable, as long as it is provided by an authorised scene of crime forensic photographer, who also makes a statement as to what the evidence is.

Video

In other incidents, photographs alone would not be sufficient to prove liability. For example, a case of dangerous driving would be better supported by the use of video evidence. Police traffic cars have video equipment fitted as standard, so that evidence of offences like these can be recorded.

Forensics

Forensic scientists are often involved in the criminal investigation of serious incidents. They have the knowledge and expertise to examine scenes of crime by applying certain principles in the gathering, securing and analysing of evidence. Sources of forensic evidence are shown in Figure 14.3.

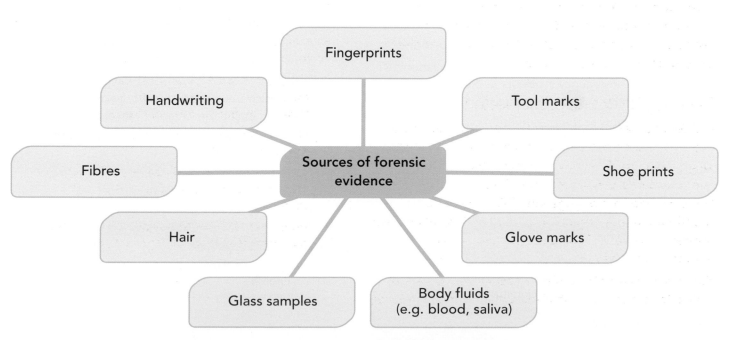

Figure 14.3: Can you think of other sources of evidence that forensic scientists might use?

Witness testimony

This involves taking statements from witnesses to the incident, who may be able to provide:

- direct evidence (what a witness actually saw in direct relation to a crime or incident)
- corroborative evidence (evidence that tends to support the testimony of what another witness says)
- circumstantial evidence (evidence that, when considered with other evidence, tends to prove the facts of the case).

At the planning stage of an incident response, each emergency service is made aware of the need to preserve evidence for a subsequent investigation, which could be for HM Coroner, a public inquiry, or civil or criminal proceedings. As part of the evidence gathering process, all the emergency services take part in the **debrief** process, as well as compiling a report on their involvement at major incidents.

Key term

Debrief – to question participants in detail after an incident.

Other agencies that may carry out their own investigations, depending upon the nature of the incident, could be:

- the Air Accident Investigation Branch
- the Marine Accident Investigation Branch
- the Rail Accident Investigation Branch
- the Health and Safety Executive
- the Environment Agency.

Assessment activity 14.3   BTEC

All emergency incident scenes are potential scenes of crime. As an experienced emergency responder you should communicate the necessity for scene preservation to your new colleagues, as well as other organisations that may be involved in attending emergency incidents.

Address the following tasks in the form of a report:

1 Describe the necessity for scene preservation units at emergency incidents as part of an incident investigation. **P5**

2 Explain how scene preservation contributes to an accident/incident investigation. **M2**

Grading tips

For **P5** you need to describe why it is necessary to preserve the scene of an emergency incident. You should also point out why this might be difficult. Carry out research into, or ask your tutor for examples of, accident investigations and gather information from the Health and Safety Executive to illustrate your report.

For **M2**, which is an extension of P5, it would be a good idea to illustrate your report with examples of what might happen if the scene was not preserved.

PLTS

By describing the necessity for scene preservation units, as well as explaining how crime scene preservation contributes to accident/incident investigation, you will be demonstrating your skills as a **reflective thinker**.

Functional skills

By writing this assignment you will develop your skills in **English**.

4.   Be able to review the health and safety considerations during an emergency response incident scenario

It is vitally important that emergency responders protect themselves from hazards and dangers, otherwise they may become part of the problem instead of part of the rescue effort.

4.1 Self-preservation

Specialist clothing

Apart from their standard uniform, the emergency services have specialist clothing to protect them from the many dangers posed by different types of emergency incidents. This is known as Protective Personal Equipment (PPE). Some PPE is common to all the services, but some is exclusive to certain emergency services (see Table 14.6 below).

All the emergency services wear high-visibility jackets to ensure they are easily seen, for example when dealing with road traffic collisions or incidents on a railway. Some members of the emergency services are trained to respond to chemical, biological, radiation and nuclear attack, for which gas-tight suits are issued.

Emergency services personnel wear protective clothing. What is the purpose of PPE?

Table 14.6: Protective Personal Equipment used by the Police, Fire and Ambulance Services

Police Service PPE	Ambulance Service PPE	Fire Service PPE
Fire suits for some specialist units	Disposable overalls where there is a risk of splashing with blood or body fluids	Fire-fighting suits, gloves and boots
Protective headwear	Protective overalls where there is a risk of severe contamination	Protective headwear for fire-fighting and building collapse
Goggles/visors	Face mask where there is a risk of transmission of a contagious disease, or risk of inhalation of dust or other particles	Self-contained breathing apparatus for entering smoke-filled buildings
Specialist riot gear and shields for public order incidents	Protective eyewear where there is a risk that blood, body fluids or dirt may get into the eyes	Visors/goggles
	Ear defenders/protection where there are noise hazards	

4.2 Scene safety measures

Even in an emergency incident, emergency services personnel have a **duty of care** to themselves, their colleagues and the public. If the scene is not made safe, then there is a chance that someone could become an unnecessary victim.

Key term

Duty of care – responsibility to ensure the safety of self and others.

The following safety measures are used at the scene of an incident to protect emergency personnel and members of the public:

- **Warning signs of an accident ahead** may be given miles in advance of an incident, for example on motorway matrix systems. Portable warning signs can be erected at the side of the road nearer to the scene.
- **Portable barriers** are an effective way of protecting personnel and the public at the scene of an emergency, although they may not be readily available to the first officer in attendance and may have to be requested.
- **Cones** can be used effectively to channel traffic into a particular lane or to close a lane of a motorway in advance of an incident ahead.
- **Road closure and diversions** are sometimes necessary because of the urgent and dangerous nature of an incident.

Activity: Preventing harm

Consider the following scenarios and say how you could prevent harm to those working at the scene.

- A large-scale traffic collision has taken place on a motorway. All three lanes are blocked and petrol from several crashed vehicles has spilled onto the carriageway.
- A suspicious package has been found in a busy shopping centre and a call has been made to the Police warning them that a bomb has been planted in one of the shops. It is a Saturday afternoon and the shopping centre is very busy.
- A light aircraft has made an emergency landing in some fields on the outskirts of a town. As it landed it collided with an overhead power cable, causing the live cable to come down into the field close to a local beauty spot that is busy with tourists.

Where would you obtain barriers if they were required?

4.3 Consideration for public welfare

There are many things to consider when there is an emergency situation, especially in large-scale incidents that could affect public welfare. Some incidents, such as burning buildings, can threaten the safety of people in the immediate vicinity. Other incidents, such as traffic collisions on motorways and main routes, can affect a much wider area, causing disruption to the road network and miles of traffic queues for several hours.

Use of the media

The media, in the form of local television and radio, can play an effective part in an emergency in three main ways. It can warn the public of:

- an emergency that could threaten their health, and advise them to keep away
- possible delays to public transport, so they can make alternative travel arrangements
- congestion on certain roads, so they can plan alternative routes.

Did you know?

The Highways Agency's website is regularly updated to show where there is congestion and how long the delay is likely to last on all motorways and main roads in England.

Ensuring the scene is safe and will not affect the local environment and its citizens

Some incidents are a greater threat to the public and the environment than others, but whatever the threat, the scene must be made safe. The public needs to be assured that there is no immediate threat to themselves, their families and friends and the environment, from the incident.

4.4 Dangers at the scene
Chemical spillage

Chemicals can be extremely hazardous to the public and to the environment. If there is an incident involving hazardous chemicals, the emergency services need to know what course of action to take to prevent danger to the public and to the environment.

All vehicles that transport hazardous substances, and all buildings that store them, must display a HAZCHEM plate (see Figure 14.4).

This is a warning system that informs the emergency services, through an Emergency Action Code (EAC), how to deal with hazardous substances that are carried in vehicles or stored in buildings. (HAZCHEM is an abbreviation of the term hazardous chemicals.)

If there is an optional second letter 'E' in the EAC, this indicates that the incident presents a threat to the public beyond the immediate vicinity. In this case, the public may need to be evacuated or warned to stay indoors with doors and windows closed.

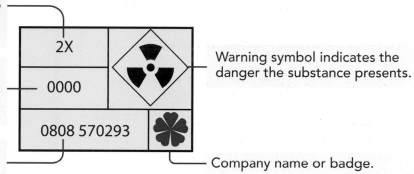

Emergency Action Code (EAC). The number tells the service which fire suppressant to use, while the letter tells them which equipment to wear, whether there will be a violent reaction and how to dispose of the substance.

United Nations Identification Number, which identifies the dangerous substance. These are assigned by the United Nations Committee of Experts on the Transport of Dangerous Goods.

Telephone number if specialist advice is required.

Warning symbol indicates the danger the substance presents.

Company name or badge.

Figure 14.4: HAZCHEM plate and explanation. What can you tell about this substance?

Table 14.7: Key to numbers and letters of the Emergency Action Code

Number	Suppressant	Letter	Violent reaction (V)	Equipment (liquid-tight suit [LTS], breathing apparatus [BA])	Disposal (dilute or contain)
1	Coarse water spray	P	V	LTS	Dilute
2	Fine water spray	R		LTS	Dilute
3	Foam	S	V	BA	Dilute
4	Dry agent	T		BA	Dilute
		W	V	LTS	Contain
		X		LTS	Contain
		Y	V	BA	Contain
		Z		BA	Contain

Electrical cables

Electrical cables run above and below the ground and carry thousands of volts of electricity. Overhead cables can be brought down by storms, air accidents or train derailments that collide with wooden, cable-bearing poles. Underground electrical cables may be accidentally exposed by excavating vehicles. Any live cables that are on or near the ground can conduct electricity through dampness or metal objects. If any of these events occur, dial 999 and ask the Police to help keep passers-by well clear.

Railways and railway crossings

There are thousands of miles of railways in the UK, with more than 8000 level crossings. Accidents on the railway are more frequent than people realise.

Activity: Railway accidents

Visit the following website and find out about the number of railway accidents in the last ten years: www.rssb.co.uk. From the Home page, click on 'Press Releases' to access safety figures.

Research some of these incidents and make notes.

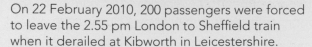

Case study: Train derailment in Leicestershire

On 22 February 2010, 200 passengers were forced to leave the 2.55 pm London to Sheffield train when it derailed at Kibworth in Leicestershire.

Initial inquiries found that two of the 56 wheels of the train had derailed. All seven carriages remained upright and no injuries were reported. However, there were disruptions to the normal timetable, with some trains having to be diverted and some services between Nottingham and Leicester to London cancelled.

1　**Name three organisations that you would expect to investigate this accident.**
2　**Which organisation would you expect to take the lead role in the investigation?**
3　**Research some of the railway accidents that have occurred over the last few years.**

Case study: Suspicious package at Bristol Airport

In July 2005, Bristol Airport was evacuated when a suspicious package (unattended bag) was found in baggage handling. Passengers were moved away from the main terminal building to the old terminal and an army bomb disposal team were sent for to deal with the package.

Planes continued to land at the airport but passengers were not allowed to leave the planes. Roads leading to the airport became gridlocked as flights were grounded and check-in suspended. Police directed arrivals at the airport to the old terminal, as well as warning motorists of the congestion surrounding the airport.

The main terminal was closed for four hours with 15 flights being affected by the alert and seven flights being cancelled. It was believed that the suspicious package got to the airport through a connecting flight.

1　**Which other agencies might have been involved in this incident?**
2　**What would their roles have been?**

Fires

Fire is one of the largest causes of accidental death in the UK with around 500 deaths a year from house fires and 250 deaths a year from vehicle fires. Each year, the Fire Service attends over 600,000 fires in the home and there are around 93,000 vehicle fires.

Fire incidents are particularly dangerous because people can become trapped and lose consciousness through smoke inhalation, one of the biggest causes of death in fire-related incidents. Therefore, evacuation is often necessary for the safety of the public.

Bombs and explosive devices

Today terrorism is frequently in the news and bomb threats are common. Terrorist bombs in particular are intended to cause the utmost devastation to people, the country or the economy. Even though many calls warning of imminent terrorist attack are hoaxes, all such calls have to be taken seriously.

Bomb warnings may or may not come with a coded message – a way of proving the authenticity of the call. The calls may come from terrorist organisations or from individuals with a grudge against society, so the targets of bombers vary from government ministers to businesses. The calls may be received at police stations, newspaper companies or by businesses, and may come in the form of telephone calls, emails, text messages or faxes.

4.5 Legislation and regulations

The emergency services, like all employees, are governed by legislation and regulations relating to their health and safety at work. Legislation is designed to protect workers and their colleagues from injury and hazards while performing their duties.

Impact of legislation and regulations

Unlike most other occupations, the work of the emergency services often involves a certain amount of risk and danger. For their own protection, and that of the public, the emergency services have to manage the risks and make decisions based on their evaluation. The emergency services also have to comply with health and safety laws, which can have an impact on the way they carry out their duties. Consider the following examples of how legislation has had an impact on the Fire Service.

- In 2006, fire-fighters in the Devon Fire Service were told to use the stairs instead of sliding down their poles because health and safety officials decided the poles were a hazard, even though using stairs would add vital seconds in responding to an emergency.

- Fire-fighters in Humberside are not allowed to use stepladders to install smoke alarms in people's homes, even though this is a popular and important fire prevention method. Installing alarms using stepladders is a contravention of the Health and Safety Executive Work at Height Regulations (2005).
- The emergency services are being told not to attempt to save drowning people because of health and safety restrictions. In September 2007, two Police Community Support Officers in Wigan stood by while a 10-year-old boy drowned in a pond. Because of health and safety rules, they had been ordered by their Control Room not to attempt a rescue. A fire-fighter in Scotland who saved a woman from drowning was later informed he could face disciplinary action for breaching safety rules.

- the Control of Substances Hazardous to (COSHH) Health Regulations 2002
- the Management of Health and Safety at Work Regulations 1999
- the Personal Protective Equipment (PPE) at Work Regulations 1992.

Did you know?

Police pursuits of stolen vehicles or disqualified drivers are covered under HASAWA. The Control Room supervisor can instruct the pursuit driver to abandon the pursuit if it is believed that the risk of danger in the pursuit (whether to the public, the police pursuit driver or the occupants of the vehicle being pursued) is greater than the risk of bringing the pursuit to a safe conclusion.

Activity: The impact of health and safety laws on the emergency services

Using the Internet, find another three examples of the impact of health and safety law on the emergency services. You could use this research for your assignment.

Activity: Health and safety restrictions on fire-fighters

1   Is there any legislation to prevent fire-fighters from rescuing cats from trees? (You should consider HASAWA.)
2   If fire-fighters were prevented from rescuing a cat because of legislation, do you think this is wrong?
3   Carry out some research using the Internet to find an article titled 'Cat up tree victim of fire regulations' appearing in the *Daily Mail* in July 2006. Make a few notes of why the cat was not rescued. You might want to use this evidence in your assignment.

Health and Safety at Work Act 1974 (HASAWA)

HASAWA set basic principles to be followed by both employees and employers to ensure a safe working environment by:

- protecting the health, safety and welfare of people at work
- protecting others against risks to health or safety in connection with the activities of persons at work
- controlling the keeping, use and possession of dangerous substances.

When it became law in 1974, HASAWA did not apply to police officers, but the Police (Health & Safety) Act (1997) brought all police officers within the scope of the Act.

HASAWA is an enabling act, which means that further health and safety legislation can be made law without having to pass through Parliament. New regulations made under HASAWA include:

- the Reporting of Injuries, Diseases and Dangerous Occurrences Regulations (RIDDOR) 1995

The Reporting of Injuries, Diseases and Dangerous Ocurrences Regulations (RIDDOR) 1995

RIDDOR enables the HSE and local authorities to identify risks in the workplace by placing a legal obligation on employers, the self-employed and people in control of premises to report:

- work-related deaths
- major injuries or injuries lasting more than three days (including fractured limbs, loss of sight, electric shock, burns)
- work-related diseases (including lung disease, skin disease and infections)
- dangerous occurrences (including explosions and the failure of breathing apparatus).

Near misses must also be reported under the regulations. A 'near miss' is when something happens that could result in injury or death but fortunately did not. This is classed as a dangerous occurrence and must be reported under RIDDOR.

The Control of Substances Hazardous to Health Regulations (COSHH) 2002

COSHH is designed to protect employees from hazardous substances that are stored or used in the workplace. These include oils, bleaches, paint, solvents and any by-products emitted from burning, as well as biological agents. The regulations require exposure to hazardous substances to be prevented or adequately controlled so that the health of workers and others exposed to them is not threatened.

Hazard Analysis Critical Control Points (HACCP)

Besides ensuring the health and safety of workers, there is also legislation that protects the consumer from contaminated or unfit food. Since January 2006, food production and preparation in the UK has been subject to European Regulation on Hygiene of Foodstuffs. This requires all food business operators

to implement and maintain a permanent procedure based on the principles of hazard analysis critical control points (HACCP).

HACCP is a method that relies on the identification and close monitoring of Critical Control Points (CCPs) during the production and preparation of food, to ensure that food is safe and fit for human consumption. It relies on the following principles:

- identifying hazards and eliminating or reducing them to acceptable levels
- identifying the critical control points at which control is essential
- establishing critical limits of acceptability from unacceptability
- establishing and implementing effective monitoring procedures
- establishing corrective actions when CCP is not under control.

PLTS

Assessing the health and safety measures taken when attending an emergency incident will help you develop your skills as a **reflective learner**.

Assessment activity 14.4   P6 M3 D2   **BTEC**

Make sure that you understand health and safety legislation/regulations and their impact on your own, your colleagues and the public's safety. Then imagine that you are part of a review panel investigating the standards of safety maintained at incidents. Create a wall display that addresses the following tasks:

1   Assess the health and safety measures to be taken to ensure personal safety and that of others when attending an emergency incident scenario, with reference to the relevant health and safety legislation. **P6**

2   Review the need for measures to be taken to ensure personal safety and that of others when attending an emergency incident scenario, with reference to relevant health and safety legislation. **M3**

3   Evaluate the impact of health and safety measures on services responding to an emergency incident scenario, with reference to relevant health and safety legislation. **D2**

Grading tips

For **P6** you should consider the steps that are taken for personal safety when attending emergency incidents, such as high-visibility clothing and protective footwear. You need to relate this to the relevant health and safety legislation.

For **M3** explain why it is necessary to ensure personal safety and that of others when attending emergency incidents. You will need to refer to the relevant legislation and/or regulations and illustrate your points with examples.

D2 requires you to weigh up what is good and what is not so good about the key health and safety legislation/regulations and how they impact on workers attending emergency incidents. You do not need to give a detailed explanation of the legislation and regulations here, but aim for a balanced conclusion. Give examples to back up your points by researching cases where the emergency services have been prevented from doing what people thought was the right thing to do because of health and safety legislation.

Jonathon Marriot
Paramedic

I was 22 years old when I joined the Ambulance Service. Before that I was a hospital porter for four years, three of which I spent in the Accident and Emergency Department. My heart used to go out to some of the casualties I saw and I wanted to do more to help them.

I've been in the Ambulance Service for eight years now, and a paramedic for six years – and I've never looked back. Every day is exciting and different. I've been to lots of major emergencies, some of which have lasted all night. A lot of the time you are working alone. It can be a little unnerving when you're the first one at the scene of a serious incident, because you're always aware that you need to pass on the right information so the necessary support arrives. It's just a case of staying calm, even though the adrenalin's going.

I love my job and I wouldn't swap it for anything.

A typical shift

I work a rota at the moment, with three on the night shift, two on the afternoon shift, two days off, and then back on the day shift for five days. I'm not sure that I could say I have a typical shift. When I'm not responding, I'm on standby near the motorway roundabout, but we have a busy area and you can never predict what will happen. Last year, during the floods, I was heavily involved in attending to the elderly for days on end – there were quite a few cases of hypothermia, which we get in cold weather as well.

When the motorway's foggy you can guarantee several RTCs and you just hope they're not too bad because I've seen some horrendous pile-ups.

The best thing about the job

During my service I've attended about twelve major incidents. Teamwork is essential and when you've finished and everything's sorted out it's a marvellous feeling. I love the teamwork element, but I also like working alone and making my own decisions, though help isn't far away if it's needed.

The job satisfaction is enormous and so rewarding. To me, there's nothing better than saving lives or making people more comfortable – and getting them on the road to recovery when they've been injured.

Think about it!

- What topics have you covered in this unit that might give you the necessary background knowledge to become a member of the emergency services?
- What knowledge and skills do you think you will need to develop further if you want to become a member of the emergency services?

Just checking

1. According to the Civil Contingencies Act, what is an 'emergency incident'?
2. How many grades of response are there for the Police?
3. List four of the common objectives when responding to emergency incidents.
4. Which agency is responsible for setting the standard for the driving of emergency vehicles?
5. What is the mnemonic CHALET used for?
6. List six of the roles and responsibilities of the Police when dealing with an emergency incident.
7. What is the Highways Agency responsible for?
8. Who investigates accidents on the railway?
9. What is the HSE responsible for?
10. What are the objectives of crime scene investigation?
11. What details are contained within a HAZCHEM plate?
12. Which regulation prevents fire-fighters from standing on stools and householders' stepladders in order to fit smoke alarms?
13. What is the fundamental principle of the HASAWA (1974)?
14. What does RIDDOR stand for?
15. What does COSHH stand for?

edexcel

Assignment tips

- This unit gives you the basic outline of how emergency incidents are responded to by the emergency services and other agencies. It would be a good idea to carry out your own research into any emergency incident that you have heard about recently or read about in the media. You could read about relevant incidents in past editions of newspapers, which may be kept in your library. Your tutor or librarian should be able to help, so don't be afraid to ask.

- When you carry out your research, see if you can apply the understanding you have developed, especially of the roles and responsibilities of the services, the level of command and control sequence (operational, tactical and strategic) and the mnemonic CHALET.

- Researching a topic for yourself gives you greater insight into a subject, as well as a better chance of achieving the higher grades in your assignment.

- Any of the services outlined in this unit require certain qualities of character, and because of this they have quite demanding selection and recruitment procedures. Some of those qualities are teamwork, problem solving and working with others, which are excellent skills to have in any career, but especially in the emergency services. How could you develop these qualities? Can you make the right decision when under pressure? How could you practise and develop this skill?

15 Planning and management of major incidents

A good deal of the work of the public services, that is, the emergency services, armed services, local authorities and health agencies, involves planning and preparation for major incidents, which can take many forms. If you are considering a career in the public services, then this unit will help you develop a firm grasp of the concept of major incidents.

After learning what a major incident is, you will be able to investigate the different causes and types, and see what effects they have in terms of loss to the individual and the wider community. You will then be able to look at the various agencies that are involved in dealing with major incidents and examine their roles and responsibilities, as well as seeing how the different agencies are legally obliged to cooperate and interact with each other.

In the next section you will have the opportunity of looking in detail at the main considerations of emergency planning and preparation, including the potential disasters that need to be planned for.

Finally, you will be required to take part in an actual emergency planning exercise, namely, a tabletop scenario, which is one of several exercises carried out by the emergency services and other agencies when preparing for major incidents.

Learning outcomes

After completing this unit you should:

1. know the effects of recent major incidents
2. know the type of work carried out by the public services during major incidents
3. understand the considerations for emergency planning and preparation for possible major incidents
4. be able to prepare for a particular major incident by using tabletop scenarios.

Assessment and grading criteria

This table shows you what you must do in order to achieve a pass, merit or distinction grade, and where you can find activities in this book to help you.

To achieve a **pass** grade the evidence must show that you are able to:	To achieve a **merit** grade the evidence must show that, in addition to the pass criteria, you are able to:	To achieve a **distinction** grade the evidence must show that, in addition to the pass and merit criteria, you are able to:
P1 define the term 'major incident' **See Assessment activity 15.1 page 68**		
P2 describe different types of major incidents and the cause of each **See Assessment activity 15.1 page 68**	**M1** investigate recent major incidents and identify their cause **See Assessment activity 15.1 page 68**	
P3 outline the effects of recent major incidents on people, communities and the environment **See Assessment activity 15.2 page 73**	**M2** explain the short- and long-term effects of the major incidents on people, communities, environment and the wider impacts they may have had **See Assessment activity 15.2 page 73**	
P4 identify the agencies that were involved in different major incidents **See Assessment activity 15.3 page 78**	**M3** explain how UK agencies involved in a specific major incident worked together in accordance with their legal duties **See Assessment activity 15.3 page 78**	**D1** analyse the importance of inter-agency emergency planning for major incidents **See Assessment activity 15.4 page 87**
P5 describe the work of agencies at UK incidents and their legal duties **See Assessment activity 15.3 page 78**		
P6 explain the main considerations when planning and preparing for major incidents **See Assessment activity 15.4 page 87**	**M4** explain the role of the organisations involved in planning for major incidents **See Assessment activity 15.4 page 87**	
P7 carry out a tabletop scenario of a major incident **See Assessment activity 15.5 page 94**	**M4** analyse the tabletop scenario **See Assessment activity 15.5 page 94**	**D2** evaluate the tabletop scenario **See Assessment activity 15.5 page 94**

How you will be assessed

This unit will be assessed by an internal assignment that will be designed and marked by the staff at your centre. The assignment is designed to allow you to show your understanding of the learning outcomes for planning and management of major incidents. Assignments can be quite varied and can take the form of:

- portfolio of evidence
- wall display
- learning journal
- video diary
- role play
- presentation
- leaflet
- report.

Adam reflects on emergency planning

I found this unit very interesting and informative, and I think it's helped me with my future career choice. I wasn't sure which service I wanted to join, but now I think it's a choice between the Fire Service and the Police. I didn't realise the amount of work that went into planning and dealing with major incidents. In fact, I'd never really thought about it until I studied this unit. It was good to look at some of the major incidents and it made us think about the different causes and the knock-on effects they have on people and communities.

If I don't join the uniformed services I think I would like to work in emergency planning, with the local authority or something like that, because I thought the section on planning and prevention was one of the best parts of the unit. This made me aware of how planning for emergencies can make a big difference. I think this unit has taught me a good lesson about planning for anything, not just emergencies.

The assignments were easy to understand and I actually enjoyed the practical tabletop exercise we did. We had some good ideas but you don't realise how much is involved until you've actually tried it.

Over to you!

- **Where do evacuees go when they have been asked to leave their homes because of the threat of an explosion?**
- **Who is responsible for investigating rail crashes?**
- **How do the emergency services and other agencies know what to do during a major incident?**
- **Is there any point in planning and preparing for something that might not happen?**
- **By studying this unit you will be able to give reasoned answers to these questions, as well as having a comprehensive understanding of the concept of major incidents.**

1. Know the effects of recent major incidents

Do you know the difference between a disaster and major incident?

Well, don't be confused because the terms 'major incident' and 'disaster' both refer to the same thing. It is just that **disaster** is a media term and refers to what the emergency services and local authorities in the United Kingdom know as a 'major incident'.

In this unit, any reference to 'disaster' and 'major incident' amount to the same thing. But what is a major incident?

1.1 Major incident: definition

Where there is a threat to human welfare, the environment or security of the UK, the emergency services are obliged to respond. It is the number of emergency service personnel who have to respond to the emergency, and the special arrangements they need to make, that makes it a **major incident**. In other words, a major incident is an emergency situation that demands special arrangements by one or all of the emergency services for:

- the rescue and transportation of a large number of casualties
- the organisation and mobilisation of the local authority and other organisations to respond to the threat of death, injury or homelessness on a large scale.

This means that one, or more, of the emergency services attend the incident in greater numbers than they would normally attend a routine incident on a day-to-day basis. This puts a strain on the emergency services.

For the purposes of this unit, an emergency situation is considered only in terms of a major incident. This includes an emergency outside the UK that has consequences in the UK. For example, if known

terrorists were boarding a plane in, say, Germany, and heading for the UK to commit an act of terrorism, then this would be classed as an emergency.

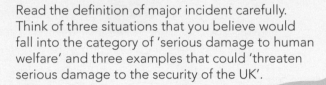

Activity: Exploring the definition of major incident

Read the definition of major incident carefully. Think of three situations that you believe would fall into the category of 'serious damage to human welfare' and three examples that could 'threaten serious damage to the security of the UK'.

Major incidents in the United Kingdom

Look at the case studies of recent major incidents in the United Kingdom on the next page and answer the questions at the end of each case study.

1.2 Causes and types of major incidents

There are many causes of disasters, but they generally fall into one of five categories:

- natural
- hostile acts
- technological
- health-related
- epidemics and pandemics.

Key terms

Disaster – great or sudden misfortune.

Major incident – an event or situation which threatens serious damage to human welfare in a place in the UK, the environment of a place in the UK, or war or terrorism which threatens serious damage to the security of the UK.

Case study: The Boscastle Floods, 2004

Boscastle is a coastal village in north Cornwall, with sea on one side and high ground with a river valley running through the village. Boscastle relies on the tourist industry for its economy.

During the afternoon of Monday 16 August 2004, record levels of torrential rain fell on the village (8.9 cm in one hour). A short distance up the valley, twice as much rain fell. This caused the river to rise 2.2 metres within an hour. However, the real problem was that just up from the village, debris had collected under a bridge and was holding back water coming from higher ground, thus causing a blockage. The bridge collapsed under pressure, releasing the debris and an estimated 2 million tonnes of water, which surged through the village, causing trees to be uprooted, boats and cars to be lost, and buildings to be washed into the sea.

Many buildings and businesses were damaged by the force of the water and had to be demolished because they were unsafe.

The emergency services, including seven helicopters from the Royal Navy and Royal Air Force, dealt with the immediate response until 2.30 am the following morning, rescuing people from treetops, roofs of buildings and cars.

There were no deaths or serious injuries reported, though approximately 60 people were evacuated from the village and taken to hospital.

1 There was no loss of life at Boscastle, so why was this classified as a major incident?

2 What problems would have been experienced in the immediate aftermath by both villagers and tourists?

3 What were the wider effects and consequences for Boscastle?

Case study: The London bombings, July 2005

During the morning rush hour of Thursday 7 July 2005, a series of coordinated terrorist explosions killed a total of 52 people and injured 700, 22 of them seriously. The explosions also killed four suicide bombers.

At 8.50 am that morning, three bombs were exploded on three trains in the London Underground within 50 seconds of each other. The first two bombs exploded on two trains travelling on the Circle Line, one eastbound and the other westbound, and the third bomb exploded on a train travelling on the Piccadilly Line. Two of the trains were travelling through underground tunnels at the time of the explosions and another one had just left a platform. Almost an hour later, a fourth bomb exploded on a London bus in Tavistock Square, causing extensive

damage to the top and rear of the bus. Some of those who were on the bus had been evacuated from a nearby station because of the earlier explosions.

The explosions brought London's transport system to a halt for over a day and the emergency services were stretched to deal with the situation.

1 Given the devastation, shock and confusion brought about by these bombings, what do you think would have been one of the main priorities of the emergency services?

2 Why would the rescue attempts have been particularly difficult?

3 Apart from the obvious effects on individuals, what other effects would there be in the capital?

Natural causes

Disasters with natural causes can be some of the most devastating in terms of loss of life, loss of property or damage to the environment, not to mention the economy. Volcanic eruptions, for instance, can have terrible consequences, such as the one at Mount St Helens in 1980 where ten million trees were destroyed leaving a desolate and infertile landscape.

Volcanoes are caused when magma is formed deep within the earth and then rises to the surface and erupts as lava.

Another natural cause of disaster is an earthquake, which is the violent shaking of the ground as a result of the movement of tectonic plates. While some earthquakes are worse than others, they can all have dreadful consequences if they occur in heavily populated areas, such as the one in Kobe City in Japan in 1995.

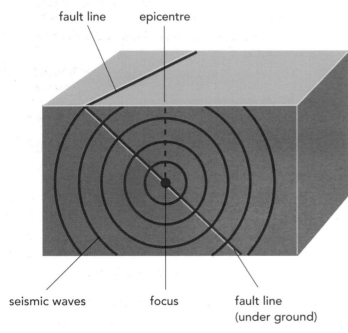

Figure 15.1: Fault lines result from tectonic plate movement

Hostile acts

These are aggressive or violent acts that can cause havoc to communities or even nations. Such acts can involve terrorism, where buildings or civilians are attacked with bombs or other explosive devices. For example, the attack on the USA of 11 September 2001 was an act of terrorism where four planes were hijacked and two of them were flown into the Twin Towers in New York, killing almost 3000 people.

Civil war

This is a war between people of the same country. It causes members of society to live in constant fear because of the threat of harm, theft, damage or loss of property. People naturally become anxious because they cannot expect the same protection that they normally experience in peacetime and there could be a strong temptation for people to take the law into their own hands. Civil war can stretch the emergency services and military to their absolute limit.

Fortunately, the UK does not have a history of regular civil war, but there have been several violent clashes of communities. For example, the Bradford Riots of 2001 were battles between white and Asian gangs which left 120 police officers injured with 36 people arrested.

Technological causes

Technological disasters are those that result from, say, defective rail tracks or the faulty components of an airplane. They could also be caused by the emission of radiation (see the case study opposite) or computer failure.

Health-related causes

Some major incidents can result from the spread of infectious diseases, which can be either **epidemic** or **pandemic**.

Activity: Kobe earthquake

What is it that makes earthquakes dangerous? Is it only the shaking of the ground? Carry out some research on the Internet to see what caused the fires in the aftermath of the Kobe earthquake.

Key terms

Epidemic – the spread of disease throughout a community. It is normally contained within that area.

Pandemic – the spread of disease over a much larger area, possibly an entire country or even the world, for instance swine flu.

Case study: The Chernobyl nuclear disaster, April 1986

Chernobyl is located in north central Ukraine, quite near to the border with Belarus, in the former Soviet Union.

In the early hours of 26 April 1986, one of the plant's nuclear reactors exploded causing clouds of radioactive fallout to contaminate huge areas of the northern hemisphere, including parts of the Western Soviet Union, Eastern Europe, Western Europe, Northern Europe and parts of North America. The contamination was so severe in Ukraine, Belarus and Russia that over 300,000 people had to be evacuated and re-housed.

This incident is regarded as the worst accident in the history of nuclear disasters, and it resulted in a dramatic increase in thyroid cancer in young people. A report by the Chernobyl Forum in 2005 stated that as many as 9000 people who were highly exposed to the radiation may die from cancer. However, according to Greenpeace, there is likely to be 270,000 cases of cancer as a result of the accident, 93,000 of which will probably be fatal.

Apart from the increases in cancer, people developed psychological problems because of the effects of radiation, social upheaval and lack of communication regarding the economic situation since the division of the Soviet Union.

The impact on the environment was phenomenal, with evidence of radiation pollution covering the entire northern hemisphere. This pollution meant

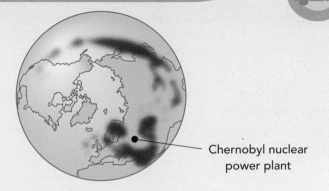

Chernobyl nuclear power plant

Figure 15.2: The extent of the nuclear fallout following the Chernobyl disaster of 1986 (shown in red)

the contamination of soil, water systems (including drinking supplies), vegetation and animals. Restrictions were placed on the sale and movement of livestock which reached as far as western Scotland, north Wales and Cumbria, where levels of contamination were above the recommended dose. Today, a total of 369 farms in England, Scotland and Wales are still restricted in the use of land for rearing sheep because of the effects of radioactive fallout from Chernobyl.

1   **What would you say were the worst effects of the Chernobyl disaster?**

2   **Could this type of major incident ever happen in the UK? Carry out some research, using the Internet, to see if we have nuclear power plants and any history of leaked radioactive materials.**

Avian flu

Avian flu, otherwise known as 'bird flu,' is one of many different types of flu that is common in birds, but it is the H5N1 flu virus strain that is of greatest concern. Avian flu is highly contagious, especially with poultry, and while it can be fatal to humans, some experts believe that it can only be passed from human to human if there are two simultaneous mutations, something that is unlikely. Furthermore, avian influenza viruses do not thrive in humans because it is thought that at 32 degrees Celsius the temperature inside a human's nose is too low. Therefore, avian flu has not reached a pandemic, even though it was predicted that it could kill between 5 million and 150 million people.

Swine flu

Swine flu is a new strain of the Influenza A (H1N1) virus. Despite its name it is not certain that the virus originated from pigs. The outbreak began in Mexico in 2009 and the virus quickly spread around the globe,

making it a pandemic. While the virus has proved relatively mild in most cases, up to May 2010 there had been over 14,000 deaths worldwide including 457 in the UK. Britain spent £1.2 billion on vaccines against the swine flu virus but 21 million flu shots remain unused as the pandemic was not as bad as predicted.

Severe Acute Respiratory Syndrome (SARS)

SARS is a respiratory disease in humans caused by the corona virus, a family of viruses that causes the common cold but which has mutated to become dangerous to humans, killing almost 800 people so far. The first SARS epidemic is believed to have started in a province of China in 2002, but there have been reported cases in over 25 countries, including the USA, the UK and India. The disease has been contained since 2006, with the last known case in 2003, but this does not mean that the disease will not return to infect humans in the future.

Assessment activity 15.1

As a member of the emergency services you will need to understand the concept of major incidents, because you will almost certainly be required to respond to one during your career. You will also need to understand the different types and causes since they may require various responses and procedures in the way they are dealt with. As well as using the Student Book, carry out some research from the Internet so that you can answer the following questions in the form of a presentation:

1 Define the term 'major incident'. **P1**

2 Describe different types of major incident and how each type is caused. **P2**

3 Investigate recent major incidents and identify their cause. **M1**

Grading tips

For **P1** you need to say precisely what a major incident is – what it is that makes it a major incident as opposed to any other routine incident.

For **P2** it would be a good idea to give different examples of major incidents and classify them into types, saying how they are caused.

For **M1** you need to look at recent major incidents in more detail and give an explanation of what happened. Although the criteria do not specifically tell you how many major incidents to investigate, you ought to cover at least three.

PLTS

By investigating recent major incidents and identifying their cause, you will be demonstrating your skills as an **independent enquirer** and **self-manager**.

Functional skills

By carrying out research on the Internet and using presentation software, you will be developing your functional skills in **ICT**.

1.3 Effects of major incidents

Effects on individuals

The effects of major incidents on individuals can be devastating. Floods, for instance, could ruin a business, meaning a loss of income for the owners as well as anyone employed by that business. Similarly, an outbreak of avian flu could result in the destruction of thousands of birds, meaning loss of income for the owner in addition to the threat to human health or life.

In some areas of the world, people lose their homes as well as their businesses. For example, the tsunami in South East Asia in 2004 not only destroyed homes and businesses it also destroyed entire villages. The same destruction could happen in the event of an earthquake or the eruption of a volcano. Flooding damages people's homes, leaving them uninhabitable for months. In recent years, people in the UK whose homes have been built on flood plains have experienced the devastating effects of flooded property.

Effects on rescue workers

At many major incidents people die or are seriously injured; some are trapped in wreckage while others might be badly burned or lose limbs. People of all ages can be casualties in disaster situations; this includes young children and babies. The emergency services and other rescue agencies witness all kinds of injuries to victims of major incidents. They can see casualties suffering terrible injuries and even dying as a result of their injuries.

When responding to a major incident, the emergency services' priority is to deal with it as efficiently as possible; they do not have time to consider their own feelings or emotions. However, when the incident has been dealt with and the individual members of the emergency services have had time to reflect on the scenes they have witnessed, then it is possible that they become psychologically stressed. This condition is known as post-traumatic stress disorder (PTSD) and it can make an individual mentally and physically ill, leaving them unfit for duty.

How might you feel after witnessing the injuries and trauma caused by a major incident?

Effects on communities

Loss of law and order

During a major incident it is inevitable that a strain is placed on the uniformed public services because the incident uses most of their human resources and normal routine is disrupted. The Police, for instance, while directing their efforts on dealing with the major incident, cannot control their area as normal. Consequently, there could be a temporary loss of law and order and an increase in crime, such as theft and looting, especially where buildings or vehicles have had to be abandoned.

Different types of major incidents can have different effects on communities. Civil wars, for instance, can bring about loss of law and order to a community or even a country. Natural causes of major incidents can also bring about civil unrest, especially where victims become agitated because they believe that the government is not doing enough to help them, as in the floods in Kentucky in the USA in 2005. A situation such as this could lead people to take the law into their own hands.

Loss of power and utilities

Loss off electricity could result from an incident involving damage to overhead power cables, for example a plane crash. Sometimes it is necessary to turn off the electricity to prevent another dangerous incident. For example, if gas pipes are ruptured, either accidentally or by falling masonry, then an electrical spark could be disastrous.

In the event of severe flooding, electricity is automatically switched off because of the extensive damage water will cause to electricity as well as the risk of electric shock. This means that those living in a flooded area may be without electricity for days, until the electricity company considers it safe to turn on the supplies again.

Disease

Following a major incident there can be prolonged periods where normality cannot be restored because of secondary effects. Floodwater, for example, can lead to disease if contaminants such as sewage mix with tap water, which is then drunk. Typhoid and cholera are two serious, infectious diseases caused by drinking contaminated water.

1.4 Wider impact of incidents

Reviews of disasters

After a major incident, the emergency services and other agencies involved hold a review to determine if the incident was responded to in the most efficient way. A review is part of a process for improving performance, where questions are asked and suggestions for improvement put forward. There are several components to the reviewing process.

Public enquiry

A **public enquiry** is an open investigation which allows members of the public to seek information about the major incident. Members of the audience are free to ask questions and raise issues about what they may have read or heard, and to voice their concerns regarding any short- or long-term effects the incident is likely to have. An enquiry may be adjourned (delayed) because further information might be needed regarding issues that have been raised at the enquiry.

Key term

Public enquiry – an open investigation held in front of a public audience by a government body in the UK or Ireland. Interested members of the public and organisations may make written submissions as evidence, as well listen to evidence given by other parties.

Public enquiries have a chairperson and a panel, usually consisting of heads of personnel who attended the major incident, representatives of government departments, specialist agencies such as Aviation Authority representatives, medical personnel and other interested parties.

Debriefs of incidents by agencies

A debrief is a method of analysing the response by an agency to an incident. Debriefs are common practice throughout all uniformed public service organisations. They are intended to assess the efficiency of how a particular service responded to an incident, with the intention of highlighting mistakes and thereby improving future performance.

Debriefs may be headed by the senior officer attending the incident, though not necessarily so. They take the form of question and answer followed by an evaluation and recommendations for future major incidents.

At a debrief following a major incident, the emergency services (Police, Fire and Ambulance) would give their response times and an account of their actions in dealing with the incident.

Other agencies, such as local authority emergency teams, also have debriefs where they answer questions regarding their involvement in major incidents.

Prevention

It is impossible to prevent some serious events from happening. Phenomena such as earthquakes and volcanoes are part of the nature of the Earth and are beyond human control. However, not all emergencies need turn into disasters where human life or the environment is threatened.

Better planning

With careful consideration, an emergency situation can be prevented from turning into a disaster. In areas where earth tremors and earthquakes occur frequently, for instance, it would be prudent to construct buildings and bridges that can withstand them. Indeed, in certain areas of the world, such as Japan, it is a legal requirement that buildings are constructed to withstand earthquakes.

In the UK, especially after the floods of 2007 and 2009, the need was recognised for better planning in the construction of new homes and communities, so that they are not built on flood plains. However, where flooding is a risk in established housing

and communities, then plans to prevent flooding are required to ensure the safety of residents and communities.

Activity: Flood prevention

What sort of plans could be put in place to prevent flooding?

Improved technology

Technology plays a large part in most people's lives these days and can help in the prevention of disasters in several ways. Highly technical equipment can forecast severe storms, gales and snow, just as it can, with some accuracy, track earthquake and volcanic movement. Furthermore, government and military intelligence have the technology to intercept emails and telephone calls from terrorist suspects, which helps to prevent terrorist activities.

Better funding

Since the terrorist attack on the World Trade Center in September 2001, more government funding has been given to emergency planning. This includes funds for the training of the fire and rescue services in chemical and biological contamination techniques, as well as for the restructuring of the government's emergency planning department. However, the recent severe flooding in the UK has highlighted the fact that funding is needed not only to defend against acts of terrorism but also to rebuild businesses and communities following any disaster.

Government funding is given to those areas where immediate aid is required following a disaster. The floods in the UK in 2007 resulted in the government distributing £3.6 million between 21 local authorities, with the largest payments going to Worcestershire, Gloucestershire and Warwickshire. Funding is also available from the European Union Solidarity Fund (EUSF), and in August 2007 the British government applied for £46 million to help with the recovery from the extensive flooding in the UK. While funding from the EUSF would help enormously, it could take up to a year for the funding to be approved and granted. Other sources of funding include grants from the Lottery Fund and donations through national appeals.

Did you know?

The Bellwin Scheme is an emergency assistance fund set up to help those local authorities who have experienced sudden and extensive upheaval as a result of an unforeseen event, such as flooding.
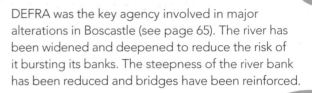

Environmental initiatives

Many disasters have an effect on the environment, whether these are oil spillages at sea, air pollution from nuclear fallout, contamination of rivers or foot and mouth outbreaks. The government department responsible for the environment is the Department for the Environment, Food and Rural Affairs (DEFRA). DEFRA has the authority to take whatever action is necessary in order to prevent a disaster or stop its escalation. For example, during the foot and mouth outbreak of 2001, DEFRA ordered the closure of footpaths in many parts of the countryside, compulsory disinfecting of vehicles and footwear when entering controlled areas, the prohibition of the movement of certain farm animals and the eventual slaughter and burning of thousands of cattle.

DEFRA also has the authority to prevent access to certain areas of open moorland in periods of prolonged hot, dry weather. At such times there is a high risk of fire, which could threaten the moorland environment. While such measures may appear to be more like coping strategies, they are, nonetheless, initiatives that are designed to prevent potential disasters from becoming reality.

Did you know?

DEFRA was the key agency involved in major alterations in Boscastle (see page 65). The river has been widened and deepened to reduce the risk of it bursting its banks. The steepness of the river bank has been reduced and bridges have been reinforced.

Education by authorities

Part of the Fire Service's role is community education in the prevention and detection of fire, and most local authorities issue leaflets to householders on the action to take during an emergency. However, while local authorities and the emergency services prepare emergency and contingency plans, some would say that not enough has been done to educate the public. The problem with educating the public is that authorities have to balance the likelihood of causing panic, by constantly telling the public what steps they should take to prevent a disaster, with information about what they should do in the event of a disaster.

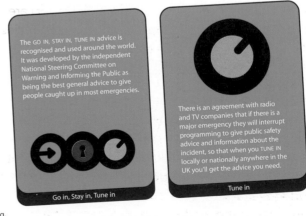

general advice about what to do in an emergency

If you find yourself in the middle of an emergency, your common sense and instincts will usually tell you what to do. However, it is important to:
- Make sure 999 has been called if people are injured or if there is a threat to life
- Not put yourself or others in danger
- Follow the advice of the emergency services
- Try to remain calm and think before acting, and try to reassure others
- Check for injuries - remember to help yourself before attempting to help others

If you are not involved in the incident, but are close by or believe you may be in danger, in most cases the advice is:
- Go inside a safe building
- Stay inside until you are advised to do otherwise
- Tune in to local radio or TV for more information

Of course, there are always going to be particular occasions when you should not "go in" to a building, for example if there is a fire. Otherwise: GO IN, STAY IN, TUNE IN.

The GO IN, STAY IN, TUNE IN advice is recognised and used around the world. It was developed by the independent National Steering Committee on Warning and Informing the Public as being the best general advice to give people caught up in most emergencies.

Go in, Stay in, Tune in

There is an agreement with radio and TV companies that if there is a major emergency they will interrupt programming to give public safety advice and information about the incident, so that when you TUNE IN locally or nationally anywhere in the UK you'll get the advice you need.

Tune in

Figure 15.3: *Preparing for Emergencies*, a leaflet issued to all householders in 2004. Do you have something similar in your home?
(*Source*: Cabinet Office. Crown Copyright material reproduced with permission of the Controller of HMSO and the Queen's Printer for Scotland.)

Costs

In terms of hardship, suffering and personal loss, it is impossible to calculate the cost of major incidents on a personal level. In monetary terms, however, the cost is calculated according to the amount of damage, the cost for rebuilding and any compensation that might be owed. The cost of the damage caused by flooding in the UK in 2007 is estimated at £3 billion in insured properties and £3 billion in uninsured properties.

Insurance companies are facing their heaviest losses in history. While they have promised to pay claimants, the process is slow because properties cannot be assessed until they have completely dried out. Furthermore, many insurance companies are considering refusal to cover flood damage claims if the government fails to invest in flood prevention.

New investments

The government has promised to invest in building better flood defences, but some experts estimate that the investment falls short by more than £8 billion. However, it is not only flood defences that need investment; it is essential for the prevention of other major incidents, such as terrorist atrocities, which require investment in security and the uniformed public services.

Lack of investment can have a drastic effect on a country's economy, as well as preventing the rapid recovery of a major incident.

Firstly, it is in the interests of private companies to invest in such things as defence and security systems so that their businesses are affected as little as possible in the event of a major incident.

Secondly, utilities, such as water and electricity companies, need to invest in their infrastructure so that they can provide adequate services during times of need. For instance, water companies need to invest in draining systems that are capable of carrying away excessive amounts of rainfall, thus minimising the risk of flooding. Electricity companies need to ensure that power stations are located in areas that are not prone to flooding.

Furthermore, with the growing concerns over the effects of global warming, careful consideration needs to be given to the location of the development of housing. The English Partnership is the National Regeneration Agency that aims to bring together the public and private sector in providing safe, sustainable housing and amenities.

Resultant legislation

Legislation is designed to give the security services, Police and other organisations the authority to take whatever measures they deem appropriate to prevent a major incident or to prevent an emergency from escalating into a disaster. Not all new legislation is the result of potential or actual major incidents, though it is often the case that they are upgraded or amended to deal with any inadequacies that may have been highlighted in view of recent events, such as the London bombings in 2005, for example.

Since 2000, there have been several Acts of Parliament designed to give the Police and security services the authority to prevent terrorism. The Terrorism Act, which became law in March 2006, made amendments to previous statutes, namely the Prevention of Terrorism Act (2005) and the Terrorism Act (2000).

The Terrorism Act (2006) makes it a criminal offence to:

- directly or indirectly incite or encourage others to commit acts of terrorism
- sell, loan or distribute terrorist publications, including publications that encourage terrorism or assist terrorists
- give or receive training in terrorist techniques
- go to a place of terrorist training
- possess or make any radioactive device
- sabotage nuclear facilities
- make threats or demands to be given radioactive materials.

Activity: The Terrorism Act (2006)

1 If you lent your mobile phone to a terrorist, and it was used to make a call or send a text for the purposes of committing an act of terrorism, would you be guilty of an offence under the Terrorism Act (2006)? Explain.

2 What does it mean to incite or encourage others to commit acts of terrorism? Discuss.

3 Why would some terrorists seek to use radioactive materials?

4 Carry out research using the Internet to find an example of when terrorism has been glorified.

Procedures

The new terrorism laws give the Police extra powers, including:

- warrants to search any property owned or controlled by a terrorist suspect
- extending stop and search powers to cover bays and estuaries
- the right to detain suspects after arrest for up to 28 days
- improved search powers at ports
- the power to prosecute groups that glorify terrorism.

Did you know?

Home Office ministers want to make it a criminal offence where people, who have been stopped by the Police, fail to answer questions about their movements and their identity.

Secure airport check-in

Since the terrorist attacks of September 2001, airport security at home and abroad has increased, with the searching and scanning of passengers and the X-raying of hand luggage and personal items prior to check in. On long-haul flights, all luggage is X-rayed and searched at random. The tighter security measures have inevitably caused long delays at all airports. Similar processes apply at ferry ports.

In August 2006, following an alleged plot to detonate bombs on up to 10 aircraft flying from the UK to the US and Canada, airport security was again increased and liquids, other than essential medication, were prohibited from being taken onto aircrafts. A one-bag rule was introduced for hand luggage. Essential travel documents had to be carried in clear, plastic bags.

Improvements

In order to deal with security risks, airports have had to make various improvements including screening of employees, better training of staff and updating security equipment, such as communications and closed-circuit television. In the USA, airports have introduced biometric testing in the form of iris recognition. This is intended to eliminate human error in identifying suspects who may use facial disguise. Currently Heathrow airport in London is conducting fingerprint and iris recognition tests with a view to strengthening security and reducing the queuing time.

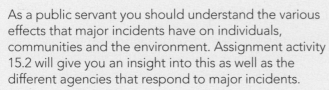

Assessment activity 15.2   P3 M2   BTEC

As a public servant you should understand the various effects that major incidents have on individuals, communities and the environment. Assignment activity 15.2 will give you an insight into this as well as the different agencies that respond to major incidents.

Create a leaflet which:

1 outlines the effects of recent major incidents on people, communities and the environment P3

2 explains the short- and long-term effects of these major incidents on people, communities and the environment, and the wider impacts they may have had. M2

Grading tips

For P3 you need to give a brief description of the effects of major incidents on people, communities and the environment, using the content already covered since assignment activity 15.2.

While M2 is an extension of P3 , you will also need to explain the wider impact of major incidents, which covers such things as improved security, legislation and so on.

PLTS

By outlining the effects of recent major incidents on people, communities and the environment, you will be demonstrating your skills as an **independent enquirer** and a **reflective learner**.

Functional skills

Creating a leaflet for Assessment activity 15.2 will help you develop your functional skills in **Reading** and **Writing**.

2. Know the type of work carried out by the public services during major incidents

2.1 Inter-agency cooperation

There are many agencies involved in major incidents and disaster recovery. Here is a list of just some of them:

- local authorities
- emergency services (Police, Fire and Ambulance)
- Red Cross
- military
- utilities (gas, water and electricity companies)
- WRVS (formally Women's Royal Voluntary Service).

Activity: Red Cross and WRVS

1 Carry out research using the Internet to find out how the Red Cross and WRVS might be involved in major incidents.

2 Name three other agencies that could be involved in major incidents.

Interaction between emergency and other services

Agencies involved in major incidents know how to interact with each other through liaison, cooperation and careful planning. Within each Police area, representatives from the agencies likely to be involved in major incidents attend Emergency Planning Resilience Forums, where they produce a comprehensive, multi-agency emergency procedures guide. The guide:

- states the aims and objectives of the forum
- defines the responsibilities of the agencies involved
- advises on the use of voluntary agencies
- gives recommendations for training.

The emergency procedures guide is a plan that the emergency and other services follow in the event of a major incident. This means that, before the onset of a major incident, the agencies involved will know their roles and responsibilities and will also have carried out joint training.

2.2 Responsibilities at the scene

Regardless of the agencies' specific roles and responsibilities, they all share common objectives when dealing with major incidents. These include:

- saving life and lessening suffering at the scene
- protecting property
- preventing the escalation of a disaster
- protecting the environment
- sharing information between all agencies involved in the incident
- protecting and preserving the scene
- contributing to the debriefing and subsequent investigation and enquiries into the incident
- restoring normality
- maintaining normal services where possible
- providing whatever resources are necessary for the recovery of the incident.

2.3 Agency specific objectives

Apart from the common objectives, each agency has specific responsibilities and objectives to ensure an efficient response to a major incident.

Local authority

Major incidents always bring disruption to the community. Since the community is the focus of social, family, educational and spiritual well-being, it is important for normality to be restored as quickly as possible. While it is the responsibility of the emergency services and other organisations to respond to the major incident, the local authority is responsible for ensuring, as far as possible, that the needs of the community are met by maintaining normal services. For example, during a major incident certain members of the community may still be reliant on community and social care, such as catering services.

In some cases, particularly severe flooding, members of the community may have to be evacuated. At such times the local authority is responsible for providing rest and reception centres or temporary accommodation; these might be located in schools and leisure centres.

Major incidents not only cause distress and anxiety for everyone directly involved, they are also a source of great concern for friends, relatives and loved ones who are not living in the area and have heard about the incident through the media. It is vital that there is a contact number so friends and relatives can find out the information they require, and this is usually provided by the local authority.

Local authorities have emergency planning teams. Local Authority Emergency Planning Officers play an important role in the coordination and recovery of a major incident by:

- establishing a Local Authority Control Point to ensure a standard response procedure for the smooth operation of the incident
- providing a Site Officer to deploy and coordinate on-site resources
- providing additional resources for the emergency and other services.

Table 15.1: The specific objectives of the Police, Ambulance and Fire Services at a major incident

Police Service	Fire Service	Ambulance Service
• Collate and distribute casualty information	• Fight fires and investigate the cause in a fire situation	• Perform triage
• Preserve the scene for evidence	• Conduct search and rescue using specialist equipment	• Establish a casualty loading area
• Investigate the cause	• Ensure the site is safe before other emergency personnel attempt rescue	• Transport casualties to designated hospitals
• Identify the dead	• Establish decontamination units where necessary.	• Order adequate medical resources.
• Ensure the entry and exit at the incident		
• Control cordons, crowds and sightseers.		

2.4 Duties under law

The Civil Contingencies Act 2004 and the Civil Contingencies Act 2004 (Contingency Planning) Regulations 2005 set the statutory guidance for civil protection in the UK at local level. It places a legal obligation on local authorities and other organisations to cooperate in responding to, and preparing for, major incidents. The Act is in two parts, with the first part detailing the duties of those who respond and prepare. The second part makes provision for the making of special emergency regulations in order to assist with the most serious incidents.

The responders fall into two categories:

1. **Category 1** responders are the organisations at the centre of planning and responding: the emergency services (Police, Fire and Ambulance), local authorities and the Health Protection Agency.
2. **Category 2** responders are the organisations not directly involved in planning but which play a vital part in dealing with incidents. Category 2 responders include:

- utilities (gas, electric, water and sewage, and telephone service providers)
- transport (train operating companies, Transport for London, airport operators, harbour authorities and Highways Agency)
- government agencies (Health and Safety Executive)
- Strategic Health Authorities.

Emergency powers

Emergency powers permitted under the Civil Contingencies Act (2004) will be only temporary and used as a last resort. They will be available only:

- for serious incidents that threaten human welfare, the environment or national security
- if it is necessary to make urgent provision in order to resolve the emergency and existing powers are inadequate
- if the emergency powers to be introduced are proportionate to the incident.

Duties of cooperation placed on agencies by law

The legislation makes it compulsory for Category 1 responders to provide an integrated response to emergency planning. They must hold a meeting at least once every six months in the form of a local resilience forum. Category 2 responders must attend at the invitation of Category 1 responders or, if it is not possible, ensure a representative attends.

Cooperation is needed between Category 1 and 2 responders and other organisations to ensure that the legal duties placed on them can be effectively managed and executed. Cooperation is only one of the duties placed on organisations by the legislation. Table 15.2 shows the legal duties placed on responders.

Table 15.2: Legal duties of responders to major incidents

Duty	Responders
Cooperation	1 and 2
Information sharing	1 and 2
Assessing the risk of hazards and emergencies and their impact on the community	1
Maintaining emergency plans for preventing, reducing and controlling emergencies, as well as dealing with secondary effects	1
Business continuity management	1
Communicating the risk to the public and how it will be responded to	1
Advice and assistance to commercial or voluntary organisations, including management issues should the need arise during an emergency.	Local authority only.

2.5 Chains of command

When dealing with major incidents, the emergency services use three levels, or chains, of command:

- Operational (also known as bronze)
- Tactical (also known as silver)
- Strategic (also known as gold).

Operational (Bronze) Command

Operational Command deals with events at the immediate scene of an incident. It could involve such things as fire-fighting, rescuing trapped victims from wreckage, treating the injured, and so on. An inner cordon is established around the incident to prevent unauthorised access to the disaster site while operational personnel carry out their work (see Figure 15.4). Operational staff includes the emergency services, local authority representatives and other organisations as demanded by the nature of the incident. Operational (Bronze) Command is located inside the inner cordon.

Tactical (Silver) Command

Tactical Command consists of a member from each of the emergency services who takes charge of the scene. This person creates tactics for his or her service at Operational Command to successfully deal with the incident.

Tactical Command, unlike Operational Command, is not directly involved in the hands-on approach but is normally established further away from the scene in the outer cordon, possibly in mobile units designated as special operations rooms.

Strategic (Gold) Command

Strategic Command is formed if the incident is very serious and cannot be resolved by Tactical Command. However, in cases of pandemic disease or predicted incidents, such as floods, the strategic team may be the first command to be established.

This command comprises senior officers from the emergency services and other organisations as required. Their role is to form a strategy to deal with the incident and to support Tactical and Operational Commands. Gold Command, as it is more often called, is located away from the incident, possibly at a police station or council building.

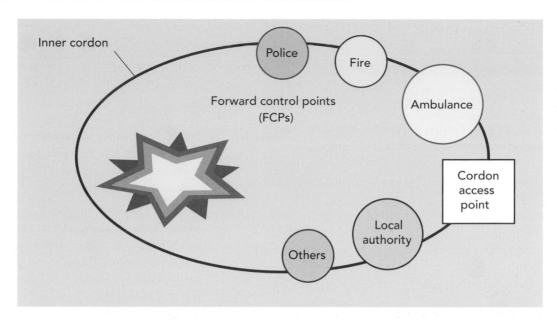

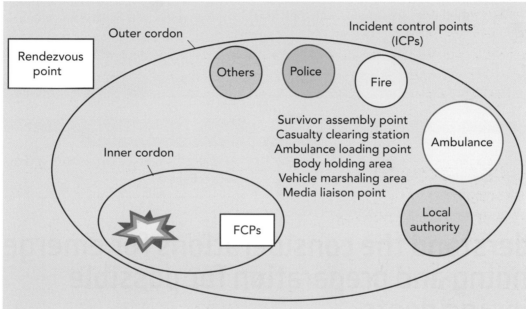

Figure 15.4: Inner and outer cordons at an emergency scene. Operational (Bronze) Command is located in the inner cordon while Tactical (Silver) Command is located in the outer cordon.

(*Source:* Cabinet Office, *Dealing with Disaster*, rev. 3rd ed., pp. 23, 24. Crown Copyright material reproduced with permission of the Controller of HMSO and the Queen's Printer for Scotland.)

Organisation

It is common practice that major incidents are coordinated by the Police Service, though strategic commanders from the other services would advise on matters where they had specialist knowledge. For instance, the Gold Fire Commander would have better knowledge of how to deal with a fire incident than a Gold Police Commander.

Each of the emergency services is coordinated and organised by their respective service commanders within the levels of command already outlined.

In terms of the organisation and involvement of local authorities, a Local Authority Liaison Officer would visit the scene to assess the level of support required by the local authority. If necessary, the Local Authority Liaison Officer would visit Silver Command to provide cooperation between the emergency services and the local authority.

In the event of a minor incident which is unlikely to escalate, the Emergency Planning Duty Manager may coordinate the local authority's response, but at large incidents the local authority will establish its own Emergency Control Centre from which to coordinate the local authority's response to the incident. This would include Chief Officers from the local authority who act at Gold Level, as well as Chief Officers from Council Departments who act at Silver Level.

Assessment activity 15.3

To be an effective member of the emergency services you must be aware of the role and responsibilities of all the agencies that may be required to attend a major incident. You should also know their duties as laid down by law.

From your knowledge so far, you should be in a position to say how UK agencies are bound by law to work together at a specific major incident.

Address the following tasks in the form of a report:

1 Identify the agencies that were involved in each of the major incidents that you described in Assessment activity 15.1, question 2. **P4**

2 Describe the work of agencies at UK incidents and their legal duties. **P5**

3 Explain how UK agencies involved in a specific major incident worked together in accordance with their legal duties. **M3**

Grading tips

For **P4** you need to identify the agencies that were involved in the disasters you described in Assessment activity 15.1, question 2.

For **P5** you need to give a description of the work of agencies that responded to UK incidents and how they were bound under the Civil Contingencies Act (2004). You should cover at least three different UK incidents.

For **M3** you need to go into more detail and explain how the agencies worked together at one UK disaster, in accordance with their legal obligations.

PLTS

By explaining how UK agencies worked together in line with their legal duties, you will demonstrate your skills as a **reflective practitioner**.

Functional skills

By writing a report you will develop your functional skills in **English**.

3. Understand the considerations for emergency planning and preparation for possible major incidents

3.1 Main considerations

The purpose of **emergency planning** is to provide an integrated response to major incidents with a view to bringing about a successful end to the incident. Planning and preparation for emergencies and possible major incidents forms a large part of the work of the emergency services and other public services. Emergency plans are drawn up so that, in the event of a major incident, the public services can respond efficiently because they are prepared for it. By sharing information and cooperating with each other at the planning stage, all responding agencies will be more effective.

Know their roles

Be competent to carry out tasks

When emergency planning personnel should:

Have confidence in other responders

Have access to resources

Figure 15.5: Essential requirements for personnel carrying out emergency planning

When emergency planning is undertaken by Category 1 responders, a great deal of thought is given to identifying possible risks. A risk is a **hazard** or **threat** that could cause serious harm to:

- the community
- organisations
- individuals
- the nation
- the environment.

Once the risks have been identified, measures can be put in place to reduce the risk or hazard. Emergency planning is a very complex undertaking, but it is broken down into five main elements:

- assessment
- prevention (including hazard prevention and minimisation options)
- preparedness
- response
- recovery.

Assessment

This is known as a **risk assessment** and forms the basis of all emergency plans. A risk assessment involves identifying a significant hazard or threat and evaluating the likelihood of it occurring and its impact shoud it occur, then formulating an overall risk score. If risks are unacceptably high then the agencies will share that information with other agencies involved in planning and decide which strategies are most suitable to reduce them.

Activity: High or low risk?

The emergency services and other public services carry out risk assessments for several potential incidents, including:

- large-scale road traffic collisions
- possible plane/train accidents
- terrorist activities
- flooding
- natural disasters such as tsunami or earthquake
- health risks including diseases such as swine flu.

Look at the above list and decide which possible risks are assessed and whether they are assessed by the emergency services or other public services. Are the risks high or low?

Prevention

Hazard prevention options

Once a potential hazard or threat has been identified and its impact evaluated as significant, then measures have to be taken to try to prevent it from causing harm. This is done by sharing information among agencies at the planning stage to decide the possible options and select the most suitable.

At the scene of an actual major incident, however, hazard prevention could be undertaken by prompt and decisive action. For example, in the Kegworth air disaster of 1989, where a passenger aircraft landed very close to the M1 motorway and a short distance from the runway, a worse disaster was prevented when the Fire Service covered the fuselage of the aircraft with foam, thereby preventing the risk of fire.

Key terms

Emergency planning – preparing for foreseen and unforeseen emergency incidents.

Hazard – anything that can cause harm.

Threat – something that is likely to cause harm.

Risk assessment – an evaluation of the seriousness of the hazard or threat, the likelihood of harm occurring and the measures needed to reduce the hazard or threat.

Hazard minimisation options

Hazards cannot always be predicted or prevented, for example the UK severe floods of 2005, 2007 and 2009. Sometimes the next best thing is to consider options for minimising harm to the public.

Flooding is a serious hazard for individuals, and in order to minimise the threat there are several options that could be put in place. Sandbags could be issued to residents, for instance, and boats could be made available to evacuate the more vulnerable members of the community. Arrangements could also be made to supply fresh drinking water in the event of domestic supplies becoming contaminated, which would minimise the risk of disease caused by drinking contaminated water.

Activity: Motorway hazards

Ice and snow on UK motorways poses a serious threat to the safety of road users. Identify four minimisation options that would serve to prevent a serious road traffic collision on UK motorways in freezing weather or snow conditions.

Preparedness

Preparedness can prevent an emergency from turning into a serious disaster, but this is only the case if there has been a proper risk assessment.

In addition to planning for known hazards, such as an explosion at a chemical plant, Category 1 responders plan for unforeseen events. These are known as contingency, or back-up, plans. They provide additional options for dealing with difficult situations where the course of action originally planned is unsuccessful. For example, in the event of radio communication failure at a major incident, the emergency services should consider alternative communication methods.

Preparation can also involve other measures, such as public awareness, community education and self-help groups – something the Fire Service is actively engaged in. If people are aware of possible hazards and how to react to them, then they are more prepared.

Activity: Preparedness and communications

Using the Internet, carry out research to identify information about communications failure during the July 2005 London bombings.

What could have been done to:

- overcome this
- make sure the services were aware of the potential problem beforehand?

Response by the emergency services

Response to an incident means the manner in which organisations respond and the way in which they set about dealing with the incident.

Police

The Police Service normally coordinates the activities of other organisations at a major incident based on land. Their primary aim is the saving and protection of life in conjunction with other emergency services, as well as preserving the scene to safeguard evidence should criminal proceedings follow.

Where possible, the Police will establish and protect inner and outer cordons to enable other responders to carry out their duties safely. The Police, in conjunction with other agencies, for instance the Highways Agency, will establish traffic cordons and diversions to keep traffic away from the scene.

It is also the duty of the Police to take witness statements, control onlookers, safeguard victims' personal property, gather evidence and oversee any criminal investigation. They also have responsibility for the identification of fatalities on behalf of HM Coroner.

Fire Service

The primary function of the Fire and Rescue Services at a major incident is the rescue of people trapped by fire, wreckage or debris. They have the necessary skills and equipment to search confined and dangerous areas for survivors, as well as having the expertise to deal with casualties. Fire Service personnel are also trained in removing large quantities of flood water, evacuation procedures and advising the other emergency services on health and safety issues at the scene. In addition they are equipped to undertake mass decontamination of people who have been exposed to chemical, biological, radioactive or nuclear (CBRN) substances.

Ambulance Service

The Ambulance Service's primary role at a major incident is to coordinate the NHS response through an Ambulance Incident Officer. Ambulance Service personnel will perform triage and designate hospitals to which injured people should be taken, as well as ensuring there are sufficient human and medical resources at the scene.

Some major incidents require the provision of specialist medical staff and scientific advice, and these are provided by the Health Protection Agency. Where an emergency is on a national or international scale, the Department of Health will take on the role of coordinating the NHS response.

Response by local authorities

Local authority planners coordinate the emergency response throughout their area, giving support to the emergency services and other organisations as well as ensuring that sufficient resources are available to deal with the incident. Local authorities assume a community leadership role and their services, such as social services and housing, are crucial to the response by providing temporary accommodation and rest centres for victims.

Response by the voluntary organisations

Within the voluntary sector, several organisations respond to major incidents and provide an array of skills and qualities. St John Ambulance, for instance, offers extra medical resources. Other voluntary services include the WRVS, who offer counselling, food and rest stations, while Mountain and Cave Rescue provides expert search and rescue support in difficult and inaccessible areas.

Recovery

The recovery phase deals with the aftermath of a major incident and returns the community to normality. This can take several forms depending on the type and scale of the incident, and could involve several agencies. In cases of severe flooding, for example, people not only face the devastating prospect of losing their belongings, they also have to be advised against entering their properties because of contamination by polluted water and the risk of disease.

The local authority takes a leading role in restoring the community to normal, but large-scale incidents, such as foot and mouth disease or extensive areas of flooding, will require the intervention of government agencies, building contractors, civil engineers, voluntary organisations, and so on. For example, in the floods in Cockermouth, Cumbria, in November 2009, six bridges were washed away, isolating Cockermouth from neighbouring towns, with little prospect of returning to normality for several years.

Where there has been soil contamination, the local authority, under the guidance of a government department, might have to excavate and replace contaminated soil. In cases of damage to wildlife because of, for example, an oil slick, the RSPCA and RSPB might become involved.

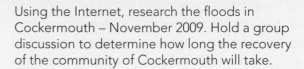

Activity: Cockermouth, Cumbria

Using the Internet, research the floods in Cockermouth – November 2009. Hold a group discussion to determine how long the recovery of the community of Cockermouth will take.

Types of plans

It is quite common for organisations to have more than one **emergency plan**, depending upon the risks and threats of their particular area. Different types of plans include:

- multi-agency emergency procedures guides
- generic plans
- specific plans
- multi-agency plans
- single-agency plans.

Key term

Emergency plan – a detailed outline of the procedures to be followed in the event of an emergency.

Multi-agency emergency procedures guides

These are comprehensive guides which are produced by Category 1 and Category 2 responders at emergency planning forums at Metropolitan District Council level. The guides detail the roles, responsibilities and procedures to be followed by responding agencies to a variety of major incidents. However, such guides are not plans and they have no operational status; they are prepared so that responders can fulfil their obligations under the Civil Contingencies Act (2004).

Generic plans

These are general plans that outline procedures for organisations to respond to and deal with a wide range of possible emergencies. Such plans describe the strategy which would be used in all instances, such as ensuring sufficient resources are made available for those responding to, say, a road traffic collision.

Specific plans

These are specific and detailed plans that relate to particular types of incidents, or to a specific site or location for which generic plans would be insufficient. For example, an incident involving toxic chemicals would require a more detailed plan than a road traffic accident in terms of dealing with the chemicals and minimising risk.

Specific plans may be used in conjunction with generic plans. For example, an evacuation procedure would be covered in a generic plan, but the response to an incident would be covered in a specific plan.

Multi-agency plans

These are required for an integrated response by several agencies. Such plans describe the roles and responsibilities of various responding agencies, as well as procedures and guidelines.

Single-agency plans

These are plans prepared by a single organisation, for instance Mountain and Cave Rescue.

3.2 Organisations involved in planning

Government agencies involved in emergency planning include:

- **DEFRA** – for incidents affecting the environment (flood or pollution incidents)
- **Health and Safety Executive** – for ensuring the health and safety of the responding emergency services and its specialist expertise in CBRN (chemical, biological, radiation or nuclear attack) and major hazard industrial sites
- **Highways Agency** – for incidents affecting the road network in England
- **Maritime and Coastguard Agency** – for incidents requiring civil maritime search and rescue

- **Government Decontamination Service** – to provide advice and guidance to those responsible for dealing with decontamination following a major hazardous materials incident.

Other organisations involved in emergency planning include:

- local authorities
- the NHS
- inter-faith groups
- Fire Service
- Police Service
- Ambulance Service
- military
- Red Cross and Red Crescent
- Radio Amateurs' Emergency Network (RAYNET)
- coroner
- Salvation Army
- Mountain and Cave Rescue
- utilities.

Organisations' roles, responsibilities and objectives during planning

It is the objective and responsibility of all organisations involved in planning to contribute to reducing the effects of a major incident and preventing its escalation. It is important to consider the roles of different organisations so that their skills and expertise can be called upon immediately in order to bring about a successful response.

Local authorities

Local authorities have large numbers of employees with skills and expertise, including structural engineers who can advise on the safety of buildings after an incident, and social workers who can assess the counselling needs of victims. Local authorities also have access to a variety of equipment and buildings, such as depots, recreation centres and schools, all of which could be called into use during and after an emergency. Part of the preparation and prevention planning involves making lists of what resources are available and how they could be used, should an emergency arise.

National Health Service (Primary Care Trusts)

Primary Care Trusts (PCTs) are responsible for local healthcare throughout England and they have a key role to play in emergency planning. It is the responsibility of PCTs to ensure that there are adequate community resources at any time in response to a major incident. Therefore, PCTs need to outline how they can contribute in responding positively to a major incident and what their role will be. For example, in the event of, say, a train crash involving many casualties, a strain is placed upon receiving hospitals. The pressure could be relieved by the PCTs discharging less seriously ill patients to make room for those in urgent need of medical attention.

Depending upon the type of incident, PCTs may need to administer drugs to people who have come into contact with hazardous materials, or vaccinate or isolate people in the event of a disease outbreak.

Key term

Primary Care Trust – a statutory body that provides healthcare by bringing together medical personnel and resources to improve the health of the people they serve.

Military

The military has a wide selection of vehicles (helicopters and reconnaissance aircraft) which may be available during an emergency. In incidents such as flooding and foot and mouth outbreaks, the services of the military are invaluable. However, military assistance to the civil community can never be guaranteed because of operational commitments, though where possible, military assistance will be provided in terms of responding to incidents as well as offering expert advice. Consequently, the military are not directly involved in planning for major incidents in the civilian community.

Voluntary organisation involvement

Voluntary organisations, such as the Red Cross and Red Crescent, RAYNET, Salvation Army and Mountain and Cave Rescue teams, are involved in emergency planning with Category 1 and 2 responders. In this way they can share information and make other organisations aware of the resources they have to offer.

The main objectives of emergency planning as far as voluntary organisations are concerned are to identify:

- at which phase of an emergency they may be called upon to assist
- what is expected of them
- who will call them out.

The response from voluntary organisations can be either operational or supportive. An operational response would involve direct assistance in dealing with the emergency by, for example, taking part in a search and rescue operation or providing comfort and guidance to casualties. A supportive response might include an organisation such as the WRVS providing care and refreshments for the operational teams at a disaster site.

Multi-agency involvement in real-life exercises

Once plans have been prepared they have to be tested, otherwise there is no way of telling if they would be adequate in the event of a major incident. Part of emergency planning involves testing the plans in major incident scenarios.

A real-life exercise involving multi-agencies is a live rehearsal of the emergency response to a major incident. It is a means of testing and validating an emergency plan. It will test such things as logistics, communications, adequacy of resources, cooperation and physical capabilities. Such exercises are helpful, especially for inexperienced personnel, because they develop confidence and provide a realistic insight into what major incidents are like.

Planning for a multi-agency response is very difficult and requires care and cooperation. This is encouraged through local resilience forums under the Civil Contingencies Act (2004). Category 1 responders are responsible for their own plans, but it is essential that the different responders' plans complement each other. Category 2 responders are governed by their own legislation in regard to emergency planning, but under the Civil Contingencies Act (2004) they are also obliged to provide Category 1 responders with information regarding their duties.

Regulations require that plans include provision for carrying out exercises, since it is only by doing this that organisations can test their effectiveness.

Exercises may focus on a number of aspects, including:

- all aspects of a generic plan
- all aspects of a specific plan
- those plans that address the most probable risks
- those plans where the least training has been done.

A real-life exercise is designed to make responders aware of other responders' roles and responsibilities, and to build morale.

3.3 Other organisations involved in prevention

Health and Safety Executive

The Health and Safety Executive (HSE) is a government agency and the enforcing authority that supports the Health and Safety Commission (HSC) in ensuring that risks to workers and members of the public are properly controlled by:

- conducting and sponsoring research
- promoting training
- providing an information and advisory service
- submitting proposals for new or revised regulations and approved codes of practice.

It is the duty of the HSC to look after many aspects of health and safety, as shown in Figure 15.6.

Large and small businesses

Any business, large or small, can experience a serious incident that prevents it from continuing to operate. For example, the severe floods of 2005, 2007 and 2009 have had a drastic impact on both small and large businesses

Case study: Manchester bomb explosion

At 11.20 am on Saturday 15 June 1996, a bomb exploded in a busy shopping area in the centre of Manchester. Two hundred and seven people were injured, some of them seriously, by flying glass as shop windows shattered.

Police evacuated hundreds of people from the city centre as army bomb disposal experts used a remote-controlled device to examine a suspect van parked outside one of the stores as the bomb exploded.

Many of those injured were outside the police cordon and suffered deep glass wounds which required surgery. Seventy bystanders were ferried to three hospitals in ambulances, while others walked or were taken by friends.

1 **What was the problem with the police cordon?**
2 **Could the management have done anything?**
3 **What would you have done if you had been in charge?**

throughout the UK. In Sheffield, South Yorkshire, the cost to businesses from the floods of 2007 was in the region of hundreds of millions of pounds (and this does not include the loss to the economy).

Business managers have a responsibility to prevent major incidents from causing major disruption, not only to their business but also to their employees and members of the public. Furthermore, businesses have a duty to protect their employees and members of the public from the threat of terrorism.

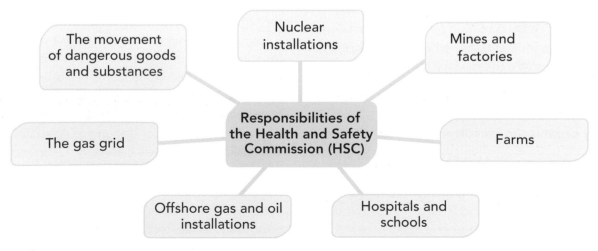

Figure 15.6: The HSC looks after many aspects of health and safety

Media agencies

Media agencies play an important role in the preparation and prevention of major emergencies because the Civil Contingencies Act (2004) requires Category 1 responders to communicate with the public regarding emergencies. Communicating with the public has two aims:

- to warn the public of any potential or current emergencies

- to provide information and advice to the public, including how they will be responded to.

Media management involves releasing factual information to warn, inform and advise the public but without causing alarm. Where casualties are involved, only numbers are given to the media; no initial statements are made about the condition of casualties, numbers of dead or their identities.

Possible future disasters

Earthquakes

Earthquakes are not something that spring to mind when considering emergency planning in the UK. However, as Table 15.3 (on page 86) and the case study below show, the UK does occasionally experience an earthquake strong enough to cause considerable damage.

According to the Environment Agency, buildings are considered to be at risk from earthquakes over 5 on the Richter scale. While earthquakes of this magnitude are rare in the UK, as can be seen in Table 15.3, they are not unknown. Although the quake of June 1931 was in the North Sea the effects were felt inland with many buildings in the north of England suffering structural damage.

Case study: Largest earthquake for over 25 years in UK

Just before 1.00 am on 27 February 2008, an earthquake measuring 5.2 on the Richter scale sent shock waves across most of the UK, causing fear and distress. The epicentre of the quake was near Market Rasen in North Lincolnshire, and earth tremors were felt as far away as Northern Ireland, Holland, Edinburgh and Plymouth.

A 19-year-old student from Barnsley, South Yorkshire, received a broken pelvis when he was pinned under fallen masonry in his bedroom. While there were no reported deaths from the earthquake, the largest since one in Wales in 1984, there were several reports of structural damage and police stations were inundated with phone calls from frightened residents. In Gainsborough, Lincolnshire, the Fire Service attended 50 calls, including a fire, as a result of the quake.

A spokesman for the British Geological Survey said that quakes of this magnitude were quite rare and would occur in the UK approximately every 10 to 20 years.

1   **Would this earthquake be classed as a major incident? Explain.**

2   **Could anything be done to prevent the effects of such tremors in the UK?**

3   **Which emergency services would you expect to attend such incidents?**

4   **What type of assistance would people require?**

Figure 15.7: Epicentre of the earthquake that struck the UK on 27 February 2008

Table 15.3: Previous earthquakes in the UK

Date	Location	Magnitude on Richter Scale
April 2007	Folkestone, Kent	4.3
December 2006	Dumfries and Galloway, Scotland	3.5
September 2002	Dudley, West Midlands	5.0
October 2001	Melton Mowbray	4.1
September 2000	Warwick	4.2
April 1990	Bishop's Castle, Shropshire	5.1
July 1984	Nefyn, North Wales	5.4
June 1931	In North Sea near Great Yarmouth	6.1

Coastal erosion

The main cause of coastal erosion is the action of waves, tides and currents on the foreshore, though it can also be affected by rainfall, drought, and freezing and thawing cycles in coastal cliffs.

In addition to being a natural defence against the sea, the UK coastline serves as natural habitat for a variety of birds and other wildlife. Coastal erosion is relatively slow to develop, so while it may not always seem proper to describe it as a major emergency, it is, nonetheless, a serious incident that has a drastic impact on the environment.

Flooding

There was extensive flooding in several parts of the UK in 2005 (for example Carlisle, Cumbria), in 2007 (for example Gloucestershire and Oxfordshire) and in 2009 (for example, Cockermouth, Cumbria). Whether this is as a result of global warming or not, flooding in the UK is currently a major problem.

Table 15.4: Richter scale of earthquake magnitude

Magnitude level	Category	Effects	Earthquakes per year
Less than 1.0 to 2.9	Micro	Generally not felt by people, though recorded on local instruments	More than 100,000
3.0–3.9	Minor	Felt by many people; no damage	12,000–100,000
4.0–4.9	Light	Felt by all; minor breakage of objects	2000–12,000
5.0–5.9	Moderate	Some damage to weak structures	200–2000
6.0–6.9	Strong	Moderate damage in populated areas	20–200
7.0–7.9	Major	Serious damage over large areas; loss of life	3–20
8.0 and higher	Great	Severe destruction and loss of life over large areas	fewer than 3

Activity: Preventative options

1 What preventative options can be taken for coastal erosion?

2 What preventative options can be taken for large-scale road traffic collisions?

3 Can you think of any preventative options for train/plane crashes? If not, what are the minimisation options?

Link

You can read about the possible effects of global warming on the UK climate, and how this has increased the likelihood of flooding, in *Unit 34: Environmental Policies and Practices*, pages 279–280.

Did you know?

There are between 200 and 300 quakes each year in Britain, but only about 10 per cent are strong enough to be felt.

Assessment activity 15.4

P6 M4 D1 · BTEC

Emergency planning is essential to prevent an emergency situation from escalating into a full-scale disaster, as well as ensuring that various agencies know what to do.

Address the following tasks in the form of a wall display:

1 Explain the main considerations when planning and preparing for major incidents. P6

2 Explain the role of the organisations involved in planning for major incidents. M4

3 Analyse the importance of inter-agency emergency planning for major incidents. D1

Grading tips

For P6 you need to explain the main elements taken into account by the agencies involved in planning for major incidents.

For M4 you need to explain the different roles of the organisations that participate in major incident planning.

For D1 you need to give a detailed account of why it is important for various agencies to join together to carry out emergency planning for major incidents. For this you might want to refer to case studies and examples of major incidents to illustrate what is positive about inter-agency emergency planning.

PLTS

By explaining the role of organisations when planning for major incidents, you will demonstrate your skills as a **reflective learner**.

Functional skills

By creating a wall display you will develop your functional skills in **English**.

4. Prepare for a particular major incident by using tabletop scenarios

4.1 Tabletop scenarios

A tabletop scenario is a cost-effective simulation of a realistic scenario, used in emergency planning.

These exercises are not necessarily based around a tabletop, though they are usually conducted indoors and may occupy one or several rooms. All the responding agencies would be present, including the media if required.

A timeline is developed, and as the simulation unfolds the participating responders are expected to implement the emergency plan and outline their roles and responsibilities in relation to the simulated incident.

Tabletop scenarios are effective in that once different organisations have exercised together, they are more likely to provide an effective response to a genuine disaster than if they had come together for the first time when a disaster occurs.

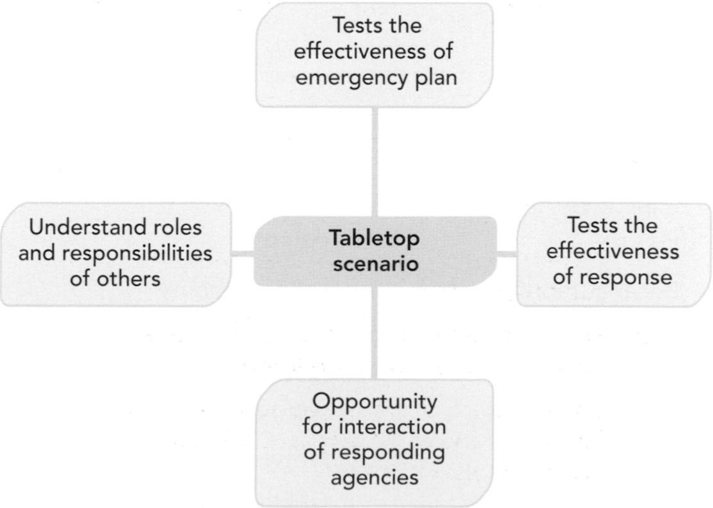

Tests the effectiveness of emergency plan

Understand roles and responsibilities of others — **Tabletop scenario** — Tests the effectiveness of response

Opportunity for interaction of responding agencies

Figure 15.8: The purpose of a tabletop scenario

Agencies that may be involved in a tabletop scenario

In accordance with the recommendations of the Civil Contingencies Act (2004), all Category 1 responders or their delegates will be involved, and Category 2 responders may be requested to participate by Category 1 responders. Voluntary services would be invited and expected to participate, depending on the type of scenario (for a list of agencies see Table 15.5). For example, mountain rescue organisations may be called to take part in a tabletop exercise that is based around an avalanche scenario in mountainous terrain.

4.2 Types of tabletop scenarios

To be of any value, tabletop scenarios are driven by an emergency plan, which could be generic, site specific, multi-agency, single-agency or an Emergency Procedures Guide. For example, while a train/plane crash scenario might test a multi-agency plan as well as the Emergency Procedures Guide, a building collapse might test a specific and single-agency plan. The Fire Service prepares such plans as they are the emergency service that would deal with such an incident.

It is only when exercises are simulated that plans can be tested and validated.

Figure 15.9: Sequence for validating an emergency plan

Table 15.5: Organisations that may respond to different types of incident

Chemical/fuel spillages	Train/plane crash	Building collapse	Terrorist attacks
Health and Safety Executive	Health and Safety Executive	Health and Safety Executive	Health and Safety Executive
DEFRA	DEFRA	Local authority	DEFRA
Local authority	Local authority	Utilities	Local authority
Health Protection Agency	Health Protection Agency		Health Protection Agency
Water authority	Salvation Army		Salvation Army
Highways Agency.	WRVS		WRVS
	Network Rail		Network Rail
	Utilities		Utilities
	Civil Aviation Authority		Civil Aviation Authority
	British Transport Police.		British Transport Police
			Military.

Section 3 (page 79) examined how the emergency services carry out risk assessments for a range of possible major incidents. When the plans have been prepared from the risk assessment, a tabletop exercise is carried out and includes the following:

- chemical/fuel spillages
- train/plane crash
- building collapse
- terrorist attacks
- large-scale road traffic collisions.

4.3 Issues for consideration in the scenario

Cause of incident

The cause and type of major incident will have a bearing on how organisations respond.

Chemical/fuel spillages

The release, or the potential release, of hazardous chemicals into the atmosphere is a risk to the public and the environment. A chemical or fuel spillage could be caused by a road traffic collision involving a vehicle carrying hazardous chemicals or fuel. Alternatively, it could be a chemical spillage from a COMAH site (location of a site where hazardous chemicals are manufactured or stored under the Control of Major Accident Hazards Regulations 1999), or even the result of a terrorist attack.

Train/plane crash

Such incidents could be caused by a technical fault, human error or an act of terrorism. Train/plane crashes are always very serious and require an immediate, combined response.

Building collapse

Building collapse can have several causes, including:

- faulty construction
- coastal erosion
- earthquake
- terrorist attack
- flooding
- fire.

Terrorist attacks

Terrorist attacks can take several forms, including bombings of busy public places, biological weapon attacks and sabotage of public transport. Terrorist attacks are usually committed with the intention of causing the maximum harm and disruption to members of the public, the government and the economy.

Agency response

The emergency services would always respond to all of the above scenarios, but some of them would call for different specialist organisations, as shown in Table 15.5.

The first priority of the emergency services is the safety of personnel and of the public. They will also try to ensure, as far as possible, that the incident does not escalate. Following an initial assessment, a major incident may be declared unless the situation is such that no further assistance is required by other organisations. However, if the incident is declared a major incident then procedures are followed according to the emergency or contingency plans. For example, most bomb threats are dealt with by the Police and they fall into three stages as follows.

Stage 1: Possibility of a bomb

If the Police suspect the threat is not a hoax they may decide to evacuate the area and call upon the local authority to arrange temporary accommodation. The local authority would then assist the Police in diverting traffic, providing barriers to control crowds and liaising with local transport companies to safely remove people from the scene. At this stage, the Police may carry out a search of premises to identify any suspicious packages.

Stage 2: Suspect device identified

Where a suspicious device has been identified, the Police would contact the Explosive Ordnance Disposal Team (Army Bomb Disposal Unit), who would decide if the device was a real threat.

A bomb disposal expert with a robot. At which stage in the agency response to a bomb threat would the Explosive Ordnance Disposal Unit be contacted?

Stage 3: Bomb explodes

The Police would work closely with the Fire Service to secure the area with an inner cordon and carry out fire-fighting and rescue operations. A security cordon would be established to protect the scene for evidence, as well as to safeguard the emergency services and members of the public from the possibility of a secondary device. The Ambulance Service would be on hand, outside the protected area, to perform triage and transport any casualties to hospital.

Resources that may be required

Where an incident involves chemicals or hazardous materials, the Fire Service will mobilise a hazardous materials (HAZMAT) unit so that victims who have come into direct contact with hazardous materials can be decontaminated. Where incidents such as train/plane crashes are prolonged or a rescue is required during the hours of darkness, then lighting and generators will be required at the site. In the case of a building collapse, props and supports will be necessary. Oxygen supplies will be needed for victims trapped in confined spaces with little air.

Extra human resources are often called for at very serious incidents, including voluntary services such as the WRVS and Salvation Army, to provide support and counselling, as well as refreshments, to victims and emergency personnel.

Inner and outer cordons

Inner cordons protect the safety of personnel where Operational Command is situated. The outer cordon contains the following posts, while others are located outside of the cordons, as shown in Figure 15.4 (page 77).

- The **casualty clearing station** is an area established by the Ambulance Service in consultation with the medical incident officer, within the outer cordon. Here triage is performed and a decision is made about the medical condition of casualties before they are evacuated.

- A **rendezvous area** is located close to, or within, the outer cordon. Vehicles attending the incident are directed here. Rendezvous points are staffed by the Police, who receive the vehicles and direct them either to the site of the incident or to the vehicle marshalling area.

- A **marshalling area** is situated inside the outer cordon and is set aside for emergency vehicles and any specialist vehicles that are required to deal with the incident. Therefore, the marshalling area should be large enough to accommodate several vehicles and in close proximity to the rendezvous point.

- The **press information centre** is located outside the outer cordon. Here press, television reporters and radio reporters gather for a press release.

Command and control

Where the incident is very serious and on a large scale, the three levels of command and control need to be established so a strategy can be formulated to deal with the incident effectively (see Figure 15.10).

Activity: The levels of command

Do you remember what the three levels of command are?

Communications network

Good communications are essential at the scene of an incident. All the emergency services will have direct access to their control room through radio communication, as well as radio handsets which

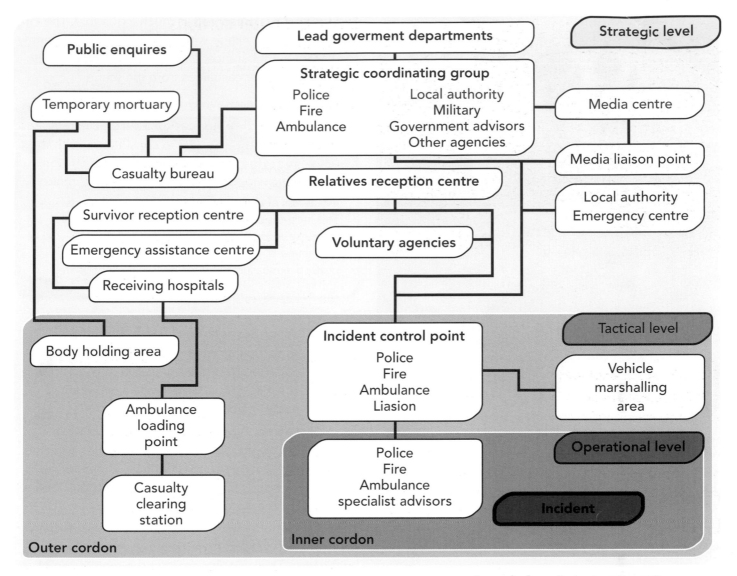

Figure 15.10: The coordinated response to a major incident, showing the responsibilities and chains of command

(*Source:* Home Office, *Dealing with Disaster*, 3rd ed., p. 10. Crown Copyright material reproduced with permission of the Controller of HMSO and the Queen's Printer for Scotland.)

enable them to coordinate with other agencies at the site. Along with local authorities, emergency services and the health service have mobile telephones which are protected under the Mobile Telecommunication Privileged Access Scheme (MTPAS). This enables mobile phones to continue operating when restrictions have been imposed on their use. Major incidents often bring severe congestion to telephone networks, but the MTPAS allows essential users to make and receive calls by placing restrictions on non-essential users.

The Internet also provides organisations with an effective means of communication, including electronic mailing, and is a source of information.

Environmental considerations

It is difficult to say which type of incident can do most environmental damage. For example, while chemical spillage can pollute watercourses, the atmosphere and plant and animal life, so, too, can acts of terrorism. Train/plane crashes can also affect the environment adversely, especially when large amounts of aviation fuel are spilt over land and water. Wetland areas and Sites of Special Scientific Interest (SSSI) with rare fauna and flora can all be threatened with chemical pollution. Furthermore, marine life and beaches can suffer pollution from such incidents as oil tankers running aground and breaking up.

What emergency services and agencies would be involved in clearing up after a major oil spill?

and the scene is preserved as much a possible. The Fire Service would also liaise with onsite chemists to identify the hazardous substance, and assist other emergency services to recover casualties from the scene.

Did you know?

The Fire Service has direct access to a computer system called Chemdata, which contains data on thousands of chemicals and tradename products. This includes essential information for emergency response, such as physical properties, hazards, containment, decontamination, basic first aid, protective measures and action in the event of fire.

The Ambulance Service's specific responsibilities include triage, the immediate treatment of casualties and transportation to receiving hospitals. It is also responsible for coordinating the health service response to the incident.

The Environment Agency has the responsibility of advising and giving information on the disposal of the substance once it has been identified. The agency will also work with the local authority and water authorities to safeguard the water supply.

The local authority has the responsibility of providing accommodation for persons temporarily displaced by the leak. They will also assist in the monitoring of chemical dispersal, advising the public and helping to reduce the pollution to watercourses. Furthermore, the local authority has a responsibility to assist the Police in implementing traffic diversions and signposting.

Public health doctors have a responsibility to work closely with hospitals, environmental health and other bodies to gather information on patients receiving medical care, either at hospitals or their own general practice. They also help to identify chemicals present in the environment.

Where there is a threat to a SSSI, country parks and woodlands, the local authority will work in consultation with English Nature to undertake to preserve, and where necessary, replace flora and fauna affected by chemical contamination.

The Health Protection Agency would provide a Consultant in Communicable Disease Control (CCDC) to assess the problem and the long-term consequences.

Common and agency specific responsibilities at the scene

Chemical/fuel spillage

It is the common objective of all responding agencies to a chemical/fuel spill to save lives and prevent the incident from escalating. However, they all have different skills which enable them to carry out specific responsibilities at the scene.

Specifically, the Police would inform the various statutory bodies, such as the local authority, the Environment Agency, the water authority and the Health and Safety Executive (HSE). They would also coordinate the response outside the immediate area of the spillage. Other specific responsibilities would include:

- controlling and diverting traffic
- making public announcements
- undertaking casualty identification
- preserving the scene for investigative purposes.

The Fire Service's specific response would be to protect and control entry and exit from the immediate scene, thereby ensuring that safety procedures are followed

4.4 Post-incident responsibilities

When the emergency services have dealt with the major incident, there are still lots of things to be done by certain organisations. The Health and Safety Executive, for instance, carries out extensive enquiries into the causes of major incidents to ensure that the risk of future incidents of a similar nature is reduced. In the event of air crashes, the Aviation Authority has a responsibility to investigate the cause. Where there has been a chemical spillage, the local authority, together with the Environment Agency, has a duty to ensure that soil and watercourses are restored to normality. The local authority also has the responsibility of monitoring air quality.

Debrief of situation by all agencies

A debrief is held after all major incidents in order to assess the effectiveness of the agency response. Debriefs may be held separately – that is, Gold Command, Silver Command and Bronze Command may have their own debriefs, but there could also be a joint debrief of all commanders.

Reviews of response procedures

Remember, a review is an assessment of how efficiently a major incident was responded to. Part of the review involves taking statements of witnesses and members of the organisations involved in the incident. Some reviews are carried out by independent Police Services – that is, a Police Service that was not involved in the incident.

When the statements have been analysed, a report is compiled. This is dispatched to the senior ranks of the emergency services so that good practice can be disseminated or lessons learned can be taken on board.

It is important to note that a review of a disaster is not meant to be a critical analysis; it is intended to serve as a learning aid with the purpose of making organisations more efficient in the future.

Scene investigation

Scene investigation is necessary to determine the cause of an incident and to see if criminal proceedings are necessary. Therefore, the more a scene is protected during an incident, the better the likelihood of finding the cause. Following some air crashes, for instance, the pieces of wreckage are collected and reassembled like a huge jigsaw puzzle.

Scenes may be investigated by the following:

- Police Service
- Fire Service
- forensic scientists
- Civil Aviation Authority
- Health and Safety Executive.

Long-term social service, victim support and NHS aftercare of victims and relatives

Physical and mental injuries may mean that victims of major incidents require long-term support from the social services and NHS, because they are no longer able to look after themselves. Victims of major incidents include not only casualties who were innocently caught up in a major incident, but also members of the emergency services who may have become injured. This long-term **aftercare** can also extend to relatives of victims who, while not suffering from any physical disability, may have become so traumatised by witnessing the injuries to their loved ones that they too have become unable to look after themselves.

Criminal and inquest proceedings support

When the scene of a major incident has been investigated and there is sufficient evidence to suggest criminal intent or negligence, proceedings are then brought against the person or organisation responsible. This could mean, as with the case of the Lockerbie air disaster of 1988, that the people responsible are **extradited** to stand trial.

An inquest is held into all sudden, suspicious and unnatural deaths by HM Coroner. If, during the course of the evidence, the coroner decides that there has been criminal negligence, then he or she can direct that a person be investigated and charged.

Key terms

Aftercare – the short- or long-term care of victims of major incidents.

Extradite – when the government of one country sends a citizen accused of a crime to stand trial for that crime in another country. For example, the Lockerbie bomber was sent from Libya to face trial in the UK.

Clear up of scene and/or environment

We have already mentioned that several agencies are involved in the clear up of the scene. The main organisations, depending on the type of incident, are the Environment Agency and the local authority.

Evaluation

When a major incident has been dealt with it, an evaluation of the incident is prepared by the coordinating officer and the local authority. The evaluation will highlight the things that went well and the things that did not go so well, together with recommendations for the future.

Assessment activity 15.5

When emergency plans are prepared, there is no way of knowing if they are adequate unless they are tested. It is far better to test them in a simulated scenario and discover in a safe environment that the plans need amending, than to find out they are inadequate in a real major incident.

Address the following tasks in the form of a group role play:

1 Carry out a tabletop scenario of a major incident.

2 Analyse the tabletop scenario. **M5**

3 Evaluate the tabletop scenario. **D2**

Grading tips

For **P7** you should first organise yourselves into groups and decide on a potential incident from the following:

* chemical/fuel spillages
* train/plane crash
* building collapse
* terrorist attacks
* large-scale road traffic collisions.

Prepare a sketch of the scene and a plan on a large sheet of paper.

Once the scenario has been agreed, each member of the group should assume the role of a responder and explain what they would do as the incident unfolds.

For **M5** you need to explain the tabletop scenario in detail, taking care to consider all the points mentioned in the last outcome.

For **D2** you will need to give an evaluation of the scenario. This should be a review of what went well and what improvements could be made to make it more effective.

PLTS

Carrying out a tabletop scenario will develop your skills as a **team worker** and an **effective participator**.

Functional skills

Participation in the group role play will develop your functional skills in **English**.

John Noble
Police Constable

I joined the Police Service six years ago. After my probation I went on a driving course to be a first responder. Although we're always incredibly busy, I wouldn't change my job for anything. The diversity of the work is fascinating. You might be dealing with a shoplifter one minute and going to a major incident the next; you just never know. As a first responder, I'm normally at the scene first and have to take charge until a senior officer arrives.

A typical shift

At the moment I work three shifts – nights, afternoons and days – and they can all be very busy. The night shift always starts busy, especially at weekends when the clubs turn out, and that's when I'm tasked to do routine patrol.

The afternoon shift is always busy from start to finish. I can remember during the floods last year I worked round the clock and I never had a break, grabbing something to eat when I had a minute. You can't just walk away when your shift is due to end, not when people need help.

While my main duty involves routine patrol and responding to incidents, there is no such thing as a typical shift.

The best thing about the job

The job satisfaction is second to none because you really feel as though you're doing a worthwhile job. I've seen some disturbing sights, but you have to stay calm and organised. When you're the first at the scene you have to send for other agencies, so you really have to know what you're doing.

When you go to a major incident you have to stay focused on those who need help first. You can't panic or get too involved because you have to take charge until back-up arrives and be accurate with the information you pass to the control room. Then you see the team working together and it normally goes like clockwork. When it's all over and things are back to normal, you get a real sense of achievement, especially if there are no fatalities. If I had to say anything, then I'd say that's the best thing about the job.

Think about it!

- What topics have you covered in this unit that might give you the background to become a member of the emergency services?
- What knowledge and skills do you think you need to develop further if you want to become a member of the emergency services?

Just checking

1. What is meant by a 'major incident'?
2. List four different causes of major incidents.
3. What is the difference between epidemic and pandemic?
4. What is PTSD and how is it caused?
5. What does DEFRA stand for?
6. List six new offences created by the Terrorism Act (2006).
7. Give three responsibilities of the Police, Fire and Ambulance Services at a major incident.
8. What is meant by 'Category 1' and 'Category 2' responders?
9. Which legislation creates such responders?
10. What are the three chains of command and where would they be located in the event of a major incident?
11. What is the purpose of a risk assessment?
12. What does RAYNET stand for?
13. What is the role of HM Coroner?
14. What is a tabletop exercise?
15. Where would you expect to see a casualty clearing point and a marshalling yard in the event of a major incident?

Assignment tips

- This unit gives you a basic outline of how the emergency services and other agencies respond to major incidents. You could carry out your own research into any major incident you have heard about recently, or read about in the press. Researching a topic for yourself gives you greater insight into a subject and a better chance of achieving the higher grades in your assignment.

- When carrying out your research, see if you can apply your understanding from this unit, especially of the roles and responsibilities of the services and the level of command and control sequence (operational, tactical and strategic). You could read about them in past editions of newspapers, which may be kept in your library. Your tutor or librarian should be able to help.

- Any of the services outlined in this unit require certain qualities of character, and because of this they have quite demanding selection and recruitment procedures. Some of those qualities are teamwork, problem solving and working with others, which are excellent skills to have in any career but especially in the emergency services. How could you develop these qualities? Can you make the right decision when under pressure? How could you practise and develop this skill?

- Critical thinking is vital when faced with a problem (sometimes called a dilemma). You will need to decide what would be the best solution, if indeed there is a best solution. Senior officers are often faced with difficult decisions in life-threatening situations. How do they decide which course of action is best? Some people believe that the correct course of action is one that brings about the greatest good for the greatest number, or one that brings about the least amount of suffering. Does that mean, then, that it is acceptable to let a few people die as long as there are more who survive? Or does everyone have a right to life?

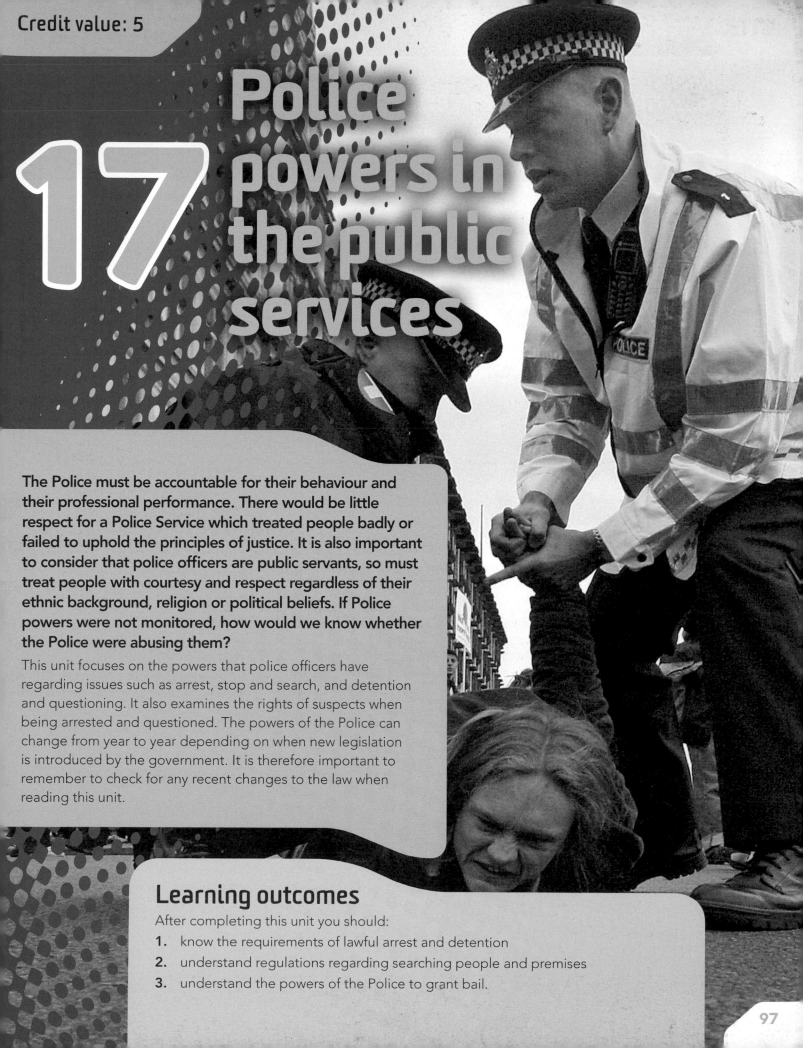

17 Police powers in the public services

The Police must be accountable for their behaviour and their professional performance. There would be little respect for a Police Service which treated people badly or failed to uphold the principles of justice. It is also important to consider that police officers are public servants, so must treat people with courtesy and respect regardless of their ethnic background, religion or political beliefs. If Police powers were not monitored, how would we know whether the Police were abusing them?

This unit focuses on the powers that police officers have regarding issues such as arrest, stop and search, and detention and questioning. It also examines the rights of suspects when being arrested and questioned. The powers of the Police can change from year to year depending on when new legislation is introduced by the government. It is therefore important to remember to check for any recent changes to the law when reading this unit.

Learning outcomes

After completing this unit you should:

1. know the requirements of lawful arrest and detention
2. understand regulations regarding searching people and premises
3. understand the powers of the Police to grant bail.

Assessment and grading criteria

This table shows you what you must do in order to achieve a pass, merit or distinction grade, and where you can find activities in this book to help you.

To achieve a **pass** grade the evidence must show that you are able to:	To achieve a **merit** grade the evidence must show that, in addition to the pass criteria, you are able to:	To achieve a **distinction** grade the evidence must show that, in addition to the pass and merit criteria, you are able to:
P1 describe the difference between arrest with and without a warrant **See Assessment activity 17.1 page 114**	**M1** explain the requirements of lawful arrest and detention **See Assessment activity 17.1 page 114**	**D1** evaluate police powers of arrest, detention and search **See Assessment activity 17.1 page 114**
P2 state the rights of a detained person **See Assessment activity 17.1 page 114**		
P3 explain the powers the Police have to search people and premises **See Assessment activity 17.1 page 114**		
P4 explain police powers to grant bail **See Assessment activity 17.2 page 116**	**M2** assess why the Police have the powers to grant bail **Assessment activity 17.2 page 116**	

How you will be assessed

This unit will be assessed by an internal assignment that will be designed and marked by the staff at your centre. The assignment is designed to allow you to show your understanding of the learning outcomes for police powers in the public services. Assignments can be quite varied and can take the form of:

- reports
- leaflets
- presentations
- posters
- practical tasks
- case studies
- discussions.

Dalit learns what powers the Police have

I liked this unit because a lot of it was law-based and I'm planning to go to university to study law after I've finished my BTEC National in Public Services. I think it's really important to know what powers the Police have and how they are allowed to use them. If we didn't have this information, how would people know whether the Police were doing their job properly and reducing crime in our country?

The interesting sections of this unit for me were on the powers of stop and search for both people and premises. A lot of my friends have been stopped and searched, and it was interesting to see how that process is governed by rules and procedure rather than just being done on the whim of a police officer. It is vital that the Police have guidance and rules on issues which affect the freedom and privacy of the public.

Over to you!

- **What areas of Police powers might you find interesting?**
- **Do you know any of the powers the Police have?**
- **Do you think the Police have too many or not enough powers?**
- **What preparation could you do to get ready for your assessments?**

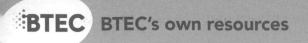

1. The requirements of lawful arrest and detention

Talk up

The Police have a great deal of power over the general public.

What would happen if they abused this power?

Find a newspaper report that deals with a **breach** of police power. What power was breached, and how could this potentially affect the reputation of the Police Service?

This learning outcome deals with how the Police and the public can make arrests and the laws and rules which govern that process. It also discusses what happens after a person has been arrested in terms of how long they can stay in **custody** and what rights they have.

1.1 Arrest with or without a warrant

An arrest is the removal of a person's liberty for a temporary period. Arrests can be carried out in order to:

- have the person answer to a charge
- prevent a breach of the peace
- have **DNA** samples taken
- return a person to prison
- have a person appear in court.

Differences between arrest made by police officers and an arrest by a private citizen

All citizens of the UK have the legal right to arrest another person. This right is given to the public by Section 24 of the Police and Criminal Evidence Act (PACE, 1984), but it actually dates back far before this to medieval times and English Common Law.

There are clear rules as to when citizens can and cannot make an arrest. For example, you cannot make an arrest if you only *suspect* someone is guilty of a crime, no matter how strong your suspicions are. Suspicion alone is not enough – and if you do make an arrest which is incorrect, you might find yourself in trouble with the Police.

The circumstances where you can make a citizen's arrest are:

- *during the offence* – if a person is in the act of committing an **indictable offence**
- *after the offence* – you may arrest the person who is guilty of the offence.

Key terms

Breach – to break or violate a law, agreement or other regulation. Also, failing to fulfil a duty or obligation.

Custody – the exercise of power to deprive a person of his or her liberty.

DNA – deoxyribonucleic acid. Genetic coding, found in the body's cells.

Indictable offence – a serious criminal offence which must be tried in Crown Court.

Case study: Citizen's arrest

In 2006, chip shop owner Nicholas Tyers and his son Lee made a citizen's arrest on a 12-year-old boy who had spat a chip at one of his customers and smashed a window. The boy was picked up by Mr Tyers and his son in their car and driven to their shop, where the Police were called. The boy complained about his treatment and both Mr Tyers and his son were charged with the offence of kidnap, which carries a maximum jail sentence of life imprisonment. The case was dismissed at Hull Crown Court in January 2007 after the judge argued that since the boy was only held for between 2 and 6 minutes the evidence did not support the charge. Mr Tyers and his family had to wait six months for the charges to be dismissed during which time Mr Tyers lost his business and his son Lee, who was a serving Royal Marine, could not join his unit in Afghanistan. No charges were ever brought against the 12-year-old boy for the original offence.

1   **Do you think Mr Tyers should have been charged with an offence in the first place? Explain your answer.**
2   **What does this case highlight about the problems with making a citizen's arrest?**
3   **Are citizen's arrests still needed in the UK?**
4   **What would you have done in Mr Tyer's circumstances?**

There are several differences between police arrests and citizen's arrests, as shown in Table 17.1.

Table 17.1: Differences between citizen's arrests and those made by the Police

Citizen's arrests	Police arrests
You cannot make a citizen's arrest if you believe a crime is about to be committed, but only if one is being committed or has been committed.	The Police can arrest if they believe a crime is about to be committed.
Citizens can only arrest another person for 'indictable' offences – these are more serious offences.	The Police can arrest for any offence.
Citizen's arrests are not carried out often by the general public and should not be carried out at all if there is a risk of danger of violence. In such circumstances the safest thing to do is to call the Police and allow them to do their job.	The majority of arrests are made by the Police. The Police are trained to carry out arrests where there is a risk of danger of violence.

Remember!

The powers of citizen's arrest are still really important in the UK as they form the basis of the powers of arrest which belong to Police Community Support Officers (PCSOs).

Arrest with a warrant

The Police apply to a Magistrates' Court for a **warrant** to arrest a suspect or to ensure that a witness attends a court hearing. The warrant can be issued under Section 1 of the Magistrates' Courts Act (1980) and must contain the name of the suspect and the offence they are alleged to have committed. The decision to issue a warrant rests solely with the magistrate.

If the magistrate issues a warrant, the police officer may then make the arrest, even if they have to use reasonable force to enter premises where they think the suspect might be. The majority of warrants issued in England and Wales are for matters such as:

- failure to appear in court
- breach of bail conditions
- failing to pay fines.

Key term

Warrant – a legal document signed by a judge giving the Police permission to carry out a particular action, for example carrying out an arrest or searching a suspect's property.

Did you know?

Warrants can be carried out by civilian agencies such as approved enforcement agencies (AEA) or civilian enforcement officers (CEO). A police officer does not necessarily need to do this work.

Arrest without a warrant

In reality, many arrests are carried out without a warrant. This is either because the Police are called to the scene of a crime and must act rapidly, or because they do not know who is about to be arrested before they deal with an incident and therefore could not get a warrant.

Section 24 of PACE (1984) sets out the general powers of arrest which may be exercised by the Police as well as the public. However, S24 of PACE was substantially changed by the Serious Organised Crime and Police Act (SOCPA, 2005). Section 110 of SOCPA replaced most of the existing powers of arrest with a new general power of arrest. It also created Code G of PACE (see below), which sets out when an officer might arrest. This power of arrest is only exercisable if the officer has reasonable grounds for believing that it is necessary.

The following extract is taken directly from Code G of the Police and Criminal Evidence Act (PACE, 1984) and identifies when an arrest might be necessary.

POLICE AND CRIMINAL EVIDENCE ACT (PACE, 1984)

Codes of practice – Code G: Statutory power of arrest by police officers

2.9 The criteria are that the arrest is necessary:

(a) to enable the name of the person in question to be ascertained (in the case where the constable does not know, and cannot readily ascertain, the person's name, or has reasonable grounds for doubting whether a name given by the person as his name is his real name)

(b) correspondingly as regards the person's address

an address is a satisfactory address for service of summons if the person will be at it for a sufficiently long period for it to be possible to serve him or her with a summons; or, that some other person at that address specified by the person will accept service of the summons on their behalf.

(c) to prevent the person in question –

   (i)   causing physical injury to himself or any other person;

   (ii) suffering physical injury;

   (iii) causing loss or damage to property;

   (iv) committing an offence against public decency (only applies where members of the public going about their normal business cannot reasonably be expected to avoid the person in question); or

   (v)   causing an unlawful obstruction of the highway;

(d) to protect a child or other vulnerable person from the person in question

(e) to allow the prompt and effective investigation of the offence or of the conduct of the person in question. This may include cases such as:

   (i) Where there are reasonable grounds to believe that the person:

   • has made false statements;

   • has made statements which cannot be readily verified;

   • has presented false evidence;

   • may steal or destroy evidence;

   • may make contact with co-suspects or conspirators;

   • may intimidate or threaten or make contact with witnesses;

   • where it is necessary to obtain evidence by questioning; or

   (ii) when considering arrest in connection with an indictable offence, there is a need to:

   • enter and search any premises occupied or controlled by a person

   • search the person

   • prevent contact with others

   • take fingerprints, footwear impressions, samples or photographs of the suspect

   (iii) ensuring compliance with statutory drug testing requirements.

(f) to prevent any prosecution for the offence from being hindered by the disappearance of the person in question. This may arise if there are reasonable grounds for believing that:

   • if the person is not arrested he or she will fail to attend court

   • street bail after arrest would be insufficient to deter the suspect from trying to evade prosecution.

By extending the powers of arrest, Code G of PACE (1984) provides police officers with the ability to use arrest to deal with most situations they encounter. However, just because a police officer *can* arrest, this does not always mean that they *must* arrest. Code G makes it clear that the decision to arrest is at the discretion of the arresting officer and they may choose a range of other options open to them, such as a **fixed penalty notice** or a report for **summons**, depending on the nature of the offence.

Reasonable grounds for suspicion

A police officer cannot stop, search or detain anybody without first having **reasonable suspicion**. The difficult question police officers face is what actually is reasonable suspicion? It could be an individual moving along a line of cars peering through the windows. It could be an individual running off when spoken to, or someone who cannot account for why they are out alone in the early hours of the morning. However, it is important to remember that there may be perfectly reasonable explanations for all of these actions. This places tremendous significance on the judgement of the police officer at the time of the arrest.

To arrest a suspect under current law (SOCPA, 2005), a police officer must be able to prove reasonable grounds for making the arrest.

Activity: Powers of arrest

1 What kinds of things might make an arrest necessary?
2 How can arrest be used as a preventative measure?
3 Why might the Police arrest someone if they are not certain of their name or address?
4 Summarise the key reasons why an officer might arrest someone.

Did you know?

Being told to arrest someone by a more senior officer is not reasonable grounds for doing so.

Key terms

Fixed penalty notice – a set penalty issued on the spot by the Police, usually an amount of money.

Summons – a formal request to attend court.

Reasonable suspicion – police officers must have reasonable grounds to suspect you have been, currently are, or will be involved in a criminal act.

1.2 Other statutory rights of arrest

Arrest as a preventative measure

This is covered in PACE (1984) Code G, section C, on page 102.

Breach of the peace

The concept of breach of the peace has a long history dating back to the common law of medieval times. It is very difficult to define and the courts often prefer a loose definition so that the term keeps pace with changing social behaviour.

The key case that helps frame what a breach of the peace is, **R v Howell** (1982). The definition provided in this case is:

We are emboldened to say that there is a breach of the peace whenever harm is actually done or is likely to be done to a person or in his presence his property or a person is in fear of being so harmed through an assault, an affray, a riot, unlawful assembly or other disturbance.

Police officers should only arrest for a breach of the peace when there is no other statutory power to do so, for example under Sections 4 and 5 of the Public Order Act (1986). It is a quick and convenient way of removing someone from a potentially violent situation, for example in a domestic disturbance.

The usual sentence for a breach of the peace is that you will be 'bound over'. This means you will have to assure the Magistrate that you will conduct yourself in a peaceful manner for a set period of time.

Key term

R v Howell – in criminal law, cases are written as R v Smith or R v Jones. The R stands for Rex if a king is on the throne and Regina if a queen is on the throne. The v stands for versus, and then the surname of the person who is accused of the crime, such as Smith or Jones, is given.

Did you know?

Breach of the peace dates back to the 1361 Justices of the Peace Act, which described rowdy and riotous behaviour that disturbed the peace of the king.

Public order offences

Public order offences are those such as:

- riot
- violent disorder
- affray
- drunk and disorderly behaviour
- use of threatening behaviour and language.

The key piece of legislation that covers public order incidents is the Public Order Act (1986).

1.3 Time limits

The Police have to conform to the law when a person is arrested. This means that the person cannot be held indefinitely at the police station – the Police must follow strict timelines and the suspect must be released or charged at the end of the time limit. Generally speaking the Police can hold a person for up to 24 hours without charging them with an offence. In serious cases where more time is needed by the Police to question the suspect or gather additional

information, the Police themselves can extend the time limit for another 12 hours. This means a possible total of 36 hours for questioning a suspect.

However, the courts can also extend the time a person spends in police custody without charge. The Police can apply to the courts to get the custody period extended to a maximum of 96 hours. In terrorism cases, Sections 23–25 of the Terrorism Act (2006) provides for a maximum detention period of 28 days, after which time the Police must either charge a suspect or release them.

Activity: Time limits

Is it reasonable to allow the Police up to a maximum of 28 days without charging someone in custody? Human rights campaigners argue that this period is too long, and that if the Police have sufficient evidence in the first place they wouldn't need to detain people for this length of time. What are your views?

1.4 Rights of a detained person

Once a person is **detained** at the police station they should be informed of their legal rights. There are three main rights that a detained person has, as shown in the spider diagram below.

The right to legal advice: to speak privately with a **solicitor**, provided free of charge at any time while being detained

The rights of a detained person

The right to read the codes of practice about how detainees are treated

The right to have someone informed: to notify someone that they have been arrested (S54 of PACE, 1984)

Figure 17.1: The three main rights of a detainee

Link

The right to legal advice and the role of solicitors are covered in more detail in *Unit 22: Aspects of the Legal System and the Law Making Process* (pages 119–236).

Did you know?

Many people think they are entitled to a phone call when arrested. Code C of PACE (1984) states that a detained person should be allowed to speak on the telephone for a reasonable time to one person. However, this is not a right and the Police can refuse.

The right to silence

The right to silence is the right to say nothing when asked questions by the Police without later penalty. This right was severely eroded by the Criminal Justice and Public Order Act (1994), which changed the law so that if a person chose to remain silent at interview they could later find themselves in difficulty in court for not raising information which they knew earlier. This includes:

- the failure, when questioned **under caution** before charge, to mention a fact which is relied on in your defence

- the failure, on being charged with an offence or informed of likely **prosecution**, to mention a fact which it would have been reasonable for you to mention at the time.

Key terms

Detained – held in custody.

Under caution – an interview where you are informed of your rights. Information provided while under caution can be used in court as evidence.

Prosecution – when legal proceedings are established against a person or organisation.

Solicitor – lawyer who deals with a whole range of legal matters.

Activity: The right to silence

In essence, the Criminal Justice and Public Order Act (1994) still means that suspects can remain silent if they wish. However, it will harm their defence if they do.

Some would question whether this is really a right to silence or a way to punish suspects who say nothing. What is your view on this?

Case study: R v Grant (2005)

In October 2000 the wife of Edward Grant left him to live with a new partner, Ian Dowling, taking their three children with her. On 15 March 2001 Mr Dowling answered a knock at the door and was confronted with a gunman who shot him in the thigh and chest. He died later that same night, and Mr Grant was subsequently arrested for Dowling's murder. The prosecution's case was that, full of bitterness at the breakup of his marriage, Edward Grant had recruited some associates to murder Ian Dowling. In 2003 Edward Grant was convicted of conspiracy to murder and sentenced to 18 years in prison.

A fundamental principle of the UK's legal system is the professional privilege accorded to legal representatives such as solicitors. This means that conversations between a **solicitor** and their client must be absolutely confidential. In the case of R v Grant (2005), Edward Grant was able to successfully appeal his conviction on the grounds that the police officers investigating him had abused their powers by planting covert listening devices in a corridor and a yard of Sleaford police station. These were able to pick up conversations between Grant and his solicitor.

1   **Why would the Police want to monitor conversations between a client and their legal representative?**

2   **Why is it important that conversations between a solicitor and their client are confidential?**

3   **How does the police officers' behaviour breach the rights of detainees set out earlier in this unit?**

4   **What are the implications for the Police Service when police officers break the law?**

DNA and other samples

If a person has been arrested for an offence that carries a possible prison sentence, the Police are entitled to take the suspect's photograph, fingerprints and DNA. Since the majority of crimes in this country carry the potential for a prison sentence, the Police routinely take DNA and fingerprint samples, and a photograph, from virtually all of the individuals they arrest.

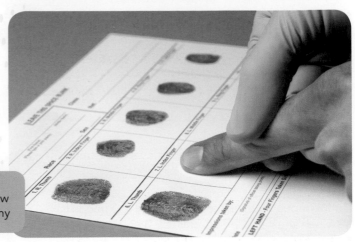

The Police are entitled by law to take the fingerprints of any suspect.

Case study: The national DNA database

Before 2001, all DNA samples taken from individuals who were not charged or who were found not guilty had to be destroyed. The law was then changed by the Criminal Justice and Police Act (2001), which allowed all DNA samples to be retained on a national database of offenders. The UK's database is the largest of any country – by the end of 2005 over 3.4 million DNA profiles were held on the database. This amounts to 5.2 per cent of the total population of the UK.

Responses to the national DNA database are mixed. Human rights groups argue that innocent people are having personal information about them retained against their wishes, while government agencies insist that the invasion of privacy experienced by those people who are on the database is outweighed by the benefits it brings in helping to track down offenders.

1 **Should there be a national DNA database at all? What are the pros and cons of the database?**

2 **Should innocent people have the right to have their DNA sample destroyed? Explain your answer.**

3 **Should everyone in the country be registered on the DNA database? Why?**

4 **How might a national DNA database lead to an abuse of human rights?**

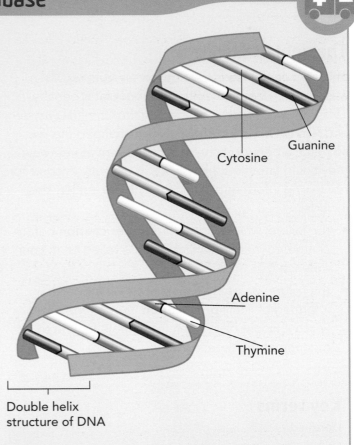

Double helix structure of DNA

Figure 17.2: DNA is unique in that it is specific to each individual

1.5 Police interviews

A police interview is a process whereby a person who may have information regarding a crime is questioned about what they know. Police interviews with suspects are usually conducted at a Police station.

Codes of practice

Police interviews are very tightly regulated by Section 66(1) of the Police and Criminal Evidence Act (PACE, 1984), specifically the following codes of practice:

- Code of Practice C: the detention, treatment and questioning of persons by police officers
- Code of Practice H: the detention, treatment and questioning by police officers of persons under Section 41 of, and Schedule 8 to, the Terrorism Act (2000).

Tape recording

It is important that police interviews are tightly regulated so that:

- the tapes can be used as evidence in court to secure a conviction
- the Police are protected against claims that suspects were bullied, beaten, tricked or coerced (forced) into confessing to a crime.

Prior to PACE (1984), statements were often handwritten by the police officers conducting the interview. This sometimes led to problems when the officers' honesty and integrity came into question, as it was relatively easy to change the statements.

Rights of interviewee

The suspect must be:

- informed as to the offence they are being questioned about
- reminded that they have the option of free legal advice.

During each 24-hour period that the suspect is held at the police station, they have the right to a continuous eight-hour rest period in which they are not questioned. They must also have rest breaks and refreshment breaks approximately every two hours or at mealtimes.

Activity: Questioning of suspects

If suspects are entitled to a continuous eight-hour rest period, this would mean they could be questioned for up to 16 hours. Do you think this timescale is appropriate? How would you feel after being questioned for this length of time? Is it likely that the Police would actually do this?

Appropriate adult for young offenders

An appropriate adult is someone, usually a parent or guardian, over the age of 18 years who sits in on an interview with anyone who is 16 years or under.

Appropriate adults also sit in on interviews with individuals who have mental health difficulties or who are deemed to be mentally vulnerable. The appropriate adult can also be a social worker or volunteer, and they help the suspect understand what is happening during the process of interview.

Link

In this unit we have already looked in detail at the following aspects of police interviews:
- the right to silence (page 105)
- fingerprints and body samples (page 106).
Searches are covered in detail in Section 2 of this unit.

1.6 Legislation

In the UK there are some vital pieces of **legislation** which govern the powers of the police.

Key term

Legislation – law which has been created and enacted by a governing body, such as the government.

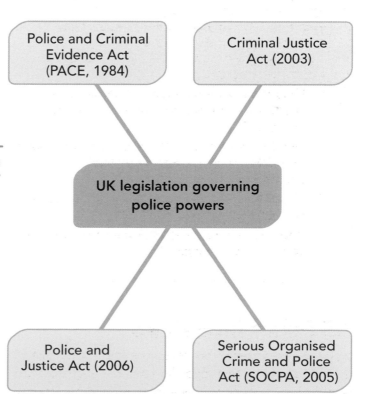

Figure 17.3: Laws which determine police powers in the UK

Police and Criminal Evidence Act (PACE, 1984)

Criminal Justice Act (2003)

UK legislation governing police powers

Police and Justice Act (2006)

Serious Organised Crime and Police Act (SOCPA, 2005)

Police and Criminal Evidence Act (PACE, 1984)

PACE (1984) is one of the most critical acts governing police powers. It established a balance of power between what the Police could do in the course of their duties and the rights of individual citizens to go about their business free from interference by the Police (see also pages 102–103 of this unit.)

PACE (1984) and the PACE codes of practice described under Section 66 of the Act set out the framework of police powers in terms of:

- stop and search
- detention
- arrest
- interviewing.

Its key purpose is to strike a balance between the powers of the Police and the rights of the public.

Criminal Justice Act (2003)

This Act amended and widened some aspects of PACE (1984), particularly in relation to stop and search. One of the most significant changes was the introduction of a trial without jury in cases of complex **fraud** or when **jury tampering** was suspected. Another key aspect was the exception to the **double jeopardy** ruling that meant that an **acquitted** defendant could be tried again for the same offence if new evidence came to light.

Key terms

Fraud – an act of deception intended for personal gain or to cause loss to another person.

Jury tampering – when a jury's decision about a defendant's guilt or innocence might have been influenced by financial bribes or intimidation.

Double jeopardy – the rule which prevents defendants being tried twice for the same crime. It is expected to be scrapped in murder cases after a major inquiry published by the Law Commission.

Acquitted – found not guilty of a crime.

Human trafficking – the movement of people across borders, usually by force or deception, in order to exploit them for financial gain.

Serious Organised Crime and Police Act (SOCPA, 2005)

One of the most controversial new laws which provide the Police with powers is the Serious Organised Crime and Police Act (SOCPA, 2005). This has become incredibly contentious because of its approach to human rights and the powers it provides to the Police.

- The Act created a serious organised crime squad to deal with the most severe crimes in society, such as **human trafficking**, which are often conducted by underworld gangs.

- It introduced significant changes to the powers of arrest (see page 102 of this unit).

- It banned public protest within a kilometre of Parliament. This was hugely controversial as the right to protest is a basic human right.

- The Act also allowed the Home Secretary to designate sites as key to national security if necessary, at which point trespassing on those sites would become a criminal offence. However, there is no clear guidance on what constitutes national security in this matter or how the Home Secretary would decide if it were necessary. This means that the government can effectively ban public protest in any area by designating it a site of national security.

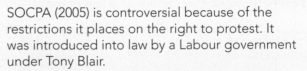

Activity: The right to protest

SOCPA (2005) is controversial because of the restrictions it places on the right to protest. It was introduced into law by a Labour government under Tony Blair.

In April 2002 during a speech made in the USA, Tony Blair said: 'When I pass protestors every day at Downing Street... I may not like what they call me, but I thank God they can. That's called freedom.'

1 How is SOCPA (2005) compatible with freedom and the right to protest?

2 How was the Act justified by the government that introduced it?

3 Produce a leaflet describing the origins of SOCPA (2005) and how it impacts on the right to protest.

Police and Justice Act (2006)

This legislation:

- created the National Policing Improvement Agency (NPIA)
- made amendments to PACE (1984) in the area of police **bail**
- sets out the powers of Police Community Support Officers (PCSOs)
- supports crime and disorder reduction partnerships in reducing anti-social behaviour.

Key term

Bail – after being charged with an offence, bail is being granted liberty under certain conditions until the next stage in your case.

1.7 Regulation

Independent Police Complaints Commission (IPCC)

The IPCC was created in 2004 to replace the Police Complaints Authority, although it gains its regulatory powers from the Police Reform Act (2002). It is an independent body, free of government influence. Since 2006 it also deals with complaints against the UK Border agency, HM Revenue and Customs and the Serious Organised Crime Agency.

The IPCC can investigate in several different ways. First, it can choose to supervise a case being investigated by a police service internally, or it can independently investigate if the complaint is about a serious matter. Serious complaints might include:

- incidents involving death or injury
- police corruption
- police racism
- perverting the course of justice.

The IPCC has teams of investigators allocated to certain regions so that it can deal with complaints quickly and efficiently. In 2008–2009 a total of 31,259 complaints were received, representing a 15 per cent increase on the previous year. The most common causes of complaints are shown in Table 17.2.

Activity: The work of the IPCC

Find out more about the work of the IPCC via their website (www.ipcc.gov.uk). By clicking on the 'News & Press' tab on the website, you can access recent IPCC press releases about their investigations.

Table 17.2: Police Complaints Statistics for England and Wales, 2008–2009 (Source: Independent Police Complaints Commission (IPCC) 2009)

Category of complaint	Percentage frequency of complaint
Neglect or failure in duty; includes allegations such as a failure to record or investigate matters and keep interested parties informed	24%
Incivility, impoliteness and intolerance; includes allegations of abusive, offensive or rude language or behaviour	21%
Assault; includes allegations that more force was used than was reasonable	13%
Oppressive conduct or harassment	7%
Unlawful/unnecessary arrest or detention	5%
Lack of fairness and impartiality	4%
Breach of Code C PACE on detention, treatment and questioning	4%
Discriminatory behaviour	3%

Case study: The G20 protests

In April 2009 leaders from the world's richest and most influential nations met in London to coordinate global action on pressing financial and economic problems, such as the recession and banking crisis. The G20 summit attracts many protesters who are unhappy at the way the global economy is run and the financial inequalities that cause so much poverty in the Third World.

There were numerous complaints about police tactics made to the IPCC in the days after the event. Many of these focused on direct assaults made by the Police on peaceful protesters and civilians who were trying to make their way home after work. The controversial tactic of '**kettling**' also came under scrutiny. Some protesters and passers-by in London accused the Metropolitan Police of keeping them 'kettled' for up to eight hours without access to food, water or toilet facilities. This included parents with children and the elderly. Liberal Democrat MP Martin Horwood, who was an eyewitness, has said he saw the Police use dogs on the protesters.

Perhaps the most controversial of all is the death of Ian Tomlinson, a newsagent trying to make his way home on the day of the protests. He tragically died after an alleged assault on him by a Metropolitan Police officer. This is a matter which is still under investigation by the IPCC.

1 **Research the police response to the G20 protests of 2009 using sources such as YouTube, broadsheet newspapers and the** Metropolitan Police statements. Do you think the response to the protesters was appropriate? Explain your answer.

2 **Why are independent commissions like the IPCC necessary?**

3 **What might happen to the public if there was no way to complain about unfair police treatment?**

4 **Many of the protesters had camera phones and were able to record police actions on the day. Is this a good thing or might it lead to a 'trial by media' once the clips are shown?**

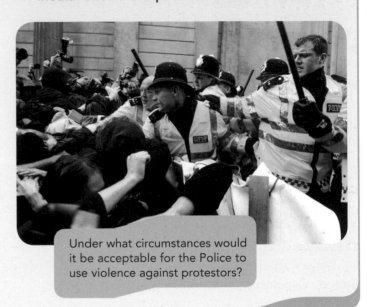

Under what circumstances would it be acceptable for the Police to use violence against protestors?

Key term

Kettling – the penning in of protesters to a confined area and not allowing them to leave for significant periods of time.

HM Inspectorate of Constabulary (HMIC)

Her Majesty's Inspectorate of Constabulary for England, Wales and Northern Ireland (HMIC) is one of the oldest inspectorates in England, dating back to the County and Borough Police Act of 1856. Like the other inspectorates it is funded by and reports to the Home Office, but is independent of it.

The role of the HMIC is:

- to formally inspect and assess the 43 police services in England and Wales
- to support the Chief Inspector of Criminal Justice in Northern Ireland
- inspection roles with:
  - Central Police Training and Development Agency
  - Civil Nuclear Constabulary
  - British Transport Police
  - Ministry of Defence Police
  - Serious Organised Crime Agency.

HMIC is able to conduct several types of inspections; some of these are described in Table 17.3.

Table 17.3: Some types of inspection carried out by HM Inspectorate of Constabulary (HMIC)

Type of inspection	Description
Thematic	Measures a particular aspect of performance, for example dealing with child protection or training of police officers, across several different police constabularies.
Best value	Ensures that the police authority is allocating and spending money in a manner which could be considered best value.
Command unit	Focuses on leadership and management.
Baseline assessment	Monitors the improvement or deterioration in performance against a pre-established baseline.

2. Regulations regarding searching people and premises

This learning outcome requires you to be familiar with:

- the powers the Police have when undertaking a search
- what the public can do if they believe they have had their person or their property searched unlawfully.

2.1 Stop and search

The right to stop and search people and vehicles in a 'public place'

A stop and search is when a police officer stops you in a public place as you are going about your business and searches your person and any bags or items you might be carrying. The Police can stop and search any member of the public at any time as long as they abide by the law and codes of practice. You can also be stopped and just questioned; this is simply called a 'stop'.

'Stop and search' can happen for a variety of reasons, but generally it will be because:

- you fit the description of somebody the Police want to talk to about a crime
- there has been crime nearby and the Police want to determine whether you were involved
- the Police suspect you to be carrying stolen property or something illegal, such as drugs
- it is thought that you are carrying something you could use to commit a crime, such as knives, firearms or other weapons.

In addition, under Section 44 of the Terrorism Act (2000) the Police have powers to stop and search anybody within a particular area when there is the potential for serious violence, for example evidence of an imminent terrorist threat on the London Underground.

A police officer can also stop and search a vehicle at any time for the reasons identified above. They may ask the driver and/or the occupants questions about where they are going.

During a vehicle stop and search the Police can ask to see identity documents such as a driving licence. Interestingly, the Police can search your vehicle without your permission and without your presence, but they must leave you a form saying what they have done and why.

Did you know?

You are entitled to claim for compensation if the Police damage your vehicle while searching it (provided they find no evidence to connect you to a crime).

Reasonable grounds

A police officer's suspicion that an offence has been or will be committed must be based on 'reasonable grounds' before he or she can exercise a number of police powers. This means an objective assessment of the situation must be made by the officer at that moment in time. The objectivity is crucial otherwise officers may allow their own subjective opinions to decide who they stop, leading to a situation where certain individuals are stopped and searched based on the prejudice of the officer involved.

You should not be stopped or searched because of:

- age, race, gender, sexual orientation, disability, religion or faith
- the way you look or dress
- the language you speak
- a prior conviction for a crime.

Prohibited articles

Prohibited articles are outlined in legislation such as Section 1 of PACE (1984). They include:

- offensive weapons
- an article made or adapted for use in connection with one of a list of offences including burglary, theft, taking a conveyance (vehicle) without authority (or being carried in one), obtaining property by deception and criminal damage.

The Misuse of Drugs Act (1971) also enables a police officer to stop and search people or individuals for **controlled drugs**.

Key term

Controlled drug – any substance whose availability and use is restricted by law. Controlled drugs are organised into categories depending on their usefulness as a medicine and their potential for misuse (dependency).

Procedures to be followed

While carrying out the 'stop', a police officer will normally ask some simple questions about who you are, where you are going and what items you are carrying. If they are satisfied with the answers you have given, they may decide not to search you at all. However, if your answers give them suspicion that you may have committed or be about to commit a crime, then they can search you.

A public search will normally take place in the street. You will be asked to turn out your pockets, open your bags and take off items such as coats, scarves and gloves to allow the Police to check you are not carrying anything illegal.

The police officer must normally tell you that you are about to be searched, what piece of law they are using and your rights regarding the search. Before you are searched, the officer must tell you their name and which station they work at. They must also tell you what made them suspicious in the first place and what they are looking for.

2.2 Searching an arrested person

Rights of police to search a person when arrested

Search after arrest can take place when the Police:

- believe you may be a danger to yourself or others
- suspect you to be carrying an item that might help you escape
- think you may be carrying evidence of a crime, for example a weapon
- need to check the belongings you have brought to the police station.

Time limits

Police searches must be carried out as soon as possible after arrest. This is necessary to:

- prevent any risk to the safety of officers and the public
- protect evidence that may otherwise be destroyed.

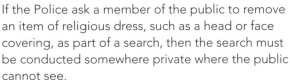

Did you know?

If the Police ask a member of the public to remove an item of religious dress, such as a head or face covering, as part of a search, then the search must be conducted somewhere private where the public cannot see.

2.3 Searching premises

The Police can enter and search your house or premises when there are reasonable grounds for suspicion (as described above for stop and search). The Police do not always need a search warrant to enter and search your premises, but they always need to have a good reason for doing so.

The Police must be careful in how they conduct a search, because if the search is conducted improperly they will not be able to use anything they find as evidence – a court of law will not allow it. Police searches of premises are governed by PACE (1984) Code B.

The three main ways in which the Police may search your premises are shown in the spider diagram below.

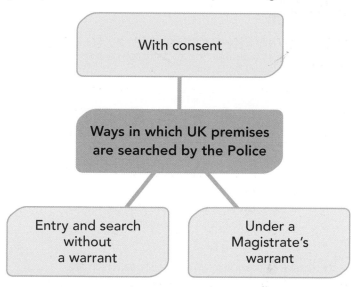

Figure 17.4: Ways in which the Police can search premises in the UK

Search with your consent

The Police can search your property if you have given them permission to do so. The permission should be in writing and you should have been told why the search is happening. The Police can take items that they consider to be evidence.

Search warrants and requirements of a warrant

Magistrates can issue the Police with a warrant to enter premises in order to search for evidence of serious offences. This means that the Police can enter and search a building even without the consent of the owner. In such circumstances the material is likely to be very important to the investigation of the offence.

Before issuing a warrant a Magistrate has to be satisfied under Section 8 of PACE (1984) that there are reasonable grounds for believing that:

- a serious offence has been committed
- there is material on the premises specified in the application which is likely to be of substantial value (whether by itself or together with other material) to the investigation of the offence
- the material is likely to be relevant evidence
- it does not consist of or include items subject to legal privilege, excluded material or special procedure material (things such as legal papers, medical samples, journalistic materials)
- entry to the premises will not be granted unless a warrant is in place
- permission for the search cannot be sought in advance as it might enable evidence to be moved or destroyed.

Powers to enter premises without a warrant

The Police can enter property without either the owner's consent or a warrant. These powers are given under various acts of law, such as:

- Gaming Act (1968)
- Misuse of Drugs Act (1971)
- Firearms Act (1968).

However, the Police and Criminal Evidence Act (PACE, 1984) is one of the most relevant laws in this regard. It allows the Police to enter and search a property without a warrant for the following reasons:

- to arrest someone
- to recapture a person who has escaped from lawful custody
- to arrest a child or young person who has been remanded or committed to local authority accommodation
- to save life or limb
- to prevent serious damage to property.

Seizing of goods

Under PACE (1984) the Police have a right to seize anything for which the search was authorised. They may also seize anything which they have reasonable grounds for suspecting is evidence of an offence.

2.4 Unlawful entry and searches

Remedies for those affected by unlawful entry and searches

Individuals who feel that they or their property have been searched unlawfully can complain to the Independent Police Complaints Commission (IPCC). Complaints must be made within one year of the incident and must refer to particular officers rather than just a general complaint against the whole constabulary or a particular policy. These complaints are usually dealt with in one of two ways: local resolution and investigation.

- Local resolution is where the complainant has the opportunity to speak with the officers concerned and hear an explanation of their behaviour or receive an apology if appropriate.

- When the alleged police misconduct is more serious, such as in a police shooting or allegations of police racism or homophobia, the IPCC will conduct an investigation into the conduct of the officers concerned. If the complaint is upheld the officers can face disciplinary proceedings or even criminal charges.

Did you know?

Searching property without proper authority leaves the Police open to being sued in a **civil court**. This may result in the police officers involved having to provide compensation to the victim of their actions.

Key term

Civil court – a law court which deals with the private affairs of citizens such as marriage and property ownership.

Assessment activity 17.1

You are a recently recruited police officer undergoing probationer training. You must demonstrate to your instructors that you understand the key issues they have been teaching you during your training. They have asked you to produce a written report that shows you understand the following issues relating to police powers:

1 Describe the difference between arrest with and arrest without a warrant. **P1**
2 State the rights of a detained person. **P2**
3 Explain the requirements of lawful arrest and detention. **M1**
4 Explain the powers the police have to search people and premises. **P3**
5 Evaluate police powers of arrest, detention and search. **D1**

Grading tips

In order to show your instructors you know about police powers, your report should:

- be clear and logical
- make reference to all of the issues which are described in this unit, such as legislation, time limits, samples, rights and interviews
- have an introduction
- include a clear sub-heading for each task you are required to do.

PLTS

Assessment activity 17.1 may be useful for practising your skills as an **independent enquirer** when you describe the difference between arrest with and arrest without a warrant. When stating the rights of a detained person, you can practise your skills as a **reflective learner**. You can practise your skills as an **independent enquirer**, **effective participator** and **creative thinker** when evaluating police powers of arrest, detention and search.

Functional skills

By using a software package, including presentation software, to present your report, you will be developing your functional skills in **ICT**.

3. Understand the powers of the Police to grant bail

Police powers to grant bail before charge and after charge

Bail means that following charge you are freed from police custody until the next stage in the process of your case.

After a suspect has been charged the Police must release him or her on bail unless:

* there is doubt about the suspect's name or address
* the Police suspect that the person charged will interfere with witnesses or evidence
* the suspect is thought to require custody for his or her own protection or the protection of someone else
* the Police believe the person will fail to attend court if released on bail.

Bail is given at the discretion of the custody officer under guidance from various pieces of legislation, as listed below.

* Bail Act (1976)
* Criminal Justice Act (2003)
* Police and Justice Act (2006).

Bail can be given both before and after a person has been charged. If the police investigation is ongoing, they may not have enough evidence to make a charge in which case they will bail a suspect with instructions to return to the police station at a later time and date.

If the Police refuse bail to a suspect they must present him or her at the Magistrates' Court as soon as possible. If the magistrate cannot deal with the whole case at that time, then the magistrate makes a further decision as to whether to grant bail or **remand** the suspect in custody until the matter can be resolved.

Did you know?

According to Martin (2000), five out of six defendants are given police bail.

Restrictions on bail granted by the Police

The Police may impose conditions on the bail that they give, such as:

* surrender of passport
* reporting to the police station at regular intervals
* **curfew**.

The Police and Justice Act (2006) allows the Police to attach conditions to bail given before charge and bail issued elsewhere than at a police station, such as street bail or bail for referral to a youth offending team.

Surrender of passport

This is set as a bail condition if there is any possibility that you may try and escape to another country to avoid punishment for a crime you have committed in the UK. If your passport is handed into the Police you will not be able to use it to travel outside the border of the UK.

Reporting to the police station

By reporting to the police station at regular intervals, such as once per week, the Police are able to ensure that:

* you are abiding by the conditions of your bail
* you have not tried to escape attending court by leaving the area.

Key terms

Remand – if you are placed on remand it means you are imprisoned until your trial.

Curfew – a set deadline by which young people have to return to a certain place such as their home.

Curfews

Like ASBOs, curfews were introduced by the Crime and Disorder Act (1998), although they had existed since 1997 in Scotland. These stated that children under a certain age must not be out on the streets after a certain time in the evening, usually between 6 pm and 9 pm depending on the age of the child.

Curfews can be used against all young people under the age of 16 years. They are applied for by local councils and enforced by the Police, who have the power to take young people home who break their curfew and are caught on the street after a specific time. Curfew orders last for 90 days. After this time the council has to reapply for another order.

The idea behind curfews is that with less young people on the streets, there will be less juvenile crime committed, and less young people will become victims of crime. However, curfews have not proved themselves particularly popular with local councils and they are not used with any great frequency.

Case study: Bail

You are a custody officer at a large town centre Police station. You must decide on the following bail issue.

A 21-year-old crack addict has been brought in on a burglary charge. He has been positively identified by the owners of the property, who discovered him in the process of burgling. The suspect has an existing warrant for his arrest for failing to attend court on a similar charge. In addition, the householder has made threats against the suspect's life if he is released.

1 **What factors must you consider in general when evaluating the bail application?**
2 **What are the particular risk factors involved in this case?**
3 **What would your decision be?**
4 **Which pieces of law currently govern the process of bail?**

Assessment activity 17.2 :BTEC

You have started working voluntarily at a local law firm so that you can learn more about the role of a solicitor before you decide what future career you want to take. Your supervisor wants you to produce a public information leaflet that can be given to clients which tells them about the powers of the Police to grant bail.

Your leaflet should be clear, well organised and informative. It should address the following task:

1 Explain police powers to grant bail. **P4**
2 Assess why the Police have the power to grant bail.

Grading tips

To support your work it is important that you understand the verbs for each task:

For **P4** you need to explain – state the facts and give reasons for them. Use examples to back up the points you make.

For **M2** you need to assess – consider the various reasons why, weighing up which are the most and least important.

Functional skills

Assessment activity 17.2 requires you to produce a leaflet. If you use an IT package such as Microsoft Publisher, you may be contributing to your functional skills in **ICT**.

Monica Jervis
Police Special Constable

Volunteering with the Police Service

I volunteer with a Police Service that covers both rural and inner city areas, and I am assigned to a town centre on the day I work. Although I am a volunteer rather than a regular police officer, a full understanding of Police powers is vital to my work.

A typical day

There isn't really a typical day! My colleagues and I can be faced with any number of situations, ranging from searching people, vehicles and premises to dealing with domestic incidents to investigating suspect packages. Anything can happen on a shift – which is why it is essential that I know what powers I have to deal with the different situations I face. This knowledge provides me with clear boundaries for what I can and cannot do.

The best thing about the job

Being a special constable allows me to give something back to my community without the upheaval of working shifts that a full-time officer faces. I teach at an infant school full-time and have a young family as well, so volunteering as a police officer allows me an outlet to contribute to community safety without disrupting my career or family.

Think about it!

- What topics have you covered in this unit that might give you valuable background knowledge to work as part of the Police Service?
- What knowledge and skills do you think you would need to develop further if you wanted to work as part of the Police Service in future?

Just checking

1. What is reasonable suspicion?
2. What are the rights of a detained person?
3. What does the IPCC do?
4. What is a search warrant?
5. What is the DNA database and why is it controversial?

edexcel

Assignment tips

- Legislation and police powers are subject to change, so one of the best things you can do to help improve your grade for this unit is to keep up-to-date with current events. Blackstone's Police Manuals provide up-to-date and accurate information the Police use when studying for their exams.

- Make sure you have read your assignment thoroughly and understand exactly what you are being asked to do. Once you are clear about this you can move on to your research.

- Thorough research based on reliable sources of evidence is essential. Many learners rely too much on the Internet and neglect other sources of information, such as books, newspapers and journals. Always double check the information you find – don't just accept it at face value.

18 Behaviour in public sector employment

The public sector offers a diverse range of employment opportunities that require individuals to adapt their behaviour from that which they might normally display in their private lives. Working within a disciplined and structured environment is a challenge and can be a source of stress. Understanding how and why certain behaviour happens can help you to understand your own reactions as well as the reactions of others.

This unit covers several important issues, including psychological approaches to behaviour and how these can benefit both a public service organisation and you as an individual working in a pressurised job role. Another key topic is communication. Uniformed public servants are often in the public eye and need to communicate clearly, for example when advising or warning people. They must also be able to coordinate public service operations and teams in order to provide a more effective service. Linked to this is the idea of managing and dealing with conflict effectively. In this regard you will consider types of conflict which you might be called upon to deal with in the course of your duties as well as disagreements and differences with colleagues, friends and family members. Learning how to deal with conflict is a key transferable skill you can use in many areas of life.

Learning outcomes

After completing this unit you should:

1. know the approaches to psychology
2. know behaviour and its management.

Assessment and grading criteria

This table shows you what you must do in order to achieve a pass, merit or distinction grade, and where you can find activities in this book to help you.

To achieve a **pass** grade the evidence must show that you are able to:	To achieve a **merit** grade the evidence must show that, in addition to the pass criteria, you are able to:	To achieve a **distinction** grade the evidence must show that, in addition to the pass and merit criteria, you are able to:
P1 identify approaches to psychology and their theorists **See Assessment activity 18.1 page 133**	**M1** analyse one approach to psychology **See Assessment activity 18.1 page 133**	
P2 describe two studies in psychology **See Assessment activity 18.1 page 133**		
P3 outline different types of behaviour and how these can be managed **See Assessment activity 18.2 page 142**	**M2** assess the benefits of understanding behaviours for public services and their personnel **See Assessment activity 18.2 page 142**	**D1** evaluate how an understanding of psychology and behaviour can benefit public services and their personnel **See Assessment activity 18.2 page 142**

How you will be assessed

This unit will be assessed by an internal assignment that will be designed and marked by the staff at your centre. The assignment is designed to allow you to show your understanding of the learning outcomes for behaviour in public sector employment. Assignments can be quite varied and can take the form of:

- reports
- leaflets
- presentations
- posters

- practical tasks
- case studies
- discussions.

Asha explains the benefits of understanding behaviour

I really enjoyed this unit. It's all about knowing how and why people behave in the ways that they do. Considering the types of behaviour people in the public services have to deal with during the course of a working day, this is really useful information for anyone who wants to work with the public.

The best part of the unit for me was the approaches to psychology. I found it fascinating how certain behaviour can be examined from various perspectives and interpreted differently. This highlights how tricky it can be to understand why people behave in the way they do. If you are working with the public you need to be patient and have an open mind.

I also particularly enjoyed the conflict management and resolution part of the unit. This would be a really great skill when working with the public. Conflict can happen quite often, so knowing how to avoid it or how to resolve it effectively would make you a better employee.

Over to you!

- **What areas of understanding behaviour might you find interesting?**
- **Have you ever been involved in conflict?**
- **Do you have strong opinions on how conflict can be dealt with?**
- **What preparation could you do to get ready for your assessments?**

1. Approaches to psychology

Have you ever experienced conflict in your life, or caused conflict through poor communication?

Look in newspapers and on news websites to see if you can find a recent example of a situation when communication or conflict was managed badly in the uniformed services. What were the consequences of this situation? What could be done to ensure it doesn't happen again?

1.1 Approaches

There are various approaches to the subject of psychology. This unit examines the approaches shown in Figure 18.1 in order to provide you with a broad cross-section of knowledge.

Behaviourist, including:

- classical conditioning (learning by association)
- operant conditioning (learning from the consequences of behaviour)
- scientific methodology

Humanistic, including free will

Key psychological approaches

Psychodynamic, including:

- unconscious mind
- defence mechanisms
- id, ego, superego

Social Psychology, including:

- group behaviour
- prosocial behaviour
- social influence

Cognitive, including:

- perception
- attention
- memory (problem solving, reasoning)
- language

Figure 18.1: Key psychological approaches

Behaviourist approach

The principles of **behaviourism** were developed by researchers such as John B. Watson (1878–1958). In his behaviourist proposal *Psychology from the Standpoint of a Behaviourist* (1919), Watson argued that the mind could not be studied because it is unobservable – its workings cannot be seen, documented or analysed. According to Watson, the only aspect of mind that can be studied is an individual's actual physical behaviour, which can be monitored in laboratory conditions.

The behaviourists' approach to psychology was therefore the first to use **scientific methodology**, and this brought psychology closer towards the 'hard' sciences such as chemistry or physics.

The theory that Watson proposed was based on the following features:

- Behaviourism is concerned with how environmental factors (stimuli) affect observable behaviour (responses).
- The focus of behaviourism is on learning. The interaction between stimulus and response is how learning occurs.
- The ultimate aim of behaviourism is to be able to predict and control behaviour.
- There is no fundamental difference between the behaviour of humans and the behaviour of animals. Each organism learns via the stimulus–response mechanism.

Learning is a key aspect of behaviourism. Behaviourists have identified two main ways in which learning can happen:

- classical **conditioning** (learning by association)
- operant conditioning (learning from the consequences of behaviour).

Remember!

A stimulus is an outside influence and a response is what we do about the outside influence. For example, if a wasp lands on your arm this is the stimulus. If you use your hand to bat the wasp away this is the response. In behaviourism all learning happens because we have received a stimulus and we respond to it.

Classical conditioning

The principle of classical conditioning is that a stimulus which wouldn't ordinarily produce a response in an individual comes to do so by being linked or paired with a stimulus which does provoke a response. The main theorist who developed this idea was Ivan Pavlov (1849–1936).

Pavlov was a physiologist (a scientist who studies the functions of the body) who was interested in the digestive processes of dogs. Pavlov noticed that dogs salivated when they received their food and he wondered if dogs could be taught to salivate at something that wouldn't normally cause them to salivate – such as a bell.

Pavlov conducted an experiment where each time the dogs received food a bell rang. Eventually the dogs associated the sound of the bell with their food and would salivate at the sound of it. Figure 18.2 on page 124 illustrates this process of classical conditioning.

Although the dog's behaviour (salivating) doesn't change, the reason why it salivates does.

- Initially the dog naturally salivates to food. This is called an **unconditioned response** – it occurs quite naturally.
- At the second point the bell is linked with the food. The bell is not a natural stimulus to the dog and is called a **conditioned stimulus**. The dog, however, is still salivating at the food in an unconditioned response.
- By the last stage of the experiment the dog has associated the conditioned stimulus of the bell with the food and will salivate at the sound of the bell alone. This is called a **conditioned response**.

In this way the dog has moved from an unconditioned response to the food to a conditioned response to the bell.

Key terms

Behaviourism – the study of human behaviour.

Scientific methodology – a rational method of investigation based on recording observable and measurable evidence. Scientists seek to record data about the environment and in this way test theories and draw conclusions.

Unconditioned response – a behaviour we perform automatically, such as scratching an itch.

Conditioned stimulus – an environmental factor that an organism can be taught to respond to in a certain way.

Conditioned response – behaviour an organism has learned to carry out in response to a conditioned stimulus.

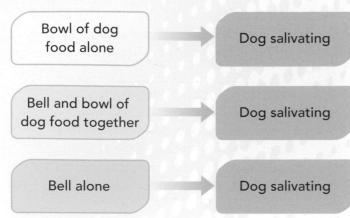

Figure 18.2: Process of classical conditioning

Following on from Pavlov's experiment with dogs, the next step for the behaviourists was to find out whether humans could be conditioned in the same way. The following case study is a classical conditioning experiment conducted by John B. Watson and Rosalie Rayner (1920) on a little boy.

Case study: Little Albert

Watson and Rayner's study of 1920 was conducted on a young child aged 11 months called Albert. Its principle was very much the same as that described in Pavlov's experiment with dogs (see above). Albert was given a white rat to stroke. As the child reached out to pet the animal, one of the researchers brought a hammer down on a metal bar causing a sudden and extremely loud crashing noise. This was repeated on a number of occasions. In time the child learned to associate the rat with the terrifying noise and eventually the sight of the rat alone was enough to frighten him. Watson and Rayner had artificially created a **phobia** in a young child through classical conditioning.

1 **Watson and Rayner's experiment with Albert has been described as ethically unsound. What do you think this means?**

2 **What could be considered improper, or wrong, about Watson and Rayner's experiment on Albert?**

3 **What do you think the possible long-term implications for Albert of the experiment were?**

4 **Could Albert's phobia have been removed in the same way that it was created?**

Activity: Classical conditioning

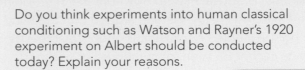

Do you think experiments into human classical conditioning such as Watson and Rayner's 1920 experiment on Albert should be conducted today? Explain your reasons.

Operant conditioning

Operant conditioning is based on the work of Edward Thorndike (1874–1949) and B. F. Skinner (1904–90).

Thorndike's cats

Like Pavlov, Thorndike experimented with the conditioning of animals. He placed a hungry cat into a box which then had to find its way out. The cat was rewarded with food when it escaped. After the cat had escaped and eaten its reward, it was placed back in the box and the process began again. What Thorndike noted was that each time the cat was placed in the box it took less time for it to escape.

Thorndike's research showed that the cats were making an association between being able to escape from the box and getting a reward.

Positive and negative reinforcement

B. F. Skinner built upon Thorndike's findings of animals being rewarded or punished to reinforce and encourage learning in rats and pigeons. He argued that an animal's future behaviour is shaped by the consequences of its current behaviour. Therefore, if behaviour is rewarded or **positively reinforced**, the animal will repeat it. For example, a dog is more likely to sit on command if it is rewarded with a food treat every time it carries out the desired behaviour. Conversely, if behaviour is punished, or **negatively reinforced**, the animal is less likely to repeat the behaviour. For example, a cat that is put outside every time it jumps up onto a kitchen work surface will soon learn not to do so.

Key terms

Phobia – intense fear of something.

Positive reinforcement – when the rate of a learned behaviour increases following the application of a conditioned stimulus.

Negative reinforcement – when the rate of a learned behaviour decreases following the application of a conditioned stimulus.

Activity: Positive and negative reinforcement

Consider how positive and negative reinforcement (rewards and punishments) have been used by others, such as your parents or employer, to modify your behaviour.

- Have you been given treats, money or privileges as rewards? Did these encourage you to behave differently?

- Have you been punished by being denied money, being grounded or verbally reprimanded? Did these encourage you to behave differently?

Work in small groups to discuss the issues. Evaluate whether positive or negative reinforcement has had the biggest influence on your behaviour and conduct.

Remember!

Scientific methodology is a rational method of investigation based on recording observable and measurable evidence. Scientists seek to record data about the environment and in this way test theories and draw conclusions.

Psychodynamic approach

The **psychodynamic** approach to the study of human behaviour is based on the work of Sigmund Freud (1856–1939). Freud developed the use of a therapy called psychoanalysis, which is still widely used today in helping people identify the causes of their **psychological** problems and suggesting ways in which they could be overcome.

Key terms

Psychodynamic – *psyche* means mind, and psychodynamic theory views the mind as exerting a powerful influence on human behaviour in terms of an individual's motivation and drives.

Psychological – relating to mental states and emotions rather than the physical body.

Repressed – information or experiences that are buried deep in the mind such that the individual concerned is not aware of their existence.

Conscious, preconscious and unconscious

Freud's psychodynamic theory suggests that the majority of human behaviour is influenced by factors we are not consciously aware of – that many of our deeper motivations are hidden from us. Freud called the part of the mind, or *psyche*, that we do know about the 'conscious', and the part of the mind that we don't know about the 'unconscious'. Between the conscious and unconscious parts of the mind lies the preconscious, from which thoughts and feelings can be recalled to awareness. Figure 18.3 shows the relationship between these three 'levels' of mind.

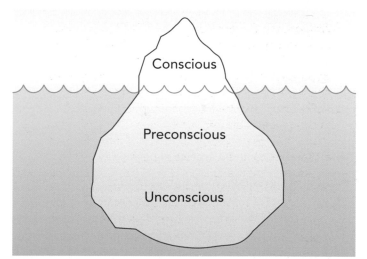

Figure 18.3: A Freudian iceberg – diagram to show the conscious, preconscious and unconscious levels of mind

Table 18.1: Freud's three levels of mind

Level of mind	Characteristics
Conscious	This is the part of the mind that is currently aware of itself. For example, it includes the awareness that you are reading this book and of your circumstances and feelings right at this moment.
Preconscious	This is the short-term storehouse for memories and thoughts. It contains information, ideas and beliefs that are not currently on your mind or are temporarily forgotten, but can be recalled easily when needed. This might include information such as names, phone numbers, addresses or the answers to your last assignment.
Unconscious	According to Freud, this is the most substantial part of the psyche (mind). It contains emotional experiences, ideas and memories that are **repressed**, or hidden from view. Freud theorised that the contents of the unconscious exerts a powerful influence over people's actions and behaviour. Sometimes the contents of the unconscious mind try to break through to consciousness, for example through anxieties and dreams or Freudian slips.

Activity: Dream diary

Keep a dream diary for one week. At the end of the week use a Freudian-based dream interpretation dictionary or website (such as http://cognitions.net/dreams-basics.html) to see what your unconscious mind is trying to tell you.

Id, ego and superego

Freud viewed the personality as having three distinct aspects: the id, ego and superego (see Table 18.2 below). He argued that these three aspects must work together and be in balance if a person is to have a healthy personality.

Activity: Id, ego and superego in action

Can you think of a situation where your id, ego and superego have all played a part in your behaviour? Compare your answer with others in your class.

Humanistic approach

The humanistic approach emerged in the 1950s and 1960s from the work of Abraham Maslow (1908–70) and Carl Rogers (1902–87). In contrast to behaviourism and the psychodynamic approach, humanists argue that individuals are responsible for choosing their own behaviour rather than simply responding to the environmental or unconscious forces that act upon them. In essence, people have **free will** and make their own choices about how to behave.

Carl Rogers suggested that people have two basic needs: the need for **self-actualisation** and the need for **positive regard**.

Key terms

Free will – the ability to choose one's actions free of external constraints.

Self-actualisation – the achievement of a person's potential in life.

Positive regard – the sense of acceptance or approval one person has for another.

Table 18.2: Freud's three aspects of personality

Aspect of personality	Characteristics
Id	This is present in an individual from birth and is made up of a person's basic needs and desires. It is the part of the personality that wants instant gratification – whatever it wants it must have immediately. Freud called this the 'pleasure principle'. The id can be seen in action in small children and babies who haven't developed other aspects of their personality. If they are hungry or thirsty they will cry until their needs are met.
Ego	This is the part of the personality that deals with reality. If the id wants something immediately then it's the ego's job to satisfy that desire in a socially acceptable manner. Freud called this the 'reality principle'. For example, the id may be angry with someone and want to punch that person; the ego knows you will end up in court charged with assault if you do.
Superego	The superego tries to suppress the unacceptable urges of the id. According to Freud the superego begins to develop around the age of five years. It holds our moral ideas of right and wrong that we develop from our parents and society at large. It is concerned with making a good impression and obeying the rules. It also controls feelings such as guilt and remorse when we misbehave. For instance, if you consider the above example of the id wanting to punch someone and the ego recognising that this would be unlawful behaviour, the superego would reflect on the immorality of the desire to hurt somebody and feel guilt and shame at this.

- Self-actualisation means striving for personal development with the aim of achieving your full potential – of being all that you can be.

- Positive regard describes the need to be viewed positively by other people. It describes an attitude of acceptance, love, respect, trust and affection found within personal relationships, such as those with close friends and family and in romantic relationships.

Rogers saw self-actualisation and positive regard as the key motivating factors that shaped people's behaviour.

Cognitive psychology

Cognitive psychology is concerned with the effect of an individual's mental processes, such as perception, attention, memory, decision making and language, on their behaviour. Cognitive psychology also considers how people think and learn. It includes study of the mental processes shown in Figure 18.4.

As with behaviourism, cognitive psychology relies upon scientific methodology and **empirical** results to support its case. There is a focus on laboratory experiments as a method of providing evidence for the theory.

Remember!

As a humanist, Rogers viewed people very differently from psychoanalysts and behaviourists.

Unlike behaviourists, who isolate the component parts of an individual for study in a laboratory, Rogers saw the individual as a whole person (the **holistic** view).

Rogers disagreed with Freud's psychodynamic view of the individual as having an inherent tendency towards destructiveness and neurosis (mental imbalance). Instead he emphasised the essential healthiness of the mind, and its natural tendency to grow and develop rather than repress and destroy.

Key terms

Holistic – the view that you cannot understand something by looking at its component parts in isolation, but only by looking at the fully functioning organism or system as a whole.

Cognitive – relating to the mental processes by which a person can know, become aware of and make decisions about their self and their environment.

Empirical – knowledge gained from observation and experiment.

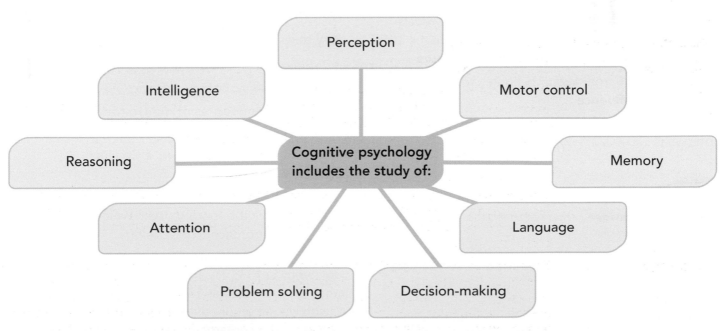

Figure 18.4: Aspects of cognitive psychology

Information processing

The dominant view in cognitive psychology is that the brain is an information processing system. This view is linked to computer science and communications theory, and compares the brain to a computer into which information is input and behaviour is output. In this way, cognitive psychology has become strongly associated with computer science and the study of artificial intelligence. It explores whether computers are capable of problem solving in similar ways to humans and examines the parallels between the human brain and computers.

Social psychology

Social psychology adopts a different position to the four psychological approaches we have already examined. It argues that to understand the individual we must look at the bigger social, political and economic picture that the person was brought up in and currently lives in.

Social psychology does not support the laboratory-based experiments and studies of the behaviourist and cognitive approaches. Instead, social psychologists argue that it is often the situation and circumstances found in the real world which give human behaviour its meaning.

Social psychology also takes into account factors outside the individual, such as:

- the influence of group behaviour on individuals which can lead to conformity, for example the effect of religious groups on **prosocial behaviours**
- the pressure from authority figures which can lead to **social influence**.

(Some of these factors are examined later in the unit on pages 130–132.)

Key terms

Prosocial behaviour – actions intended to benefit others and not for personal gain.

Social influence – when a person's thoughts or actions are affected by other people.

1.2 Theorists

Abraham Maslow

Maslow was born on 1 April 1908 in New York to a very poor Russian immigrant family. He was the first of seven children. His parents believed education was the only way for their children to become successful in their new nation and they pushed Maslow hard academically.

Maslow did not set out to be a psychologist – he initially began to study law at the City College of New York. However, following a transfer of his studies Maslow became interested in psychological research and spent time working under the direction of Harry Harlow, who researched maternal attachment in baby monkeys.

Maslow graduated with a degree in Psychology in 1930, followed by a Masters degree in 1931 and a PhD in 1934. After he achieved his PhD he returned to New York where he began research on sexuality at the University of Columbia.

Maslow had a distinguished teaching and theoretical career. He is best known for his work on self-actualisation and the promotion of the humanistic approach to psychology.

Maslow married his cousin Bertha in 1928 and they had two daughters. He died in June 1970 after years of ill health.

Key texts
- *Motivation and Personality* (1954)
- *Towards a Psychology of Being* (1962)
- *The Farther Reaches of Human Nature* (1971, posthumous)

John B. Watson

John B. Watson is best remembered for his tremendous contributions to the development of the behaviourist approach to psychology.

He was born in Greenville, South Carolina, in a farming community in 1878. His home life was troubled: his father left when he was 13 years old, and initially Watson was an unruly child and a difficult student. In spite of this he had ambition and determination, and received a Masters degree in 1901 before completing a PhD in Psychology at the University of Chicago.

By 1908 Watson was Professor of Experimental and Comparative Psychology at the prestigious Johns Hopkins University in Maryland.

Watson's personal life was nearly as troubled as his parents' had been. His first marriage in 1901 resulted in two children, Mary and John. However, he left his wife in 1920 to marry one of his graduate students, Rosalie Rayner (you may recognise the name from the Little Albert case study on page 124). The scandal surrounding Watson's divorce and subsequent remarriage caused Johns Hopkins University to ask for his resignation. This exclusion from academia led him to New York, where he applied his expert knowledge of psychology to the field of advertising. He was employed by several prestigious advertising agencies and spent the latter half of his career outside academia. Watson retired in 1945 and died in 1958.

Key texts

- *Behaviour: An Introduction to Comparative Psychology* (1914)
- *Psychology from the Standpoint of a Behaviourist* (1919)
- *Behaviourism* (1925)

Carl Rogers

Rogers was born in 1902 in Chicago as part of a large family. Although he was to become one of the founding fathers of humanism, he began university as an agriculture student and then switched to theology. After graduating and getting married, he moved to New York. While training to enter a religious ministry, Rogers questioned his religious beliefs and decided on another change in direction, this time towards psychology. He returned to education, enrolling on a Masters Degree at Columbia University, and received his PhD in 1931. He taught at various academic institutions, such as Ohio State University, the University of Chicago and the University of Wisconsin.

Rogers is best known for developing the humanistic approach to psychology. This contrasts sharply with the deterministic views of psychoanalytic theory and behaviourism. Indeed, so new was humanism that it was described as 'the third way'. Rogers' theory is based on a person's need for self-actualisation (see pages 126–7). Humanism spawned the huge growth in counselling and therapy seen throughout the latter half

of the 20th century. Rogers was active in the field of psychology until his death in 1987.

Key texts

- *Client-Centred Therapy* (1957)
- *On Becoming a Person* (1961)
- *A Way of Being* (1980)

Sigmund Freud

Sigmund Freud was born on 6 May 1856, in Moravia, in what is now the Czech Republic. The Freud family moved to Vienna in Austria when Sigmund was around four years old. Vienna would be Freud's home for most of his life.

Freud was a brilliant student and did exceptionally well at school. He opted to progress to medical school and studied medicine at the University of Vienna, concentrating on the study of **physiology** and **neurology**. Vienna at this time was a breeding ground for **anti-Semitic** feeling and, as a Jew, Freud began to feel this discrimination.

Freud married in 1886, and over the next nine years he and his wife had six children. The change in his family status did not put a halt to Freud's research: he continually published papers and books on topics such as dream interpretation and sexuality. During the 1930s Nazism began to move through Austria. This placed Jews like Freud in a very difficult and dangerous position. Freud chose to escape and emigrated to England, where he died in September 1939.

Key terms

Physiology – the scientific study of the body's physical, biochemical and mechanical systems.

Neurology – the scientific study of the nervous system.

Anti-Semitic – characterised by hostility or prejudice towards Jewish people

Sigmund Freud, the 'father of psychoanalysis', in 1905. Why do you think his impact on the field of psychology has been so great?

Key texts

- *Studies of Hysteria* (1895) (with Joeseph Brever)
- *The Interpretation of Dreams* (1900)
- *Three Essays on the Theory of Sexuality* (1905)
- *Beyond the Pleasure Principle* (1920)
- *The Ego and the ID* (1923)

1.3 Studies in psychology

There are some fascinating studies in psychology that highlight how individuals can behave in particular circumstances. The case studies below describe some of the key behavioural issues that can be relevant to those working in the public services.

Key term

Confederate – someone who takes part in a study but is not a genuine participant. Confederates are given instructions by the researcher to play a specific role.

Case study: The Asch paradigm (1951)

This classic study was conducted by Solomon Asch in 1951. A class of students was asked to take part in a test in which they looked at a line and compared it with a series of three other lines. They needed to decide which two lines were of matching length. One example of Asch's test is shown in Figure 18.5.

However, the experiment was not all that it seemed! All of the students *except one* had been briefed by Asch before the experiment began to give particular answers to the test. The majority of the **confederates**' answers were wrong, but they consistently gave the same answers as each other. Asch's experiment was in fact a test of how the one participant who had not been briefed would respond in this situation – would he or she conform to the confederates' incorrect answers or give the right answer?

Asch found that participants (i.e. those who were not confederates) conformed to the group answers, even if they were clearly incorrect, a high proportion of the time. Of all of the participants, 75 per cent gave the wrong answer to at least one question. By contrast, in a control group with

no pressure to conform to an incorrect view, only 3 per cent of participants gave a wrong answer to at least one question. Asch's experiment indicates a high tendency of individuals to conform when in a group.

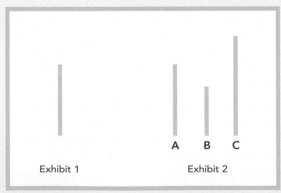

Figure 18.5: Example of Asch's test

1. Why do you think the individuals went along with the wrong answers of the group?
2. Why is understanding conformity useful to the public services?
3. How could conformity be used by the public services to control criminal or anti-social behaviour?

Case study: Obedience to authority (Milgram, 1963)

Stanley Milgram's 1963 study was designed to assess the level of obedience people showed to an authority figure. Forty men aged 20–50 years were recruited and paid to attend the study. They were not told the real reason for the experiment, but that it was designed to determine the effect of punishment on learning.

Each participant was paired with another person who was, unknown to them, a confederate in the study. Each confederate was asked to memorise pairs of words, which they later were asked to match correctly. If the confederate failed to match the pairs when asked, they were given an electric shock by the participant. The electric shock generator was designed to look realistic and went up to a maximum of 450 volts with switches labelled as follows:

- slight shock
- moderate shock
- strong shock
- intense shock
- extreme intensity shock
- danger: severe shock
- XXX (two switches had this label).

No shock was actually given – the confederate simply acted as though they had received an electric shock – but the participant did not know this and thought the shocks were genuine. The confederate deliberately gave wrong answers in order to see what level of shocks the participants would be prepared to give a complete stranger, simply on the say so of an authority figure (in this case the researcher). It is also worth noting that the confederate gave a convincing performance and begged to be released, showed significant signs of pain and even complained of heart trouble.

All forty participants gave a shock of up to 300 volts (a shock level which could be fatal) and 65 per cent of participants gave shocks up to the maximum 450 volts on the scale, despite hearing the pain and upset of the confederate.

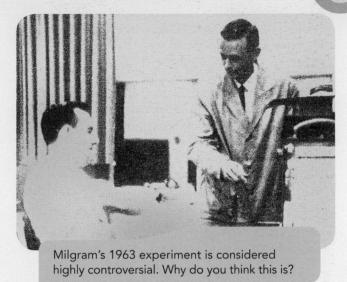

Milgram's 1963 experiment is considered highly controversial. Why do you think this is?

1   Why do you think people obeyed the researcher rather than refuse to hurt the confederate?

2   Why do you think only 35 per cent of people stopped before the maximum voltage?

3   What does this experiment tell you about obedience to authority?

4   Why is unquestioning obedience like this potentially dangerous in a public service context?

5   Can you think of a historical or current situation where the public services of a country have hurt civilians and have claimed they were 'just following orders'?

Case study: Nurses (Hofling, 1966)

Hofling's experiment was also designed to test obedience to authority. Hofling wanted to know whether nurses would disobey nursing protocols on the administration of medicines if they were asked to do so by a doctor. A fictitious drug called 'Astroten' was placed in the drug cabinet of the ward. A doctor whom the nurses did not know then called them up and asked for a specific patient to be given 20 mg of Astroten. The nurses should have refused for three reasons:

Should nurses always follow instructions from senior staff such as doctors?

- Astroten was not on the list of approved medications and no paperwork had been completed to allow it to be given to a patient.

- Hospital policy was that nurses should only take telephone instructions from doctors known to them.

- The fake bottle of Astroten said clearly on the label that 10 mg was the maximum dose.

Of the 22 nurses who were called by the doctor, 21 would have given the patient an overdose of the medicine.

1 What are the implications of the findings of Hofling's 1966 experiment for the medical profession?

2 How could a study like this lead to better training for nurses?

3 In a public service career, what are the benefits and drawbacks of questioning or refusing orders?

Case study: Stanford Prison Experiment (Zimbardo, 1973)

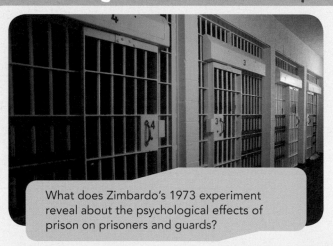

What does Zimbardo's 1973 experiment reveal about the psychological effects of prison on prisoners and guards?

Philip Zimbardo's 1973 experiment explored the psychological effects of prison on both guards and prisoners. The participants were 24 university undergraduates who were given the role of either guard or prisoner randomly, based on the toss of a coin. A mock prison was constructed at Stanford University, where the experiment was conducted. Those students who were prisoners were arrested by the Police and processed as potential criminals before being sent to the mock prison at the university, to make the experience seem as real as possible.

The prison simulation was also kept as realistic as possible. On arrival the 'prisoners' were stripped naked, searched and deloused. They were then issued a uniform and a number and had their ankle chained. The guards had been given no specific training so they were free to act as they thought a prison guard would. They also wore a guard-style uniform, a whistle and mirrored sunglasses. They carried a club as a weapon.

The guards gave punishments to prisoners who they thought had broken the rules. By the morning of the second day, the prisoners had had enough and barricaded themselves into their cell. The guards used force to break this rebellion. Once they had access to the prisoners they stripped them naked and began to harass and intimidate them. Thirty-six hours into the experiment one prisoner had to be released because he was suffering acute emotional distress. The behaviour of the guards became more brutal and the prisoners began to show clear signs of distress. The planned two-week experiment had to be abandoned after six days.

1 Why do you think the guards behaved in this way?

2 What are the ethical implications of a study such as Zimbardo's?

3 What does the Stanford Prison experiment reveal about power and authority?

In addition to the case studies in this unit, you might wish to research the psychology studies summarised in Table 18.3 below for your assignment.

Table 18.3: Further studies in psychology

Subject/title	Researcher and date	Aim and nature of experiment	Findings
Auto kinetic effect	Sherif (1936)	To demonstrate that people conform to group norms even when the norms aren't clear. Sherif used an auto kinetic effect – a light projected onto a screen in a dark room which appeared to move, although in reality it was stationary.	Participants tested individually on how far the light had moved gave a wide variety of answers. When asked in groups, answers tended to cluster around the same estimate – seeming to conform to a perceived group answer.
Conformity	Crutchfield (1955)	Crutchfield built on the Asch paradigm (see page 130) by ensuring that participants could not see the confederates, and by changing the lines to multiple-choice questions.	Crutchfield found evidence to support the idea of conformity in groups, which backed Asch's findings.
Blue green study	Moscovici (1969)	To discover whether one confederate could induce conformity in a large group of participants. Participants were asked to decide the colour of 36 slides, all of which were various shades of blue.	When the confederate consistently said the slides were green, over 8 per cent of the participants agreed - with 32 per cent conforming at least once. This shows that a minority can influence a majority.
Brown eyes, blue eyes	Elliott (1968)	To explore racial prejudice in children. Elliot divided her class into blue-eyed and brown-eyed and told the blue-eyed children they were more likely to succeed. Brown-eyed children were given ribbons to identify them and denied privileges. A few days later Elliott told the class she had made an error and in fact brown-eyed children were superior.	Initially, the blue-eyed children became arrogant, bossy and unpleasant to their brown-eyed classmates. The brown-eyed children lost confidence and their work suffered. When Elliott told the children about her mistake, the situations immediately reversed. Elliott's study shows that children are taught to discriminate by others, but that this discrimination can be unlearned.

Assessment activity 18.1

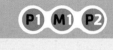

1   As a newly qualified prison psychologist, you have been asked to produce an information booklet for prison officers that will help them to understand the behaviour of inmates from a psychological perspective. Your booklet should:
   - Identify the approaches to psychology and the theorists who developed those approaches. **P1**
   - Analyse one approach to psychology in greater detail to provide the prison officers with the level of knowledge they need. **M1**

2   The case studies described on pages 130–3 highlight some of the issues that can arise when looking at behaviour. These studies have significant implications for the public services in terms of obedience, social influence and conformity.

   You have been asked by your local army cadet group leader to give a presentation to a cadet group that describes two studies in psychology. **P2**

Grading tips

For **P1** and **M1** your booklet should include the behaviourist, humanist, cognitive, psychodynamic and social approaches to psychology described on pages 123–8, and go into detail about one of them. You should also discuss the different theorists, such as Maslow, Watson, Freud and Rogers, discussed on pages 128–30.

For **P2** you will need to think about your audience and choose the studies that might have most relevance or be most interesting to them in terms of their future careers. Consider producing a handout to accompany your presentation.

PLTS

By analysing one approach to psychology in detail, you will demonstrate your skills as an **independent enquirer**.

Functional skills

By producing a booklet and a presentation you could be providing evidence towards your functional skills in **English**. Speak with your tutor about this.

133

2. Behaviour and its management

Knowing how to deal with the public, especially in difficult or stressful circumstances, is a key aspect of any public service career. This means that understanding why people behave the way they do and how that behaviour can be managed, for example what you can do to calm a situation, is essential knowledge when working in the public services.

2.1 Behaviours

The four key types of behaviour that you will examine in this section are shown in Figure 18.6.

Aggression

Individuals who use an aggressive style of communication and behaviour may be generally disliked because they intimidate, or threaten, others. An aggressive style is associated with:

- threatening body language, for example standing too close to another person (invading their personal space) and using hostile gestures such as pointing
- speaking in a loud, forceful and abrupt way
- often interrupting and shouting over others, indicating poor listening skills.

Some people may become physically abusive, for example pushing and hitting others.

As a public service employee it is likely that you will encounter aggressive behaviours, whether verbal or physical, from members of the general public as you conduct your duties. Less frequently you may encounter such behaviour in a colleague or boss. This form of behaviour can be considered bullying and should never be accepted. However, the best way to deal with it is rarely to respond in kind. Responding to aggression with aggression simply leads to a worse situation for all concerned. In addition, you should never behave in an aggressive manner to the public, even on occasions where you may be called upon to restrain someone or to stop certain behaviours. A good public service officer will maintain a calm temperament and take action based on the situation, rather than acting on feelings of anger or resentment.

Individuals who demonstrate aggressive behaviour may have low self-esteem and feel unable to control a situation without showing anger and aggression. By doing so they put their own rights above the rights of anyone else and avoid responsibility for the way they behave. Aggressive managers may give destructive feedback to employees that harms their confidence and work performance. They also tend to create confrontational situations or initiate conflict to suit them. This can have a detrimental effect on the workforce and the organisation itself.

Avoidance behaviours

Avoidance behaviours are techniques that people use to avoid or evade conflict, communication and responsibility. They include behaviours such as:

- failing to respond to requests
- not going to meetings
- planning situations to ensure that nothing is asked or requested of you.

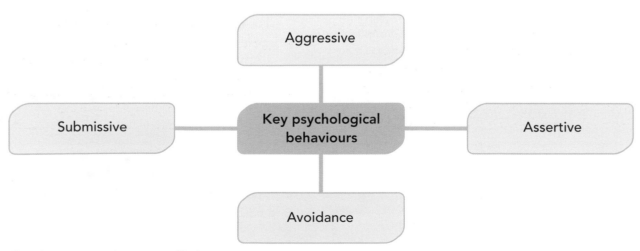

Figure 18.6: Four key types of behaviour

A person who uses avoidance behaviours is unlikely to become involved in conflict or to even recognise that there is a problem, because to do so would require effort on their part.

Managers who avoid conflict are unlikely to provide their staff with feedback on their performance, engage with the appraisal process or help with staff development. Equally, they are unlikely to take the concerns or complaints of employees seriously, which can lead to a reduction in staff morale and efficiency.

Key terms

Avoidance behaviours – techniques that people use to avoid or evade conflict, communication and responsibility.

Submissive behaviours – techniques that people use to defer to the opinions of other people who are seen as having more power. It is a means by which people avoid taking responsibility.

Submissive behaviours

Individuals who **behave submissively** generally defer to the opinions of those with more power and can be very hesitant in putting across their own message. A submissive approach is unlikely to command authority and respect, making it an inappropriate choice for the majority of public service work.

Many people use submissive communication in their daily lives without being aware of it. Submissive communicators have body language designed to make them appear smaller, for example stooping and crossing their arms, and may avoid eye contact. Often submissive individuals want to keep the peace and find it very hard to say no, as they prefer to please people by allowing them to have their own way.

Submissive managers are rare because they prefer other people to be in charge. They are not effective at resolving conflict between staff members or the public as they want to please everyone rather than address the issues at hand. Submissive managers often create more conflict because of their strategy of telling individuals what they want to hear rather than the truth. This may mean giving individuals positive feedback when their performance doesn't warrant it or allowing their own views to be misconstrued (misunderstood).

Assertive behaviours

Assertive communication strikes a balance between aggressive, avoidance and submissive behaviours.

- Communication is direct and clear, yet can include sympathy, empathy and negotiation as required.
- Body language is relaxed but alert. Eye contact is maintained but does not generate a feeling of tension in the other person.

Assertive behaviours have the capacity to calm a tense situation and command authority through respect, not fear. Assertive individuals protect their own rights while equally upholding the rights of others. They can clearly put their own viewpoints across while also acknowledging and respecting a variety of opinions.

A key component of assertive communication is confidence. A genuinely confident person does not need to shout and scream to make a point, nor do they agree with others for the sake of a quiet life. An assertive manager is able to deal with conflict effectively through communication, negotiation and compromise. They are able to provide constructive feedback on the performance of employees and their honesty can help defuse conflicts.

Remember!

- There are various styles of communication.
- Good communicators ensure that they can adapt their style to the situation.
- The most productive form of communication in the public services is assertive communication.
- Aggressive communication styles can be considered bullying and usually show an individual has little confidence.
- A submissive communicator is unlikely to be given positions of responsibility and leadership.

2.2 Behaviour management techniques

There are a variety of techniques that can be used to manage behaviour and prevent or resolve conflict. Some of these will be examined in this section.

Prevention of conflict

Conflict can occur for many reasons. Just as every person is unique, so too are the reasons why people feel conflicted. A situation in which you may feel at home may therefore cause someone else to feel very uncomfortable. It is important to remember this, because the key to managing conflict is recognising that not everyone reacts the same way to a situation.

Knowing how to resolve conflict once it has arisen is a vital aspect of any work you do with the public and with colleagues. Conflict management techniques are described in Figure 18.7.

A skilled public service officer or manager will be able to spot situations that have the potential to become confrontational and will put in place techniques to resolve them. If you work in an organisation, **prevention of conflict** might include strategies such as **teambuilding**. If you are a police officer working with the public, simply moving someone along might be enough to avoid a violent conflict with another person.

Key terms

Prevention of conflict – identifying a problem that might be occurring early enough for it to be resolved quickly and easily.

Teambuilding – strategy whereby teams work together in a different setting, for example while undertaking an outdoor sports activity, in order for them to understand how other team members work best.

Reducing escalation is another important technique that can be used to calm a potentially tense situation. This can be done in many ways, such as:

- tone of voice is soft and pleasant rather than loud, harsh and aggressive
- friendly eye contact is maintained
- body language is open and relaxed
- humour is used to lighten the situation.

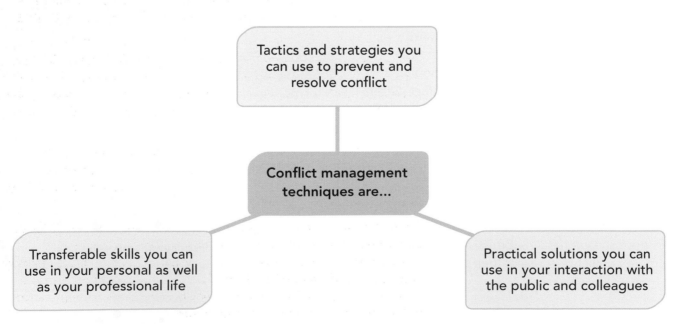

Figure 18.7: Conflict management techniques may not always be successful, but you will get better with practice

Conflict resolution

There are various methods of conflict resolution, as outlined in Table 18.4 below.

Table 18.4: Types of conflict resolution

Method	Description
Mentoring	Mentoring is the process of pairing up a more experienced member of staff with a less experienced one. In this way the inexperienced member of staff is helped to become proficient and confident in their role. Mentoring can help a new member of staff resolve conflict as they can look to their mentor for advice and guidance.
Socialisation and humour	These are some of the most useful tools in resolving conflict. A team that bonds well socially and enjoys a shared sense of humour is likely to be able to resolve conflicts more easily than a team that doesn't. However, you should always take care that humour is appropriate to the situation and will not cause offence.
Acts of gratitude and kindness	Maintaining a good atmosphere is critical to reducing conflict. Simple gestures such as saying thank you and showing appreciation for the work people do can reduce tensions and help others feel motivated.
Codes of behaviour	Organisations often produce formal codes of conduct for their employees that relate to behaviour. These can include codes for personal conduct, timekeeping, uniforms, absences and performance, to name just a few. The idea of a code of behaviour is that if everyone knows the standards of behaviour that are expected from them, then conflict will be kept to a minimum.
Internal **mediators** and advisors	These are trained people within an organisation who are used to diffuse or resolve conflict as unbiased outsiders. They can be very effective as they do not favour one side or the other – they are simply there to help resolve a problem.
Record keeping	Another method of resolving conflict is to keep records of individuals' behaviour. For example, if a manager and employee are in disagreement over an issue of punctuality, it would help if the manager had a record of lateness to which they could refer. Written records are useful tools in resolving conflict as they provide evidence for one side or the other that may put the issue to rest.
Thomas Kilmann Conflict Mode Instrument (TKI)	This is a questionnaire that helps people identify how they approach and deal with conflict. It provides strategies for developing conflict resolution skills.

Case study: The Betari Box

Betari's box, shown in Figure 18.8, suggests how our own attitudes can become stuck in a loop that is hard to recognise and hard to break. The key aspect is that your attitude affects the response of the person you are speaking to, and their attitude affects how you respond to them. In order to resolve conflict you first have to examine your own attitude and consider how your approach may be making the situation worse. The second step is to become unaffected by the attitude of others – that is, not letting someone's hostile or uncooperative behaviour make your own response hostile in return.

1 **Have you ever been in a conflict situation where your own attitude has made things worse?**

2 **How could you use Betari's box to break the cycle of conflict?**

3 **How could learning to control your own attitude and response help you in a public service career?**

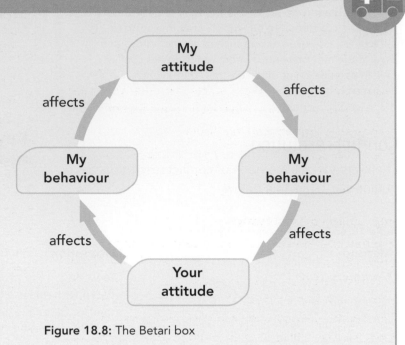

Figure 18.8: The Betari box

2.3 Benefits of understanding behaviour

There are many benefits to a sound understanding of behaviour within large organisations such as the public services. These include increased financial profit and greater staff motivation which helps:

- individuals including public service personnel
- customers and the general public
- public service teams
- public service organisations as a whole.

Table 18.5, on pages 140–1, examines these benefits in more detail.

Dealing with stress

Public service work, whether uniformed (such as the Police, fire-fighters or nurses) or non-uniformed (such as teachers, lecturers and probation officers), comes with a certain amount of stress attached to the job.

This stress may be caused by:

- low pay compared to the private sector
- dealing with a potentially hostile client group
- working in a rigid hierarchical employment structure that ensures individuals at the lowest rung on the ladder must implement policies and initiatives they have had no input in developing
- the risk of physical assault and verbal abuse
- the demands of the government to constantly work harder with fewer resources.

Remember!

Many public service workers actually thrive on stress factors such as these because they add variety and excitement to the nature of the work. Although there is no doubt that public service life can be stressful at times, it is also both personally rewarding and professionally fulfilling.

Top this off with mountains of paperwork and long hours which cause disruption to personal relationships, and you have a recipe for a workforce prone to stress-related illness including depression.

An understanding of behaviour management techniques can be used by organisations to try to reduce the impact of these stresses on the workforce. This may take the form of actively reducing stress by:

- ensuring limited working hours
- providing mechanisms to help employees deal with stress more effectively, such as sports facilities or in-house counselling.

Improving communication

If communication in your organisation is clear and direct there will be less chance of misunderstandings and mistakes that can be very expensive to correct. Your organisation should also perform more efficiently. Employees will be happier and more motivated because they will know exactly what they have to do and why. Customers will be happier because they will receive a better service.

Creating a positive environment

Customers, clients and staff need a positive environment in which to interact and perform their respective roles. A negative environment harms productivity, for example if the offices of a building are dirty and intimidating there may be increased absenteeism from staff that dislike the environment.

Professional development

Psychology has a role to play in the effectiveness of appraisal systems, which have a direct impact on the professional development undertaken by an individual. Appraisals:

- outline an individual's strengths
- identify areas that require development
- organise training to address development areas.

An effective appraisal system may mean the difference between promotion and standing still within an organisation.

Reducing conflict

Dealing with conflict is a daily part of the professional life of most individuals. However, this requirement is more pronounced in the lives of public service workers, who may deal with conflict from:

- the public
- colleagues
- superiors
- the government
- the media
- pressure groups
- their family.

An understanding of behaviour management techniques can help individuals avoid, minimise and resolve conflict. It can also provide people with a larger range of coping techniques, for example they can understand how to control their response to a difficult situation.

Case study: Dealing with conflict

PC Jensen and WPC Dev are responding to a public call about a disturbance in a local shopping centre. When they arrive on the scene they find a man in a state of disarray shouting abuse. He is bleeding heavily from a head wound. One of the local shopkeepers has left his shop and is behaving very aggressively towards the injured man, whom he believes to be drunk. Neither of the police officers can smell alcohol on the injured man and attempt to resolve the situation.

1   How could the police officers use psychology to diffuse the situation?

2   Considering your own knowledge of psychology, what advice would you give to the officers on why the man who is shouting abuse might be behaving in this way?

3   How might psychology explain the actions of the shopkeeper?

4   If you were one of the police officers in this situation, what would your first action be?

5   When resolving conflict, how important is an understanding of behaviour management?

Improving leadership

Confident and effective leadership skills are of vital importance in public service organisations. Understanding behaviour can help good leaders become better leaders; it can also help poor leaders recognise and overcome the challenges they face.

Developing self-esteem

Self-esteem and self-confidence are important components in performing stressful and difficult jobs effectively. Behaviour management strategies can usefully be employed by organisational managers to improve the self-esteem of their employees. Equally, individuals can use psychology to promote their own self-esteem.

Customer satisfaction and needs

The public services have a customer base of 60 million individuals – the entire UK population. In addition they service numerous other thousands of individuals abroad, for example in delivering humanitarian aid and engaging in UN-backed military action. Like any other organisation, the public services must ensure that their customers are satisfied with their performance. If they do not, the government could be forced to change, reform or even replace the functions that the public services currently call their own. Behaviour management approaches can provide those working in the public services with techniques on how to deal with customers effectively and sensitively regardless of how angry, upset, grief stricken or injured they may be. This understanding is vital when training officers to deal with their customers courteously and respectfully.

Table 18.5: The benefits of understanding behaviour to individuals, customers, teams and organisations

Understanding behaviour	Benefits for individuals including public service personnel	Benefits for customers and the general public	Benefits for teams	Benefits for public service organisations
Dealing with stress	Better able to do their job. Greater job satisfaction.	Receive a higher level of service and better value for money.	Team relations improve and members work more effectively together.	Saves millions of pounds lost every year due to staff absences from stress. The workforce is more efficient, not less.
Communication	Employees are happier and better motivated when communication is clear and direct. This is because they know exactly what they have to do and why.	Customers will be happier because complaints and enquiries will be dealt with more effectively.	Team relations will be more effective because there will be less chance of misunderstandings and mistakes that can be very expensive to correct.	Organisations can achieve their overall aims and objectives with greater success. The organisation should also perform more efficiently.
Creating a positive environment	Individuals work harder when they feel motivated to do so.	Customers will have a positive experience of the service provider resulting in positive feedback.	Team members will be motivated to work harder to achieve team goals. There will be a greater spirit of cooperation.	A negative environment harms productivity, for example if a police station reception was dirty and intimidating, less people would be inclined to go there to report a crime.

Understanding behaviour	Benefits for individuals including public service personnel	Benefits for customers and the general public	Benefits for teams	Benefits for public service organisations
Professional development	Individuals feel valued by organisations that recognise and reward achievement. They will feel fulfilled at work and motivated to work harder.	Customers will receive a better level of service from employees who have improved through training.	The professional development of team members will enhance the overall team's performance in terms of motivation and ability to succeed.	Organisations will be able to bring the very best out of their workforce, making them more efficient and likely to succeed.
Reducing conflict	Individuals will be happier in an environment which has reduced conflict. This can raise job performance and productivity.	Customers will feel more welcome and more confident about the service they need.	Teams will perform and bond better with reduced conflict, allowing them to focus on their core tasks.	Reduced internal conflict will allow the services to focus on their core tasks of serving the public.
Improving leadership	Individuals will be more efficient and productive if they have better leaders.	Customers will have confidence in a service that has outstanding leaders and trust them to do their job.	Teams work more effectively for good leaders. This saves money and resources in the long term.	The services need good leaders in order to be effective in operational situations where people's lives and property may depend on it.
Developing self-esteem	Increased self-esteem allows individuals to deal with stressful jobs more effectively.	The public will have a better service from an organisation which works hard to promote the value of all its employees.	Leaders can use psychology to improve the esteem of their team, and this can lead to improved productivity.	An organisation which improves its employees' self-esteem may benefit from more productive, valued and committed workers.
Customer satisfaction and needs	Ensuring customer needs are met can help keep an individual in employment.	Customers are satisfied that they are receiving the service they need and trust in the high standards of the organisation.	Teams can take pride in meeting customer needs, thereby increasing job satisfaction.	A service which meets the needs of its customers is not likely to face significant change over time.

Assessment activity 18.2

You are working as a personnel officer in your local council. Your line manager has asked you to hold a seminar discussion with frontline council staff that come into contact with the public, so they can receive training on behaviour management. Your seminar discussion must cover the following points:

1 Outline different types of behaviour, such as aggressive, submissive, assertive and avoidance, and how these can be managed. **P3**

2 Assess the benefits of understanding approaches to psychology and behaviours for public services and their personnel. **M2**

3 Evaluate how an understanding of psychology and behaviour can benefit public services and their personnel. **D1**

Covering these issues should help the frontline council staff deal more effectively and patiently with the general public.

Grading tips

For **P3** you will need to write a clear description but not a detailed one.

For **M2** you will need to consider the information then decide how important each factor is. Give evidence to support your views or statements.

For **D1** review the information then bring it together to form conclusions. Give evidence for each of your views or statements.

PLTS

By evaluating how an understanding of psychology and behaviour can benefit public services and their personnel, you will demonstrate your skills as a **reflective learner**.

Functional skills

Holding a seminar discussion will help you to develop your functional skills in **English**. See your tutor for additional guidance.

Koko Watanabe
Counsellor

My job

I'm a counsellor with the NHS. It's my role to see both NHS staff and members of the public who are referred to me with psychological or emotional problems. I use a variety of techniques to help them better understand their own and others' behaviour, in the hope that they can make positive changes to their situation.

A typical day

I see clients for most of the day. They come to me for a one-hour session in my counselling room. Each client has different needs and requirements and my approach to them has to mirror what they need. Some individuals are looking for coping strategies to help them in stressful jobs; some are struggling to cope with conflict at work or in their personal life; some suffer from low self-esteem which affects their job prospects or their interaction with others. I try and help my clients look at their own conduct and behaviour objectively. I also help them to develop a more positive attitude and behaviours that will have a positive impact on their lives.

The best thing about the job

The best part of counselling for me is seeing someone implement the techniques they have learned in order to make positive changes in their life. Usually people come to me for an initial series of six one-hour sessions. The best thing is if I don't see them again, because it means they were able to use the strategies and techniques and don't actually need me anymore!

Think about it!

- What topics have you covered in this unit that might give you the background to work in the field of psychology or counselling?
- What knowledge and skills do you think you need to develop further if you want to be involved in psychology or behavioural science in the future?

Just checking

1. How did Watson and Rayner induce a phobia in Little Albert?
2. What are the id, ego and superego?
3. List four types of behaviour.
4. Describe the use of Betari's box.
5. List the benefits of understanding behaviour for public service organisations and their personnel.

Assignment tips

- Make sure you have read your assignment thoroughly and understand exactly what you are being asked to do. Once you are clear about this you can move on to your research.

- Thorough research based on reliable sources of evidence is essential. Many learners rely too much on the Internet and neglect other sources of information, such as books, newspapers and journals. Always double check the information you find – don't just accept it at face value.

- Read as much as you can about behaviour. There are some excellent psychology textbooks available that discuss behaviour in an accessible way, such as *Psychology: The Science of Mind and Behaviour* (6th edition) by Richard Gross (Hodder Education, 2010).

- Aim to read lots of case studies and examples. These will add additional depth and detail to your assignments.

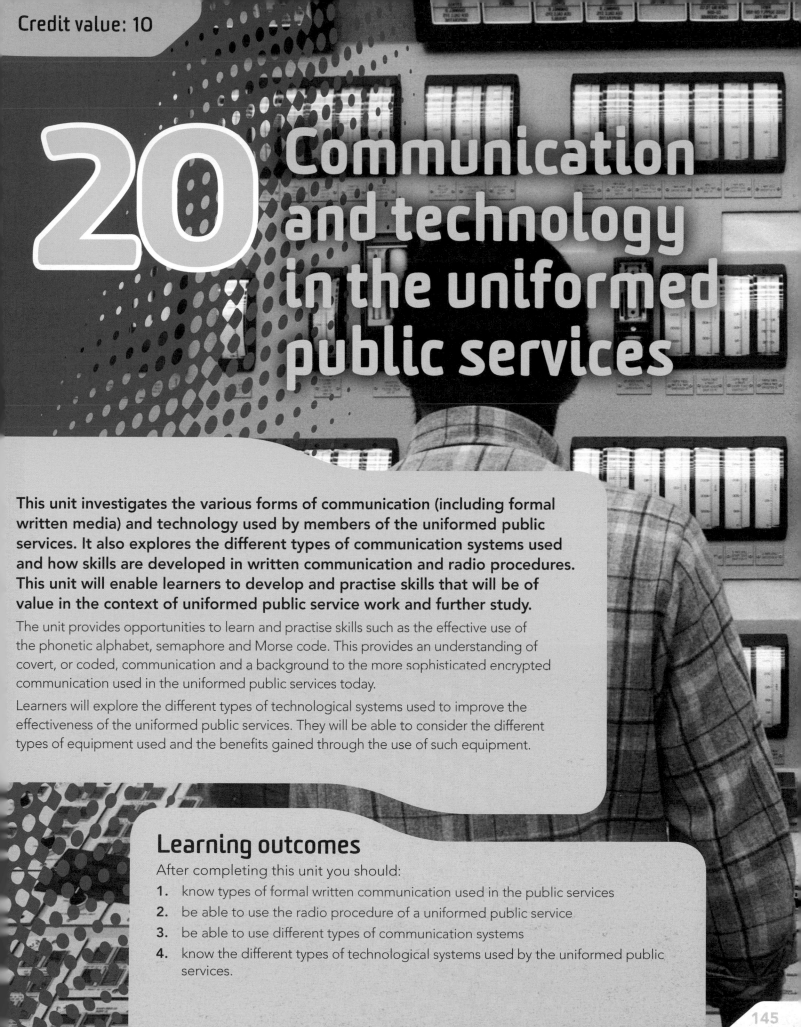

20 Communication and technology in the uniformed public services

This unit investigates the various forms of communication (including formal written media) and technology used by members of the uniformed public services. It also explores the different types of communication systems used and how skills are developed in written communication and radio procedures. This unit will enable learners to develop and practise skills that will be of value in the context of uniformed public service work and further study.

The unit provides opportunities to learn and practise skills such as the effective use of the phonetic alphabet, semaphore and Morse code. This provides an understanding of covert, or coded, communication and a background to the more sophisticated encrypted communication used in the uniformed public services today.

Learners will explore the different types of technological systems used to improve the effectiveness of the uniformed public services. They will be able to consider the different types of equipment used and the benefits gained through the use of such equipment.

Learning outcomes

After completing this unit you should:

1. know types of formal written communication used in the public services
2. be able to use the radio procedure of a uniformed public service
3. be able to use different types of communication systems
4. know the different types of technological systems used by the uniformed public services.

Assessment and grading criteria

This table shows you what you must do in order to achieve a pass, merit or distinction grade, and where you can find activities in this book to help you.

To achieve a **pass** grade the evidence must show that you are able to:	To achieve a **merit** grade the evidence must show that, in addition to the pass criteria, you are able to:	To achieve a **distinction** grade the evidence must show that, in addition to the pass and merit criteria, you are able to:
P1 describe different types of formal written communication used in the uniformed public services **See Assessment activity 20.1 page 152**		
P2 send a message by radio using standard voice procedures from one uniformed public service **See Assessment activity 20.2 page 158**	**M1** compare different types of radio communication systems **See Assessment activity 20.2 page 158**	
P3 send a message using different forms of communication **See Assessment activity 20.3 page 165**	**M2** analyse the advantages and disadvantages of other communication systems **See Assessment activity 20.3 page 165**	
P4 describe different types of technological equipment used by a selected uniformed public service **See Assessment activity 20.4 page 170**	**M3** explain in detail the benefits of using technological equipment in a selected uniformed public service **See Assessment activity 20.4 page 170**	**D1** evaluate the importance of using communication and technological equipment in the daily operation of uniformed public services **See Assessment activity 20.4 page 170**

How you will be assessed

This unit will be assessed by an internal assignment that will be designed and marked by the staff at your centre. The assignment is designed to allow you to show your understanding of the learning outcomes for communication and technology in the uniformed public services. Assignments can be quite varied and can take the form of:

- role plays and scenarios
- presentations
- tutor observations
- case studies
- written assignments

- practical tasks and demonstrations of your ability to communicate using radio and other communication systems

- witness testimony
- audio/video recordings of practical tasks
- leaflets
- posters.

Jake learns about the importance of communication in the emergency services

I was really looking forward to studying this unit because one of the careers I'm considering is with the Fire Service. I know I'm unlikely to get a job as a fire-fighter until I've got more experience, but I've been applying to work in the emergency call communications centre. I've found out that I would need to have computing skills and good communication skills, such as listening, passing on information to others and note-taking. The role would require me to log details of calls onto the Fire Service database and contact the control room to deploy Fire and Rescue Services if required.

Studying this unit has given me the opportunity to research formal written communications and practise some of these. I've also learned how to use a radio and other communication technology. It was great to be able to use things like Bluetooth, texting and email as some of my evidence, but the unit did make me stop and think about how I've used these systems in the past and how I would need to use them in a public service context.

One of the most interesting things for me was looking at the changes that are happening, partly as a result of poor communications between uniformed service personnel during events such as the London bombings in July 2005. The use of Airwave by all the emergency services is a really important development, and our class got a chance to see that in action on a visit.

This unit was very practical, which I liked, and it has made me even more determined to apply for a job in an emergency call centre. I'm more confident now that I can deal with life-or-death emergencies, such as a multiple pile-up on a motorway, as well as more routine complaints such as kids setting off fireworks in the street. Studying this unit has made me more aware of the importance of communications in the work of the emergency services.

Over to you!

- **What areas of this unit appeal most to you and why?**
- **What communications and technological equipment do you use already on a day-to-day basis?**
- **How do you think the uniformed public services use communications and technology?**
- **How could you prepare yourself for the assessment activities?**

1. Know types of formal written communication used in the public services

Formal written communications

All organisations use formal written communications, and uniformed public services are no exception. If you join a uniformed service, whether as a uniformed member of staff or as part of the support staff team, you will need to be able to complete a range of written communications including letters, memos, reports and incident reports.

With all formal communications there are certain things to keep in mind. The tone of the communication should always be polite and business-like. The content should be checked for accuracy (including spelling and use of grammar) and should be written in straightforward English that aids understanding.

1.1 Formal written communications

Letters

Letters can serve two main purposes. They can:

- inform the recipient, for example a letter giving a date and time for a court appearance
- request information, for example asking availability to book a conference location.

Public service organisations have letter templates that are used for most standard correspondence and which follow a 'house style'. Letters will include key information such as the organisation's:

- name
- address
- phone number
- email address
- website.

Normally the name and address of the recipient will be stated along with the date of writing. Often the purpose of the letter is highlighted before the main body of text, as is the name (or sometimes just the job role) of the person sending the letter.

Letters can be both:

- external communication, for example to service users, members of the public and partner public service organisations

- internal formal notification, for example a letter to all staff informing them of a change in policy.

Memos

Memos are generally for internal communication purposes. They are less formal than letters, but serve the purpose of communicating key information to the people highlighted on the circulation list. Memos are useful in situations where emails or text messages are not suitable, for example sending a report or a paper in internal post. However, in many situations email has taken over the role of the memo.

A memo usually:

- is a paper (hard copy) document
- is used for communicating inside an organisation
- is short
- contains *To*, *From*, *Date*, *Subject Headings* and *Message* sections
- does not need to be signed, but generally has the sender's name at the bottom.

Reports

Reports are usually highly structured and follow standard organisational formats. The structure and conventions used in written reports stress both the information included and the process by which the information was gathered.

Normally these stages are involved in writing a report:

- clarifying the terms of reference
- planning the report
- collecting relevant information
- organising and structuring the information
- first draft writing
- checking and re-drafting.

Generally reports follow a set structure which includes:

- a title page
- acknowledgements
- contents page (with page numbers)
- executive summary (this is vital as busy senior managers may only read this page)
- introduction (explaining why the report has been written and for what audience)
- methodology
- findings
- conclusion and recommendations
- references and any appendices.

Annual reports

All public services are required to publish annual reports. These detail the performance of the public service during the previous year and set targets for the coming year.

Are you familiar with the types of information recorded in an incident report for the emergency services?

Incident reports

Many incident reports actually require the completion of a form, recording specific information in a standard format for internal and external audit.

Other written communication

Journals

Most public service organisations have in-house journals which are usually available in both printed format and to download from the organisation's website. These can provide a range of useful information about the work of the organisation, including its successes and achievements, targets and goals. In addition there will be journals related to the area of work that personnel of a specific public service may require.

For example, the Prison Service publishes the *Prison Service News* (paper copy and online) which includes news, views and developments such as policy initiatives. The Prison Service also publishes the *Prison Service Journal* which aims to promote discussion on issues related to the work of the Criminal Justice System, including the Prison Service. This is available by subscription and selected articles are available online. In addition, Prison Service personnel may access journals such as *Howard Journal of Criminal Justice* and *British Journal of Criminology* to learn about the wider research relevant to their work.

Staff notices

Most organisations in the public sector will have staff notice boards. The problem with staff notice boards, though, is that someone has to keep them up-to-date! Increasingly uniformed public services are using global email as their key way of informing staff about important matters. Some public services use electronic notice boards at the point of entry to the building to highlight key issues. For example, in most prisons information about prisoner numbers, special events or staff news is displayed on an electronic screen in the gate.

Formal published reports

All uniformed public services are required to produce strategic plans, business plans and annual reports. These are public documents that can be accessed from the Internet and provide details of things such as achievement against government targets, expenditure, staffing or future plans. If you are researching a specific service it is well worth downloading this documentation as it can be a valuable source of information.

HM Inspection reports

All uniformed services are subject to inspections by independent bodies appointed by government to oversee their performance. These reports are public documents which are available on the Internet. Performance is graded and any deficits will result in a formal action plan that must be completed.

The Police are inspected by Her Majesty's Inspectorate of Constabulary for England, Wales and Northern Ireland (HMIC). In addition, they are subject to the Independent Police Complaints Commission (IPCC), which investigates any complaints against them.

Link

You can read more about the HMIC and IPCC in *Unit 17: Police powers in the public services,* pages 100 and 110.

Audit reports

Public services are subject to a range of audits:

- **internal audit** to ensure required performance standards are being achieved
- **external audit** which may be for a specific aspect of work, such as budget and finance
- **general audit** of performance.

Key terms

Internal audit – audit undertaken by personnel employed by or working on behalf of the public service organisation. It is not usually published for the general public.

External audit – audit undertaken by a government department, inspectorate or organisation working on the government's behalf. External audits are usually published.

General audit – this may be undertaken internally or by an external body. It would include benchmarking performance against other public and private sector organisations.

The Audit Commission is the independent body which monitors performance, seeking to improve efficiency, economy and effectiveness (the three Es) in public services. It reports on local government, health, housing, community safety and the Fire and Rescue Services.

Internet and Intranet

All uniformed public services have Internet sites which anyone can access. These give a wealth of up-to-date information about the organisation. They can also provide the public with the ability to communicate with the organisation directly.

In addition, public services will have Intranet systems. These are organisational systems which can only be accessed by personnel from that organisation.

Case study: Audit report on Fire and Rescue Services

Fire and Rescue Services (FRS) spent around £2.1 billion of public money in 2007/08. Their income comes from local council tax and grants from national government.

There are 46 FRS authorities in England serving 50 million people. Of these, 15 are provided by County Councils; the remainder are statutory bodies (Combined or Metropolitan Fire Services).

In February 2009 the Audit Commission reported that:

- Fire Services continue to improve, preventing more fires, reducing deaths and injuries and saving lives.
- The gap between the best and worst services is widening, with 37 of England's 46 FRS improving, improvement slowing in 6 services and 1 service rated as not improving.
- The focusing of prevention work on people most at risk has helped towards a 6 per cent reduction in accidental domestic fires.

- FRS have good financial management and two have top rating for value for money.
- There is scope for further savings (up to £200 million).
- Diversity in the workplace is a key issue, with the need to improve recruitment of people from ethnic minorities and women.

Research your local FRS by accessing their annual report and their performance in the 2008 Audit Commission report. You can access this report via the Audit Commission's website (www.audit-commission.gov.uk).

1 **How is your local FRS doing? Is its performance improving?**

2 **How well is your local FRS doing at reducing accidental domestic fires?**

3 **What is the gender and ethnicity composition of the workforce employed by your local FRS?**

Intranets are a very useful way of storing information for staff, such as policies, procedures and employment information. Many public services now use their Intranet systems to allow staff to do simple tasks such as claiming travel expenses, applying for annual leave and applying for internal promotions or transfers. Because they can be accessed electronically, Intranets are an effective way of keeping everyone up-to-date and informed, no matter where they are geographically located.

Email

Email (both internal and external) has become the communication method of choice for most organisations. The advantages of email are:

* speed
* being able to check information has been received
* providing an audit trail of information
* the ability to reach everyone in an organisation.

However, email also has its disadvantages, especially the need to have access to a computer terminal. This is not always practical for many frontline uniformed public service personnel, as they are often out on the road. There are also security concerns if any portable electronic device carried by frontline uniformed public service personnel falls into the wrong hands.

Effective email writing

* **Subjects.** Give the message a clear and unambiguous subject or title. Email messages without a subject may be deleted because of a fear of viruses, and if the purpose of your email is not immediately clear it may be ignored.
* **Contents.** Start the message with a greeting to create a friendly, business-like tone. If it is the first communication you should address the recipient formally, for example, 'Dear Mrs Johnson'.
  * Be clear and keep the message short and to the point. You should avoid comments such as 'Good news!', 'Guess what?'
  * Start with a clear summary of the message then give full details in the following paragraph(s). Ensure the final paragraph makes clear what should happen next. For example, 'Please let me have confirmation of your attendance at the meeting by Monday 24th.'
  * End the message politely using an accepted format, for example 'Yours sincerely', 'Kind regards', 'Best wishes'.

* **Attachments.** Make sure you refer to attachments (and make extra sure that you remember to include them!).
* **Name and contact.** Include your name at the end of the message and give your contact details including your phone number if appropriate. You should also state your role in the organisation or department.

Case study: Effective email writing

Subject: Friday 10 Sept, 11 am, meeting with ICT Dept

Dear Jackie,

I wanted to let you know that I've scheduled a meeting with the ICT department for this Friday, 10 Sept to discuss the new data base requirements.

The meeting is scheduled to start at 11 a.m. in the small conference room on the 2nd floor. Please let me know by return if you can make that time.

Many thanks,

Monica

Monica Jordan

HR Support Officer

Monica.Jordan@anyplace.gov.uk

0191 2233424 ext 219

Review the email above.

1   What do you think?

2   Is it fit for purpose?

Organisational policies and standard operating procedures

Uniformed public services have a range of organisational policies and standard operating procedures which aim to lay down standards for how the organisation and its personnel operates. They set standards or benchmarks for performance and give personnel clear guidance on how to act in specific situations.

For example, the Prison Service has prison service instructions (PSIs) and prison service orders (PSOs) which govern all its activities. These include both public documents (which can be downloaded from the Internet) and restricted documents which can only be accessed by authorised personnel.

In addition, most uniformed services have staff bulletins (sometimes known as brigade bulletins). These are news magazines circulated electronically which keep staff up-to-date on changes and important news.

Assessment activity 20.1 **P1** BTEC

Produce a leaflet for the induction of new staff which explains the types of written communications used in a specific uniformed public service. **P1**

Grading tips

To achieve **P1** you will need to describe the different types of formal written communication used in the uniformed public services, giving examples of when and where they would be used.

You will need to give a clear description that includes all the relevant features – think of it as 'painting a picture with words'. Use the unit content as a checklist to ensure you cover all the necessary criteria.

PLTS

By completing this assignment you will demonstrate your skills as an **independent enquirer**.

Functional skills

This assignment may be used to develop your functional skills in **English** and in **ICT** (if you use a word-processer to write your answer).

2. Be able to use the radio procedure of a uniformed public service

2.1 Radios

Radios typically have a number of features and some of these are described below. The main differences between different types of radios are:

- size and weight
- number of channels which they can use
- frequency range
- power supply and battery life.

An aerial, or antenna, allows the transmission and receipt of signals to the radio. Push-to-Talk (PTT) (or press-to-transmit) allows the radio operator to switch from voice reception to transmit mode. While the PTT button remains unpressed, any radio traffic that is received on the selected channel or frequency is heard through the radio's speaker.

Channel selector, or frequency selector, allows the operator to select channels or frequencies. If there is interference from other users nearby, channel selector

allows the operator to change to another frequency, although they need to ensure that all users are transmitting on the same frequency! In busy areas, such as airports or railway stations, a certain number of frequencies (known as multi-channel systems) are allocated for the site, which can all be controlled from a central base station. The microphone and speaker are built into the radio.

Channel lock is another standard radio feature which keeps the radio tuned in or locked to one channel. For connectivity many radios have optional jacks for additional headsets, microphones or speakers. Most radio systems in use by uniformed public services will use rechargeable batteries that require recharging every 12 hours, or more frequently depending on how heavily they are used. The radio should have a display showing the amount of power available.

The life of radio equipment will vary, partly depending on the use it gets and the environment in which it is being used, although the normal life for a two-way radio should be up to five years and up to two years for any accessories.

Radio systems

Radios came into widespread use in the armed forces in the 1930s and were important in the Second World War. Radio systems tend to be named after the company that developed and manufactured them, for example one of the early radio systems was developed by Pye radios. Pye was involved in the development of radar systems, including Air Interception Radar, Air-to-Surface Vessel Radar (ASV) and later the development of the commercial Private Mobile Radio (PMR) using analogue transmission.

The original 1950s Racal radio receivers were high-grade valve sets designed for use by the Royal Navy. Eventually they were used by all the armed forces and became the main radio surveillance system for Government Communications Headquarters (GCHQ).

The main radio systems currently used by uniformed public services are detailed in Figure 20.1.

Clansman

This system has been in use by the Army, Navy and RAF, primarily in land-based environments, since the 1970s. It is a family of radios and ancillaries designed for operations in combat zones anywhere in the world. Clansman equipment provides communication facilities over long and short distances for infantrymen, beach landings, parachute drops, armoured vehicles

and some ground-to-air links. It also provides access to area communications systems such as Ptarmigan. Clansman combat radios are based on **analogue technology** with limited data capacity. As this will not support the requirements of future military information systems it is being replaced by **digital technology**, such as the Bowman system (see page 154).

(see page 154)

Key terms

Analogue technology – analogue is the process of taking an audio or video signal (often the human voice) and translating it into electronic pulses. It is relatively inexpensive, but there are limits to the amount of data it can carry.

Digital technology – breaks the signal into binary code (a series of '1's and '0's) and sends it to the device at the other end (phone, modem, etc), which reassembles the code into the original signal. Because digital technology corrects any errors that occur during transfer, there is less distortion than with analogue, and digital can also carry much more data.

Ptarmigan

The Army first used this innovative and influential system in the 1980s, and it has only recently been replaced by the Bowman system. This extremely mobile, battlefield communication system uses digital microwave technology to provide secure communications networks over a large area and in a range of formats, such as voice, data, telegraph, etc.

It also provides global communication links via satellite communication systems and civilian systems. The

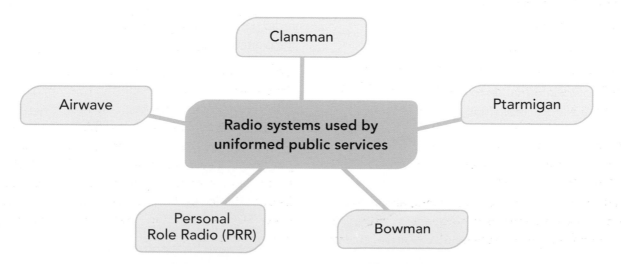

Figure 20.1: Radio systems used by uniformed public services

military technology that enabled communication to stretch from frontline soldiers to whole networks, led directly to the development of today's mobile phone networks by commercial companies.

Bowman

The Bowman system was first introduced in 2004 and is a tactical communications system designed to exploit the latest developments in radio and computer technology. The Bowman system is now generally used by the British military (having largely replaced the Clansman and Ptarmigan systems). In 2009 it was upgraded and now includes battle planning tools and a more stable tactical Internet. Bowman systems will be installed in 15,700 British Army vehicles, 60 helicopters, 141 ships, and around 75,000 service personnel will be trained in their use. Bowman radios are also in use by the Royal Marines, Royal Navy ships, RAF Regiments and specialist Army signals units.

The system incorporates both digital voice communication and data communication technology. Key features include:

- built-in geographical positioning systems which reduces the need for open radio traffic
- secure digital communications transfer systems
- secure tactical communication which removes the need to encode and decode radio messages
- resilience against electronic warfare attack.

Personal Role Radio

Personal Role Radio (PRR) is a small transmitter-receiver that allows infantry soldiers to communicate over short distances. It is effective through the walls of buildings or thick ground cover and enables infantry soldiers to react quickly to changing situations, including contact with the enemy. PRR is a short-range radio used extensively for non-core infantry tasks such as static observation points and base defence. It works with Clansman and Bowman radios, enabling information to be communicated between the platoon radio 'net' and the section.

Table 20.1: Features of Personal Role Radio (PRR)

Weight	1.5 kg
Range	500 m
Channels	256
Length	380 mm
Battery length	20 hrs (continuous use).

Airwave

Airwave is a digital radio communications network, replacing analogue radio systems, designed for the Police, to provide a secure and flexible communication network. Police authorities and forces in England, Scotland and Wales, the Serious and Organised Crime Agency and the British Transport Police piloted the system, which was taken up in full at the end of 2009 with all fire and ambulance services also using Airwave.

The system provides emergency services with a number of key features:

- an emergency button on the terminal that an officer can press if in danger
- improved radio coverage
- improved speech clarity
- improved security and encryption of communications
- private mobile radio communications network
- enhanced operational flexibility
- scope for mobile data applications
- national roaming
- improved capability for radio inter-operability between the Police and other services.

Ultra-High Frequency, Very-High Frequency and High Frequency

Ultra-High Frequency (UHF) and Very-High Frequency (VHF) are the frequency bands most commonly used for transmission of radio and television signals. Mobile phones also transmit and receive using UHF. UHF is used by most public service organisations for two-way radio communication, using both narrow band and frequency modulation (FM). VHF is also used by land, sea and aircraft communications.

All radio frequencies are in the range from 3 Hz to 300 GHz (3,000 MHz):

- UHF between 300 MHz and 3 GHz
- VHF between 300 Hz and 3 GHz
- HF between 30 Hz and 300 Hz.

Radio waves with frequencies above the UHF band fall into the SHF (Super-High Frequency) and EHF (Extremely-High-Frequency) bands, all of which fall into the microwave frequency range.

2.2 Use of radio procedures

Some of the ways the uniformed public services uses radio communication are detailed in Table 20.2.

Table 20.2: How the uniformed public services use radio communication

Army	• person-to-person contact in the field • base-to-unit contact
Coastguard	• ship-to-shore contact • ship-to-ship contact when out searching for a lost vessel or persons • contact from Coastguard to other emergency rescue services
Police	• station contacting officers who are away from base, e.g. in vehicles or on the beat • communication between officers, e.g. when undertaking surveillance or when pursuing suspects • contacting other emergency services during an emergency incident
RAF	• ground-to-air contact • contacting other armed or emergency services, e.g. during an emergency incident or joint exercise
Revenue & Customs	• customs officers working at ports and airports to communicate with each other and back to base • border patrol on HMRC fleet of boats to communicate with Police authorities and base
Royal Navy	• ship-to-shore contact • contacting other armed or emergency services, e.g. during an emergency incident or joint exercise.

2.3 Radio communication

Voice procedures

The purpose of voice procedures is to ensure messages are sent, received and correctly understood. The prowords in Table 20.3 are some of the commonly used key words.

The introduction of National (Police) Standards for radio communication has created Standard Communication Procedures (SCP). These aim to improve:

- response to incidents and emergencies
- operational performance
- communication practices.

Some of the SCP procedures are basic, but they are mandatory because of the need to standardise good practice in radio transmissions across the emergency agencies. At major incidents and life-threatening emergencies where the incident action is happening at speed, there is a need for rapid, clear, concise and accurate communication.

Security

It is important that communications are only received by the uniformed public service personnel they are intended for. Most systems used by the uniformed services are encrypted to ensure security of communication.

Accuracy and discipline

The ABCD of radio communication means that all communication should comply with:

Accuracy → Brevity → Clarity → Discipline

The need for discipline in the use of the radio is absolute. It ensures that:

- communications are short, clear and to the point
- there is no 'over talking'
- active listening takes place
- there are no misunderstandings
- allowance is made for priority use
- a number of people can communicate at the same time.

Prowords

Prowords are easily pronounced words and phrases commonly used when transmitting messages. Using a limited number of phrases helps to avoid confusion for the person receiving the message and allows the person listening to the message to concentrate on the information being communicated. For example 'hello' at the beginning of a message indicates that this is the start of the communication, that nothing has gone before and that nothing has been missed.

Prowords can save time too, which is important in emergency situations, as one proword often replaces a phrase or entire sentence. Some examples are given in Table 20.3.

Table 20.3: Prowords used in radio procedures

Word	Meaning
Affirmative	Yes.
Negative	No.
Over	I've finished talking and I am waiting for your reply.
Out	I've finished talking and don't expect a reply.
May Day	Maritime distress call which has priority over urgent calls.
Repeat all	Please repeat my message back to me so I can check your understanding.
That is correct	You have repeated back my message correctly.
Will do	I will follow out your request/instruction.
Free to talk	I'm checking if you are available and the communication is secure.
Hello	Greeting at start of communication.

Authentication

Authentication refers to the need to ensure the message and the person transmitting the message are genuine. Uniformed public services use call signs and code words (as described below) to authenticate communications and identities.

Call signs

These are used to identify individuals or groups communicating over the airwaves. They are code names aimed at making the communication more secure and ensuring that individuals are correctly identified. Call signs often include code names and numbers. The Police use the call signs of the phonetic alphabet (listed below), so if a number of units are taking part in one activity, a common call sign is used for the activity, but with a different number for each unit. For example, Delta One, Delta Two, etc.

Code words

These are accepted abbreviations or coded words used to ensure communications are both swift and secure. Some common ones in use by the emergency services are 'RTA' for road traffic accident and 'ETA' for expected time of arrival.

The armed forces use code words commonly. Some examples are given below, but a full list can be found at www.armedforces.co.uk/abbreviations.htm.

- AWOL — Absent without leave
- BMH — British Military Hospital
- CinC — Commander-in-Chief
- OIC — Officer in Charge
- NCO — Non-Commissioned Officer
- PRR — Personal Role Radio.

Phonetic alphabet

The NATO phonetic alphabet, more formally the international radiotelephony spelling alphabet, is the most widely used spelling alphabet. Though often called 'phonetic alphabets', spelling alphabets have no connection to phonetic transcription systems such as the International Phonetic Alphabet.

The NATO alphabet assigns code words to the letters of the English alphabet **acrophonically** (Alpha for A, Bravo for B, etc.) so that critical combinations of letters (and numbers) can be pronounced and understood by those who receive and transmit voice messages by telephone or radio, regardless of what their first language is.

Letter	Word	Letter	Word
A	Alpha	N	November
B	Bravo	O	Oscar
C	Charlie	P	Papa
D	Delta	Q	Quebec
E	Echo	R	Romeo
F	Foxtrot	S	Sierra
G	Golf	T	Tango
H	Hotel	U	Uniform
I	India	V	Victor
J	Juliet	W	Whisky
K	Kilo	X	X-Ray
L	Lima	Y	Yankee
M	Mike	Z	Zulu

Key terms

Acrophonically – using a word as the name of the alphabetical symbol representing the initial sound of that word.

Network – groups of equipment, individuals and agencies acting together to increase efficiency and effectiveness through shared information and resources.

Case study: Police national standard for radio communications (AirwaveSpeak)

In 2007 the National Policing Improvement Agency (NPIA) announced the launch of AirwaveSpeak to assist police forces by enhancing inter-agency operations and in support of frontline policing. Research among different police forces had highlighted concerns over the variable standards in police radio discipline and led to the call for a common national standard to be developed.

A team of professional linguists were used to develop the national standard, working in coordination with police officers and other staff involved in communications (such as emergency call centre staff).

AirwaveSpeak was developed with the aim of improving communication between radio users and different police force, as well as radio users and other emergency services. It was designed to ensure those communicating by radio had a clear and simple language to use.

AirwaveSpeak offers a number of features such as:

- provides a clear radio language which can be easily used and understood by all police forces and their personnel
- uses everyday standardised terminology
- ensures clear transmissions between police forces and other public services and on an interagency basis at emergency and national events
- shorter radio transmissions, less repeated messages and less use of air time, so cutting costs
- better radio discipline thus helping recording of information by communications room staff
- based around the principles of accuracy, brevity, clarity and discipline (ABCD, see page 155).

1   **Why do you think the uniformed services need a national standard for communicating via radio?**

2   **What are the advantages and issues of introducing a standard communication procedure?**

Net control

There are various types of net (**network**) control. These include:

- **One to one** – radios are designed to transmit one message at a time and so the most common form of communication is one radio holder communicating directly with another.
- **Radio control base** – this network communicates with a number of radio holders (or substations). The radio control base is the communications station and has the responsibility of clearing traffic and exercising circuit discipline within a network.

Leaving and joining the net

To call up an individual, their call sign must be used first to ensure their attention is engaged. To broadcast to all users, or a circulation message, the correct call signs, or group identification, must be used (for example 'All units'). This is repeated then followed by the caller's own call sign and the word 'over'.

It is useful to indicate what the content of the next part of the message will be, for example: 'All units. All units. Standby for a circulation message re: a recent RTA. Over'. This allows everyone to get into a position to receive and record the message and avoids the likelihood of a repeat message being requested.

When leaving the network or terminating the call once the full exchange is finished, the word 'Out' must be used. As good practice the prowords 'Nothing more, over' could be used to show that that part of the communication is completed. The final exchange would then be 'Thank you, out'.

Rebroadcast

Rebroadcasting occurs when the caller asks for information to be 'repeated', 'clarified', 'confirmed' or 'explained'.

'Read back' or 'acknowledge' are used to check how a message has been heard or understood, but if the receiver of the message is not sure they have heard or understood the message (or part of the message) they should ask for it to be rebroadcast. To do this they should use the prowords 'Repeat' or 'Say again'.

Radio users

There are two main types of radio users:

- Personnel use radios to assist in their work role. These include both uniformed public service personnel and those working in private organisations such as security provision.
- Private radio users (often called 'radio hams') use radio communications as a hobby.

Pass simple messages

Certain things are to be kept in mind when making calls. These include:

- Try to ensure that each transmission serves a single, easily-recognised purpose, for example by making a short, clear request or giving a manageable amount of information in each transmission.
- Take care how you phrase questions.
- Make messages simple and direct, for example 'Was she observed entering the premises?'
- Avoid indirect or complicated wording.
- Make a statement and add a question tag on the end, such as 'So he was observed entering the premises, yeah?'
- Add a suggested answer to the question, such as 'Where was the suspect heading? To the town centre?'
- Ask two questions at the same time, for example 'Did you get the witness's name and what was it?'
- Compose messages with more than one purpose.
- Avoid using informal language and speaking in a casual, chatty manner.

Urgent messages

Emergency calls will always take priority over routine message taking. It is normal practice to clear emergency traffic, then priority calls and finally those with routine messages.

Link

For more on responding to and categorising emergency calls, see *Unit 14: Responding to emergency service incidents*, pages 30 to 35.

Test calls

It is important to ensure equipment (both for transmission and receiving messages) is operating effectively. This can be done by sending and receiving test messages. Test messages should be clearly identified as such by the use of the proword 'test message'.

Battle orders

A range of radio equipment may be used by the armed forces to issue battle orders. The systems must use encryption of the messages to ensure that enemies cannot intercept the transmissions.

Weather forecasts

Radio weather forecasts are widely used by ships. The shipping forecasts, inshore waters forecasts and coastal forecasts are issued on a regular basis by the Met Office, on behalf of the Maritime and Coastguard Agency, to alert those at sea to potential dangers from changing weather patterns. As well as being broadcast on the radio network, these forecasts are also available via the Internet and are constantly updated.

Assessment activity 20.2

 BTEC

Radio communication is essential to the work of the uniformed public services and their personnel. It is important to understand radio communication and be able to use radios to communicate in practical situations.

1. Send a message by radio using standard voice procedures from one uniformed public service. **P2**
2. Compare different types of radio communication systems. **M1**

Grading tips

For **P2** you will need to demonstrate your practical skills by sending a radio message using the voice procedures of a specific public service. Ideally your tutor will record or video tape this so you have evidence that you have completed this task successfully.

For **M1** you need to identify the radio communication systems and then explain the similarities and differences and the advantages and disadvantages of those systems. One way to approach this would be to use a table listing the types of radio systems, their key features, advantages and disadvantages. You would then need to summarise the key points from your comparison.

3. Be able to use different types of communication systems

3.1 Communication systems

Reasons for use of communication systems

Much of the work of uniformed public service personnel takes place away from base. Public service personnel often work alone and in dangerous situations or are required to protect the public in a range of situations. It is vital that public service personnel can communicate with their own base and other public services quickly and effectively.

Development of communication systems

Communication is constantly changing. The use of flags and semaphore to communicate in the army and navy in the nineteenth century gave way to Morse code. By the Second World War, radio communication was well established. More recently, systems such as LinguaNet, microwave and Bluetooth have developed.

Relevance to uniformed public services

The different uniformed public services have specific needs to use communication technology, which in turn is closely linked to the work each service undertakes. We will look at these in detail in Section 4 of this unit, where we review the different types of communication used (see pages 166–70).

Practical use of different types of communication

Communication methods must be fit-for-purpose and able to be used in the specific circumstances uniformed public service personnel find themselves in. The case study *Communications and the London bombings* (page 165) describes some of the difficulties encountered by emergency workers during the London bombings of 2005. Communication systems must be easy to use, portable (for personnel away from base), have good reception and be secure and reliable.

Object video

Object video is a surveillance system used to monitor people for security and public safety. Object video is especially useful at events where large crowds of people congregate, such as at music concerts and sports events. Object video converts video images into data that can be used to identify individuals, track an individual's movements and help detect and solve crime.

Closed circuit television (CCTV) systems have intelligence software embedded in them. They are used to track a moving object using camera networks, so they can track an individual as they move from the range of one camera to the next. The systems can set up an automatic alert so that the CCTV operator is aware of problems occurring or alerted to potential issues. The operator can then use the system to analyse the situation, for example by replaying the video evidence.

Object video has a number of benefits including:

- being an effective, proactive 24-hour security system, so increasing the safety of the public
- using resources effectively as it is automated, providing real-time detection of potentially threatening events
- being suitable for use outside and indoors, using wireless or wired systems.

Object video is now widely used by a range of public services including the military (for defence and at military bases); the Police and other protection agencies; for Customs and border control; to monitor important (but vulnerable) infrastructure and protect from possible terrorist threats (e.g. at airports, transport systems, nuclear power plants, sea ports). It is used extensively not just in the UK but throughout the world.

LinguaNet

This is a specially designed messaging system that enables providing for real-time, cross border operational communication by emergency services such as police, fire, ambulance, coastguard, and disaster response teams. It provides a straightforward, cost-effective link for routine communication between operational public service units across frontiers. LinguaNet also offers online resources to help people learn a foreign language and online translation services.

Microwave

Microwaves can be found at frequencies between 300 MHz and 3 GHz and can be seen as a form of light energy. They have a number of uses. Most people are familiar with using microwave ovens for cooking, but they are also used in telecommunications and broadcasting and in mobile phone networks such as GSM. Radar systems use microwaves to detect the speed and range of objects. Before the advent of fibre optic transmission, long distance telephone calls were carried via microwave

Bluetooth

Bluetooth is an open wireless protocol which allows the exchange of data over short distances (using short radio waves) from both fixed and mobile devices, creating personal area networks (PANs). It was originally conceived as a wireless alternative to data cables. It can connect several devices together at the same time. It is used by mobile phones, PDAs (personal digital assistants) and laptops, allowing the sharing and transfer of data between devices. The main advantage of Bluetooth is that it is a no-cost, rapid method of sending data between devices. Its disadvantage is range: the devices must be in close proximity for data to be transferred.

Popular current uses of Bluetooth include:

- wireless communication using hands-free headset and mobile phone
- wireless networking between PCs
- wireless communication with PC input and output devices

What communication systems do the Police benefit from in their work?

- data transfer between mobile phones.

3.2 Standard voice procedures

As with radio communication, public service personnel need standard voice procedure to ensure that:

- communications, which are subject to interference, are not misunderstood
- communications over long distances with weak signals are not misunderstood
- protocols are followed during emergencies.

Some examples of procedures are given below.

WACCO

WACCO is used by all 'blue light' emergency services and the armed forces to provide a structured way to communicate important information over a radio system.

- **Warning**: this will cover potential hazards or particular difficulties that others coming to the scene may encounter.
- **Access**: in routine situations access is unlikely to be a problem, but for incidents in particular areas (remote locations, areas of congestion) the best access route will need to be identified. Ideally entry and exit routes will be different to ensure emergency vehicles are not blocked on exit by others arriving at the scene.

- **Casualties**: as much detail as possible must be provided to assist ambulance and other public services and voluntary services, such as the Women's Royal Voluntary Service (WRVS) and St John's Ambulance, when preparing their response. Details must include the number of people affected, the type of injuries they have and whether they are trapped or can be moved.

- **Control point**: this may need to be set up, and its location reported, so those reporting to the scene know where to assemble for briefing when they arrive on site.

- **Other information**: situations or problems such as traffic blockages, weather reports and chemical spillages may also need to be communicated.

Person descriptions and vehicle descriptions

To aid in giving descriptions of people, public services personnel use the mnemonic NASCH:

- **N**ame
- **A**ge
- **S**ex
- **C**olour
- **H**eight

An example might be:

- **N**ame: Johnston
- **A**ge: 26 years
- **S**ex: female
- **C**olour: white
- **H**eight: 5 feet 7 inches.

For vehicles, uniformed public services use the consonants in the word CoMMuTeR. The letters relate to:

- **C**olour
- **M**ake
- **M**odel
- **T**ype
- **R**egistration number.

So a vehicle may be described as:

- **C**olour: blue
- **M**ake: Audi
- **M**odel: not known
- **T**ype: saloon car
- **R**egistration number: Delta, Tango, five, one, November, Papa, Charlie.

3.3 Satellite communications

SATCOM is an abbreviation of satellite communications. The first satellite, Satcom 1, was launched in 1975. SATCOM is used for both civilian and military purposes and can communicate using pictures, words and other forms of information. There are hundreds of satellites in orbit providing services to private companies, governments and international organisations such as NATO. The armed forces use satellite communications when communicating with land vehicles, ships and planes.

Satellite communications can be especially useful in disaster situations because they can transmit information in remote areas that do not receive cell phone reception or where Internet connections have gone down. Meteorological and storm warning satellite technology can help with predicting disasters and enabling preventative actions to be taken.

Satellites for navigation were developed in the 1950s to enable ships to know their position at any given time. Sat Navs are now widely used by both uniformed services and the general public in navigation at sea, in the air and on land.

Search and rescue satellites were designed to enable communication between rescue services and vessels at sea, planes and vehicles or personnel in need of assistance. These satellites are designed to locate and detect emergency beacons, even in remote or dangerous places.

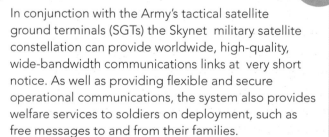

Did you know?

In conjunction with the Army's tactical satellite ground terminals (SGTs) the Skynet military satellite constellation can provide worldwide, high-quality, wide-bandwidth communications links at very short notice. As well as providing flexible and secure operational communications, the system also provides welfare services to soldiers on deployment, such as free messages to and from their families.

The first satellite of the constellation, Skynet 5A was launched in March 2007, Skynet B followed in November 2007. Skynet C (launched April 2008) will act as an 'in'orbit reserve'. The whole system will provide all three UK armed forces with the next generation military satellite services.

Video link

Video link allows different locations to be linked remotely. The technology required is simple. A camera and screen (with a microphone) needs to be installed at each location. A broadband line is used to transmit the pictures and sound electronically between the locations. Many of us use this type of technology in our homes, using webcams to communicate across the world.

In the public services context the most common use is for court hearings where offenders are held in custody. Evidence can be presented to the court electronically (such as original papers and documents) and dangerous weapons and offensive items can be shown by video so they do not have to be handled. In England and Wales there are 58 prisons linked up to 153 Magistrates' Courts and 32 Crown Courts. The potential use for this technology by uniformed public services is huge, and many are already using the technology for video conferencing and meetings.

Did you know?

Prison video links

Prison video links allow court hearings and legal visits to be managed from prison, avoiding the need to physically transport an offender to the court. They are also used for inter-prison communication and visits (both within the UK and internationally), probation visits and staff training. The benefits of video links include:

- improved security (as potentially dangerous offenders are kept securely in the prison)
- protection of witnesses and victims in court
- financial savings from not needing to transport (and escort) prisoners
- less disruption of prison regime by preparing for court appearances and receipt back from court after hearings
- reduction of escape risk while prisoners are being escorted to court
- reduction of drugs/weapons being transferred into the prison environment.

Internet telephone

These systems allow users to make free phone calls (both domestic and international) using the Internet and Voice over Internet Protocol (VoIP). VoIP is transmission technology for allowing voice communications over IP networks such as the Internet or other networks, rather than using the public switched telephone network (PSTN). Internet telephone systems have many advantages – usually there is no cost and the systems are easy to set up. The disadvantage is the time lag between transmission and receipt of messages.

Morse Code

This was created for Morse's electric telegraph in the early 1840s. It was also used from the 1890s for early radio communications. In the early twentieth century Morse code was used in high-speed communications nationally and internationally using radio circuits, telegraph lines and cables under the sea.

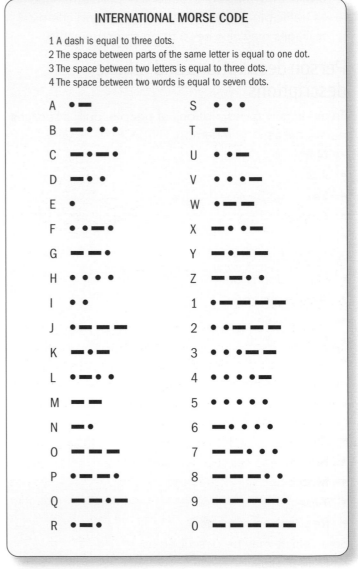

Figure 20.2: Morse code

Email

Email is the accepted standard internal method of communication in most public service organisations. Portable electronic devices allow email to be sent and received remotely and many mobile phones now have facility for email receipt and sending. Most public services also have the facility to use email in external communications, both with other agencies and with members of the public who use their services.

Wireless networking

The development of wireless connectivity in the late twentieth century has enabled electronic devices to communicate with each other without the use of cables.

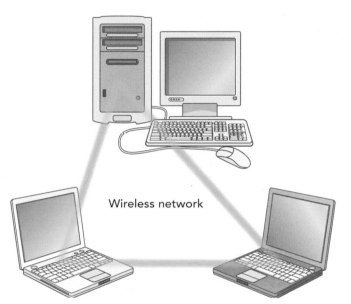

Wireless network

Figure 20.3: Wireless connectivity allows electronic devices to communicate without the use of cables.

Mobile phones

Introduced commercially from the mid 1980s, early mobile phones were large and not easy to transport. They were analogue and used for voice calls only. They had limited transmission range, relying on a network of distributed transceivers to communicate. Their signals were transmitted by frequency modulation.

Today's digital mobile phones generally have a range of built-in features such as cameras, radio and music playback. Communication to and from mobile phones includes voice, text, Internet and email communication. The latest mobile phones include the most up-to-date technology (e.g. face-to-face video calling) and owners can personalise their phones by downloading applications for a range of things, from surf reports and restaurants guides to sending packages via FedEx.

Internet

The Internet is a global collection of large and small networks, which are connected together in many different ways. The name Internet comes from the concept of interconnected networks.

The Internet was originally developed by the US armed forces during the Cold War to assist communications in the event of nuclear attack. Having no central hub reduced the possibility of an attack on or disruption to the network. Later the technology was adopted by the American National Science Foundation (NSF) and various American universities as a knowledge exchange system.

The Internet became generally available in the 1980s and has since grown to a worldwide phenomena. The World Wide Web (www) was developed during the 1990s. Today the Internet provides connections between computers and Internet search engines allow users access to a huge range of information.

All uniformed public services have websites. These can be used to store information for internal or external users to access and to allow communication with users of the services.

Paging

Pagers are wireless communication systems which send brief messages to the person holding the pager. They are one-way messaging systems. Paging may be manual or automatic. Manual systems send a message to the paging operator through a phone call which is delivered to the pager via the operating network. Automatic paging mechanically processes and delivers messages. Messages may be voice messages, alert tones (which alert the receiver to call into base) or digital messages such as phone numbers to call back.

Pagers are often used by uniformed public services to alert personnel who are on call (such as retained fire-fighters) to report for duty. An automatic message can be transmitted to all those on call if an incident occurs.

Semaphore

Semaphore is a system for conveying information at a distance by means of visual signals normally using hand-held flags (see Figure 20.4 overleaf). Information is encoded by the position of the flags; it is read when the flag is in a fixed position.

Did you know?

Semaphores were adopted in the 1800s and widely used during sea battles such as the Battle of Trafalgar. The modern naval semaphore system still uses flags and is accepted as an emergency communication system.

Figure 20.4: Semaphore is a visual system of communicating at distance using handheld flags.

Case study: Communications and the London bombings

Public services, especially emergency services, need to be able to communicate effectively. The key findings of the London Assembly report, published in June 2006 based on the response to the attacks in the city of London on 7 July 2005, found that while there were 'incredible acts of courage and resourcefulness' by the emergency services, underground workers, health professionals and members of the public, there were also failures of communication between the emergency services as well as within each organisation.

Police, fire and ambulance staff all used different radio systems. Some staff could not communicate with each other or with their control rooms, and rescuers at ground level could not talk to their colleagues underground.

The Fire Service, for example, had to use people running up and down escalators to access information. Eighteen years after the King's Cross fire of 1987, there were still no digital communications which would have enabled communication below ground level.

There was an over-reliance on mobile telephones, especially by the London Ambulance Service. Officials should have been aware that the mobile network would become congested after a major incident.

Radio systems also needed to be used more effectively. In some instances, the Ambulance Service had one member of staff monitoring two channels.

1 **Why do you think the different uniformed services had different communication systems?**

2 **Research the London Assembly report on the July bombings. Find out what recommendations were made and whether these have been implemented.**

Assessment activity 20.3

  BTEC

Communication using a range of technology and systems is vital to the work of the uniformed public services. In this assessment activity you will need to demonstrate that you can use non-radio forms of communication and you will need to analyse the advantages and disadvantages of these communication systems.

P3 Demonstrate the sending of a message using other forms of communication.

M2 Analyse the advantages and disadvantages of other communication systems.

Grading tips

For **P3** you will need to demonstrate in a practical situation your ability to use non-radio communication systems. Your tutor will probably suggest some systems you could use to demonstrate this criteria. You might consider

using systems you are already familiar with such as email, mobile phone, Bluetooth and the Internet (systems such as Skype). You may want to be more adventurous and try out semaphore. You will need to produce evidence to show you have used non-radio communications. This could be in the form of a print out of an email or Internet communication, a recording of a mobile phone message or a witness statement from the person who received your message.

For **M2** you will need to analyse the advantages and disadvantages of non-radio communication systems. You may decide to use a table to summarise the basic information. You would then need to bring your findings together and interpret those findings to reach conclusions.

PLTS

By analysing the advantages and disadvantages of non-radio forms of communication, you will demonstrate your skills as an **independent enquirer**.

Functional skills

Presenting your findings as a report will help to develop your functional skills in **English** (and in **ICT** if you word-process your answer).

4. Know the different types of technological systems used by the uniformed public services

4.1 Equipment

Frontline public services personnel use a range of electronic equipment as standard in their working day, depending on the job they are undertaking.

Listed below are some of the types of equipment employed and an outline of which public service uses each piece of equipment listed in their work.

Table 20.4: Frontline electronic and technological equipment

Equipment	Used for	History and use by public services
Electronic tagging	• Keeping track of offenders in the community • Ensuring curfews are not breached • Ensuring exclusion zones are not entered by offenders	• Probation • Prison Service • Youth Offending Team • Police • Introduced in 1990s to reduce the prison population and allow offenders to retain home and family links
CCTV	• Improving public safety • Reducing crime • Reducing fear of crime	• CCTV has been in use since the 1990s in certain public areas such as town centres, airports, roads, public transport • Images can be used as evidence in court by the Police/CPS • Managed by local authorities
Passive Radio Frequency (RF) sensors (Tags)	• Tagging/bar-coding goods • Seasonal parking permits • Passports • Traffic tagging at poll booths • Travel permits	Widely introduced in the 1980s and now used by uniformed public services in activities such as border patrols and traffic management
X-ray machines	• Widely used in medical diagnosis since invention • Security screening at ports, airport, on entry to public buildings	• Invented in 1896 and now widely used for security screening • Used in prisons to screen all people and goods on entry • Used to screen on entry to public buildings such as Crown Courts • Used in prevention of terrorism, e.g. screening at airports
Geophone	Instruments for measuring ground motion, e.g. for detecting earthquakes, machine vibrations	• First used in the early 1900s • Used in search and rescue by emergency services
Satellite navigation	Navigation aids used to locate current position and destination	• Satellites for navigation were developed in the 1950s to enable ships to know their position at any given time • Sat Navs are now widely used by uniformed services for navigation on sea, air and land

continued

Equipment	Used for	History and use by public services
Vehicle mounted data systems (VMDS)	VMDS are touch screen onboard computers, often with onboard printers attached to link emergency vehicles back to base	Introduced in recent years to emergency services such as Fire and Rescue, VMDS allow access to a range of information to assist rescues such as: • building plans • design specifications of modern vehicles • road maps • details of chemical substances
Thermal imaging cameras	These cameras convert invisible infrared radiation into visible images	• Originally developed for military use during the Korean War (1950–53) and now used by a range of uniformed public services • Used by the Fire and Rescue Service (FRS) to seek out people trapped in burning buildings where visibility is poor, to locate hidden fires/hot spots and to check that fires are properly extinguished • Used by the military and the Police in detection activity
Automatic distress signal unit	Automatic warning system activated if no movement is detected for a period of a fixed number of seconds	Used by public service personnel in dangerous situations, e.g. an automatic distress signalling unit is provided on each operational FRS BA (breathing apparatus) set so that if a fire-fighter is immobilised a warning will sound
Roaming network mobile phone	Most mobile phones are of this type and will locate the nearest network as they are moved	Mobile phones are carried as standard by many uniformed public service personnel
Simulators	Equipment used to replicate a real environment where it would be dangerous to practice on the real thing	Used, for example, in RAF pilot training and police advanced driving training
Fax machine	Machine that transmits written communications and documents	Used by most uniformed public services, although becoming less commonly used as the ability to scan and email documents becomes widely used
Hand-held metal detector	Portable equipment that enables objects made of or containing metal to be located	• Used by uniformed services in search and rescue, weapon detection • Also used to screen individuals before entry to secure locations for metal objects (which could be used as weapons)
Nuclear quadrupole resonance sensors	Equipment capable of detecting nuclear quadrupole resonance (NQR) signals in explosives and drugs	• Used by armed forces in landmine detection • Often mounted on armoured vehicles while being used
Man-portable Surveillance and Target Acquisition Radar (MSTAR)	MSTAR is lightweight, all-weather, battlefield radar	• MSTAR was developed in the 1980s by the MOD and widely used in the 1990s (e.g. Gulf War) • Main users are armed forces (artillery observation parties, reconnaissance and surveillance purposes)
Intelligence, Surveillance, Target Acquisition and Reconnaissance (ISTAR) equipment	System that links battlefield functions to help the armed forces use its sensors and manage the surveillance intelligence gathered	Used by armed forces in support of intelligence gathering on the battlefield.

4.2 Importance of using different types of technological systems

Effective communication

Effective communication is vital to all public service organisations. Often their uniformed personnel are operating away from base and need to keep in touch with their operations base or with colleagues who are also away from base. In addition, uniformed service personnel need to be able to communicate with personnel from other services.

Rapid response

In many situations which the uniformed services deal with there is a need for rapid response. There are situations on the battlefield, emergency situations, civil contingencies and disasters where it is critical to get uniformed service personnel to the incident quickly and to communicate with them at the incident. There are also situations, such as when uniformed service personnel are in personal danger, for example a prison officer being attacked by a prisoner, where having good communications can trigger rapid response.

Collaboration between services

Collaboration between uniformed services and inter-agency communication are features of all aspects of public services operations. Having a range of communication and technology systems available for use in assisting this collaborative working between services means a coordinated response can be provided to the public or other public service personnel if required. The use of vehicle mounted data systems (VMDS) by the Fire and Rescue Services means that data is instantly available to help all the emergency services when called to a road traffic accident. Without this information there may be delays in dealing with chemicals or entering buildings on fire to rescue those inside.

Advantages and disadvantages

While effective communication and technology systems have many advantages (which we have discussed) there are also disadvantages:

- **Cost:** systems are often expensive, both to buy and to maintain.
- **Training:** for these systems to work effectively, uniformed public service personnel must be trained to use the equipment. This involves cost and staff time.

- **Keeping systems secure:** surveillance gathering equipment must be protected and the intelligence gathered cannot always be readily used. For example, information gathered from phone message interception cannot always be used by prosecutors in court because of the need to keep such information secure.

Did you know?

Firelink is the digital wide-communication system for the UK Fire and Rescue Services (FRS). Put simply it helps to link up the communications of all the 'blue light' services. It was designed to help communications between different uniformed services and enhance their ability to deal with incidents such as major emergencies, terrorism and flooding. It provides FRS operational staff and fire-fighters with a radio system that has:

- excellent network coverage
- clear radio voice quality
- a secure and resilience system
- inter-operability with other FRS, Ambulance Services and the Police.

The system uses TETRA technology radios which can transmit both voice and text messages. The system also allows the control room to send mobilising instructions and operationally urgent information directly to vehicles and their crew using GPS (global positioning system) technology.

4.3 Use of technological systems in the uniformed public services

The Police

The Police use a wide range of technological systems in support of their work. One example is the Police National Network (PNN) which is designed to provide telecommunications services and data to all criminal justice organisations and police forces. Originally intended to replace the network used to access the Police National Computer (PNC), PNN is now used by all UK police forces and other CJAs (criminal justice agencies) including HM Revenue & Customs and the Crown Prosecution Service. It has brought a number of benefits including:

- providing a common communications platform
- saving costs
- improved support of information exchange required by the Police
- data and information sharing between the CJAs and the Police
- video conferencing
- secure Internet access.

Case study: Police National Computer (PNC)

The Police National Computer (PNC) was initially set up in 1974 as a stolen vehicle database, but advances in technology since 1995 mean it is now an important on-line tool that allows the Police to carry out searches for people or vehicles, even if they only have partial information. The PNC holds details of people, crimes, vehicles and property that can be accessed electronically by the Police (and other CJAs).

Some of the systems the PNC supports are:

- VODS (Vehicle Online Descriptive Search) – this allows authorised users to search the vehicles database at DVLA by owner postcode, vehicle registration number and colour to reduce the list to potential suspect vehicles in an investigation.

- ANPR (Automatic Number Plate Recognition) can take a visual image of a number plate and check for current insurance being in place on the vehicle, name of registered owner, etc.

- QUEST (Querying Using Enhanced Search Techniques) allows the search of a database of names, so helping identify suspects through information such as personal features and physical descriptions.

- CRIMELINK is a web-based system which can be used to solve serious serial-type crimes. It searches for patterns in crimes, similarities and links.

- The PNC also hold the National Firearms Register and authorised users can search the register to confirm firearms are licensed.

- The introduction of hand-held devices has enabled police officers to undertake roadside checks on information stored in the PNC database.

The PNC is a national system. It is available to be accessed 24/7 all year round. It is a vital tool for the Police (and other CJAs) in investigating and solving crime. Some 185 million enquiries were dealt with by the PNC in 2008 and this number is increasing by 10 per cent each year.

A new computerised information system called CRASH is being developed to collect, validate, transmit and store records of road traffic accidents, so eliminating the need for this to be in written format, on report forms. Officers will input data directly to a central system using hand-held devices. CRASH will link directly into the Police National Computer and the PNC can directly transfer information into the CRASH system.

1 **What are the advantages of the PNC to the Police and other criminal justice agencies?**

2 **What issues and disadvantages might there be with the storage of data on computers rather than in a paper-based format?**

Armed forces (Army, Navy, RAF)

All armed forces use technology to support their operations (military operations, peacekeeping duties and the provision of humanitarian aid). The key uses of technology are:

- intelligence and information gathering
- communications
- weapons
- defence.

The Joint Operational Command System (JOCS) provides digitised tools for controlling joint operations between the armed forces. JOCS provides a central means of communication for senior staff in the MOD, RAF, Army and Navy. It connects the permanent joint HQ in the UK with 40 sites based around the world.

The Ambulance Service

The Ambulance Service uses a wide range of technology in its work. As well as sophisticated communication technology and Sat Navs, ambulances are fitted out with medical equipment. This will vary from basic equipment for outpatient transfer vehicles to state of the art medical diagnostic and treatment systems. Emergency ambulances are equipped with ECG machines (electrocardiogram, which monitor heart rates) and defibrillators for restarting the heart after cardiac arrest.

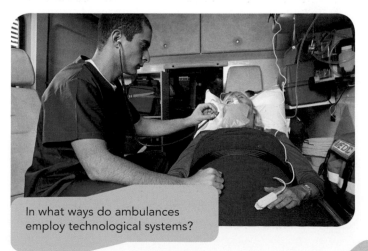

In what ways do ambulances employ technological systems?

HM Coastguard

The Coastguard use technology for day-to-day activities such as internal and external communications. Technology is also used extensively in search and rescue operations. One example of this is GMDSS (Global Maritime Distress and Safety System). This maritime communication system is used in both routine communications, such as ship-to-ship and ship-to-shore communications, and in emergencies. Commercial ships (vessels over 300 tonnes) and other vessels, such as fishing boats, are obliged to fit GMDSS. Offshore yacht races require yachts to be equipped with GMDSS and many smaller vessels voluntarily equip themselves with the GMDSS system.

Assessment activity 20.4

All the uniformed public services use a range of communications and technology. That use is vital to their effective operations, both in times of emergency and in their day-to-day operations. Some of the communications and technology equipment is common to a range of uniformed public services (indeed, this is vitally important for inter-agency effectiveness on an operational basis). Other equipment is specific to specific services, or services operating in specific sectors (for example, tagging equipment used by the criminal justice agencies).

1 Describe different types of technological equipment used by a selected uniformed public service. **P4**

2 Explain in detail the benefits of using technological equipment in a selected uniformed public service. **M3**

3 Evaluate the importance of using communication and technological equipment in the daily operation of uniformed public services. **D1**

Grading tips

P4 and **M3** are linked grading criteria. They require you to identify one specific uniformed service and to describe the technological equipment that service uses. Ideally you should select a service you have visited or where you have met service personnel. Use the unit content as a starting point, but bear in mind that your chosen service may only use a small selection of the technology listed there.

For **P4** remember that 'describe' means that you must give a clear overview that includes all the relevant features. You may want to ask yourself the questions 'what, how, why?' in relation to each piece of equipment you identify.

M3 develops this by asking you to explain in detail the benefits the use of the equipment brings, so you need to extend your 'what, how, why?' to the benefits of each piece of equipment described. For example, electronic tagging is used by the criminal justice agencies (in particular the Prison Service and the Police) to monitor the movements of offenders while they are in the community and ensure they abide by court orders and licence restrictions (such as curfews, keeping away from specific areas, etc.). The benefits of this are that all offenders in the community can be monitored 24 hours a day. Without the technology offenders would either not be monitored or would have to be kept in custody.

D1 requires you to take an overview of the whole of the unit and consider how important both communication systems and technological equipment are to the day-to-day operations of the uniformed public services. You are required to undertake an evaluation of this so you will need to review the information you have researched for the whole unit and bring this together to form a conclusion. You will need to give evidence and examples to support your views and statements.

PLTS

By evaluating the importance of using communication and technological equipment, you will demonstrate your skills as a **reflective learner**.

Functional skills

By word-processing your response to this assessment activity, you will develop your functional skills in **English**.

Jake Andrews
Communication Systems Operator, Royal Signals

I work in the Army's Radio and Information Systems out in the field. I like to think of my role as the key to ensuring the maintenance of the Army's battle-winning communications infrastructure. I joined the Army five years ago after completing my BTEC National in Public Services.

I've been trained to operate satellite communications systems, secure digital radio systems and wide-area information systems networks. All my training was certificated so I have gained a great portfolio of skills that are also recognised outside of the Forces. I also underwent extensive computer systems training and achieved my ECDL qualification.

I already had a driving licence when I joined up (otherwise the Army would have trained me) and I've since achieved my LGV licence.

Typical day

There really isn't one! As a Communication Systems Operator, I need a number of skills and qualities, including being inquisitive, being able to improvise and a love of communication systems! Like all members of the Army I need to be able to work well in a team and be well motivated, with a determination to overcome unforeseen problems.

I went to Afghanistan last autumn for eight months. I really enjoyed doing my job out there rather than being in the UK and practising.

The best things about the job

I really enjoy being part of a team and I also like the opportunities and challenges my job brings. When I joined the Army I was looking for a career and technical experience, and the Royal Signals has given me that. I also wanted to travel, see the world and test myself. Recently we went to Germany for two weeks and went skydiving. I really enjoyed that. I also love sport, and I play for our Brigade football team.

Our Regiment is capable of conducting sustainable Electronic Warfare in support of national operations anywhere in the world. In the past the Regiment has been involved in both active service and supporting NATO and UN peacekeeping operations.

Think about it!

- Why is teamwork vital in the work of Communication Systems Operators?

- Why are effective communications systems vital to the work of all uniformed services?

- Why do you think the Armed Forces support their personnel in achieving nationally recognised qualifications?

Just checking

1. Why do some communications need to be written? What are the advantages and disadvantages of written communications?

2. How have electronic communications helped the work of the public services? What are the key issues with their use?

3. How does email protocol for public services employees differ from the way an employee may use email in private correspondence?

4. Below are some key prowords. Check out what each of these means and when it would be used.
   - Back up
   - Code zero
   - Nothing more
   - Reading back
   - Urgent call
   - Yes, yes.

5. Identify two types of radio systems and describe the key features of each.

6. Explain the meaning of the abbreviations UHF, VHF and HF.

7. Outline how one uniformed public service uses radios to support their day-to-day work.

8. Explain how WACCO is used by blue light services.

9. How have CCTV and video links assisted the work of the public services?

10. Explain what thermal imaging technology is and how it is used by Fire and Rescue Services.

edexcel

Assignment tips

- Remember this unit requires you to know and understand the use of communications and technology in uniformed public services.
- You will also need to demonstrate your practical ability in communicating using a radio system and other communication systems.
- Keep a log of the communications you make, especially those that are different or unusual.
- Get your log countersigned by a reliable observer who was present and can witness what happened. Always get the observer to include their status, for example tutor, RAF Trainer, fellow learner or Cadet Leader.

21 Custodial care services

The work undertaken by the staff employed in the custodial care sector is diverse and directed at ensuring the care and control of individuals kept in custody. The aim here is to keep individuals secure while helping to rehabilitate them to lead useful lives both in custody and on release from custody. Staff operating in a custodial care environment must be able to maintain the delicate balancing act between care and control to ensure that the duty of care for individuals is not at the expense of the security and order of the establishment and the welfare of the general public.

By studying this unit you will examine how care and control of individuals is managed and maintained and the custodial environment kept secure. The need for security and the risks to both the individual and the establishment where security is not maintained are explored. You will investigate the factors that influence security, including physical and dynamic elements – for example, both the fabric of an establishment and the use of intelligence information are considered. You will also understand the procedures to be followed when offenders and their property are received into and discharged from custody.

On completion of this unit you will know how the custodial environment assists offenders with acknowledging and addressing their offending behaviour and its impacts. You will also understand how the custodial services work to help offenders to develop positive relationships both inside the custodial environment and in preparation for release from custody. This unit will also introduce you to the process of development and resettlement of offenders and build your knowledge of offending behaviour as well as the stages an offender must go through before release.

Learning outcomes

After completing this unit you should:

1. know the security measures employed in the custodial environment
2. know how control is maintained in the custodial environment
3. understand the receiving and discharging procedures for individuals and their property
4. understand how offenders can build positive relationships in custody.

Assessment and grading criteria

This table shows you what you must do in order to achieve a pass, merit or distinction grade, and where you can find activities in this book to help you.

To achieve a **pass** grade the evidence must show that you are able to:	To achieve a **merit** grade the evidence must show that, in addition to the pass criteria, you are able to:	To achieve a **distinction** grade the evidence must show that, in addition to the pass and merit criteria, you are able to:
P1 describe the physical, dynamic and procedural security considerations in a custodial environment **See Assessment activity 21.1 page 181**	**M1** justify the use of adjudications and incentive schemes in relation to addressing offending behaviour and the maintenance of control **See Assessment activity 21.2 page 188**	**D1** evaluate the need for security and control in a custodial environment **See Assessment activity 21.2 page 188**
P2 outline the types and methods of searches conducted by staff in a custodial environment **See Assessment activity 21.2 page 188**		
P3 describe control measures in place in a custodial environment **See Assessment activity 21.2 page 188**		
P4 explain the process of receiving and discharging individuals and their property into and from the custodial environment **See Assessment activity 21.3 page 191**		
P5 assess the importance of building positive relationships for offenders **See Assessment activity 21.4 page 196**	**M2** analyse how developing positive relationships and addressing offending behaviour benefits the individual and society **See Assessment activity 21.4 page 196**	**D2** appraise the impact of offending behaviour programmes **See Assessment activity 21.4 page 196**
P6 identify how offending behaviour is addressed in custody **See Assessment activity 21.4 page 196**		
P7 explain how offenders are prepared for rehabilitation and release **See Assessment activity 21.4 page 196**		

How you will be assessed

This unit will be assessed by an internal assignment that will be designed and marked by the staff at your centre. The assignment is designed to allow you to show your understanding of the learning outcomes for custodial care services. Assignments can be quite varied and can take the form of:

- role plays and scenarios
- presentations
- tutor observations
- case studies
- written assignments

- leaflets
- posters
- practical tasks
- recorded evidence (such as tape recordings, videos).

Rashid learns about working in the Prison Service

This unit helped me to understand how very complex the management of offenders in custody is. Before I studied this unit I had very little understanding of the importance of security in a prison environment – both the need to keep prisoners away from the public for their safety and also the need to keep prisoners safe while locked up.

As part of our study of this unit our class were taken on a visit to a prison. We had to go in three groups as they can only let small numbers go round a prison. It was quite scary because we had to be searched before we went through the double electronic gates, and everywhere we went we had two prison officers with us. They unlocked each gate or door and when we all passed through then the door was locked again. I felt quite claustrophobic.

We went into one of the cells and the door was locked behind us – which freaked some of the class! I sat on the bed and it was really hard.

Some parts of the building were OK, like the gym (which had state-of-the-art equipment) and the classrooms, except they had no computers – they are not allowed, which must make study very hard.

We also met some of the dog handlers. They have different types of dogs for different jobs. Dogs get trained to detect drugs and also mobile phones. They are also used to patrol the perimeter walls and find contraband that is chucked over the walls.

I learned two important things from the visit, which are that I never want to be a prisoner and also that there are loads of different jobs in the Prison Service with good promotion prospects, so I will definitely explore this further as a possible career choice.

Over to you!

- **What areas of the work of the Prison Service appeal to you?**
- **Do you think you could work with offenders convicted of serious crimes like sex offences against children?**
- **How will your study of this unit prepare you for the assessment activities?**

1. Know the security measures employed in the custodial environment

What do you know about prison security?

What do you think the terms physical, dynamic and procedural security mean?

What technology might prisons use to keep prisoners secure?

Discuss these questions in small groups, then compare your answers with the rest of your class.

1.1 Physical security

The *Prison Service Statement of Purpose* has two aspects:

- serving the public by keeping in custody those committed by the courts
- looking after prisoners with humanity and helping them lead law-abiding and useful lives in custody and after release.

To achieve the first part of serving the public and to ensure that prison Key Performance Target (KPTs) are met, it is vital that prisoners cannot escape from custody. This means **physical security** in terms of high walls, locked and patrolled entry and exit points (gates) and zoned and locked areas inside the boundary walls are vital.

Looking after prisoners humanely and helping them to lead law-abiding and useful lives can only be fulfilled if the staff and prisoners inside the prison are kept safe from violence, bullying and fear of attack. Thus additional security is required in terms of CCTV, perimeter patrols, checking prisoner locations and keeping them securely locked in the required physical areas.

Custodial environment

Physical security covers all measures that are used to deter and prevent prisoners from accessing areas where they should not be or attempting to escape from custody. These include:

- locked doors
- locked gates
- surveillance and detection equipment.

Many prison buildings were not built for that purpose – they are listed buildings or former military camps, for example. But whether prison buildings are purpose-built

> **Key term**
>
> **Physical security** – ensuring the physical prison environment is secure by the use of entry gates, walls, bars, locks and CCTV (closed circuit television).

or adapted from other uses, the basic ways a custodial environment maintains security is by physical barriers such as perimeter walls, bars and gates. Technology supports this with CCTV, lighting and motion sensors. Key to all of this is staff vigilance and regular patrols, for example patrols of boundary walls and the use of dogs.

> **Did you know?**
>
> Category D prisons hold prisoners who are not considered to be a security risk. There is little physical security and prisoners are allowed to leave the custodial environment during the day to work or study or at weekends on home visits (known as ROTL – release on temporary licence).
>
> Prisoners in category D establishments are either those convicted of offences where the public is not considered to be in physical danger (such as fraud) or prisoners coming to the end of their sentence and being prepared for release.
>
> Because these prisons are described as 'open' prisoners cannot escape from them – prisoners who fail to return after their ROTL expires are considered to have absconded.
>
> When figures were first recorded (1995–96) 956 prisoners absconded from category D prisons. Since then, 11,844 prisoners have absconded, including 261 prisoners who absconded in 2008–09.

Physical security has two key purposes:

- to create physical barriers to restrict free movement and prevent escape from the custodial environment
- to monitor and detect behaviour which arouses suspicion by using CCTV, alarms and patrols.

Physical security is therefore important in ensuring locks, cells, alarms, fences, walls and gates are kept secure. It is also critical that regular security checks are made by observation and surveillance and searches (both routine and non-routine) of all areas of the custodial environment.

The importance of searching

Searching may take place in any part of the whole establishment, but specific areas will be routinely searched or non-routinely searched when security intelligence suggests there may be an issue. Routine searching will be undertaken in areas accessible by prisoners and those where equipment that may be used in an attack or escape is stored (such as kitchens and workshops). Dogs are routinely used to assist with physical searches for illicit items such as phones and drugs.

Search equipment

Specialist equipment is used by prison staff, in particular when searching for illicit items such as mobile phones, SIM cards, drugs, illegally brewed alcohol and weapons. One of the most commonly used forms of search equipment is portable visual inspection equipment. This is designed to allow staff to undertake searches in areas where access is difficult, such as pipes, ceilings, toilets, cavities in cell doors and walls.

Searching areas such as roofs may be helped by the use of infrared technology, for example cameras and telescopes which are used to locate items in darkened areas.

1.2 Dynamic security

The concept of **dynamic security** is based on surveillance and intelligence gathering. One of the key roles of prison staff is to monitor normal everyday activities and the movement of prisoners (for example, to work, education, visits or the gym) and to look for unusual patterns of behaviour or opportunities

Did you know?

Any potential security breach will initiate a search. A serious potential breach will result in a 'lock down', where no movements of any kind into or out of the prison will be allowed (this includes all staff, prisoners, visitors, goods and supplies) until a full search has been conducted.

Key term

Dynamic security – the Prison Service describes dynamic security as the process of looking for patterns in intelligence, close monitoring of gang members, sharing of information, building close relationships with external agencies and partnerships to share intelligence, along with tackling the drug and violence issues.

Activity: Mobile phones on the inside

The Prison Service is considering introducing jamming to block mobile phone signals. Illegal phones are being used by prisoners to continue their criminal activities while in custody. Recent government data confirmed 81 phones and SIM cards were confiscated at a south west Category B prison in 2008. This compared to 40 in 2007 and 19 in 2006. A prison inspector estimated that, as phones inside prisons change hands for over £400 each, the trade in illegal phones within prisons in 2008 was worth over £9 million (more than 7000 mobile phones were discovered in prisons in England and Wales in 2008).

Small handsets mean that phones and SIM cards can be smuggled in by prisoners, staff and visitors or even thrown over prison walls. The prison inspectors say

blocking technology would make mobile phones useless and prevent their use in crime and the intimidation of witnesses.

The argument against using blocking technology is that it could also block out essential communication from the prison to outside services. It may interfere with the reception for innocent citizens living and working near to a prison. The technology is also very expensive (£250,000 per jail) and the money could be better spent on other deterrents.

1 **Do you think blocking equipment should be used?**

2 **How could the cost of this technology be justified?**

for contraband to be passed from one prisoner to another. Family and official visits (e.g. from a solicitor or probation officer) are also monitored and suspect activity investigated.

Having a constructive regime where there is a good relationship between staff and offenders is important to build trust and give prisoners the confidence to report suspicions and worries. A secure environment is important to both staff and prisoners alike. If the environment is not secure there is a risk that vulnerable prisoners may be bullied and have their possessions damaged or stolen, and these vulnerable prisoners may then self-harm or become suicidal.

Having intelligence systems which both collect and analyse intelligence data effectively is vital for the safety of all those in custody and those charged with looking after them.

As part of their dynamic security processes, prisons routinely listen to prisoner's phone calls and read both outgoing and incoming mail. For some prisoners, their conversations with visitors (including solicitors) may be recorded. Recently there was a lot of press coverage when a suspected terrorist had conversations with his visiting MP (Member of Parliament) recorded in breach of the so-called Wilson Doctrine, which has made Parliamentarians of both Houses exempt from such surveillance since 1966.

1.3 Procedural security

Importance of security procedure

Procedural security is quite simply ensuring that physical and dynamic security policies, procedures and practices are always carried out. It is no use having secure issue of keys to staff if they go through doors and gates and leave doors unlocked behind them.

All staff employed by the Prison Service (officers and civilians) and those working within the custodial environment who are employed by other organisations (e.g. healthcare staff employed by the primary health care trust or teachers employed by the educational contractors) receive training in

security procedures and practices and have the importance of security highlighted to them. Security has to be the first consideration in any activity within a custodial environment.

Security risks

The identification of possible security risks and ways to deal with them is of key importance for all personnel employed by, or working with, the Prison Service. There are risks which civilians who have not worked with offenders would probably not consider, for example the need for prison personnel to keep personal details (such as where they live, the names of their children and the type of car that they drive) secret and not disclosed to offenders.

Physical risks

Prison staff have to be aware of how to identify, deal with and isolate physical risks. For example, being alone with a prisoner creates a potential risk so should only happen if the member of staff is in an environment where assistance can be readily summoned (using radio communication or panic alarms) and the risk assessment for the specific prisoner has been completed. Activities in the custodial environment must be risk assessed and where risks are identified, controls put in place to manage those risks.

Procedural security also covers a range of events such as how violent incidents are managed. Prison staff are provided with training to deal with aggressive and threatening behaviour. They will use a range of techniques and procedures to manage such situations, including:

- the use of de-escalation techniques and acting to defuse the situation
- self-defence and breakaway techniques (which include control and restraint)
- the use of segregation and seclusion (isolating individual prisoners or locking down an entire wing or the whole prison).

Documents and records

It is vital that required documentation is completed and records are fully maintained. In a potentially volatile environment situations occur that need following up and investigation. Documentation and records provide an audit trail to show that agreed procedures have been effectively adhered to.

> **Key term**
>
> **Procedural security** – the identification, establishment, enforcement and audit of security policies.

Categorisation of custodial environments

The categorisation of offenders and establishments is a critical part of procedural security. The risk posed by different offenders and the physical security of different jails must be matched up to ensure that high risk prisoners are held in the highest security locations, while low risk prisoners can be held in category C or open conditions.

Prison categorisation

Male adult prisoners aged 21 years and over receive a security categorisation shortly after entering prison. These are based on a number of factors such as the severity of the crime they have been charged with (or convicted of), the likelihood of escape and the length of sentence given. Consideration is also given to the risk to the public if they did escape.

Table 21.1 lists the four categories of male adult prisoners in the UK.

Female adult prisoners are classified into four categories.

- Restricted Status is similar to Category A.
- Closed is for women who may attempt to escape.
- Semi-open is for those who are unlikely to try to escape.
- Open is for those who can be trusted to stay within the prison.

Offenders under the age of 21 years may be sent to:

- **Secure training centres** which are focused on education and hold offenders up to 17 years.

- **Local authority secure children's homes** which are managed by Social Services and deal with the physical, emotional and behavioural needs of vulnerable young people
- **Juvenile prisons** which accommodate 15–18-year-olds and are operated by the Prison Service, as are Young Offender Institutions which hold offenders aged 18–21 years.

Activity: Security

The Prison Service website states that 'security is the bedrock on which all of our efforts to develop positive regimes are based. We continually strive to improve our excellent security record that has seen no escapes by Category A prisoners since 1995.'

Security is an all-embracing term which incorporates:

- *physical security*: walls, bars, locks or even more modern devices such as closed circuit television
- *security procedures*: accounting for prisoners or searching cells
- *assessment procedures*: categorising prisoners to make sure that they are kept in appropriate security conditions.

1 **Discuss the implications of the need to ensure that physical and procedural security is followed in prisons.**

2 **Why do you think escapes from Category A prisons are used as the benchmark for successful security measures?**

3 **Would including absconds from open prisons give a more realistic picture of the success of security measures in prisons?**

Table 21.1: The four categories of male adult prisoners in the UK

Category	Description
Category A	Prisoners whose escape would be highly dangerous to the public or national security and who have committed very serious crimes. The types of offenders in this category are terrorists, multiple rapists and paedophiles.
Category B	Prisoners who do not require maximum security but their chance of escape has to be minimised. Prisoners will be considered for Category B if they have been sentenced to 10 years or over or have an indeterminate sentence with a tariff over 3 years. Other factors considered are having received a previous sentence of 10 years or over, previous escape from closed prison, the Police or escort, and a current or previous serious offence involving violence, threat to life, firearms, sex, arson, drugs or robbery.
Category C	Prisoners who cannot be trusted in open conditions but who are unlikely to try to escape. Prisoners with short sentences and those convicted of less serious crimes will normally be considered for open prisons (Category D) unless they: • have a previous sentence of a year plus for sex offending, drugs, violence, threat of violence or arson • have (within the past 3 years) breached bail, HDC or ROTL or absconded • have outstanding confiscation orders • face further charges at court.
Category D	Prisoners who can be reasonably trusted not to try to escape, and are given the privilege of an open prison. These prisoners are given ROTL (Release On Temporary Licence) to study, work or visit on 'home leave'.

Case study: Category A prisoners

Category A prisons hold many suspected and convicted terrorists and other dangerous prisoners. There are currently eight high security prisons holding 1000 category A prisoners in the UK. Prisoners on remand have to be presented at court for their court case to be prosecuted. However, potentially dangerous prisoners have to be kept secure at all times as they may present a threat to the public and may try to escape from custody. When high risk prisoners are moved they have to be in secure armoured vehicles accompanied by the Police (many of whom may be armed) and may also have a helicopter escort. The route may need to be checked in advance or even closed to the public.

As most high security prisons hold prisoners who have been charged by the Police in different areas of England and Wales, prisoners may need to be transported long distances for their court hearings.

There are two alternative strategies available. The first is using video links from within the prison to the court where the case is to be heard. The second is to schedule cases in the nearest court buildings – ideally those Crown Courts where a secure underground tunnel can be used to escort prisoners from the prison to the court buildings.

The court where the case is being heard may wish to have the prisoner physically present, especially for sentence, and the prisoner may feel disadvantaged if their case is heard by video link.

1 **What are the potential security issues raised by the movement of Category A prisoners?**

2 **Do you think prisoners should have the right to appear in court in person?**

Activity: Prison population

Using the data in the table below and by further research (see the Ministry of Justice website) find out:

- the most common offences
- the number of offenders with life sentences
- the number of sex offenders
- the variation in the capacity (number of prisoners that can be held) at different establishments.

Table 21.2: Prison population at June 2009 in England and Wales

Source: Ministry of Justice, Population in custody (monthly tables June 2009, England and Wales)

Total prisoners in custody	**83,887**
Adult (over 21) prisoners in custody	71,600
15–17-year-olds in custody and secure accommodation	2100
17–21-year-olds in custody	9800
Foreign nationals in prison in England and Wales	11,400
Prisoners on remand awaiting trial	8900
Convicted prisoners awaiting sentence	4500
Foreign nationals of Jamaican nationality	1060
Foreign nationals of Nigerian nationality	770
Male prisoners	79,481
Female prisoners	4296
Number with sentences of 4 years or more	24,497
Number of prisoners sentenced for offences against the person	19,950
Number of prisoners sentenced for drug-related offences	10,696
Number of prisoners held in HMP Wandsworth	1675
Number of foreign national prisoners held in HMP Wandsworth.	555

Assessment activity 21.1

The custodial care services have to hold offenders in a secure environment both to protect society and to ensure the safety of the offenders.

Produce an introductory leaflet to go into a new Prison Officer's induction pack that describes all the aspects of physical security and patrolling, dynamic security, including the role of staff and intelligence, and procedural security including the way custodial establishments are categorised **P1**.

Grading tips

The elements that contribute to security in custody are complex and to achieve **P1** you will need to describe the physical, dynamic and procedural security considerations in a custodial environment.

Describe means you need to give a clear description that includes all the relevant features – think of it as 'painting a picture with words'. Use the unit content as a checklist to ensure you cover all required information to achieve this criteria.

PLTS

By producing an introductory leaflet you will demonstrate your skills as a **self-manager**.

Functional skills

Producing a leaflet may help you to develop your functional skills in **English** (and in **ICT** if you word-process your answer).

2. Know how control is maintained in the custodial environment

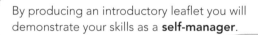

2.1 Searches

The Prison Service uses searching as part of its overall security processes. Searching can be planned and systematic or random, routine or intelligence-led.

Everyone entering the custodial environment (prisoners, staff, official visitors, prisoner's visitors, contractors, etc.) are subject to searching before entry. The type of searching will depend on the likely risk to security that a specific individual poses to the overall security and the Category of the establishment. All prisoners are searched at reception.

High security prisons (which hold Category A prisoners) will routinely search all visitors and staff. Most prisons have airport-style security gates through which all those entering the establishment must pass. They also have airport-style x-ray machines to check bags, coats and shoes being brought through. In contrast,

Category C establishments may let pre-booked official visitors through the gates with no physical searching.

In addition to searching individuals, property will be searched and any prohibited items (such as metal cutlery, scissors, computers, mobile phones, alcohol, drugs and weapons) will not be allowed entry.

All goods arriving at the establishment will be screened, including post and supplies. This is important as illegal items can be smuggled inside the prison in a huge number of ways. For example, drugs can be concealed in the spine binding of books and magazines.

Prison staff also search cells and other parts of the building on a routine and intelligence-led basis. They also patrol the perimeter walls, looking for items that have been thrown into the prison. These can include a variety of illicit items such as mobile phones, drugs and alcohol.

Searching may involve the use of various hand-held and floor-mounted detectors and both active and passive dogs. Searching aims to stop any prohibited goods entering the secure environment and to identify and confiscate any which have managed to bypass security checks. These goods could be used to undermine good order, for example to threaten, blackmail, intimidate or injure others or to assist attempts to escape.

Searches have to be conducted correctly and thoroughly, but it is vital to respect individuals and their property during the searching procedures.

Rub-down searches

All searches are used to check that the person (prior to entering the prison) has no prohibited items in their possession. Staff conducting any searches must be trained and any searches must normally be carried out by a member of prison staff of the same sex. Rub-down searches check that nothing is attached to the body externally, but they will not identify items hidden internally.

Electronic wands

Electronic wands and walk-through security portals will identify metal (and some other items) secreted on the person. The use of dogs in searching may help to identify drugs hidden on an individual. The Prison Service has recently introduced the Body Orifice Security Scanner (BOSS) chair, which may be used where there is suspicion that items have been secreted internally.

Searching of visitors

Searching procedures should always be explained before being carried out and posters outlining searching procedures should be displayed. Prisoner's visitors will be issued with a Visiting Order and this should include information about searching procedures in use at the particular establishment.

If an individual wishing to enter the establishment refuses to be searched, they will be denied entry. This applies to official visitors, prisoner's visitors and staff.

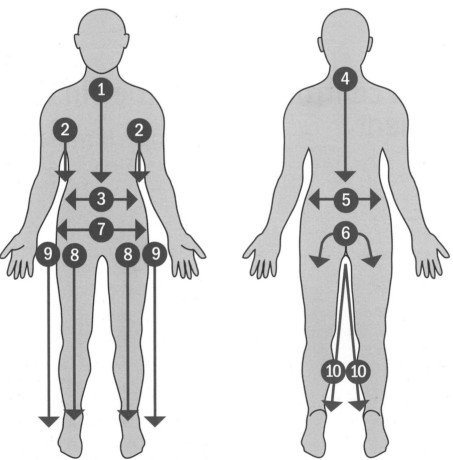

Figure 21.1: Procedure for rub-down search. Staff carrying out the search place their hands on the person being searched in the order shown, moving their hands in the direction of the arrows. This process enables them to check for prohibited items.

Case study: The BOSS scanner

In 2009 the Prison Service agreed the introduction of a new security scanner called BOSS (Body Orifice Security Scanner). The BOSS is a non-intrusive scanning system within a moulded chair, designed to detect small metallic objects, such as mobile phones and their component parts or weapons, concealed internally by individuals.

The BOSS uses the same technology as metal detecting gates used in airports. Sensors are housed in the chair frame and each sensor in the chair is wired to an audible alarm which will sound if any metal is detected. A button on the alarm panel will also light up on detection.

The equipment is not harmful to the person being scanned and its use is no more intrusive than that of a walk-through archway scanner or hand-held metal detector. It may be used to:

- scan prisoners, social, official and professional visitors and prison staff
- as a searching aid to complement a rub-down search

The individual being searched must be made aware of the purpose of the BOSS and how it works.

BOSS information notices are distributed to prisoners and staff and made available to social, official and professional visitors. Prisoner's visitors should be advised that they may be subject to a search using the BOSS on entry to the prison.

The person being searched should be asked if they are in possession of an unauthorised item before the search is conducted and given the opportunity to dispose of any secreted item in private. Two staff members must conduct the search: one to explain the process and observe the subject of the search, and the other to monitor the equipment alarm panel.

If BOSS gives a positive indication, the subject of the search must be allowed to provide an explanation. For example, it is possible that an intimate body piercing or a medically inserted metal plate may set off the alarm.

What are the advantages and disadvantages of using this type of electronic detection equipment?

Activity: Prison security

A tutor (well-known to prison staff) set off the security alarms when screened for entry into a male high security prison where she was due to teach literacy to a group of prisoners. Despite removing her jewellery and shoes the alarm still activated. The prison staff refused her access until she had agreed to be physically searched. She refused.

1   **Should the tutor have been allowed in to the prison?**
2   **What security risks might she pose?**

Prohibited items such as computers, cameras, memory sticks, phones, SIM cards, drugs, alcohol and weapons will be refused entry (and may be confiscated). It is an offence to take a prohibited item in to a prison. Anyone found taking a prohibited item into an establishment is liable to be prosecuted.

Searching of prisoners

If a prisoner refuses a search they will be given a direct order to comply. If they refuse to comply the prisoner would normally be located in the segregation unit (or the equivalent) and fully searched. Prison officers are allowed to use 'reasonable force' when undertaking the search, in accordance with prison rules.

2.2 Control measures

The need for prisons to be a safe and secure environment for both staff and prisoners means that a clear set of policies and procedures have to be in place for an effective response when there are any breaches of prison rules.

Minor breaches of prison rules will be dealt with informally. Often this involves the prisoner's Personal Officer discussing with the prisoner the importance of not breaking rules and the possible consequences if the rule breaking persists.

Breaches of rules may involve things like fighting, stealing property, racial abuse, being found in possession of illegal items like drugs, alcohol, mobile phones and failing mandatory drug testing.

Prison managers are authorised to operate Minor Reports systems to deal with some charges brought against prisoners aged under 21. If these charges are proved the punishments available include a caution, loss of privileges, loss of earnings or extra work.

The formal prisoner discipline process is known as 'adjudication'. There are approximately 100,000 disciplinary hearings held in prisons each year. These adjudications are carried out by either prison managers or by independent adjudicators, who have the power to award up to 42 extra days imprisonment for each offence.

An adjudication serves two purposes:

* It aims to help maintain discipline, control and order and keep the custodial environment safe.
* It aims to make sure the use of authority by prison staff is fair and just.

Report writing

The procedures for prison discipline are set out in the *PSO 2000 (amended 2008) Prison Discipline Manual*. This Manual must be made available to all prisoners to ensure adjudications are conducted in accordance with the law and without discrimination.

A Notice of Report (or form F1127A – see Figure 21.2) will be completed by the member of staff who witnessed the offence or against whom the offence was committed. This charge must be made within 48 hours of the offence being discovered.

Adjudication

The adjudication heard by a Governor may permit the accused to have legal assistance or a **McKenzie friend**.

The prisoner is entitled to appeal against the finding of such a hearing.

At an adjudication heard by an independent adjudicator the prisoner is entitled to request legal assistance. There is no appeal against the decision of this hearing.

Key term

McKenzie friend – a member of the chaplaincy, a probation officer, a tutor or a fellow prisoner.

Verbal caution

A verbal caution is available as a punishment for any case where a warning seems sufficient to recognise the offence and to discourage its repetition. A verbal caution cannot be combined with any other punishment as a result of the same charge.

Other punishments include:

* additional days (only permitted if sentenced by the independent adjudicator)
* being confined to the cell
* exclusion from association
* loss of privileges
* removal from the wing
* loss of earnings.

Case study: Prison rules

Under Section 51 of the prison rules, the following behaviours are some of those classified as offences:

* assault (including racially aggravated assault)
* detaining another against their will
* denying access to any part of the prison to any officer or any person (other than a prisoner) who is at the prison for the purpose of working there
* fighting
* intentionally endangering the health or safety of others
* intentionally obstructing an officer in the execution of duty
* escapes or absconding from prison or from legal custody
* using controlled drugs or being intoxicated
* possession of any unauthorised article
* taking improperly any article belonging to another
* setting fire to any part of a prison or any other property
* absenting self from any place where he is required or being present at any place where he is not authorised to be
* being disrespectful to any officer or any person working at or visiting a prison
* using threatening, abusive or insulting words or behaviour
* disobeying any lawful order, rule or regulation.

1 **Do you think this list of offences is reasonable?**
2 **What other offences might breach the rules?**

F1127A - NOTICE OF REPORT
COPY FOR PRISONER

Charge number [   ]

First name(s) .... Surname ....

Number..

You have been placed on report by ....

for an alleged offence which was committed at..................... hours on..(date)

at .... (place)

The offence with which you are charged is that you:

Contrary to Rule .... Paragraph........................ Prison/YOI Rules
(Delete as appropriate)

The report of the alleged offence is as follows:

Signature of reporting Officer ....

Your case will be heard at .... hours on..(date)

You will have every opportunity to make your defence. If you wish to write out what you want to say you may

ask for writing paper. You or the adjudicator may read it out at the hearing.

You may also say whether you wish to call any witnesses.

This form was issued to you at... hours on...(date)

by...(name of issuing officer - block capitals)

....☐

OR016 Printed by HMP Albany

Figure 21.2: Notice of Report (form F1127A), to be completed
within 48 hours of the offence being committed by the prisoner

Incentives for good behaviour

In contrast to punishment for poor behaviour, the Prison Service also operates a scheme of incentives and earned privileges (IEP). This means that prisoners have the opportunity to get extra privileges through good behaviour but lose those privileges if they misbehave.

The range of privileges available depends on which jail the prisoner is in. Local IEP schemes must include the following privileges:

- access to in-cell television for standard and enhanced prisoners
- access to own cash to spend (on top of their prison wages) on phone calls or in the prison shop (canteen)
- additional visits
- eligibility to participate in higher rate pay schemes
- wearing own clothes
- more time out of cell for socialising.

Every prison's regime is based on a system which places each prisoner on one of the following three levels:

- basic
- standard
- enhanced.

Most prisons operate a system which starts prisoners on the basic level. Privileges can then be earned which enhance a prisoner's daily life in prison. These privileges vary, but the key ones are listed in Table 21.3.

How effective do you think incentives for good behaviour are in encouraging prisoners to behave well while in prison?

Table 21.3: Levels of privilege awarded in prison

Level	Description
Basic	The minimum standard of facilities to which someone is entitled to regardless of their behaviour. It includes visits, letters, telephone calls, provision of food and clothing, access to the prison shop, exercise and socialising. Prisoners will be expected to take part in activities such as education, work programmes, exercise and religious observance.
Standard	Provides the prisoner with more privileges and facilities such as in-cell TV, more visits and phone calls and more out of cell association time.
Enhanced	Prisoners have further privileges such as access to more personal money, better prison jobs and higher rates of pay.

Restraint techniques

Prisons are a closed and unnatural environment and on occasions staff will need to exercise a range of techniques, including physical restraint, to maintain control. Any use of force must be reasonable and not excessive. The aim is to restore control with minimum physical intervention. Officers are highly trained in a range of control and restraint techniques and are skilled at assessing the level of danger and the need for control and restraint in any given situation.

As part of their training prison officers learn:

- how to identify possible areas of conflict and minimise conflict situations
- how to deal with aggressive and unwanted behaviours and reduce tension
- techniques of non-verbal, verbal and physical intervention
- how any incidents must be recorded
- legal requirements in relation to restraint.

All members of staff involved in the use of control and restraint (C&R), including the supervising officer, must complete a *Use of Force Form* after any incident.

Activity: Appropriate control and restraint (C&R) techniques

Control and Restraint (C&R) techniques are used by the Prison Service as a last resort in order to bring a violent or disobedient prisoner under control while minimising risk of injury to staff or prisoners. The techniques must be applied for as short a time as is possible and throughout any incident staff must continue to attempt to de-escalate the situation.

C&R techniques are detailed in a training manual which is issued to prison Governors and local C&R instructors. Basic techniques are used by a team of three or four officers in order to manage a violent prisoner. C&R must only be used as a last resort after all other means of de-escalating the incident (such as negotiation) have failed.

The use of force is lawful only if it is:

- reasonable
- proportionate
- necessary
- no more than necessary in the circumstances.

1   **Do you think it is reasonable for staff to use physical force and restraint against a prisoner?**

2   **What controls need to be in place to ensure prisoners are not unnecessarily restrained?**

Assessment activity 21.2

1 Outline the types and methods of searches conducted by staff in a custodial environment. **P2**

2 Describe control measures in place in a custodial environment. **P3**

3 Justify the use of adjudications and incentive schemes in relation to addressing offending behaviour and the maintenance of control. **M1**

4 Evaluate the need for security and control in a custodial environment. **D1**

Grading tips

For **P2** you need to write a clear description or give a summary of the essential points, but you do not have to give a detailed response. Make sure you refer to all aspects listed in the unit content.

For **P3** you need to provide a clear description that includes all the relevant features of the control measures, both sanctions imposed for breaches of rules and incentives provided for good behaviour.

For **M1** you should develop what you have described in P3, giving reasons and examples to support your opinion or views to show how you arrived at your conclusions.

For **D1** you will need to go a stage further and evaluate the need for security and control. This means you will need to present a reasoned case as to why these measures are necessary in the custodial environment, giving arguments to support your opinions. You will need to include a conclusion based on your views of the need to have such measures in place.

PLTS

By evaluating the need for security and control in a custodial environment you will demonstrate your skills as a **reflective learner**.

Functional skills

Using clear descriptions and reasoned arguments in your writing will help you to develop your functional skills in **English**.

3 Understand the receiving and discharging procedures for individuals and their property

3.1 Receiving individuals

Most prisoner escort is now carried out by private companies. Once the courts have decided an individual is to be remanded in custody or given a custodial sentence, the prisoner must be transported to a custodial environment. When the prisoner arrives at a prison they will be taken to the reception area where the following activities must take place.

- The prison staff must confirm the prisoner's identity and verify the legality of the prisoner's detention. For this to take place there must be documentation from the court, for example a warrant, that names the prisoner and gives information such as their address and date of birth and the reason for their detention.

- Prison staff must check and record essential information such as the name, address and

Case study: Prison rules

Each prison decides what items prisoners are allowed and this list is governed by volumetric control (see page 190). Typically the following are allowed subject to security checks:

- newspapers, magazines and books
- a combined sound system, or a radio with records, cassettes or CDs
- smoking materials (where smoking is allowed)
- electronic games and players
- materials related to hobbies
- one birdcage and one small bird
- writing and drawing materials
- a wrist watch
- an electric shaver
- toiletries for personal use

- a plain ring
- one medallion
- religious texts and items
- photographs and pictures
- unpadded greetings cards
- a calendar
- a diary
- an address book
- postage stamps and envelopes
- prescribed medication
- disability aids.

1   **Why do you think prisons have lists of allowed items?**

2   **Why do you think volumetric control is needed?**

---

telephone number of the prisoner's next of kin and the prisoner's religion. The prisoner must have fingerprints and photographs taken and recorded. Other information such as being a foreign national, not being able to speak English or being a member of the armed forces must also be recorded.

- Reception staff have to identify if a prisoner may be at risk of suicide or self-harm, and ensure such prisoners are kept safe. Vulnerable prisoners must not be placed in shared cells (so a single cell risk assessment should be completed) and first-time prisoners should be identified (as they may be at particular risk of self-harm).

- Prisoners and their property then need to be searched. Prisoners will receive a rub-down search immediately on reception followed by a full search undertaken by two prison officers of the same sex as the prisoner (in accordance with the local searching strategy of the prison and the National Security Framework). Property will be searched for items which are not allowed (these vary between establishments and a list of prohibited items should always be displayed in Reception).

Health checks

During prisoner reception, prison staff must also identify any immediate potential risk the prison may pose to themselves, other prisoners, staff and the public. The following activities must take place before the prisoner is locked up for their first night:

- suicide/self-harm screening
- cell-sharing risk assessment
- medical risk assessment.

Most of this assessment is undertaken by reception staff or staff on a dedicated induction unit or the personal officer. Medical assessments are undertaken by a member of the healthcare staff.

Induction

Prisoner induction may take place by admitting the prisoner to a special induction unit for the first night(s) of their imprisonment, or induction may take place on the wing the prisoner has been allocated to.

Induction should cover the basic rights the prisoner has and the basic information about the prison regime, for example, meal times, washing facilities, times of religious worship, association and exercise.

Most prisons have a written induction pack which is given to new prisoners and explained to them either by their Personal Officer (a prison officer who takes responsibility for monitoring and reporting on named prisoners) or by another prisoner (a Listener, who is specially trained to assist new prisoners on arrival and help them settle in to the routine of the particular establishment).

As many prisoners are foreign nationals, publications are often available in a range of languages. Some prisons have made videos to show prisoners the layout and facilities and to help where prisoner reading and language skills are poor.

3.2 Property procedures

A full inventory of the prisoner's property must be taken. Reception staff must check any property bags received with a prisoner against the property seals listed on the Prisoner Escort Record (which will be received by the prison when the prisoner is handed over to the custody of prison staff). Any discrepancies must be dealt with at Reception. Prisoner property which is to be stored must be searched and resealed with the establishment's own unique property seal.

All property (including cash) must then be recorded on property record cards and any items that a prisoner claims to be valuable must be separately listed. Reception staff should explain how and where the prisoner's property will be stored. Finally, individual records of prisoner property must be signed by staff and the prisoner concerned.

Prisoners are allowed to keep items listed on the establishment's list of approved property in accordance with **volumetric control** (clearly there is limited storage space in a prisoner's cell so maximum volumes of property are set). Prisoners are not allowed to bring food and other perishable items into the custodial environment so these must be destroyed in the prisoner's presence.

During their period of custody prisoners may have access to their property (if it is an approved item) and may exchange property held in the cell and stored property to maintain volumetric control limits.

On discharge from custody the prisoner's property will be returned to them. On transfer to another establishment, prisoner property will also be transferred.

Key term

Volumetric control – the amount of property a prisoner is allowed in their cell is measured by volume. Property must fit within these set guidelines.

3.3 Discharging prisoners

Before discharging a prisoner, a similar procedure must be completed, including:

- full document check
- prisoner identity check
- prisoner search
- return of property
- issue of any discharge grant and travel documents
- issue of any prescription medicines
- issue of discharge clothing
- signing (by prisoner) of their discharge certificate.

Did you know?

Prison staff take a proactive role in coping with the differing needs of foreign national prisoners.

- Many establishments hold regular meetings between staff and prisoners to discuss the challenges facing foreign nationals (immigration status, staying in contact with family, language difficulties and resettlement).
- Many prisons produce magazines providing helpful advice and points of contact for prisoners during their time in custody.
- The booklet *Information and Advice for Foreign National Prisoners* is available across the prison estate in 22 languages and contains substantial information on issues including prison regimes, support organisations and contacting families.

Did you know?

The number of foreign nationals in prison has doubled and now represents over 14 per cent of the total prison population in England and Wales. There are a huge range of nationalities and languages to be considered alongside the cultural and religious diversity that the foreign nationals already bring.

- As of the end of June 2007, 10,097 foreign nationals were in British jails.
- These prisoners come from 169 different countries. The largest groups are prisoners from Jamaica, Nigeria, Vietnam, Pakistan and the Irish Republic.
- The majority of foreign national prisoners have committed drugs offences.

Activity: Procedures for the reception and discharge of prisoners

Use the three documents referenced below to find the answers to these questions:

1 What essential information must be recorded at first reception?

2 What actions must be taken by staff when a prisoner is received into custody?

3 What rights do prisoners have when being received into custody?

4 What are the Reception procedures for prisoner property?

5 When discharging a prisoner from prison, what must prison staff confirm?

6 What is the Multi-Agency Public Protection Arrangements (MAPPA) and how does it allow the Criminal Justice Agencies to manage the assessed risk posed by the offender on their release into the community?

7 What are the three categories of offenders who are managed by MAPPA?

8 What rights do prisoners have when being discharged from custody?

The following documents can be accessed from HM Prison Service website (www.hmprisonservice.gov.uk). From the Home page, click on the 'Resource Centre' tab, then select 'List PSOs' from the 'PSIs and PSOs' drop-down menu on the left of the screen.

- Prison Service Order 6400: Prisoner Discharge
- Prison Service Order 1250: Prisoners Property
- Prison Service Order 0500: Prisoner Reception.

Assessment activity 21.3

Depriving someone of their liberty is a serious matter so it is vital that checks are put into place to ensure the law and procedures are followed. Similarly it is vital to ensure that those discharged from custody are the correct individuals and that they are supported on discharge to comply with any conditions attached to their discharge.

For this assessment activity you will need to explain the process for the receipt and discharge of prisoners and property.

Task

Prepare a PowerPoint presentation for prison officers about to transfer to Reception, to help them learn the requirements of their role there.

Your presentation should explain the process of receiving and discharging individuals and their property into and from the custodial environment.

P4

Grading tips

To achieve P4 you need to include in your presentation the following key points:

- *When receiving prisoners*: recording of essential information, searching and security requirements, listing of property and property procedures, health checks, reception interview with Personal Officer, induction into prison.

- *When discharging prisoners*: required procedures including identification of individual's security needs on release, terms of release, any pre-release conditions and completion of all documentation and records.

PLTS

By organising your explanation into an effective PowerPoint presentation, you will demonstrate your skills as a **creative thinker**.

Functional skills

Creating a PowerPoint presentation will help you to develop your functional skills in **ICT**.

4 Understand how offenders can build positive relationships in custody

4.1 Relationships

The importance of building and maintaining positive relationships between prisoners and those they come into contact with, both while in custody and on release, cannot be over stressed.

- If a prisoner has been mixing with other offenders before being convicted and imprisoned, and has little positive support or role models in the community they come from, the danger is that on release they will return to that environment and will begin offending again. But if the prisoner can build positive relationships which lead to opportunities for work or constructive study, the chances of reoffending are greatly reduced.

- Prisoners may well have alienated family and friends and may find it difficult to reintegrate into society on release. Inevitably there is a social stigma attached to those who have served custodial sentences, and by being taken into custody, jobs, family links and housing may have been lost.

- Other prisoners may be positive role models, for example prisoners who act as listeners for those involved in delivering the Toe by Toe reading programmes (see next page). These schemes encourage prisoners to take responsibility for themselves, which is not an easy thing to do in an institution like a prison where life is largely dictated by the prison regime.

- Maintaining relationships with family and friends is especially important. Prisoners are entitled to visits, although these take place in a supervised environment which can make them stressful for both prisoner and visitor. Children are generally allowed to visit, but this can also create stresses. Initiatives to build and retain relationships between prisoners and their children include open days and encouraging offenders to tape bedtime stories for their kids or write stories and letters to send to them.

- Probation officers are important for the prisoner's rehabilitation, both while in custody and on release. Probation officers work with prison staff to agree the programmes the prisoner needs to complete as part of their attempt to address their reoffending. They also help to plan the prisoner's reintegration into society on release.

- Volunteers can help prisoners both during custody and on release. Schemes like Toe by Toe and Storybook Dads rely on volunteers, and the Samaritans are active in prisons, supporting prisoners and training Listeners. Prisons have multi-faith Chaplaincy departments which are staffed by paid staff and volunteers, thus ensuring all prisoners of faith groups can be supported and links with families maintained.

Activity: Storybook Dads

Storybook Dads (covers mums too!) gets the imprisoned parent to record stories and a message which is then downloaded onto a computer. Using digital audio software, trained prisoners then edit out mistakes and background noises and add sound effects and music.

The advantage of the editing process is that parents who are poor readers or non-readers can still participate. A mentor simply reads each line for them to repeat and then the mentor's voice is edited out.

Finally, the CD or DVD is burned off, a personalised cover is created and the finished disc is sent to the child. The prisoners do not have to pay for the CD, but many choose to make a donation.

Story writing workshops are also held where prisoners are encouraged to create a personalised, fully illustrated story book and CD where their child is the main character. The children are thrilled with these gifts and it helps to keep them in touch with their absent parent.

Find out more about Storybook Dads by visiting their website (www.storybookdads.co.uk).

1 **Produce a leaflet which explains the work of Storybook Dads to volunteers who would like to help with this project.**

2 **Write a letter to the local press explaining how this project could help the Prison Service in its aim of rehabilitating offenders.**

4.2 The prison environment

Prison is a difficult environment so it is vital that there is provision of support for all prisoners throughout their sentence.

Toe by Toe

Prisoners who have problems communicating or developing relationships with others within the custodial environment need special support. This may be provided by fellow prisoners through mentoring and buddy schemes and schemes such as Toe by Toe and Support for Literacy. Listeners who have been trained by the Samaritans are a vital support to other prisoners who feel depressed and vulnerable or who are missing family links.

Chaplaincy

The Chaplaincy in every prison establishment is committed to serving the needs of prisoners, staff and faith communities. Chaplains from a wide range of faith traditions work with the Prison Service, including:

- Buddhist
- Church of England
- Free Church
- Hindu
- Jewish
- Muslim
- Roman Catholic
- Sikh.

Chaplains are appointed on the basis of their skills and abilities, and to meet the need of prisons and their particular populations. One of the key roles of the Chaplaincy is to meet every prisoner after reception into custody and talk to them about family links, emotional and spiritual needs and the prisoner's personal well-being.

Personal Officer scheme

The Personal Officer scheme was introduced to ensure that when prisoners first arrive at prison a named officer is there for the prisoner to turn to for help and advice. All Youth Offender Institutions have Personal Officer schemes, as do most adult prisons. The Personal Officer is a prisoner's first port of call if they have questions, complaints or need advice. They also get involved in developing and managing the prisoner's sentence plan, helping the offender to make the best use of their time in prison and preparing them for a law-abiding life on release.

4.3 Dealing with offending behaviour

Assessment of individual behaviour

To achieve the Prison Service's statement of purpose, the individual's offending behaviour and its causes must be addressed. Depending on the offence the prisoner has been convicted for and the analysis undertaken of that prisoner when received into custody after sentence, a plan will be drawn up that helps the individual attend various offending behaviour programmes and receive education and training to enable them to start to prepare for life on release.

Provision to address offending behaviour

Basic literacy and numeracy education may be offered, as are programmes such as shopping, nutrition and cooking, and training and skills development linked to qualifications such as NVQs. These tend to be in practical subjects such as catering, sports management, environmental management, plumbing and brick laying. Prisoners may also be offered the opportunity to study for GCSEs, A Levels and degrees by distance learning, computer-based learning or formal education classes.

Offending behaviour programmes aim to identify what has caused the prisoner to offend and what behavioural factors (physical, social, psychological, emotional) have contributed to the offence. Programme planning for an individual also looks at triggers to the offending and patterns of offending.

Changing behaviour positively is not easy. It requires a commitment by the offender to work with the psychologists and programme staff in the establishment to take ownership and responsibility for their own behaviour and the decisions they make, both positive and negative.

Recent initiatives (called restorative justice) have encouraged offenders to address the impact of their crimes on the victims and the need for those victims to be protected from further offences.

Psychologists conduct individual offender risk assessments or oversee and assist with the delivery of interventions based on their initial findings. They advise on the best location for relevant prisoners (based on the need for specific programmes, which are only available in certain establishments). They also provide lifer reports and parole reports for prisoners applying for early release.

Offending behaviour programmes

Enhanced Thinking Skills

Enhanced Thinking Skills (ETS) is a relatively short programme which addresses thinking and behaviour associated with offending. This includes impulse control, flexible thinking, social perspective taking, moral reasoning, inter-personal skills and problem solving. Over 40,000 offenders have completed this course over the past 12 years.

Controlling Anger and Learning to Manage It (CALM)

CALM is a programme for offenders whose offending is associated with poor emotional control. CALM works to enable prisoners to manage the emotions (such as anger, jealousy and anxiety) which are associated with their offending.

Sex Offender Treatment Programmes (SOTP)

SOTP is a range of programmes intended for sex offenders. The specific programme is designed according to the needs of the individual offender and the level of risk they pose to society.

Choices, Actions, Relationships and Emotions (CARE)

CARE is a programme for female offenders where their offending behaviour is linked to the need to manage emotions. The programme aims to develop a positive self-identity to help offenders on release.

Activity: The Shannon Project

The Shannon Project aims to set up Toe by Toe reading schemes in prisons.

- 67 per cent of prisoners do not have the reading and writing skills necessary to do 80 per cent of the jobs in the labour market, so the chances of them returning to crime are high.
- 48 per cent of the prison population have a reading ability below that expected of an 11-year-old.
- The Toe by Toe Reading Plan is a peer mentoring programme which encourages and supports prisoners who can read to give one-to-one tuition to prisoners who struggle to read.
- In both 2007 and 2008 the Project provided resources to teach over 5000 prisoners to read or to improve their reading skills.
- Trained volunteers help staff and prisoners set up and maintain a reading plan that is tailored to the needs of the specific establishment.
- Copies of Toe by Toe are provided to every learner and every prisoner involved in mentoring others.
- Mentors ensure learning takes place five times a week and lasts no more than 20 minutes each session.
- Mentors ensure learning is one-to-one and takes place in a suitable environment.

Why does the scheme work? The scheme costs the establishment very little money and staff time and gives prisoners (both mentors and learners) responsibility for learning.

1 **Produce a FAQ sheet to give out to new prison staff explaining the Toe by Toe project. Include information to explain why improving literacy skills will help prisoners on release and contribute to reducing reoffending.**

2 **Work in pairs to write a script for a radio interview where a newly released prisoner explains the benefits to him and his family of completing the Toe by Toe programme. If possible record your interview to play to the rest of your group.**

4.4 Preparation for resettlement

Resettlement is more than simply discharging the prisoner from custody. It also involves offering support with drug and alcohol misuse, financial exclusion, temporary accommodation, homelessness, chaotic lifestyle, separation from children and families, domestic violence and abuse. Research has identified that these issues, if not addressed, are likely to result in the prisoner reoffending. It is therefore vital that the professionals involved in resettlement take a joint approach. Prison and probation staff work closely with local authority housing sections, job centres, educational providers and charities (such as NACRO and Bridging the Gap) to ensure the prisoner has accommodation and employment or training available on discharge.

Supporting a crime-free life

Once released the offender will need to be supported to help avoid returning to a life of crime. This support will include the provision of somewhere to live, a job, training or further education opportunities and help with building new social networks.

Resettlement is where the prisoner is given support and help from the probation and prison services and voluntary agencies to help prepare for life after release. They are given information about such things as state benefits, training, education and work experience. The aim is to help prisoners return to normal life, get a home and job and not re-offend.

Preparation outside the custodial environment

Prisoners preparing for release may be asked to attend groups or courses to help them with any behaviour problems they may have, such as alcohol or drug abuse, gambling, financial pressures, depression, aggression or lack of temper control, or sexual problems. These courses help prisoners deal with the issues they may face after being released.

NACRO has a computer-based service (called EASI) that provides up-to-date information on housing, employment, training, money, education and benefits. It also provides a counselling service.

> ### Did you know?
>
> NACRO is a charitable organisation that works with disadvantaged people, offenders and those at risk of offending. It runs a wide range of services, from working with young people in trouble to providing accommodation for ex-offenders and helping people develop new skills and qualifications. For more information visit www.nacro.org.uk.

Resettlement units

Resettlement units are designed to help prisoners, particularly those serving longer sentences, prepare for release. As part of the resettlement arrangements some prisoners are able to go out to training or work from the unit or prison and return when they have finished.

Working in the local community

Working in the local community can also give prisoners the chance to build self-confidence and at the same time develop a sense of social responsibility. The work can include local environment projects, working with the elderly or people with disabilities, sports activities and fundraising.

Many prisons run their own job clubs in which advice and assistance are available to prisoners on how to look for jobs, including how to prepare a CV and interview technique.

Advice and support

Advice and support is available to prisoners on financial matters during custody to assist in their resettlement after release. Prisons work in partnership with Jobcentre Plus, who are able to help prisoners with benefit claims such as Housing Benefit and will advise on claiming benefits when released. At discharge, prisoners may be eligible for money in addition to a discharge grant to help secure accommodation.

Prisoners released on licence

Prisoners released on licence have to clearly understand the terms of that licence and that they can be recalled to prison if they breach the licence terms.

Assessment activity 21.4

(P5) (P6) (P7) (M2) (D2) **BTEC**

Part of the rationale for custody is to work with offenders and enable them to address their offending behaviour and the consequences of that behaviour to themselves, their victims, their families and wider society. Produce a report that:

1 assesses the importance of building positive relationships for offenders **P5**

2 identifies how offending behaviour is addressed in custody **P6**

3 explains how offenders are prepared for rehabilitation and release **P7**

4 analyses how developing positive relationships and addressing offending behaviour benefits the individual and society **M2**

5 appraises the impact of offending behaviour programmes. **D2**

Grading tips

For **P5** you need to give careful consideration to all the factors or events that apply to building positive relationships, highlighting the most important or relevant. Your answer should cover relationships both inside the custodial context and external relationships.

For **P6** you need to give a list of the main methods employed to address offending behaviour, but you do not need to provide detail.

For **P7** use the unit content as a checklist and set out in detail what happens to prepare offenders for release and why.

For **M2** you will need to identify the key points and how these benefit both the individual offender and society overall. It may help to use examples to illustrate your answer.

For **D2** you will need to consider the positive and negative points of offering offender management programmes and reach a reasoned judgement about whether their overall impact is beneficial. To answer this effectively you will need to research data relating to reoffending and the costs of providing programmes for offenders. You should also consider the potential impact on society of offenders being released without being made to take responsibility for their crimes.

PLTS

By appraising the impact of offending behaviour programmes, you will demonstrate your skills as a **reflective learner**.

Functional skills

Producing a report will help you to develop your functional skills in **English**. If you word-process your response, you will also develop your functional skills in **ICT**.

Rachel Clarke
Forensic Psychologist

I work in a busy team of psychologists, psychology assistants, prison officers and administrative support staff. Together we are responsible for delivery and assessment of a range of offending programmes offered in the prison, and for assessing the suitability of specific prisoners to undertake each of those programmes.

Although I am part of this multi-disciplinary team I also have a lead role in managing the assessment process for individual prisoners. We carry out one-to-one assessments with prisoners to identify the risk of re-offending (especially for sex offenders after a treatment programme or lifers being released into the community) or the risks of self-harm, suicide, or other behaviour which has the potential to harm the offender, other prisoners or staff.

In my eight years working for the Prison Service I've delivered a range of programmes, including enhanced thinking skills and CALM, and have worked with female offenders, prisoners with life sentences and sex offenders. I've also been involved in research projects in which the Prison Service has tried to assess the effectiveness of specific programmes.

Typical day

Our work has a routine because the programmes we offer have to be planned and timetabled well in advance. This is because we need to ensure that we have appropriately qualified staff to deliver the programme as well as suitable classrooms for delivery. We also need to check that the work of our department fits into the overall prison regime. Assessments also have to be planned and are often needed by a parole board or the probation service, since the reports can be used when deciding if early release or release on licence is appropriate.

Twice during my career I have been involved in hostage negotiation situations, advising the prison Governor throughout the crisis period.

The best things about the job

I really enjoy being able to undertake research and working on a one-to-one basis with individuals. I initially joined the Prison Service as a psychology assistant and have received fantastic training which has given me the opportunity to progress to my current role. I love working in a multi-disciplinary environment but that can have its frustrations. Other staff, especially uniformed colleagues, can be quite dismissive of the role of the psychology department and the importance of programmes, so I spend a fair bit of time developing awareness sessions for the whole of the prison's staff. This includes running a session as part of new staff induction. To me the key is that all of the staff in an establishment are essential parts of the overall team and we need to work together!

Think about it!

- How does the work of the psychology department support addressing offending behaviour?
- How do psychologists support the courts and their decision making?
- Why is it important that staff in the Prison Service work in multi-disciplinary teams and understand the roles of all their colleagues?

Just checking

1. Explain the terms listed below:
   - Offending behaviour
   - Pro social modelling
   - Resettlement.
2. Why is it important that Reception complete a single-cell risk assessment when a prisoner is received into custody?
3. Identify three behaviour modification programmes and summarise the purpose of each.
4. Explain the different categories of male prisons and how prisoners are categorised.
5. Define the three key types of security considerations the prison estate operates to.
6. What Licence Conditions might apply to a sex offender on discharge?
7. Explain the purpose of Youth Offender Institutes and the types of prisoners these hold.
8. What is the National Security Framework? Why it is important to the work of HMPS?
9. Summarise the role of forensic psychology in addressing offending behaviour.
10. Hold a class discussion reviewing the merits and issues of a liberal prison regime which permits prisoners access to TV, play stations and PIN phones.

edexcel

Assignment tips

- Make sure you refer to the unit content section of each unit when you are writing your assignments. This will give you a good idea of the topics you need to cover for each of the pass criteria.
- When you are researching for your assignments (both classroom tasks and formal assessed assignments) look out for government websites (that end .gov.uk) as these will provide reliable information or will lead you to other reliable sites.
- Prison service policies can be located at www.hmprisonservice.gov.uk. They are found by clicking on the 'Resource Centre' tab and then selecting the 'PSIs and PSOs' menu on the left of the screen.
- Information about prisons run by private sector organisations can be found at www.hmprisonservice.gov.uk/prisoninformation/privateprison. These prisons are regulated in the same way as public (state run) prisons in England and Wales.

22 Aspects of the legal system and the law making process

The legal system of England and Wales can appear very complex and daunting at times, with its long history, traditions, and use of Latin and legal language. However, understanding this system will give you a strong foundation if you want to study any area of law or to work in uniformed public services. The legal system is essentially a practical tool that helps to provide solutions when problems occur.

The first part of this unit explores the structure and framework of the civil and criminal courts in England and Wales, as well as the roles of the lay and paid personnel who work within them. You will learn about the role of the Crown Prosecution Service, the use of juries, the different types of judge, what they do and how they are appointed.

The final parts of the unit examine how legal rules are made, the categories of offences, the criminal trial processes and the rights of the defendant to bail and legal representation.

Attendance in court can be part of the job for many individuals who have a career in the uniformed services, so it is really important that you are familiar with the courts and the people you are likely to encounter there.

Learning outcomes

After completing this unit you should:

1. know the hierarchy of the courts system
2. know the role undertaken by the personnel of the courts
3. know how legal rules are created by precedent
4. understand how the criminal trial process works.

Assessment and grading criteria

This table shows you what you must do in order to achieve a pass, merit or distinction grade, and where you can find activities in this book to help you.

To achieve a **pass** grade the evidence must show that you are able to:	To achieve a **merit** grade the evidence must show that, in addition to the pass criteria, you are able to:	To achieve a **distinction** grade the evidence must show that, in addition to the pass and merit criteria, you are able to:
P1 outline the hierarchies of the civil and criminal courts in England and Wales **See Assessment activity 22.1 page 212**		
P2 describe the roles of judges, lawyers and lay people in criminal trials in England and Wales **See Assessment activity 22.2 page 220**	**M1** compare the roles and functions of paid and lay personnel within the court system of England and Wales **See Assessment activity 22.2 page 220**	**D1** critically analyse the role of lay personnel within the court system of England and Wales **See Assessment activity 22.2 page 220**
P3 describe how legal rules are created by precedent **See Assessment activity 22.3 page 224**		
P4 outline the rights of the defendant to legal representation and bail **See Assessment activity 22.4 page 227**		
P5 describe how the criminal trial process works for both a summary and an indictable offence **See Assessment activity 22.5 page 233**	**M2** compare the trial process in the Magistrates' and Crown Court, using a summary, either way and indictable offence **See Assessment activity 22.5 page 233**	
P6 outline the powers of the courts in sentencing offenders, using one example of a summary offence and one indictable offence **See Assessment activity 22.5 page 234**	**M3** explain the grounds for appeal from the Magistrates' Court and the Crown Court in England and Wales **See Assessment activity 22.6 page 234**	

How you will be assessed

This unit will be assessed by an internal assignment that will be designed and marked by the staff at your centre. The assignment is designed to allow you to show your understanding of the learning outcomes for aspects of the legal system and the law making process. Assessments can be quite varied and can take the form of:

- reports
- discussions
- leaflets
- presentations
- posters

- practical tasks
- case studies
- diaries
- action plans.

Cho learns more about the legal system

I really liked this unit because we had studied Police powers in Unit 17 and this unit linked very closely to some of the things we had learned there. I haven't decided which career path I would like to follow yet. My parents suggested I might make a good solicitor or barrister, and I know they are keen for me to go to university and to study law, so this unit really gave me a chance to see if I enjoyed the subject.

I found looking at the courts really interesting. My tutor took us to visit the local Magistrates' and Crown Courts so we could see what happens inside. I was very impressed with the way the barristers spoke in court and how they built a case, based on the evidence. We also got the chance to speak with a local magistrate about their role and how they decide on a person's guilt or innocence.

The best thing about this unit was when we did a mock court trial. We all wore gowns and rearranged the classroom to look like a courtroom. I was the judge, and once the jury had decided on the case, I had to choose a sentence. I learned so much about the trial process and now I think I will be applying to study law at university next September.

Over to you!

- **What areas of the law might you find interesting?**
- **Have you considered a career as a legal professional?**
- **What preparation could you do to get ready for your assignments?**

201

1. Know the hierarchy of the courts system

Thinking about the law

Did you know that in the past it was illegal to have an abortion, to perform homosexual acts and to commit suicide?

These laws have changed to reflect the needs of individuals and society.

Discuss which laws you would change now if you could. Which laws do you think are fair and which do you think are unfair? Why do you think this?

Share your findings with the rest of your class. Did you come up with the same kind of things or was each person's assessment different? Why do you think this is?

One of the most important things you will learn from this unit is that the law is not static – it does not stay the same forever. The law is dynamic and changes in response to the needs of the public and government of the time. This is crucial for the development of a modern and energetic society in which morals and ideas about how we should live change constantly.

1.1 Structure of the civil courts

This section examines the structure and function of the civil courts of England and Wales. The structure in Scotland and Northern Ireland is different from that outlined here. Although the courts in England and Wales are notionally split into two halves – criminal and civil – in actual fact there are many links and crossovers between them. You will see below, when we look at the civil and criminal sections in more detail, that each has its own court structure. See Figure 22.1 to understand how the two court structures fit together.

The civil court structure is complicated and (see Figure 22.1), depending on the nature of the case, the following courts may be involved:

- Magistrates' Court
- Crown Court
- County Court
- High Court
- Court of Appeal
- the Supreme Court
- European Court of Justice.

Civil procedure is used when one person or organisation decides that they have been wronged by another person or organisation. It does not deal with criminal matters, which are when the state has been wronged by an organisation or individual. Civil claims are usually about getting financial compensation for a wrong that has been committed. The **plaintiff sues** the **defendant** for an amount of money to correct the breach of civil law that they claim has been committed against them.

Key terms

Plaintiff – the person or organisation claiming to be a victim.

Sue – to institute legal proceedings against a person or institution, typically for redress (financial compensation).

Defendant – the person or organisation that is accused or being sued.

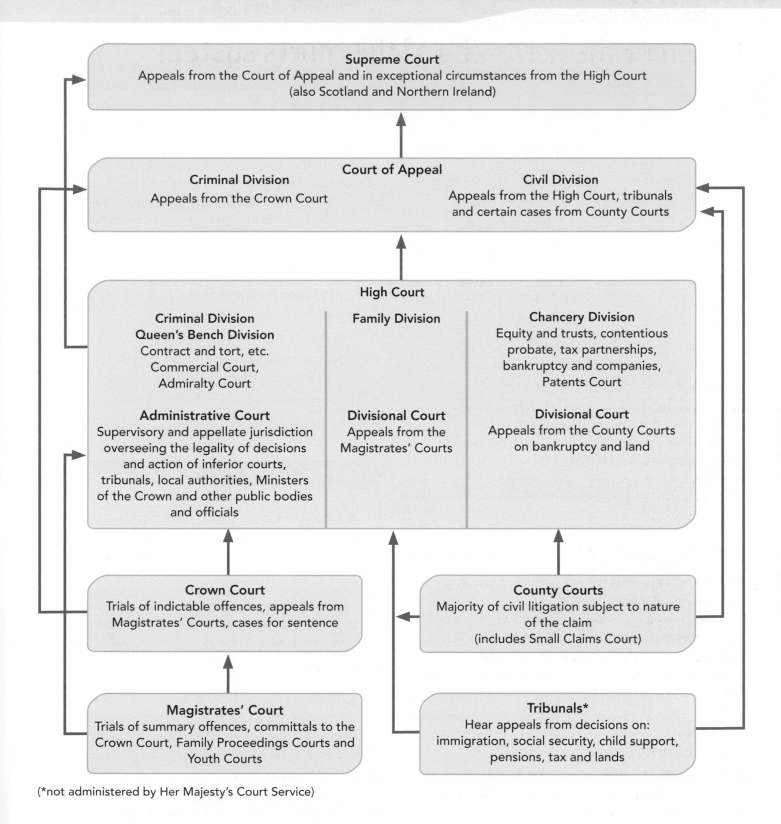

Figure 22.1: The structure of the courts system in England and Wales. Can you see the relationship between the civil and criminal courts? The arrows show the movement of cases up the hierarchy of the courts, which is also the Appeals route from each court.

(*Source:* Her Majesty's Court Service. Crown copyright material reproduced by permission of the Controller of Her Majesty's Stationery Office and the Queen's printer for Scotland.)

Function and jurisdiction of the courts

Claims usually start in the court in which they are likely to be tried, and this depends on two issues:

- the size and nature of the claim
- the complexity of the legal issues.

As shown in Table 22.1, smaller cases are normally heard in the County Court and larger ones in the High Court.

Table 22.1: The courts where civil claims are heard

Size of claim	Where case will be heard
£5000 or less	Small Claims Court (which is within the County Court)
£5000–£25,000	Usually County Court
£25,000–£50,000	High Court or County Court, depending on the complexity of the case
£50,000 and above	Usually High Court

The functions and jurisdictions of the various Civil Courts are described below.

Remember!

Key facts about civil law

- Civil law exists to resolve disputes between companies or individuals.
- Civil law has its own civil courts: Small Claims Court, County Court and High Court.
- Civil law has many divisions, each dealing with a specialised branch of the law.
- The main purpose of civil law is financial redress (compensation).
- The parties involved are called plaintiff and defendant.

Small Claims Court

Firstly, you should remember that the small claims track is actually part of the County Court, not a separate court in itself. It is called 'the small claims track' because it is a process, or 'track', that small claims move through. It is designed to deal with claims worth less than £5000, but it can be a greater sum if all parties agree to have the small claims track hear their case and the case does not require a great deal of legal preparation.

The most common cases heard by the small claims track are compensation claims for faulty goods or services, and disputes between landlords and tenants. Before anyone goes to court they should try and make every effort to have resolved the issue themselves. This is because court cases cost time and money and can be very inconvenient. Sorting out disputes without going to court may save a lot of unpleasantness.

The first step in the small claims procedure is to complete a claim form and pay a small fee, based on the amount being claimed. The form contains written details of the claim and it must be clear to the defendant and the court why the claim is being made and how much the claim is for. Once the defendant receives the claim form, they then have 14 days in which to send back a defence. At this point the defendant has several options:

- They may choose to pay the claim.
- They may make an admission and agree arrangements to pay at a later date.
- They may make a defence to the claim.
- They may choose to do nothing.

Did you know?

The fee paid for issuing a claim through the small claims track varies depending on the amount you are claiming. For sums up to £300 the cost is £30; for a claim of £3000–£5000 the fee is just over £100.

If no response is received, the court may choose to rule in favour of the plaintiff automatically. If the defendant defends themselves, a hearing follows. This hearing can be either public or private, depending on the wishes of the people involved and the decision of the court. Each party will have a fair and equal opportunity to state their side of the dispute to the presiding judge, who is likely to be a district or deputy district judge. Both parties are also entitled to take a representative to speak on their behalf if they wish.

This procedure can be quite quick and straightforward. Elliot and Quinn (2002) note that 60 per cent of cases take less than 30 minutes. After both parties have presented their case, the judge then makes a decision as to whether or not to award compensation.

It is unusual for a **solicitor** to present a small claims case because the procedure is designed to be accessible by the general public, and for them to be able to present their own case. However, someone might have an initial meeting with a solicitor to decide if their case has merit.

It is difficult to appeal against small claims judgements unless there has been a significant irregularity affecting the proceedings, or the judge is incorrect on a matter of law.

County Court

County Courts deal with low-level civil law matters. They were created by the County Courts Act (1846) and a large number of civil claims are heard in these courts every year. There are around 250 County Courts in England and Wales, each of which is presided over by a **circuit judge**, who sits alone to make judgements. It has **jurisdiction** over matters such as contract, **tort**, recovery of land, partnerships, **trusts** and inheritance, as well as the small claims track, which was discussed in the previous section.

Table 22.2: There are advantages and disadvantages to the small claims procedure, as shown below

Advantages	Disadvantages
Quick, simple and cheap	It may involve complex cases
Increases public confidence by seeing justice done	The paperwork could be simplified
It is fully accessible to all members of the public	There are problems enforcing successful claims, for example if the person being sued for compensation doesn't have any money
	The financial limit needs regular updating to keep it in line with inflation.

Key terms

Solicitor – lawyers who deal with a whole range of legal matters.

Circuit judge – sits in either County Court or Crown Court and is based on one of the six court circuits in England and Wales.

Jurisdiction – a court's authority to hear and decide on a case.

Tort law – the branch of law that covers civil wrongs, such as trespass or product liability.

Trust – a legal arrangement where one party transfers the ownership of assets to another party who manages the assets for the benefits of others. It is sometimes used in place of a will.

Case study: A case of bad workmanship

Genna and Sam bought a kitchen from a local kitchen company and found a fitter who advertised in their local newspaper to install it. The builder agreed a set price with Genna and Sam and told them the work would take five days to complete. Both Sam and Genna were at work all day and left the fitter in charge of the property. They also paid him half of the money in advance, with the other half to be paid when the job had been done.

Initially the work looked as if it was progressing well, but by mid week it became obvious that there were some problems with the quality of workmanship. Some of the worktops were chipped and scratched and several of the cupboard doors wouldn't close fully. There was also a crack in the glass of the kitchen window near where some cabinets had been removed.

Genna and Sam contacted the builder and asked him to correct the work. When the fitter arrived he claimed there was nothing wrong with the workmanship and demanded the 50 per cent balance of payments he was owed. Genna and Sam refused to pay and asked him to leave the house.

The following day Genna and Sam engaged another fitter to complete the job and spent money on

replacement work surfaces and doors. They also received a quote for a replacement double-glazed window in the kitchen.

Genna issued a small claim in the local County Court against the kitchen fitter claiming:

- the 50 per cent payment he had received in advance
- the cost of replacing the double-glazed window
- the cost of the replacement fitter
- the cost of the additional work surfaces and door.

The fitter did not issue a defence and did not attend the court hearing. The judge found in Genna's favour and awarded her the costs for replacement work surfaces and doors, but he did not award costs for the cracked window as there was no evidence that the fitter was responsible. The judge did not award the 50 per cent payment as not all of the work was substandard.

1   **Why is the small claims track important in cases such as this?**

2   **What defence could the fitter have offered? Could the fitter have issued a counterclaim? If so, what for?**

3   **If the fitter refused to pay the costs, what could Genna do to ensure payment?**

The County Court has a fast-track procedure that can be used to reduce the waiting time. This is mainly used for cases for claims of between £5000 and £15,000.

The main difference between small claims procedure and County Court procedure lies in the **arbitration** stage. Small claims are dealt with in an informal manner by a judge who undertakes the role of **arbiter**, whereas County Court proceedings are heard in open court in a much more formal manner.

High Court

The High Court is based at the Royal Courts of Justice in London, but it also sits at 'district registries' across England and Wales, which are usually located inside existing Crown or County Court buildings. These district registries mean that High Court cases can be heard anywhere in the country without the necessity of going to London.

The High Court is split into three divisions:

- Queen's Bench
- Chancery
- Family.

Procedure in the High Court

The procedure in the High Court is much more formal than in the small claims track or County Court. The first stage in this procedure is to issue a **writ**, which is drafted by a **barrister** or solicitor and is then **served** on the defendant. A writ is a document that is similar to a County Court summons and it is the most common form of starting an action in the High Court. The writ tells the defendant who the plaintiff is and why they are making a claim. If the defendant does not respond within 14 days, the judge may make a decision by default on behalf of the plaintiff.

If the defendant intends to defend themselves against the claim, they must complete and return an 'acknowledgement of service' form, which states their intention to defend. The defendant must then submit a document called a 'defence'. This document answers the claims made by the plaintiff and sets out any new facts that the plaintiff did not know, or did not disclose. The plaintiff can then deny the defendant's 'facts' or reply to them in a document called a 'reply'.

This procedure will continue until both parties have exchanged every point they think is relevant. At this point the pleadings are closed and the judge can clearly see the matter that he or she must decide on. Following this a trial is conducted, with each side having its own witnesses. The judge then makes an appropriate decision regarding the case. The cost of a High Court trial can be very expensive and this can stop people making a claim.

Court of the first instance

You may also hear the term '**Court of the first instance**' or 'first instance court'. This is the court that has jurisdiction over an offence. For example, for a serious criminal offence the Crown Court would be the court of first instance and for a minor criminal offence, such as a traffic violation, the Magistrates' Court would be the first instance court. The system is identical in civil cases; the court of the first instance in civil cases is whichever court has jurisdiction over the claim and where the claim will be tried.

The civil courts track is not without its problems. Some criticisms of the civil procedure are outlined in Table 22.3.

Table 22.3: Criticisms of civil procedure

Criticism	Detail
Expense	The costs of the case can amount to more than the original claim was worth. This means people or companies can end up losing money in civil proceedings, even if they win the case. Lord Woolf's 1996 Access to Justice Report found that this happened in 40 per cent of cases where the original claim was worth £12,500 or less.
Delays	The civil justice procedure deals with a tremendous volume of cases and it is over-stretched. According to the Woolf Report, the current average waiting time in the County Court is 79 weeks.
Injustice	If people cannot afford a lengthy trial they may have to accept an out-of-court settlement from the other party for a lower sum. This can create a sense of injustice.
Too complex	The procedure can be difficult to track and follow.
Enforcement	It can be difficult to enforce judgements and make sure that people who are successful in the civil courts can actually get their money from the other party.

Activity: Which court?

Susan has had a disastrous haircut in a town centre salon. She complained at the time, but the salon refused to put the problem right. Susan was left £90 out of pocket for the haircut and had to pay a further £100 to another salon to have her hair put right. She wants to sue the original hairdresser, but doesn't know how to go about it.

1 **Which court would Susan use to sue her hairdresser?**

2 **Describe the steps she would have to go through to conduct a claim.**

3 **What amount could Susan claim in compensation?**

1.2 Criminal Courts structure

The criminal court structure contains some of the same institutions we examined in the civil court system. Figure 22.2 shows the main courts in the criminal court system.

Function and jurisdiction of the criminal courts: Youth Court

Magistrates' Courts may deal with cases that involve people under 18, but only if they are tried with an adult. Young people also appear in the Crown Court if they are being jointly tried with an adult whose case needs to be heard in that Court. Homicide (murder) and rape cases will always be heard in the Crown Court. The Youth Court may also send a young

person to the Crown Court if the offence is very serious and the sentencing powers of the Youth Court are thought to be insufficient to punish the young offender properly.

However, unless the case is one of those mentioned above, 10–17-year-olds will have their case dealt with in the Youth Court. This is a specialised form of Magistrates' Court. As in the Magistrates' Court, the case will be heard by magistrates sitting in a panel of three (usually one magistrate will be female in the Youth Court), or by a district judge (in a Magistrates' Court).

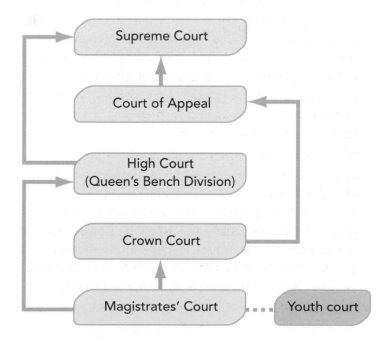

Figure 22.2: The structure of the criminal courts system. The arrows show the movement of appeals up the hierarchy of the courts.

The Youth Court is not open to the general public, in order to protect the young people involved, and only those directly involved in the case will normally be in court. A hearing in the Youth Court is similar to one in the Magistrates' Court, though the procedure is adapted to take account of the age of the defendant. The magistrates and district judges who sit in the Youth Court receive specialist training on dealing with young people.

Magistrates' Court

The Magistrates' Court is the most junior of all the courts in the English legal system. The country is divided up into 'commissions', which are then further divided up into petty sessional areas, or **benches**. Each bench has its own courthouse and clerk. Although this is the most junior court, it is a vital part of the legal system because of its caseload. There are over 400 Magistrates' Courts in England and Wales and each deals with business happening in the local area.

Magistrates' Courts deal with:

- 97 per cent of all criminal cases
- civil family matters such as adoption, custody and maintenance
- granting of **warrants**, **summonses** and bail applications
- granting of licenses, e.g. for the sale of alcohol
- juvenile jurisdiction (offenders aged 10–17)
- **summary jurisdiction**
- jurisdiction over some **triable either way offences**
- committal for trial for **indictable offences**.

The courts are staffed by magistrates whose job it is to decide guilt or innocence and to provide appropriate punishments to those defendants they convict. The maximum sentence that magistrates can give for an offence is six months' imprisonment and/or a fine of up to £5000. If they feel an offence needs a stronger punishment than they are able to give they may send the case to Crown Court, which has the power to deliver harsher sentences. Around 90 per cent of people appearing before a Magistrate's Court plead guilty, which simplifies and speeds up matters considerably.

Magistrates have a long history in the English legal system. They date back to the Justices of the Peace Act (1361) which gave certain judicial powers to lay people. This meant that they had the ability to deal with criminal matters and some civil issues, but unlike

magistrates today they were also entrusted with the running of local government.

The magistrates and judges found in this court will be discussed later in this chapter.

Case study: Arrested for assault

Charlie was out celebrating his older brother's 21st birthday with a group of friends when a fight broke out in a club. The Police were called and began to arrest those involved, including Charlie's brother. Charlie, who had been drinking and had taken drugs, tried to prevent the Police arresting his brother and ended up assaulting a police officer. Charlie was arrested. As he is only 16 years old his case will be examined in the Youth Court. Charlie has a very good academic record, is due to begin college in September and has never been in trouble before.

1 What will be the key factors the Youth Court will take into account?

2 How does a Youth Court differ from an adult court?

3 What is likely to happen to Charlie if he is found guilty of assault?

Key terms

Bench – an area where a court has jurisdiction. Each bench has its own court house and jurisdiction.

Warrant – an order from the court which instructs the Police to perform a duty, such as an arrest or a search.

Summons – a request to attend the court regarding a particular issue.

Summary jurisdiction – responsibility for less serious criminal matters.

Triable either way offences – offences that can be tried in either the Magistrate's Court or the Crown Court.

Indictable offences – the most serious criminal offences which are dealt with in the Crown Court.

Activity: Magistrates' Courts

What are the advantages of pleading guilty in a Magistrates' court?

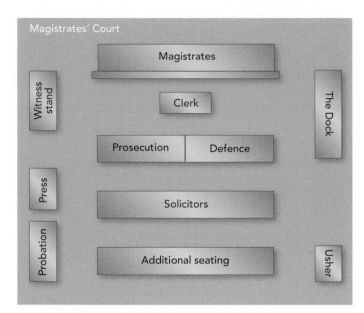

Figure 22.3: The inside of a Magistrates' Court

Link

See pages 216–7 and 218–9 for information about the roles, selection and training of magistrates and judges.

Remember!

Key facts about Magistrates' Courts:

- There are over 400 Magistrates' Courts in England and Wales.
- They deal with less serious criminal offences and some civil matters.
- They deal with juveniles aged 10–17 (in the Youth Court).
- There are two types of magistrate: lay justice and district judge.
- Magistrates have maximum sentencing powers of six months' imprisonment and a £5000 fine per offence.

Crown Court

The Crown Court was established by the Courts Act (1971). It was created to replace the system of Assizes and Quarter Sessions that was outdated and unable to cope effectively with increasing numbers of criminal cases. There is only one Crown Court, and this is called the Central Criminal Court, or sometimes the 'Old Bailey'. This one Crown Court has around 77 centres from which it operates throughout cities in England and Wales.

The Crown Court deals with four main area of work:

- criminal trials of indictable and some triable either way offences

- appeals against the decisions of magistrates
- sentencing from Magistrates' Court
- some High Court civil matters.

Offences dealt with in the Crown Court also fall into four categories, as shown in Table 22.4 below.

Table 22.4: Offences dealt with in the Crown Court

Category	Offences
Class 1	Murder, treason, offences under the Official Secrets Act. Usually tried by a High Court judge or circuit judge.
Class 2	Manslaughter, rape, etc. Again, may be tried by a High Court or a circuit judge.
Class 3	A wide variety of indictable and triable either way offences. May be tried by a High Court, circuit or recorder judge.
Class 4	Robbery, assault, grievous bodily harm, etc. Usually tried by a circuit judge or a recorder.

The Crown Court also operates a tier system for its external centres that dictates the kind of work they are allowed to do. There are three tiers of the Crown Court:

- The first tier deals with High Court civil matters, any kind of triable either way or indictable criminal offence and hears appeals from Magistrates' Courts.
- The second tier deals with triable either way offences and indictable offences and hears appeals from Magistrates' Courts.
- The third tier deals only with class 4 offences and appeals.

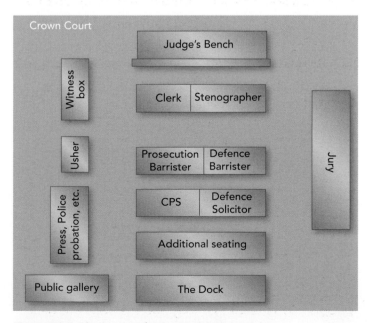

Figure 22.4: The layout of a Crown Court room

European Court of Justice

The European Court of Justice has 27 judges and 8 advocate generals who are appointed by the collective governments of the European Union for a term of 6 years. They are chosen from the best judges each nation has and they must be completely independent and very skilled at their role.

The European Court of Justice has very clear jurisdiction on what it can and cannot do, and it is not an enforcement agency. As you can see from Table 22.5, the European Court of Justice actually has very little to do with anything in the British legal system, as it deals only with European law. The court has the task of ensuring that EU law is applied equally throughout the 27 member states. The majority of cases heard by the Court of Justice are referred to it by the national courts of the member states.

The impact of some of the decisions of the European Court of Justice on the uniformed public services in the UK is described in Table 22.6.

The Court of Appeal

This court has two divisions, criminal and civil, which hear appeals from the lower courts within each structure (see Figure 22.1 on page 204). Like the High Court, the Court of Appeal also sits within the Royal Courts of Justice in London.

The appeals system has two main functions:

- to put right any incorrect or unjust decisions made in the courts below them
- to help promote consistent development of the law.

Table 22.5: Jurisdiction of the European Court of Justice

Jurisdiction	Explanation
Preliminary rulings	This is when the member states of the EU ask the European Court of Justice to clarify the meaning of a piece of European law so that it can be correctly interpreted and applied in all of the member states. This guarantees cooperation between the European Court and the national courts.
Actions for failure to fulfil obligations	This type of action allows the court to monitor how the member states are fulfilling their obligations under European Union law. If the member state is found to be failing in their legal obligations to either their citizens or other member states, they must rectify this at once.
Actions for annulment	This allows the European Court of Justice under certain circumstances to annul (get rid of) a piece of law set by another EU institution.
Actions for failure to act	This is when member states can lodge a complaint against the European Union itself for failing to reach a decision on a given issue. If upheld this is then officially recorded.
Appeals	Appeals on points of law only can be brought before the Court of Justice against judgments and orders of the court of first instance.
Reviews	Decisions of the court of first instance on appeals against decisions of the European Union Civil Service Tribunal may, in exceptional circumstances, be reviewed by the Court of Justice.

Table 22.6: How decisions of the European Court of Justice have impacted on uniformed public services in the UK

Decision	Impact
European Working Time Directive	The working time regulations affect all uniformed public services as they state that there should be a limit on the average working week for all employees. This limit is 48 hours, with minimum daily and weekly rest periods and a limit on night workers' average working hours. However, the public services do have special provisions within the regulations in order to protect operational effectiveness. For example, a war or riot doesn't stop in accordance with the European Working Time Directive and neither should the response to the incident.
European Security and Defence Policy (ESDP)	In 1999 the ESDP resulted in the setting up of a European rapid reaction force, which was needed to target trouble spots in Europe. The aim was to address the problems of European armed forces strategic cooperation and utilisation of equipment – for example, most of the equipment and telecommunications technology used in Kosovo in the mid 1990s was American. The rapid reaction force is a 60,000-strong force that can be deployed within 60 days and can operate for up to a year. It is also better value for money to pool military resources across EU nations and split the cost. This has affected the armed services in the UK by potentially enabling a faster, more coordinated response to European incidents of conflict.
Europol	Europol is the EU cross-border police organisation. It coordinates cooperation between all the EU policing agencies including customs and immigration. Europol has several key priorities in assisting the police forces of member states, and mainly deals with drug, vehicle and human trafficking, illegal immigration and terrorism. Police, customs and immigration in the UK can access this information network across 27 nations, which can be used to share intelligence and coordinate joint policing operations.
Eurojust	Eurojust is an EU organisation which was created to help judicial authorities such as courts in dealing with cross-border offences such as organised crime. To this end Eurojust supports investigations and prosecutions across the EU and aims to develop Europe-wide cooperation on criminal justice cases. For example, Eurojust can help member states by working to overcome language barriers in extradition proceedings.

Table 22.7: Appeals in the civil and criminal divisions of the Court of Appeal

Civil division of the Court of Appeal	Criminal division of the Court of Appeal
Presided over by the Master of the Rolls	Presided over by the Lord Chief Justice
Hears appeals mainly from: • the High Court • the County Courts • certain tribunals, such as employment and immigration.	Hears appeals from the Crown Court on a variety of matters, such as: • appeals against conviction • appeals against unduly lenient sentences • points of law.

The Court of Appeal may allow an appeal to go ahead if:

• it is thought that a conviction may be unsafe

• the judge in the original case interpreted the law incorrectly

• there was some sort of irregularity in the course of the trial.

The court can recall all the witnesses and evidence that were used at the original trial, and new evidence can be submitted. Many countries have an automatic right to appeal built into their criminal justice system, but this is not the case in England and Wales where permission to appeal must be given by the courts.

The Court of Appeal hears cases where the plaintiff or defendant is not happy with the original results of the case in the lower courts. Not just any case can go to appeal; there must be a sound reason why the plaintiff or defendant needs to appeal, such as the first trial was not conducted correctly or brand new facts have come to light. There are approximately 40 judges who sit in the Court of Appeal. These judges often sit in both the civil and criminal appeal courts.

Activity: Rights of appeal

Should criminal convictions have an automatic right of appeal? What are the advantages and disadvantages of this?

Make notes about your views on these questions and discuss them with the rest of class.

Key term

Judiciary – the collective name for the judges who work in courts and decide on legal cases.

The opening of the newly renovated Supreme Court of the United Kingdom, October 2009

The Supreme Court

The Supreme Court is the final court of appeal for all UK civil cases and criminal cases from England, Wales and Northern Ireland. In England and Wales it hears appeals from the Court of Appeal (Civil and Criminal Divisions) and some cases from the High Court (see Figure 22.1 on page 203).

The Supreme Court replaced the House of Lords as the highest court in the UK in October 2009. The House of Lords was part of the government. Having an appeal court that is completely separate from the government is important because it helps to ensure the independence of the **judiciary**.

Assessment activity 22.1

P1 **BTEC**

Understanding how the courts operate in a hierarchy is a key issue when you are looking at the legal system. Working in pairs, produce a wall chart that outlines the hierarchies of the civil and criminal courts in England and Wales. **P1**

Grading tip

Remember to include all the different courts on the civil and criminal trees and include some annotation about the role and jurisdiction of each court.

PLTS

By working in pairs to produce your wall chart you will demonstrate your skills as a **team worker**.

2. Know the role undertaken by the personnel of the courts

The courts system in England and Wales deals with thousands of cases each day, many of them legally complex. The legal profession manages and deals with these cases on behalf of the parties involved.

2.1 The legal profession

This section looks at the work, training and regulation of barristers and solicitors and their roles in the court systems of England and Wales.

Solicitor

Solicitors may work alone or in a partnership with other solicitors. They deal directly with the public and offer a wide variety of legal services, such as:

- pre-trial work
- accident claims
- conveyancing, contracts
- wills
- representation in court
- divorce and family matters.

There are around 80,000 solicitors in England and Wales who are regulated by The Law Society. The Society has the power to discipline or **strike off** a solicitor for professional misconduct.

The training of a solicitor usually starts with a law degree, followed by the Legal Practice Course (LPC) that lasts one year and then a training contract that lasts two years.

There are other methods of becoming a solicitor if you have a non-law degree, or indeed if you have no degree at all.

Solicitors are able to act as **advocates** in the Crown Court if they have an additional qualification called an advocacy certificate.

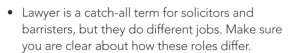
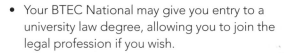

Did you know?

- Lawyer is a catch-all term for solicitors and barristers, but they do different jobs. Make sure you are clear about how these roles differ.

- Your BTEC National may give you entry to a university law degree, allowing you to join the legal profession if you wish.

Barrister

Barristers are considered to be self-employed individuals and are not allowed to form partnerships with other barristers. However, in practice they usually share a set of offices, called 'chambers', with other barristers, in order to share costs and gain professional support and advice.

Barristers are generally associated with advocacy work, which is representing people in court, but they may also deal with matters such as drafting documents and offering expert advice on legal issues. Barristers are not allowed to deal directly with the public; they must take their instructions from a solicitor.

Like a solicitor, the training of a barrister normally starts with a law degree. They must then join one of the four Inns of Court (listed below) and complete the Bar Vocational Course (BVC), which is usually a one-year course. They must also complete 12 qualifying sessions with their Inn. After this they must complete a pupillage, which is an additional year's training, with a set of chambers.

There are over 9500 barristers in England and Wales and they are governed by the General Council of the Bar, which acts in much the same way as other professional bodies, such as The Law Society, or the General Medical Council. Barristers must be a member of one of the following four Inns of Court, which are based in London:

- Middle Temple
- Inner Temple
- Gray's Inn
- Lincolns Inn.

Key terms

Strike off – when a professional organisation such as The Law Society can remove a solicitor from an approved list of practitioners. It effectively removes the solicitor's right to practice law.

Advocate – the person who speaks on your behalf in court and presents your case. This can be a solicitor in the Magistrates' Court but it is usually a barrister in the Crown Court and the superior courts.

There are two ranks of barrister:

- **Queen's Counsel (QC)** – senior and experienced barristers who take on more complicated cases. A barrister must have at least ten years' experience before being appointed as a QC. The majority of the judiciary are promoted from within the ranks of the Queen's Counsel. Since very few QCs are women, or from ethnic minority backgrounds, this has significant implications for the composition of the judiciary. Becoming a QC is called 'Taking Silk'.

- **Juniors** – less experienced barristers who deal with less complicated cases. Juniors also help QCs deal with cases in court.

Remember!

Key facts about the legal profession:

- Solicitors have direct contact with clients.
- Solicitors deal with a wide range of legal matters including crime, family and civil issues.
- The general public cannot contact a barrister on their own; a solicitor must do it for them.
- There are two kinds of barrister: QCs and Juniors.
- Barristers deal with the majority of advocacy work in the Crown Court.

Activity: Being a barrister

1 Once you have finished your National Diploma, what steps would you have to take if you ultimately wanted to become a barrister?

2 List the top six skills you think are important to be a successful barrister.

2.2 Prosecutors

The role of the Crown Prosecution Service

In England and Wales criminal prosecutions are conducted by the Crown Prosecution Service (CPS). The CPS was created by the Prosecution of Offences Act (1985) to take the role of prosecution away from the Police and put it in the hands of an independent body. The CPS work closely with the Police and have several key roles:

- advising the Police during investigations
- determining the charge in criminal cases
- reviewing cases submitted by the Police for prosecution

- preparing and presenting the prosecution's case in court.

The Code for Crown Prosecutors

The CPS bases its decisions to prosecute on the Code for Crown Prosecutors. This is a document that sets out the basic principles a prosecutor must follow when making decisions about a case. There are two main tests set out in the code that prosecutors use to decide whether or not to charge a suspect.

1. The evidential test. The prosecutor must decide if there is sufficient evidence for there to be a realistic chance of getting a conviction. If there is insufficient evidence, and a court would be unlikely to convict on the basis of that evidence, then the case must not go ahead.

2. The public interest test. A prosecutor must decide if moving the case forward to court is in the public interest. This can be a difficult judgement to make because the prosecutor must decide whether the public would benefit from a person being prosecuted for their offence.

Case study: The public interest test

In July 2008 5-year-old Megan Liggins-Mills was knocked down and killed by her half-brother Martyn Mills. Mr Mills had driven to his mother's house where his 8-year-old daughter and his half-sister, Megan, were playing in the driveway. As he turned the car into the drive he struck both girls. Jessica suffered leg injuries, but Megan suffered more serious head injuries and died a short time later.

The Crown Prosecution Service decided not to bring charges against Mr Mills as it was not in the public interest to do so. They considered it to be 'a genuine error of judgement'. Megan's family were extremely unhappy with the CPS decision, arguing that Mr Mills should have been charged with manslaughter.

1 What are the difficulties in deciding what is in the public interest?

2 Why do you think the CPS decided a prosecution was not in the public interest in this case?

3 Conduct some research into other cases where it has not been in the public interest to prosecute. Do you agree with the decisions? Why?

Other prosecutors

Although the CPS conducts the vast majority of prosecutions, there are other agencies who can prosecute. For example, breaches of the Health and Safety at Work Act (1974) can be prosecuted by the Health and Safety Executive, the local authority or the Environment Agency. Other agencies that can prosecute include the Benefits Agency and the Revenue & Customs Protection Office.

Private prosecutions

A private prosecution is started by an individual who is not associated with the CPS, the Police or any other prosecuting agency. Victims have no right to review the decisions made by the CPS regarding charging, so they may decide to take out a private prosecution if the CPS does not wish to prosecute. The CPS can decide to take over or discontinue a private prosecution at any time and, as these cases are not subject to legal aid, they can be very expensive to deal with.

Key term

Right of audience – for potential High Court judges, this is the legal right to act as a lawyer in the High Court. For potential circuit judges it is the right to appear in court as an advocate.

Plea bargaining

This may also be called plea acceptance. It is a process where a defendant may plead guilty to a lesser offence in return for a more serious offence being dropped. This has the advantage of avoiding a long and expensive trial that may or may not produce a conviction. By accepting a guilty plea to a lesser charge, time and money can be saved by both the defence and the prosecution.

2.3 The judiciary

Judges have a very important role in the court system, because they are legal experts on points of law if the prosecution and defence are in dispute. The judiciary manage and oversee the conduct of trials and sum up to the jury in criminal cases. They also pronounce sentence if a defendant is found guilty.

The roles, selection and appointment of judges in civil and criminal cases

Table 22.8 below shows how the roles of the different judges vary, and also how they are selected and appointed.

Table 22.8: The types of judges, their roles and how they are appointed

Type of judge	Roles and where they work	Selection and appointment
High Court judges, also called Puisne (pronounced 'puny') There are currently 106 High Court judges.	Usually based in London, but also travel to the major court centres in the rest of the country to try complex and/or serious criminal cases and important civil cases in Crown Courts. Also assist the Lord Justices to hear criminal appeals. High Court judges sit in one of the three divisions of the High Court: • the Queen's Bench • the Chancery • Family.	Appointed by the Queen, who takes recommendations from the Lord Chancellor. Before they can be considered, potential High Court judges have to: • have had the **right of audience** for at least 10 years • have been a circuit judge for two years.
Circuit judges There are over 600 circuit judges in England and Wales.	Travel around an area of the country called a circuit. There are six circuits in the country. Listen to middle-range Crown Court cases; also sit in the County Court to hear civil matters. In some circumstances they might also be found in the Court of Appeal criminal division. Deal with a wide range of legal matters including civil, criminal and family matters.	Like High Court judges, they are appointed by the Queen on the basis of a recommendation from the Lord Chancellor. Before a legal professional can be appointed a circuit judge, they must have: • held the right of audience for at least 10 years • served as a part-time recorder on criminal matters • served as a full-time district judge.

continued

Type of judge	Roles and where they work	Selection and appointment
District judges There are currently 434 district judges in post, including 18 who sit in the family division of the High Court in London.	Like circuit judges, they sit on one of the six geographical circuits. Full-time judges who do a wide variety of civil work, such as family matters, property matters and bankruptcy. They deal with the vast majority of cases heard in civil courts, which often involve small claims.	In order to be appointed a district judge they must: • have held the right of audience for seven years • usually have been a deputy district judge for two years.
Recorders and assistant recorders	Part-time judges who often still work as barristers or solicitors. They deal with some of the least serious Crown Court cases and can sit in either County or Crown Courts.	Recorders are selected from barristers and solicitors who apply for the position and who have had at least seven years' experience. Becoming a recorder is often seen as the first step to becoming a judge.
District judges (Magistrates' Court) Previously called stipendiary magistrates and still known as justice of the peace.	Deal with the longer and more complex cases that appear in the Magistrates' Court. This type of judge has a very wide jurisdiction in Magistrates' Court, including criminal cases, youth court and family matters. They also sit as **prison adjudicators.** Unlike **lay magistrates,** they sit alone to hear a case.	As with all judges, they are appointed by the Queen on the recommendation of the Lord Chancellor. Before becoming full-time district judges (Magistrates' Court) they must have: • had the right of audience for at least two years • usually sat as a deputy judge for at least two years.

Key terms

Prison adjudicators – deal with offences and charges against prisoners.

Lay magistrate – 'lay' in the context of magistrates means 'ordinary'. Lay magistrates are ordinary people who volunteer and are trained for the role.

Judicial immunity – when judges are protected from the legal consequences of their decisions.

Superior judges – judges who operate in the superior courts, such as the Court of Appeal or the High Court.

Inferior judges – circuit judges, district judges and other judicial officers.

Judicial independence and immunity

In order for the public to have faith and trust in the justice system it is important that judges are seen as being completely independent when making decisions. This means that they cannot allow themselves to be influenced (or perceived by others to be influenced) by a variety of factors such as:

- the state
- the media
- other judges
- religion
- politics
- money.

Judges are also traditionally immune from legal actions arising from their judicial role. This is called **judicial immunity** and it means that they cannot be sued or prosecuted for a decision they made in the course of their duties, even if new evidence comes to light in later years that shows that the decision they made at the time was incorrect.

Removal of judges from office

It is actually very difficult to remove a judge from office, and how a judge may be removed differs for **superior judges** and **inferior judges**. Superior court judges can only be removed if both houses of parliament pass a resolution requiring them to go, but this is an extremely rare occurrence and last happened in 1830. Superior judges can be removed if they experience a significant illness or disability which affects their ability to be a judge, but again this is not used often. Judges would far prefer to resign than be dismissed and resignation and retirement at age 70 are the main ways judges leave office.

Inferior judges can be disciplined and removed from office by the Lord Chief Justice. The type and jurisdiction of cases they oversee may also be restricted.

Case study: Removing a judge from office

Although a superior court judge has not been removed from office since 1830, there have been a handful of cases where inferior court judges have been removed. In 1983 Judge Bruce Campbell was removed for smuggling whiskey from Guernsey to England, and more recently District Judge Margaret Short was removed from the bench in 2009 after a judicial investigation into her conduct. Research both these cases then answer the questions below.

1 Why are so few judges removed from office?

2 Why is it important that judges obey the law?

3 What are the implications for the judiciary if judges are rude and unprofessional?

2.4 Lay people

Lay magistrates

Magistrates are sometimes referred to as lay magistrates and, like district judges (Magistrates' Court), they are also known as justices of the peace (JP). Magistrates are unpaid volunteers who are trained to serve as representatives of their local community. They sit in panels of three and have a trained legal advisor on hand at all times when in court (this is the clerk of the court).

There are approximately 30,000 magistrates in England and Wales and they are based across 300 courts. Even though they are volunteers, they must commit to a minimum number of days in order to be able to fulfil their role; currently this is a minimum of 26 half days.

Selection of lay magistrates

Magistrates apply for the role from the local community and normally undergo a two-stage interview process. The purpose of the first interview is to find out more about the person, their skills and attitudes. The second interview is designed to test their judicial abilities by looking at case studies of criminal cases. Lay magistrates can be of any gender or ethnic background, but must be aged between 18 and 65 years. It is important to remember that magistrates are unpaid volunteers; they serve the community and the criminal justice system for reasons that are not financially orientated.

Training of lay magistrates

Although magistrates are not legally trained in the sense that they don't have a law degree, they have to undertake ongoing training throughout their time on the bench. This is because the law can change frequently and they have to keep up to date. The Judicial Studies Board decides which areas of training are required and the actual training is usually carried out by the Clerk of the Court where the magistrate sits. In general, a new magistrate will have undergone about three full days of training before they sit for the first time. They will also be mentored during their first sessions.

Activity: Lay magistrates

The backbone of the justice system is dependent on volunteers. What is your view on the use of volunteers in such an important service?

1 List and describe five personal characteristics that you think would be useful if you intended to become a lay magistrate.

2 How do these characteristics compare with the characteristics needed in other public service roles?

3 Why is there a need for district judges (Magistrates' Court) when lay magistrates do the job for free?

4 What reasons might someone have for volunteering as a lay magistrate?

The jurisdiction of lay magistrates in civil and criminal cases

Magistrates are often referred to as the backbone of the criminal justice system, because they deal with 97 per cent of all criminal cases. A magistrate's main duty is to ensure the defendant receives a fair and public hearing within a reasonable time.

As they do not have legal training, lay magistrates do not deal with complex or difficult cases. Instead they try low-level criminal offences in the Magistrate's Court, as shown below. Magistrates also refer more serious cases to the Crown Court, which does have the power to deal with them.

• A magistrate's jurisdiction is local, which means that it covers the area to which they are appointed.

- All hearings for criminal cases commence in the Magistrates' Court, but the magistrate must send serious crimes, such as murder, rape and robbery, to the Crown Court to be dealt with.

- A magistrate will hear all summary (less serious criminal) offences involving people over the age of 18 – which can only be dealt with in the Magistrates' Court – such as motoring offences, less serious assaults and public order offences, such as anti-social behaviour.

- Magistrates decide what will happen to the defendant while their case is being prepared. For example, remanding in custody, setting bail (or not) and imposing any bail conditions.

- During the trial, magistrates hear the evidence and decide whether the accused is guilty or innocent.

- If the defendant is found to be guilty, the magistrate decides on the most appropriate sentence.

A magistrate's sentencing options include:

- absolute discharge – usually for a first offence, when a further offence is unlikely

- conditional discharge – where a further offence within 3 years means the defendant can be sentenced for both crimes

- community sentence

- fines up to £5000 (the most common sentence)

- compensation to a victim of up to £5000

- a prison sentence.

Magistrates also work in:

- Youth Court – for cases involving young people aged 10-17

- Family Proceedings Court – for cases involving some types of family dispute

- Civil Court – for civil cases, plus enforcing Council Tax demands, licensing requests e.g. for the sale of alcohol, betting shops

- Magistrates sit in Crown Courts when appeals are being heard against a conviction from a Magistrates' Court.

Link

See page 208 and pages 228–9 for more about the role of magistrates.

Table 22.9: Advantages and disadvantages of the use of lay magistrates

Advantages of using lay magistrates	Disadvantages of using lay magistrates
A very cost-effective and efficient way of administering justice	Inconsistent decision-making between benches
Involvement of ordinary people makes the justice system appear fairer	Magistrates tend to have a bias towards the Police and are more likely to believe their evidence than the evidence of the defendant
Groups of three are likely to give more balanced decisions	Magistrates tend to be white, middle class and middle aged
They have local knowledge and understanding	Cases are not heard in much detail and magistrates tend to rely very heavily on the Clerk.

Removal of lay magistrates from office

Section 11 of the Courts Act (2003) gives the Lord Chancellor the power to remove a lay magistrate if:

- they fail to meet the standards of competence needed

- they misbehave

- they refuse or neglect to do the duties of a lay magistrate.

In January 2010, the Office for Judicial Complaints recommended Magistrate Iris Josiah be removed from the bench after she failed to declare she had two separate court proceedings against her.

The role of juries in the criminal and civil courts

The use of a jury has a long and distinguished history, but it has seen a decline in both civil and criminal cases over recent years. A jury is made up of 12 people in a criminal case and eight people in a civil case. In a criminal case the jury appears in Crown Court when a defendant pleads not guilty.

Juries are a fundamental principle of the legal system because the exercise of justice is by the people, not the state. The guilt or innocence of a person is not decided by a judge who is in the employ of the state, but by ordinary people from the community at large. Juries are not required to justify their verdict and there have been cases where juries have acquitted defendants despite strong evidence of guilt, as a way of showing their disapproval of the law.

Qualification and disqualification for jury service

To qualify for jury duty you must be:

- aged between 18 and 70
- registered on the electoral roll
- have lived in the UK for at least five years since the age of 13.

Even if you fulfil these qualification criteria, you may still not be allowed to serve on a jury, or your personal circumstances might mean you can be excused from jury duty.

You are considered ineligible for jury duty if you:

- have a mental disorder
- are a member of the clergy
- are a judge or otherwise connected with the criminal justice system.

You will be automatically disqualified for jury duty if you:

- have certain criminal convictions
- are currently on bail in a criminal case.

You can choose to be excused if you:

- are aged 65–70 years
- have already done jury service in the last two years
- are an MP
- work in the medical profession
- are in the armed forces.

You can also be excused if you provide the judge with a good reason why you cannot serve or you have a lack of capacity to understand the case (for example, you don't understand English or you are hearing impaired).

Summoning, vetting and challenging jury members

If you are called to jury duty you will receive a **summons** from the Lord Chancellor to attend your local court. Once there you will undergo a series of **vetting** checks to make sure you are eligible for service, which might include criminal record checks.

The defence and prosecution may also make challenges to the potential jurors. This is where a prospective juror is removed because they are considered unsuitable. Challenges are quite rare in the UK, but a juror would be considered unsuitable if they were biased in a particular way, such as they personally knew the people involved in the court case.

Implications of trial by jury

- Juries usually look at the evidence and testimony to determine what the facts of the case are, while judges usually rule on points of law.
- A judge cannot order the jury to convict, no matter how strong the evidence is.
- Typically, the jury only decides whether the defendant is guilty or not guilty, but the actual penalty is set by the judge.
- In highly emotional cases, such as child rape, the jury may be tempted to convict based on personal feelings, rather than on conviction beyond reasonable doubt.
- One criticism of juries is that they do not usually have to give a reason for their verdict. Opponents argue it is unfair for a person to be deprived of life, liberty or property without being told why.
- Juries are fair, efficient and effective. They convict almost two-thirds of those they try. They convict more defendants than they acquit in rape, they do not exhibit any racial bias and they only fail to reach verdicts in less than 1 per cent of cases.
- Despite the failings of individual jurors, juries get it right most of the time. They make the right decisions on the evidence and come to the right verdicts.

Table 22.10: Advantages and disadvantages of the jury system.

Advantages	Disadvantages
Ordinary people are represented in the justice system	Juries are untrained
Group decisions give fairer results	Complex cases may be difficult to understand, particularly in civil cases
Public representation makes the system more open to scrutiny	It is a compulsory system.

Key terms

Summons – a request to attend court.

Vetting – process of checking prospective jury members to ensure they meet the eligibility criteria.

Assessment activity 22.2

Produce a leaflet that includes the following information on the legal system in England and Wales:

1 a description of the roles of judges, lawyers and lay people in criminal trials **P2**
2 a comparison of the roles and functions of paid and lay personnel within the court system **M1**
3 a critical analysis of the role of lay personnel within the court system. **D1**

Grading tips

For **P2** be sure to cover all the different personnel you might find in courts, such as barristers, solicitors, juries and lay people.

To achieve **M1** you should include a section in your leaflet where you compare the roles and functions of paid and lay personnel in the court system.

To achieve **D1** you should critically analyse the role of lay personnel (both lay magistrates and juries) within the court system of England and Wales. Include both the positive and negative aspects of using lay personnel before giving your conclusion regarding the benefits and disadvantages to the court process.

PLTS

Assessing the advantages and disadvantages of using lay personnel within the court system will demonstrate your skills as a **reflective learner**.

Functional skills

By producing an information leaflet you will develop your functional skills in **English**.

3. Know how legal rules are created by precedent

3.1 Judicial precedent

The development of the legal system

Much of English law is unwritten. It was developed over the centuries by the decisions judges made in important cases. The legal system that we know now began its development during the Norman conquest of 1066, but it really started to become an organised system during the reign of Henry II (1154–89). When Henry came to the throne, justice was usually dealt with in local courts. These were:

- *Feudal Courts* – local lords dealing with issues arising from the peasantry or tenants on their land.
- *Courts of the Shires and Hundreds* – county sheriffs, often sitting with a bishop or earl, to hear more serious cases.

According to most sources of information, these early courts were based on local customs that, as you would expect, often differed from county to county. This lack of consistency in the law at the time meant that courts in different areas might settle the same dispute in entirely different ways.

Common Law

Henry II wanted a more standardised system of law in England and so he introduced the *General Eyre* which literally means 'a journey'. This was a system whereby representatives of the king went out to the counties of England to check on the legal administration there. They would sit in local courts and observe how legal problems were dealt with in each area. Over time these representatives came to be seen as judges themselves and were called Justices in Eyre.

Activity: Primogeniture

The right of the eldest son to inherit his father's land, known as primogeniture, was almost universally applied across England. However, if you lived in Nottingham or Bristol, the youngest son inherited the land. If you lived in Kent, all of the landowner's sons inherited the land in equal shares.

1 What is primogeniture?
2 Why were customs different across the country?
3 Why would a standardised system of law be better than a fragmented system?
4 Why did sons inherit but not daughters?

By selecting the best local laws from all over the country, the judges gradually changed differing local laws into a system of law which was 'common' to the entire kingdom – this is how common law originated. So in summary, common law is a judge-made system of law originating in ancient customs that were brought together and extended by judges operating over many centuries.

The development of judicial predecent

The decisions made by judges create new law for future judges to follow, i.e. decisions made by a judge in a certain case are 'binding' on the decisions of future judges when the facts of the cases are the same. This procedure is known as judicial precedent.

Judicial precedent is an important part of common law. It is based on the Latin saying: *Stare decisis et non quieta movere*. This can be interpreted as 'stand by what has been decided and do not change the established'.

The English legal system follows the rules of judicial precedent quite rigidly when compared with other countries. This means that courts in England and Wales must follow decisions already made in a higher or superior court, and appeal courts are bound by their own past decisions. In order to understand judicial precedent you must be aware of the hierarchy of the courts. Figure 22.5 clearly shows which courts are binding on the decisions of other courts.

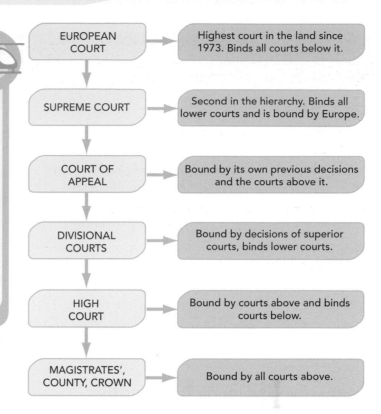

EUROPEAN COURT	Highest court in the land since 1973. Binds all courts below it.
SUPREME COURT	Second in the hierarchy. Binds all lower courts and is bound by Europe.
COURT OF APPEAL	Bound by its own previous decisions and the courts above it.
DIVISIONAL COURTS	Bound by decisions of superior courts, binds lower courts.
HIGH COURT	Bound by courts above and binds courts below.
MAGISTRATES', COUNTY, CROWN	Bound by all courts above.

Figure 22.5: The binding relationships between the courts

Case study: R v R (1991)

A husband had sexual intercourse with his wife without her consent. The married couple had separated, but the husband forced his way into his wife's home and made her have intercourse with him. Up until this time the common law rule was that a husband could not be criminally liable for raping his wife, as the woman's marriage vows constituted ongoing consent for sexual relations. The judge in R v R (1991) recognised the changed attitudes of society towards the status of women and created judicial precedent that outlined that all non-consensual intercourse was rape, regardless of marital status.

1 Why was rape within marriage not a crime until 1991?
2 Why did the judge create a new precedent in this case?
3 What were the implications on society of this new precedent?
4 Do you think the judge made the right decision in R v R?

Law reporting

Law reports are books that contain judicial opinions and decisions from cases decided by the courts. This provides a comprehensive work of reference for judges and lawyers who are seeking to find a precedent for their case.

Persuasive and binding authorities

Persuasive authority is a matter of precedent which is not legally binding. This means that, although a court is likely to take the information into account when making a judgement on a case, it is not necessarily bound to follow it. This might mean that the precedent came from a court in another country, such as an EU member or a military court. Although the precedent is not binding on courts in England and Wales, persuasive authority might be used as guidance by our judges.

As discussed above, binding authority is a matter of precedent that all lower courts in the hierarchy must abide by.

Ratio decidendi

This Latin phrase means 'the reason for the decision'. When it is used by the legal profession it means the legal, moral and social principles a court uses to make a rationale for a particular decision in a court case. Usually the *ratio decidendi* is binding on the lower courts. This is because under the principle of judicial precedent, lower courts must abide by the decisions of the higher courts.

Obiter statements

An *obiter dictum* is a Latin phrase used in the legal profession to mean comments made by a judge about a case that do not form part of the rationale for a decision and are said 'by the way'. These comments are not legally binding on the courts below, but could be seen as a 'persuasive authority' in helping lower courts to make a decision.

3.2 Avoiding judicial precedents

How judicial precedent works and avoiding it if required

When a judge encounters a case where there may be a relevant previous decision made by either the court they are currently in or another one in the hierarchy, the judge has four possible courses of action.

- **Follow** – if the facts are very similar to the previous case then the judge will choose to follow the precedent which has already been set.
- **Distinguish** – if the facts are quite different from the previous case, then the judge can distinguish between the two cases and doesn't need to follow the original precedent.
- **Overrule** – if the original precedent was set in a lower court the judge may overrule it if he or she disagrees with it. This means that, although the original case still stands, the judge does not have to follow its precedent.
- **Reverse** – if the decision made by a lower court is appealed to a higher court, the higher court may reverse the decision if they think the lower court has misinterpreted the law. The higher court will then substitute its decision for the previous one.

The last two courses of action can be problematic because if higher courts overrule or reverse the decisions of lower courts they can weaken their power. Judges think extremely carefully in these circumstances and it is relatively rare that these options are taken.

Although most law today is created through Acts of Parliament, the law may still be made and refined through judicial decisions. Indeed, interpreting the Acts of Parliament themselves often calls for judges to give clarity to the law by interpreting complex legislation.

Table 22.11: The advantages and disadvantages of judicial precedent

Advantages of judicial precedent	Disadvantages of judicial precedent
• **Consistency** – consistency in the law helps to provide a sense of equality and justice. • **Certainty** – because of the high number of recorded cases that have gone before, lawyers are able to advise their clients with confidence. • **Flexibility** – the options available to judges ensure that the law can develop and be applied fairly.	• **Rigidity** – judicial discretion can be limited. • **Bulk** – the sheer volume of prior cases can make understanding the law very time consuming. • **Illogical distinctions** – judges may look for justifications not to follow a precedent and create illogical distinctions to support them. • **Accident of litigation** – the court relies upon a suitable case appearing if it wishes to alter the law.

Did you know?

Most laws these days are created by statute. Put simply, statute law is law which has been formally written down and recorded as an Act of Parliament. Statute law has become increasingly important over the last 150 years or so and differs from common law in the following ways:

- It is created by Parliament, not by judges.
- It is not bound by judicial precedent.
- It can abolish and replace common law made by judges.
- It is formally recorded in an Act of law, rather than as a statement by a judge.

Remember!

The Supreme Court took over the functions of the House of Lords in October 2009.

Case study: Interpreting legislation

The Dangerous Dogs Act (1991) created all sorts of problems which the courts had to resolve. For example, the Act specifically referred to 'dogs', which left the courts having to interpret the legislation regarding bitches. In addition, the law made reference to the control and destruction of various breeds of dog, but failed to give guidance on mixed breed dogs. This left the courts in a very difficult position when interpreting the law.

1 **What were the difficulties in implementing this Act?**

2 **Do you think the Act was designed to control bitches as well as dogs?**

3 **Do you think dog owners were right to challenge the government on the grounds that this Act was flawed?**

Practice statements

Practice statements were designed as a way of allowing the House of Lords (and now the Supreme Court) to move away from a previous decision if they thought it necessary. It did not change the rules of precedent in the lower courts, just in the House of Lords (and now in its successor the Supreme Court). Before practice statements were allowed the only way for the Lords to depart from previous decisions was by an Act of Parliament. They are called practice statements because they allowed the Lords to change its practice.

'Their Lordships nevertheless recognise that too rigid adherence to precedent may lead to injustice in a particular case and also unduly restrict the proper development of the law. They propose therefore, to modify their present practice and, while treating formal decisions of this house as normally binding, to depart from a previous decision when it appears to be right to do so.'

Lord Gardiner's statement in the House of Lords, 26 July 1966.

Activity: Judicial precedent

Based on the advantages and disadvantages of judicial precedent described in Table 22.11 above, do you think the use of judicial precedent is a positive or negative feature of our legal system? Write a 500-word argument to explain your case.

4. Understand how the criminal trial process works

4.1 Categories of criminal offence

All court cases proceed in the first instance to the Magistrates' Court, but the offence may eventually be dealt with by another court. Which court an offence will ultimately be tried in depends on the type of offence. All criminal offences can be divided into three categories:

- summary offences
- triable either way offences
- indictable offences.

Summary offences

These are dealt with only in a Magistrates' Court. Generally these offences are considered less serious and are punishable by a maximum of 6 months' imprisonment, and/or a £5000 fine. Summary offences include:

- minor assaults
- driving without insurance
- indecent exposure
- assault on a police officer
- taking without owner's consent (TWOC).

Triable either way offences

These offences can be tried in either the Magistrates' Court or the Crown Court, depending on what the prosecution thinks is appropriate, what the defendant wishes and the nature of the case, i.e. the value of stolen property or the extent of injuries. These tend to be middle-range crimes, such as:

- indecent assault
- making off without payment
- obtaining services by deception
- going equipped for stealing
- handling stolen goods
- possession of a controlled drug.

Indictable offences

These offences appear in Magistrates' Courts first, but are then committed automatically for trial in the Crown Court. Generally these are the most serious offences and they are punishable by the penalty prescribed by law, which could be anything up to life imprisonment for certain offences. Indictable offences include:

- murder
- manslaughter
- rape
- blackmail
- aggravated burglary.

4.2 Bail

Police powers to grant bail

Bail means that following charge, you are freed from police custody until the next stage in the process of your case.

Bail can be given both before and after a person has been charged. If the police investigation is ongoing, they may not have enough evidence to make a charge in which case they will bail a suspect, with instructions to return to the police station at a later time and date.

Bail is given at the discretion of the custody officer under guidance from the Bail Act (1976), the Criminal Justice Act (2003) and the Police and Justice Act (2006).

> ### Link
>
> For more on the powers of the Police to grant bail, see page 115 of *Unit 17: Police powers in the public services.*

Right of defendant to bail

After a suspect has been charged, the Police must release him or her on bail unless:

- there is doubt about the suspect's name or address
- the Police suspect that the person charged will interfere with witnesses or evidence

- the suspect is thought to require custody for his or her own protection or the protection of someone else
- the Police believe the person will fail to attend court if released on bail.

If the Police refuse bail to a suspect they must present him or her at the Magistrates' Court as soon as possible. If the magistrate cannot deal with the whole case at that time, then the magistrate makes a further decision as to whether to grant bail or remand the suspect in custody until the matter can be resolved.

Conditional and unconditional bail

Unconditional bail means that bail is given without any conditions attached. In certain circumstances the Police may impose conditions on the bail that they give, such as those outlined in Table 22.12 below.

> ### Key term
>
> **Curfew** – an order that children under a certain age must not be out on the streets after a certain time in the evening, usually between 6 pm and 9 pm depending on the age of the child.

Breaches of bail

Breach of bail conditions, such as failure to report to the Police station, is not an offence as such, but the responsibility of the court is to reach a decision

Table 22.12: Conditions which can be imposed on bail

Condition	Explanation
Surrender of passport	This is set as a bail condition if there is any possibility that you may try and escape to another country to avoid punishment for a crime you have committed in the UK. If your passport is handed into the Police you will not be able to use it to travel outside the UK.
Reporting to the Police station at regular intervals	By reporting to the Police station at regular intervals, such as once per week, the Police are able to ensure that: • you are abiding by the conditions of your bail • you have not tried to escape attending court by leaving the area.
Curfews	**Curfews** were introduced by the Crime and Disorder Act (1998), although they had existed since 1997 in Scotland. They can be used against all young people under the age of 16 years. They are applied for by local councils and enforced by the Police, who have the power to take young people home who break their curfew and are caught on the street after a specific time. Curfew orders last for 90 days. After this time the council has to reapply for another order. The idea behind curfews is that with less young people on the streets, there will be less juvenile crime committed, and less young people will become victims of crime. However, curfews have not proved themselves particularly popular with local councils and they are not used with any great frequency.

on whether the bail conditions have been breached and then decide whether to remand the person into custody or grant them bail again, perhaps with different conditions. There is no penalty that can be given for a bail breach.

Right to liberty under Human Rights Act

Article 5 of the Human Rights Act (1998) states that everyone has the right to liberty and security. However, this should not be taken to mean that everyone has the right to freedom, as the extract from Article 5 of the Act states very clearly below.

Everyone has the right to liberty and security of person. No one shall be deprived of his liberty save in the following cases and in accordance with a procedure prescribed by law:

(a) the lawful detention of a person after conviction by a competent court;

(b) the lawful arrest or detention of a person for non-compliance with the lawful order of a court or in order to secure the fulfilment of any obligation prescribed by law;

(c) the lawful arrest or detention of a person effected for the purpose of bringing him before the competent legal authority on reasonable suspicion of having committed an offence or when it is reasonably considered necessary to prevent his committing an offence or fleeing after having done so;

(d) the detention of a minor by lawful order for the purpose of educational supervision or his lawful detention for the purpose of bringing him before the competent legal authority;

(e) the lawful detention of persons for the prevention of the spreading of infectious diseases, of persons of unsound mind, alcoholics or drug addicts or vagrants;

(f) the lawful arrest or detention of a person to prevent his effecting an unauthorised entry into the country or of a person against whom action is being taken with a view to deportation or extradition.

As the above extract shows, there are multiple occasions where the state can legally deprive a person of their freedom and liberty.

4.3 Access to legal advice and representation

Funding and respresentation for defendant

Civil law issues: Community Legal Service (CLS)

This service exists to provide assistance in matters of civil law, such as providing advice on civil matters, resolving or settling disputes involving legal rights and helping to enforce legal decisions involving compensation. It does not cover some of the most common areas of civil law such as:

- allegations of negligence
- conveyancing
- wills
- company/business laws
- boundary disputes.

The money for the CLS is provided by the Community Legal Service Fund (CLSF). The budget of the CLSF is capped; once it is gone it is gone and people may be refused assistance if the funding has run out.

The Criminal Defence Service (CDS) and legal aid

The CDS came into being in April 2001. Its job is to ensure that those involved in criminal proceedings have access to advice, assistance and representation. The CDS provides for free **duty solicitor** access at Police stations. Duty solicitors are available on a 24-hour rota to assist those who are being charged, questioned or placed in Police custody. Although this initial assistance is free, it must be in the interests of justice for further representation to continue to be free.

Key term

Duty solicitor – a solicitor whose services are available to a person suspected or charged with a criminal offence for free.

Did you know?

You can find more information about the Community Legal Service and the Criminal Defence Service on the legal services commission website (www.legalservices.gov.uk).

Table 22.13: The new system of legal aid has many advantages and disadvantages

Advantages	Disadvantages
The new system is intended to increase access to justice for those who need it most.	Budget-capping may lead to some people being refused access to justice.
There is increased control of the costs and resources of legal aid.	Choice of legal representatives will be restricted due to limited legal service contracts being issued.
It ensures free and impartial representation for the defendant in accordance with the right to a fair trial established under the Human Rights Act (1998).	Some of the most common civil cases are now ineligible for funding.
It results in higher standards of work from legal professionals.	

The level of funding in criminal cases is not capped and continues to be demand-led. Only solicitors' firms who have a contract with the CLS are able to offer state-funded criminal defence. This defence falls into three categories:

- **Advice and assistance** – this is the provision of advice and assistance from a solicitor. It covers aspects of criminal defence such as general advice, preparing a written legal case and getting legal opinions from barristers. It does not cover representation in court.
- **Advocacy assistance** – this form of help covers the cost of preparing a case and the initial representation in a Magistrates' Court and Crown Court. This form of assistance is not means tested, but it is merits tested. This means the provision of defence must be in the interests of justice.

- **Representation** – this covers the cost of a solicitor to prepare the case and represent the defendant in court. It may also cover the cost of a barrister in Crown Court and the cost of appeals.

What is a fair trial under the Human Rights Act (1998)?
Principles of fairness:

1. A fair and public hearing within a reasonable time by an independent and impartial tribunal established by law.
2. Judgement should be pronounced publicly.
3. Everyone charged with a criminal offence should be presumed innocent until proven guilty according to law.
4. The defendant should be informed promptly, in detail and in a language they understand, about the nature of the accusation against them.
5. The defendant should be allowed adequate time and facilities to prepare a defence.
6. The defendant should be allowed to defend themselves, or appoint a defence team of their choosing. If they cannot afford to do this they should be given free legal representation.
7. The right to examine and cross-examine witnesses.
8. Free assistance of a court interpreter if the defendant cannot understand or speak the language used in court.

Assessment activity 22.4

Using the information in this section of the unit and your own research, produce a frequently-asked-questions booklet which outlines the rights of a defendant to legal representation and bail, in accordance with the Human Rights Act (1998). You should also include what the Act says about the right to a fair trial and to liberty. **P4**

Grading tip
Ensure your booklet is written at the right level to be understood by a defendant and that it answers any questions they might have clearly.

PLTS

By creating a booklet on the rights of the defendant you will help develop your skills as a **creative thinker** and **effective participator**.

4.4 Magistrates' Courts trials

The process of a Magistrates' Court case varies depending on whether a defendant pleads guilty or not guilty, and upon the type of offence.

Why plead guilty?

A defendant can plead guilty for a number of reasons. For example:

- They may be happy to admit they committed a crime and stand trial for it. Very occasionally this is done to challenge an unfair or unjust law. The resulting court case and publicity surrounding it can sometimes lead to changes being made to the law.

- A defendant may plead guilty if the evidence against them is so convincing that they realise there is no hope of a not guilty verdict. The defendant hopes that the judge or magistrate might take their admission of guilt into account when sentencing them.

- Some defendants might be coerced or paid into pleading guilty in order to ensure the real criminal remains free.

> ### Did you know?
>
> In 2010, around 66 per cent of Crown Court defendants plead guilty to some or all of their offences.

Guilty and not guilty pleas in a Magistrates' Court

Guilty plea

If a defendant in a Magistrates' Court indicates that they will plead guilty, the court immediately acts as if the defendant has pleaded guilty. This means that the person loses the right to take the case to the Crown Court, where it would normally be tried by a jury, as well as a judge.

The Magistrates' Court will then hear some more details of the case and can then either:

- send the case to the Crown Court for sentence, when the case will usually be adjourned so the prosecutor can prepare appropriate papers

- adjourn for a pre-sentence report

- sentence there and then.

Representations on the defendant's behalf can then be made about sentencing in the light of the circumstances of the case or any previous convictions.

Not guilty plea, or no plea

If a not guilty plea, or no plea has been indicated, the magistrates will go ahead and decide whether to deal with the case. The magistrates give the defendant the choice of where the case should be dealt with, either at the Magistrates' Court or at the Crown Court.

The magistrates can choose to have the case dealt with by the Crown Court. If the case is not suitable for the Crown Court, the magistrates will be able to choose the sentence.

Even if a defendant decides to have the matter dealt with by the Magistrates' Court, the magistrates can still choose later to send the defendant to the Crown Court if they have insufficient sentencing powers for the case.

Summary trial process

If a guilty plea is entered to a summary offence, then it is normally very straightforward: the defence solicitor may put forward some mitigation in order to reduce the severity of the punishment, and the magistrates will issue a sentence, with guidance from the clerk. If there is a not guilty plea the general process is as shown in Figure 22.6 below.

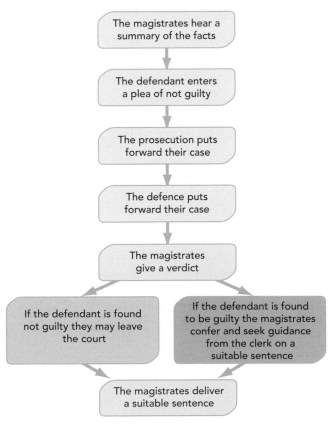

Figure 22.6: This is the general process for summary offences in a Magistrates' Court if a not guilty plea is entered. How would it differ if a guilty plea had been entered?

Triable either way offences

The situation is different for triable either way offences. As you may recall from page 208, a triable either way offence is one that can be tried in either the Magistrates' Court or the Crown Court. A decision has to be made about where the case will be tried and this is done via a procedure called **plea before venue**.

Plea before venue was introduced by the Criminal Procedure and Investigations Act 1996 to provide clear stages for the process of deciding in which court a trial should take place, taking into account the defendant's plea. As all criminal cases start life in the Magistrates' Court, the plea before venue procedure also begins here. The process is described in Figure 22.7 below.

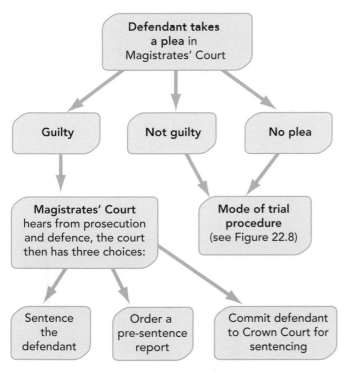

Figure 22.7: Flowchart of plea before venue

Key term

Plea before venue – the process by which it is decided in which court a criminal case will be heard.

Mode of trial

Mode of trial is a procedure used to determine which court a case is tried in if the defendant pleads not guilty, or enters no plea (see Figure 22.8).

Figure 22.8: The mode of trial procedure determines where a case will be heard

Link

See page 231 for information about committal proceedings from Magistrates' to Crown Court.

Link

Refer back to page 207 to read about Youth Courts, which are held within Magistrates' Courts.

4.5 Crown Court

This section of the unit requires you to look at juries, which you read about on pages 218–19 earlier in this unit. Look for information there about the following topics:

- trial by jury
- composition of juries
- the implications of trial by jury
- the advantages and disadvantages of the jury system.

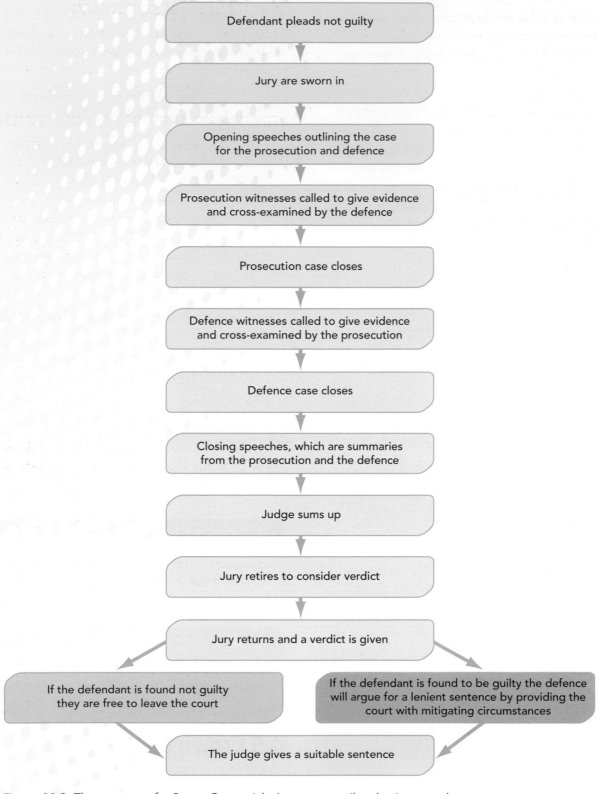

Figure 22.9: The progress of a Crown Court trial where a not guilty plea is entered

4.5 Indictable trial process

The progress of a Crown Court trial where a not guilty plea is entered in an indictable offence is shown in Figure 22.9. (Only indictable offences go the Crown Court.)

Where a guilty plea is entered, the court may adjourn for pre-sentence reports or choose to sentence immediately. A jury is not used where a defendant pleads guilty.

4.6 Sentencing powers

Magistrates' Court sentencing powers and limitations

Magistrates' Courts may sentence a defendant for summary or triable either way offences to a maximum of six months' imprisonment and a £5000 fine per offence (see chart below) However, magistrates are given very clear guidelines on how to sentence by the Sentencing Guidelines Council, which tries to ensure that sentencing across England and Wales is consistent.

As discussed earlier in this unit, the fines that can be imposed by magistrates must not exceed certain maximum levels depending on the severity of the offence. These levels are outlined in the chart below.

Level 1	£200
Level 2	£500
Level 3	£1000
Level 4	£2500
Level 5	£5000

Committal from Magistrates' Court to Crown Court for sentencing

If magistrates feel that an offence requires a larger punishment than they are able to give out, they can send the offender to Crown Court for sentencing. This is called committal for sentencing.

Crown Court sentencing and restrictions

Crown Court sentencing powers are different from the powers of magistrates. Crown Courts are able to sentence more serious offences, but again they must take into consideration guidance from the Sentencing Guidelines Council. All offences have a maximum penalty which is set out in law, but some also have a minimum sentence. For example, in the case of murder, a judge has no choice but to give a life sentence.

There are a range of penalties available to judges in Crown Court including:

* fines
* community sentence
* custody
* suspended sentence.

Figure 22.10 shows the number of criminal cases which passed through the Magistrates' Courts and the Crown Court in 2008.

Did you know?

Guidance on sentencing can be found at www.sentencing-guidelines.gov.uk.

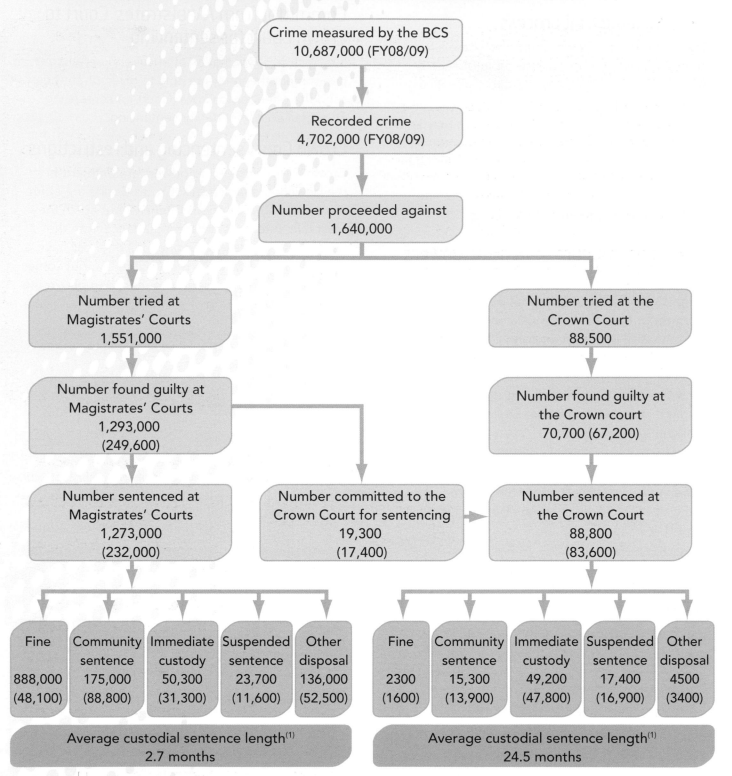

Crime measured by the BCS
10,687,000 (FY08/09)

Recorded crime
4,702,000 (FY08/09)

Number proceeded against
1,640,000

Number tried at
Magistrates' Courts
1,551,000

Number tried at the
Crown Court
88,500

Number found guilty at
Magistrates' Courts
1,293,000
(249,600)

Number found guilty at
the Crown court
70,700 (67,200)

Number sentenced at
Magistrates' Courts
1,273,000
(232,000)

Number committed to the
Crown Court for sentencing
19,300
(17,400)

Number sentenced at
the Crown Court
88,800
(83,600)

Fine	Community sentence	Immediate custody	Suspended sentence	Other disposal
888,000 (48,100)	175,000 (88,800)	50,300 (31,300)	23,700 (11,600)	136,000 (52,500)

Fine	Community sentence	Immediate custody	Suspended sentence	Other disposal
2300 (1600)	15,300 (13,900)	49,200 (47,800)	17,400 (16,900)	4500 (3400)

Average custodial sentence length[1]
2.7 months

Average custodial sentence length[1]
24.5 months

Note: Figures are rounded to the nearest hundred for indictable offences and nearest thousand otherwise. Due to time lags between appearances in court, numbers convicted and sentenced may not match. Numbers in brackets indicate figures for indictable offences.

[1] Excludes life sentences and other indeterminate sentences

Figure 22.10: This chart from the Justice Department website gives a breakdown of the number and categories of criminal cases that passed through the Magistrates' Courts and Crown Court in 2008

Source: Justice Department website, www.justice.gov.uk

Assessment activity 22.5

Understanding the criminal trial process and the possible consequences of a trial are important if you choose to work in the public services, particularly if you are considering a career in the Police or law. Working in pairs produce a PowerPoint presentation which addresses the following tasks:

1   Describe how the criminal trial process works for both a summary and an indictable offence. **P5**

2   Outline the powers of the courts in sentencing offenders, using one example of a summary offence and one indictable offence. **P6**

3   Produce a set of supporting notes for your presentation which compare the trial process in the Magistrates' Courts and Crown Court using a summary, triable either way and an indictable offence. **M2**

Grading tips

You could produce a flow chart on your slides to show the trial processes and possible sentencing options. This would help you cover the required content for **P5** and **P6**.

A case study approach with examples of summary and indictable trials would work well for **P5**. The case study could then be expanded into a comparison for **M2**, in which you could highlight the similarities and differences between the processes in Magistrates' Courts and Crown Court for different offences.

PLTS

By creating a flow chart to show the trial processes and sentencing options, you will demonstrate your skills as an **independent enquirer** and **creative thinker**.

4.7 Appeals from criminal courts

An appeal is a request for a case to be re-examined by a higher court. Courts that can conduct appeals are known as appellate courts. Below is a list of courts and the appellate court that considers its appeals.

- Magistrates' Court – Crown Court
- Crown Court – Court of Appeal (Criminal division)
- Court of Appeal (Criminal division) – the Supreme Court.

You can also see this relationship in Figure 22.1 on page 203. The arrows show the route of appeal.

Parts of this learning outcome have been covered earlier in this Unit.

For **Appeals from the Magistrates' Courts to the Crown Court**, please see the following:

Page 207 examines the **criminal courts structure**.

Page 207 Figure 22.2 shows the structure of the criminal courts system. The arrows on the artwork show the movement of appeals up the court hierarchy.

Pages 207–209 show the function and jurisdiction of the **Youth Courts** and **Magistrates' Courts**.

Page 209 examines the **Crown Court**, including appeals from Magistrates' Courts on page 210.

Pages 210–212 deals with the **Court of Appeal** and its power.

Pages 210–211 cover the **European Court of Justice**.

Page 212 covers the **Supreme Court**.

Did you know?

Appeals 'by way of case stated' are used when a defendant and the legal team believe that either the inferior court has exceeded its jurisdiction, or the court is wrong on a point of law. They then have the opportunity to 'state their case' to a superior court.

Assessment activity 22.6

Produce an A3 annotated diagram that explains the grounds for appeal from the Magistrates' Court and the Crown Court in England and Wales M3.

Grading tip

Use actual case study examples to place the information in context.

Cherelle Brown
Trainee solicitor

Starting out

I work as a trainee solicitor in a busy city centre law firm. I originally wanted to be a police officer, but while completing my BTEC National in Public Services I really enjoyed the law units and decided that I wanted to be a solicitor. I worked really hard on my BTEC and got overall distinctions, which meant I had the grades to go and study law at university. It was a tough three years, but I graduated with a LLB (hons) Law.

A typical day

My day is really varied. The firm has been great in allocating a supervisor I get on really well with and making sure I get the opportunity to work in the various departments here. At the moment I work in the defence advocacy section and, like all trainee solicitors, I have to deal with a large amount of administration and research on behalf of the partners. But I do have my own caseload, which means I can meet with clients and take their instructions, evaluate evidence and check witness statements. I also advise clients at the Police station when they have been arrested.

The best thing about the job

Working in criminal law is really interesting as you never know what type of case you will get next. Plus I have the opportunity to spend a lot of time out of the office, either at the Police stations or the courts.

Think about it!

- What topics have you covered in this unit that might give you the background to work in law?
- What knowledge and skills do you think you need to develop further if you want to be involved in the legal profession in the future?

Just checking

1. How does the small claims track work?
2. What is an appellate court?
3. Explain the public interest test.
4. How and why might a judge or magistrate be removed from office?
5. How did common law and judicial precedent develop?
6. What is an *obiter* statement?
7. What are the advantages and disadvantages of a jury?
8. Explain how legal aid works in criminal cases.
9. Where would an appeal from the Magistrates' Court be heard?
10. What is the role of the Supreme Court?

edexcel

Assignment tips

- In a unit like this, which focuses on the legal system, one of the best things you can do to help improve your grade and your knowledge is to make sure you keep up to date with current events by reading a reputable news source on a daily basis. This means using your lunch hour or an hour after school or college to read the BBC news website, or picking up a broadsheet newspaper such as *The Times* or the *Guardian* (both of these have websites where you can read the news if you can't get hold of the paper). Not only will you become more informed about government policies and the public services, but you will also pick up lots of information that can be used across all of your National Diploma units.

- This may sound very basic, but make sure you have read your assignment thoroughly and you understand exactly what you are being asked to do. Once you are clear about this, then you can move on to your research. Doing your research well and using good sources of evidence is essential.

- Lots of students rely too much on the Internet and not enough on other sources of information, such as books, newspapers and journals. The Internet is not always a good source of information, as it is very easy to use information from American or Australian government websites without realising – but your tutor will notice. Always double check the information you find; don't just accept it at face value. Good research and preparation is the key to getting higher grades.

- Remember particularly that the law and legal procedures can change from year to year and if you use out-of-date materials you may find you don't get the grades you were hoping for.

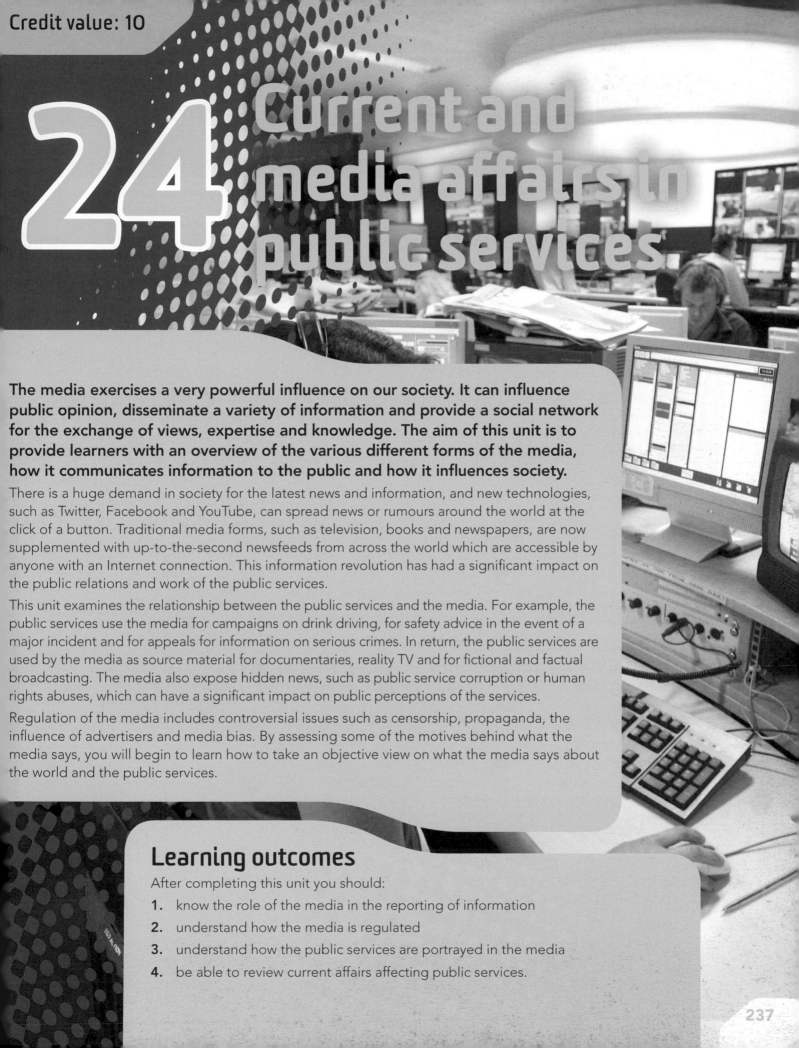

24 Current and media affairs in public services

The media exercises a very powerful influence on our society. It can influence public opinion, disseminate a variety of information and provide a social network for the exchange of views, expertise and knowledge. The aim of this unit is to provide learners with an overview of the various different forms of the media, how it communicates information to the public and how it influences society.

There is a huge demand in society for the latest news and information, and new technologies, such as Twitter, Facebook and YouTube, can spread news or rumours around the world at the click of a button. Traditional media forms, such as television, books and newspapers, are now supplemented with up-to-the-second newsfeeds from across the world which are accessible by anyone with an Internet connection. This information revolution has had a significant impact on the public relations and work of the public services.

This unit examines the relationship between the public services and the media. For example, the public services use the media for campaigns on drink driving, for safety advice in the event of a major incident and for appeals for information on serious crimes. In return, the public services are used by the media as source material for documentaries, reality TV and for fictional and factual broadcasting. The media also expose hidden news, such as public service corruption or human rights abuses, which can have a significant impact on public perceptions of the services.

Regulation of the media includes controversial issues such as censorship, propaganda, the influence of advertisers and media bias. By assessing some of the motives behind what the media says, you will begin to learn how to take an objective view on what the media says about the world and the public services.

Learning outcomes

After completing this unit you should:

1. know the role of the media in the reporting of information
2. understand how the media is regulated
3. understand how the public services are portrayed in the media
4. be able to review current affairs affecting public services.

237

Assessment and grading criteria

This table shows you what you must do in order to achieve a pass, merit or distinction grade, and where you can find activities in this book to help you.

To achieve a **pass** grade the evidence must show that you are able to:	To achieve a **merit** grade the evidence must show that, in addition to the pass criteria, you are able to:	To achieve a **distinction** grade the evidence must show that, in addition to the pass and merit criteria, you are able to:
P1 describe how changes in technology have affected the gathering and presentation of information in different types of media **See Assessment activity 24.1 page 249**	**M1** analyse how changes in technology affect the gathering and presentation of information in different types of media and its ability to affect events **See Assessment activity 24.1 page 249**	
P2 outline how the media can affect events as well as report them **See Assessment activity 24.1 page 249**		
P3 identify the methods used in the regulation and self-regulation of the media in the UK **See Assessment activity 24.2 page 258**		
P4 assess the independence of the media from owners, revenue generators and politicians **See Assessment activity 24.2 page 258**	**M2** analyse the independence of the media from owners, revenue generators and politicians **See Assessment activity 24.2 page 258**	**D1** evaluate the independence of the media from owners, revenue generators and politicians **See Assessment activity 24.2 page 258**
P5 explain how positive and negative images affect public perceptions of the public services **See Assessment activity 24.3 page 262**	**M3** analyse how positive and negative images affect public perceptions of the public services **See Assessment activity 24.3 page 262**	**D2** evaluate how positive and negative images affect public perceptions of the public services **See Assessment activity 24.3 page 262**
P6 review current case studies of media portrayal of the public services, including one factual and one fictional case study **See Assessment activity 24.4 page 266**	**M4** analyse current case studies of media portrayal of the public services, including one factual and one fictional case study **See Assessment activity 24.4 page 266**	

How you will be assessed

This unit will be assessed by an internal assignment that will be designed and marked by the staff at your centre. The assignment is designed to allow you to show your understanding of the learning outcomes for the current and media affairs in public services. Assessments can be quite varied and can take the form of:

- reports
- leaflets
- presentations

- posters
- news articles
- case studies.

Paula learns how the media affects the public

I really enjoyed this unit and found it really useful. I was able to develop a good understanding of how the different types of media can show how the public services are portrayed. I have seen different stories in the news about the public services, but have never really thought about the impact these stories have had on the services and society. I have learned a lot about why it is important that the media is regulated and to make sure that factual stories are correct.

One of the things that I really enjoyed was looking at different sources of media and case studies, and putting together my own evaluations of aspects of current factual and fictional media reports. It was interesting to see how images, text and headlines have an impact on the reader's perceptions of an article and how media reporting can influence a whole communities' views on a subject matter.

The great thing about this unit is that it is very practical and there are lots of opportunities for research and looking at topical current affairs. It was also fascinating to be able to see how the media not only affects different societies, but the world as a whole. All of this information will be really useful to me when I apply to a service, as it will show that I understand media and current affairs and its importance to the services.

Over to you!

- **When was the last time you watched the news?**
- **Where do you get your information on local, national and international events?**
- **When was the last time you read a newspaper?**
- **Do you automatically believe all the information you get from the media? If not, why not?**

1. Know the role of the media in the reporting of information

Talk up

The role of the media

How relevant do you think the media and current affairs are to the media?

Can you think of some examples?

How do you think new technology might affect this relationship?

Discuss these questions with a partner, and then with the rest of your group.

1.1 The information age

When you first start to consider and analyse the media, it does not initially seem to have particular relevance to a career in the public services. In fact, this could not be further from the truth. The media and current affairs is an essential social institution within society, which is as important as other key institutions such as the family and education, and is a fundamental part of the social structure.

The growth of information technology and the increase in demand for information

The mass media we are familiar with today, such as radio, cinema, television, magazines and the Internet are very recent developments which are the result of the technological revolution of the twentieth century.

Historically, transmitting information was quite difficult. The invention and development of the printing press in the fifteenth and sixteenth centuries is credited with revolutionising book production and the spread of knowledge, but books were still too expensive for many people. Newspapers and political pamphlets began to appear in the middle of the seventeenth century, with a 'golden age of newspapers' between 1890 and 1920. However, it is worth remembering that, before the introduction of universal free education in the nineteenth century, literacy rates were quite low.

Even though books, newspapers and other printed material were more freely available, many people would not have been able to read them.

More recently, the huge demand for information and entertainment has been met by newer forms of media, and new ways to deliver it, such as digital radio, 3-D cinema, cable and digital television and the Internet. Book publishing now includes electronic versions that can be downloaded onto small electronic devices that can hold many books at a time.

Did you know?

The oldest English newspaper still in existence is the *Observer*, which was first published in 1791. This was followed by *The Times* in 1785, the *Guardian* in 1821, the *News of the World* in 1843 and the *Telegraph* in 1855. *The Independent* is a comparative newcomer, with its first issue in October 1986.

Did you know?

The BBC (British Broadcasting Corporation) was formed in 1926 and the first television broadcast was made from the 1936 Olympic Games.

Activity: Recent developments

Consider the recent developments in media technology shown in Figure 24.1.

1 Can you say which have occurred over the last decade?

2 Which do you consider to be the most important media developments affecting your own life?

3 Which do you think would be the most important developments to the public services?

List and discuss your answers with a colleague.

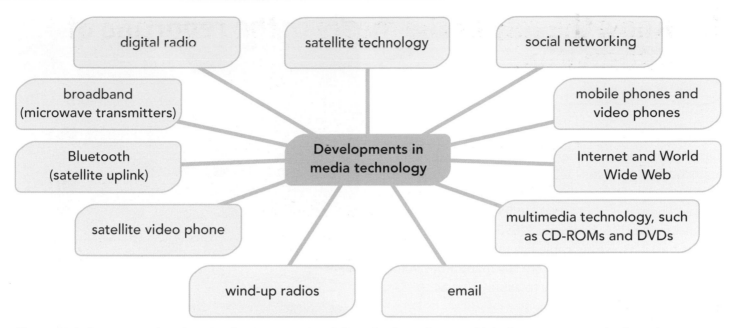

Figure 24.1: Some examples of recent developments in media technology. Can you think of any more examples from the last decade?

Recent history and technological developments

The media and technology change and evolve at an extraordinary rate. Some of the more recent media developments are shown in Figure 24.1.

The development of television

Television did not become a dominant force in the media industry until the 1950s and 1960s. The development of television actually dates back to the nineteenth century and originally there were two separate forms of development:

- *mechanical television* projected a picture using rotating disks or rods
- *electronic television* was based on cathode ray tube technology, which was proven to work better than its mechanical counterparts.

Eventually electronic television became the starting point for the television we know today.

The development of television is based around the work of many scientists, including Karl Braun who invented the cathode ray tube, Vladimir Zworykin who improved on the cathode ray tube and Louis Parker who invented television receiving equipment. However, John Logie Baird, a Scottish engineer, is generally credited as producing the world's first television system in 1923.

Terrestrial television

The 1920s saw ongoing developments to improve the first television system by scientists, such as those listed above. It became clear very quickly that television had huge mass appeal and could become commercially viable. However, there were difficulties in developing television cameras which could capture images of a high enough quality to be transmitted. Both this and the onset of the Second World War in 1939 delayed the development of a television network which could broadcast to the public. Only after the Second World War did the television system we are familiar with today develop. It is called terrestrial television because it uses ground-based transmitters to pass the signal to your home, where it is picked up by your television aerial and appears on your TV as the programme you are watching.

Satellite television

Terrestrial television is not without problems. In order to gain a clear picture you have to be located fairly near to a transmitter and even then there is sometimes distortion and interference to the picture. The solution to this problem was the development of satellite television.

Satellites are located high in the Earth's orbit, meaning a lot more customers are in its line of sight. Unlike terrestrial TV, satellite TV is entirely digital so you receive a far better picture and sound quality. In the UK it also had the advantage of offering a much wider range of TV stations and programmes than the terrestrial service can offer.

Cable television

Cable television is another way to overcome the restrictions of terrestrial television. It works by running fibre optic cables from the transmitter directly to people's homes. Cable television has been incredibly popular in the USA: by the mid 1990s over half of US homes had it. However, cable has taken time to make its mark in the UK, and there are still many areas in the UK which do not have access to cable TV at all.

Link

The development of radio is described on page 244.

What has been the impact of satellite technology on mass media in the UK?

The influence of the Internet

Although television remains the most popular form of mass media, newspapers and radio are still read and listened to by millions of people each day. However, the supremacy of television is now being challenged by online media including websites, newsfeeds and social networking. Over the last ten years, access to news and information via the Internet has become increasingly commonplace. This has been facilitated by the increased availability and decreased price of home computers, computers in the workplace and the increased use of mobile phones. News on the Internet is up-to-date and interactive, giving it distinct advantages over other forms of media.

Activity: Evaluating the Internet

It is important to understand the history of the media and evaluate how things have changed.

1 Create a list of the advantages of using the Internet to access news, entertainment, sport and social networking.

2 Are there any disadvantages of using the Internet that you can think of as a group?

Satellite technology and news reporting

The main impacts of satellite technology on news reporting relate to:

- the speed of reporting
- the ability to collect news from and transmit it to remote and difficult locations.

Communications and media signals can be beamed around the world in a matter of seconds, ensuring news and current events happening in one part of the world can be seen almost instantly in another part of the world. Examples include reporting on the frontline from Iraq or Afghanistan, on natural disasters or on terrorist incidents.

The media already extensively uses satellites so that reporters in remote or challenging locations can report live on events while also keeping in touch. Reporters are able to transmit their story via a **satellite uplink**, which is then relayed to a receiver, which may be thousands of miles away.

Key term

Satellite uplink – a communication system that creates a link between a transmitter on Earth and a satellite in space. The satellite can then transmit the information to another location.

The latest form of satellite systems do not need expensive central receiving equipment to transmit satellite signals to a receiving centre and then around the country. These newer systems are called Direct Broadcast Systems (DBS). The first DBS was Sky in 1989, which originated as a signal from the Astra satellite. DBS require a small satellite dish to be placed at a high point (usually on a roof or high wall) to receive signals. It then receives direct transmission from a satellite.

More recent examples of the media operating very quickly to collect and transmit news include reports of the earthquake in Haiti in 2009, flash floods across Europe in 2010 and the boarding of the aid ship *MV Mavi Marmara* by Israeli soldiers in 2010. These events were on television screens within minutes of happening. This would have been impossible just a few short years ago.

Link

See pages 244–7 for more information about how such media reports can influence public opinion.

It is also important to remember that the speed of reporting has been vastly improved by the use of social networking media, such as Twitter, YouTube and Facebook (see below).

Did you know?

There are over 425 million Internet users in Europe alone. According to the Office for National Statistics (ONS) in 2009, 70 per cent of all UK households had Internet access.

1.2 Types of media

Media is any form of communication that is intended to be viewed by a number of people. We have just looked at television. Figure 24.2 shows some other types of media.

Radio

Radio is the transmission of communication signals, such as sound and music, by **modulating electromagnetic waves**. These travel through the air and are picked up by a receiver which then converts them into recognisable sounds.

Radio began with the development of wireless telegraphy in the late 1890s. Initially, however, telegraph only transmitted signals, but both technologies resulted from the work of many people.

Voice radio as we know it did not really emerge until the 1920s, when the BBC received a license to transmit radio in 1922. The 1920s to1950s were the golden age of radio, when millions of people in the UK and US tuned in to

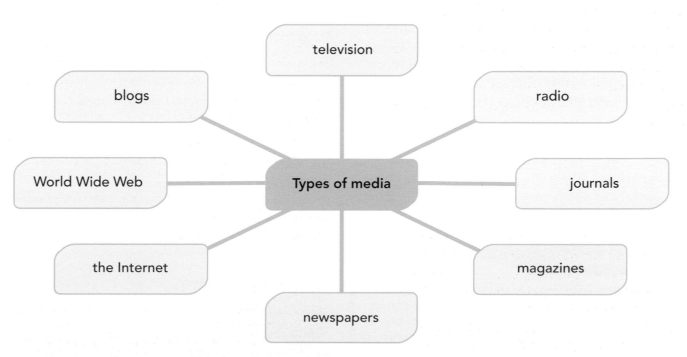

Figure 24.2: Types of media. Can you think of any more?

Link

Radio systems and procedures used in the uniformed public services are described in detail in *Unit 20: Communication and technology in the public services*, pages 152 to 155.

Key term

Modulating electromagnetic waves – radio transmitters cannot all send out the exact same message on the same carrier wave. If they did, all you would hear on your radio would be a garbled, mixed-up version of all the transmissions. So that each wave doesn't overlap with others, it is modulated, or changed, to make it unique from other signals. This is why you can pick out specific stations on your AM/FM radio.

listen to the latest news or their favourite programmes. However, by the 1950s, television began to replace radio as a source of both news and entertainment.

In the 1960s, small, battery-powered transistor radios that could be listened to anywhere became readily available. At the same time, many more hours of music were on offer – from off-shore pirate radio stations to the BBC's new Radio 1 and local radio stations.

New developments

Today there are Internet radio stations that can be received all over the world and which offer alternatives to more standardised terrestrial radio. Digital radio (DAB) continues to become more popular, and broadcasters can use this format to appeal to specialist audiences.

The way people access and listen to radio and share music has completely changed over the last few years. **MP3 players** in particular have revolutionised the way we listen to and share music. Globally, the MP3 format dominates all other audio formats, and the term is used to describe all kinds of formats and players.

Podcasts are another popular way of listening to radio programs because they can be downloaded and listened to at any time.

Bluetooth and Wi-fi technology means that devices such as phones, computers etc, can be linked to exchange files, or to download music or broadcasts. Mobile phones and the iPhone are now multipurpose devices that can also receive terrestrial radio, Internet radio, videos and access the Internet.

Did you know?

The first Police radios began to appear in the late 1920s as a one-way communication method for Police headquarters to contact officers on patrol. However, it wasn't until the 1940s that officers had their own car-based transmitters and could relay information back to headquarters.

Newspapers

The first English newspaper was the *Observer* in 1791. However, the real growth in the newspaper industry occurred in the nineteenth and twentieth centuries, as more people were able to read and there was an increased demand for information.

Newspapers come in two forms – **tabloid** and **broadsheet** – each catering to different public requirements. However, traditional forms of the media like this are in decline. The Organisation for Economic Development and Cooperation (OEDC) reported in 2010 that: in the UK newspaper circulation had declined by 25 per cent; in the USA there was a 30 per cent decline; and across all **OECD countries** two-thirds were facing a decline in newspaper circulation. This is largely the result of the availability of online news sources.

Journals and specialist magazines

Journals are specialist publications which provide information on a specific topic, such as areas of science, which may not be of interest to all people in the way that general news is. There are also specialist magazines that cater for people with particular interests, such as *Motorsport* for motor racing enthusiasts.

Key terms

Podcast – a series of audio or video media files that are released periodically and can be downloaded. The files can then be stored on a computer, iPod or other device, ready to be used offline.

MP3 players – devices that use audio compression technology originally developed in the 1990s to decrease the size of music files, without compromising quality.

Tabloid – a newspaper which is designed to provide a very broad overview of news and may focus on particular stories which are scandalous or entertaining rather than particularly newsworthy. A **broadsheet** provides more in depth coverage of the news focusing more on issues such as politics or the environment rather than entertainment.

OECD countries – those nations which have joined the Organisation for Economic Co-operation and Development.

The public services use journals to ensure their employees, such as Police officers and fire-fighters, can keep up to date with the latest news which affects them directly. Public services publications include *Police Review*, *Soldier Magazine* and *The International Fire Service Journal of Leadership and Management*.

The Internet

The history of the Internet begins in the 1950s and 1960s when computer systems began to be connected together for the first time in order to allow academic researchers to collaborate on scientific issues. The modern Internet as we know it today was developed by CERN, the European Organisation for Nuclear Research, as a way of connecting computer networks to facilitate collaboration. Essentially this is what the Internet allows us to do today.

Online media has seen tremendous growth, both in terms of news- and entertainment-based websites, but also in terms of the growth in social networking media technologies such as Twitter, Facebook and YouTube (see below). Today the public want their information quickly, without expense and at a time convenient to them. Online news sites, such as the BBC News and the *Guardian* websites, are updated many times throughout the day and can be read during a lunch break at work or even from a mobile phone. The BBC claims that 13.2 million people visit its news site every day and that it has over 2 million pages of news and archives.

Forms of Internet-based and online media are becoming increasingly popular and are being used by public services to improve their performance. In the UK the public services are very proactive when dealing with new and emergent media technologies. The case study (right) illustrates one example.

Facebook

Facebook is a social networking site which allows registered members to share messages, photos and information with other registered users. It was created in 2004 and by 2010 was estimated to have approximately 400 million active users.

Police in several countries have used Facebook as a crime-fighting tool. In New Zealand, Queenstown and Manurewa, the Police have used the social networking tool to upload videos and pictures from CCTV cameras of criminals in action. Other uses include the tracking down of criminals or suspects the Police wish to question.

Case study: Paramedic training in Second Life

Second Life is a 3D online, virtual world, where real people can create their own characters and scenarios to act out. This has proven incredibly useful in emergency services training because practising skills in a virtual world allows trainees to make mistakes and learn from them without causing harm to the general public.

Paramedic students at St George's Hospital at the University of London are provided with scenarios to deal with in Second Life, including **triage**, treating patients, assessing the scene and coordinating with other paramedics at the scene. Their performance is then monitored and graded by their assessors. This has proven to be a very valuable and innovative teaching tool, with 90 per cent of student paramedics claiming it helped them learn more effectively.

1 **Which other services could benefit from online scenarios such as this?**
2 **What are the advantages and disadvantages of using media-based simulations?**
3 **Can you think of any other new media technologies that could help the services? How could they be adapted to benefit the services?**
4 **Can you find other examples of similar training methods?**

Key term

Triage – dealing with casualties in priority order, with the most seriously injured being treated first.

YouTube

YouTube is a website which allows members of the public to upload videos which can then be viewed by any other members of the public. The site was created in 2005 and by June 2010 it was estimated that 2 billion videos per day were being viewed. This is significantly more than any other traditional video-based media, such as TV.

Mobile phone and camera technology is now widely available: most people in Europe and the USA have mobile phones with video capture capability. This means that images can be captured and shared with the world almost simultaneously. In 2009 the *Guardian* reported that a video had been uploaded to YouTube of a man being fatally shot by the Police in a San Francisco subway station. Also in 2009 *The Times* ran an article about a YouTube video of a man being tasered twice by the Police in Nottingham city centre. It had been captured on the mobile phone of a bystander and uploaded within hours of the incident, and seemed to indicate that the Police had used excessive force.

Highlighting problems with the actions of the public services and making the resulting videos available online may have the impact of providing some transparency and honesty in the dealings the services have with the public. The public services themselves also use YouTube to show safety or recruitment videos. More controversially, however, individual members of the armed services have videoed fire fights in locations such as Afghanistan and Iraq without permission and uploaded the results onto sites like YouTube.

Twitter

Twitter is a **microblogging** site created in 2006, which allows users to send text-based messages of up to 140 characters which can be seen on the Twitter website by a group of people known as 'followers'. The messages, known as 'tweets', can be restricted to a specific band of followers, such as family and friends, or can be made freely available to all Twitter users. The estimated number of Twitter users is 100 million worldwide with some 65 million tweets being posted per day.

Twitter has the potential to be a significant help to the public services. Jason Palmer published an article in *New Scientist* in 2009 which argued that blogs, photo sites (such as Flickr) and microblogging sites (such as Twitter) did a faster and more effective job of getting information out to the public during emergencies than government information, public services advice or the TV, radio and newspapers. US reporter Sandy Kieffman

Did you know?

In the US there have been instances where the authors of Twitter posts have been taken to court for defamation (saying things which harm the reputation of a person or organisation) and also for threatening violence.

noted that during the height of the swine flu panic in late 2009, some healthcare agencies were using Twitter to pass along vital information to the public on H1N1 cases.

Activity: Twitter

Do you use Twitter? If so, what do you use it for?

Do you think the public services in the UK could successfully use Twitter to provide information and advice to the public? What would be the advantages and disadvantages of this?

Working in pairs, answer these questions and then feedback verbally to your tutor and the rest of your group.

1.3 Media effects

Public perceptions of issues affecting public services

The media can have a tremendous impact on public perceptions of events related to the public services. The coverage the media provides can either strengthen public support for the services or paint the services in a very poor light. The media can:

- provoke public anger
- create further disorder
- generate public sympathy
- create **moral panics**
- expose issues or provoke discussion.

Media influence on riots and public unrest

Creating further disorder

By reporting incidents of public disorder and riots, the media can help to create further disorder. For example, by reporting on events and their locations more people may turn up to see what is happening.

Key terms

Microblogging – a form of blogging which uses much smaller pieces of content. It may be just a sentence, an image or a video fragment. Twitter is a form of microblogging.

Moral panic – the public expression of concern that results from media coverage of an event.

This could potentially lead to their getting caught up in the riots, resulting in more arrests and injuries. It could also be that some participants at a demonstration may act more provocatively because they know the event is being filmed.

Media engaging public opinion and sympathy

The media can also generate outpourings of public sympathy by showing the plight of people in other parts of the world, for example after a natural disaster such as flooding, an earthquake or famine. It can also encourage the public to explore issues further and provoke discussion of them. For example, media reports from the Balkans highlighted issues in Bosnia, which led to the UN intervening and providing help.

In these ways, media coverage affects public opinion and galvanises public pressure for services or central government to:

- make changes
- hold enquiries
- reconsider a course of action
- contribute to an international issue with financial, military or human resources.

Manipulation

The media have several tools which they can use to manipulate or influence their audience's perception of events. Table 24.1 shows the variety of techniques in producing news which can impact on the public in this way.

Is the intense media scrutiny of Police actions when dealing with riots a help or a hindrance?

Case study: The G20 riots

The G20 Summit in London (2009) was an opportunity for the financial leaders of the world's twenty richest nations to make decisions affecting the world economy. The Summit happens every year and it has often been the target of protesters who believe the wealth and power in the world are unfairly distributed, leaving the poor regions in poverty while the more powerful and wealthy nations get richer.

The 2009 riots were notable because, although the majority of the protesters were peaceful, a minority were violent and bloody skirmishes erupted between the protesters and the Police. The media were on the scene, as were individuals with mobile phones, capturing footage and uploading events as they happened. This led to intense media scrutiny of Police public order tactics such as 'kettling' (where protesters are penned into an area and not allowed to leave). The media were very critical of what they called heavy-handed Police crowd control techniques. Events culminated in the death of newsagent Ian Tomlinson, who appeared to be assaulted by officers as he walked home from work through the protests. At the time of writing the case is under investigation by the Independent Police Complaints Commission.

1   **Conduct some research online. How did the media portray the actions of the Police during the G20 riots of 2009?**

2   **In your opinion, how can media reports on Police conduct affect the public's perception of events?**

3   **What are the problems in relying on media reports in situations such as this?**

Activity: Manipulation

What does manipulation mean? Discuss in small groups what manipulation is and how it can happen. Share your ideas with the rest of the class.

Table 24.1: Different methods of media manipulation

Method of manipulation	Explanation
Suppression by omission	The media can choose to manipulate the news by omitting aspects of a story or even the story in its entirety. Stories that reflect badly on those with power do not often make the news. Examples of this include US-backed political regimes in right-wing countries such as Turkey, Indonesia and Saudi Arabia which have poor human rights records and have been implicated in large-scale human rights abuses. It has been argued that because of their political allegiance to the USA the horrors committed within their borders do not get proper media attention.
Attack and destroy the target	If a media story cannot be suppressed by omission then the media can attack the story as a fabrication and discredit evidence or witnesses.
Labelling	The media can attach a label to an individual or an occurrence, which puts it in a positive or negative light. For example, individuals who fight for freedom and justice for all may be called 'do-gooders', which instantly demotes them to the status of busybody rather than social activist. Freedom fighters who wish to liberate their country from foreign occupation may be called 'terrorists'.
Pre-emptive assumption	Media coverage makes assumptions about the way things are and does not encourage debate around these issues. For example, the media often refers to a 'flood' of asylum seekers who cost the nation millions of pounds. What the media does not question is the fact that the UK takes far fewer asylum seekers than most other nations in the EU and that many asylum seekers are repatriated if their claim is found to be bogus or their country becomes stable again.
Face value transmission	This is when the media accept, at face value, official lies put forward by corrupt governments and pass them on to the public unquestioningly.
Slighting of content	The media may ignore the actual content of a story in favour of other factors, for example an election campaign is reduced to a 'who will win' race when the actual policies and political philosophy behind the campaigns is almost forgotten.
False balancing	The media are supposed to provide a fair and balanced account of events, according equal weight to each side of the story. In actual fact the media often provide biased coverage and promote a balanced view where in fact there is no balance.

Case study: The Israeli boarding of the *Mavi Marmara*

In May 2010 a flotilla of aid ships, led by the *Mavi Marmara*, were intercepted in international waters by the Israeli military as they were preparing to deliver aid to Gaza in conflict-stricken Palestine. This was because Israel had put in place a naval blockade around Gaza on the grounds that the HAMAS government intended to import arms which would then be used against Israeli targets. International aid agencies have pointed out that such restriction on trade means very few goods can go in and out of Gaza, leading to widespread poverty, illness and extremely poor standards of living for the population.

The boarding of the *Mavi Marmara* was very controversial because it was an aid ship in international

waters. The Israeli military unit responsible for the boarding killed 9 Turkish civilians and injured about 30 more. The media response in the UK was highly critical of the Israeli action and arguably generated increased sympathy for the Palestinian cause.

1 Research the case. Can you find a media story about the boarding of the *Mavi Marmara* which might generate sympathy in the public? What type of language and images do they use to do this?

2 Can you think of any other cases where the media's reporting of an event has generated public sympathy?

3 How can the public services use the media in situations like this to their advantage?

Case study: 2009 – outbreak of swine flu

The swine flu **pandemic** of 2009 was a global outbreak of a new strain of influenza, termed a pandemic virus by the World Health Organisation (WHO).

The outbreak was first observed in Mexico in April 2009, but it was later suggested that there was evidence to show that there had been an ongoing epidemic for months before it was officially recognised as such. The Mexican government soon closed most of Mexico City's public and private offices and facilities to contain the spread of the virus. As the virus quickly spread globally, clinics were overwhelmed by testing and treating patients. On 11 June 2009, the WHO declared the outbreak to be a pandemic.

Research media reporting of the swine flu pandemic of 2009–10.

1   Why would the media create a moral panic out of the swine flu outbreak?
2   Why do the media create moral panics in the first place?
3   Do you think the public actually believe these moral panics?
4   Read a tabloid newspaper. Are there any current moral panics?
5   Can you think of other examples of moral panics

Key term

Pandemic – the outbreak of an infectious disease over a large geographic area.

Assessment activity 24.1

Understanding the media is very important if you are considering a career in the public services.

In pairs, research, prepare and present a 15-minute PowerPoint presentation with supporting notes which:

1. describes how changes in technology have affected the gathering and presentation of information in different types of media **P1**

2. outlines how the media can affect events as well as report them **P2**

3. analyses how changes in technology affect the gathering and presentation of information in different types of media, and its ability to affect events. **M1**

Grading tips

For **P1** you should try and ensure that you make use of a wide range of research methods and investigate a number of media types.

For **P2** you need to give up-to-date examples and case studies to show how the media have affected events related to the work of the public services.

For **M1** you need to give examples that show the positive and negative sides of the development of media.

PLTS

By carrying out the necessary research and thinking creatively about how you will present this information in your presentation will demonstrate your skills as an **independent enquirer** and **creative thinker**.

Functional skills

By using PowerPoint presentation software you will develop your functional **ICT** skills to present information in ways that are fit for purpose and the audience. Speaking to your audience and listening to their comments and questions about your presentation will help you develop your functional **English** skills.

2. Understand how the media is regulated

2.1 Regulation

Data Protection Act (1998)

Confidentiality and data protection is enshrined in law. The media is regulated by this legislation so that they cannot breach confidentiality and must preserve the anonymity of individuals who are protected in law. The Act that supports this is the Data Protection Act (1998), which came into force in March 2000. The main purpose of the Act is to protect the right of an individual to privacy in relation to their personal data. A good example of this in action is the preservation of the anonymity of serious criminals such as the killers of 2-year-old James Bulger, who were given a new identity when they were released from prison to protect them from vigilante attacks by members of the public in retaliation for their crime.

There are many bodies that regulate the conduct of the media in the UK, such as:

- the Broadcasting Standards Commission (BSC)
- Ofcom
- the Press Complaints Commission (PCC).

The Broadcasting Standards Commission

The Broadcasting Standards Commission was established by the Broadcasting Act (1996). Its main functions are to produce codes of conduct regarding broadcasting standards, to evaluate and assess complaints made against TV and radio programmes and to conduct research into issues of standards in TV and radio broadcasting.

Ofcom

Ofcom is funded by fees from industry for regulating broadcasting and communications networks, and by the government. Ofcom's main functions are:

- to regulate TV and radio sectors, fixed line telecoms and mobiles, plus the airwaves over which wireless devices operate, and to advise Parliament when it is setting technical aspects of regulation
- to promote the interests of citizens and consumers and make sure they get the best from their communications services by ensuring that:

  o the UK has a wide range of electronic communications services, including high-speed services such as broadband, and that the radio spectrum is used by everyone (including taxi firms, boat owners, mobile phone companies) in the most effective way

  o a wide range of high-quality television and radio programmes are provided, appealing to a range of tastes and interests, provided by a range of different organisations

  o people who watch television and listen to the radio are protected from harmful or offensive material

  o people are protected from being treated unfairly in television and radio programmes, from having their privacy invaded and from offensive and potentially harmful effects from radio or television.

Activity: Ofcom

In November 2009, Ofcom had to investigate complaints from the general public about the popular TV show 'The X Factor' when it was claimed that the judges made the wrong decision when eliminating a contestant from the show.

1 Do you think Ofcom should spend time investigating such complaints? Explain your answer.

2 Research other recent examples of complaints that Ofcom has investigated.

The Press Complaints Commission (PCC)

Ofcom regulates broadcast media, and it is the Press Complaints Commission (PCC) that responds to issues regarding written media. The PCC is an independent body that is funded by the annual levy it charges newspapers and magazines. It has no legal powers, but all newspapers and magazines voluntarily contribute to its costs and follow its rulings.

The PCC deals with complaints about the content of newspapers and magazines. All national and regional magazines are bound by a code of conduct that covers issues such as accuracy of reporting and invasion of privacy. The PCC provides a free service to the public who may have concerns about the accuracy or editorial comment of a news story that concerns them or their organisation. The PCC itself claims that there are many benefits to the way the organisation is run (see Table 24.2).

Table 24.2: The benefits of the Press Complaints Commission

Benefit	Detail
Accessibility	The PCC is free and available to all citizens. It operates a 24-hour service in a variety of languages to facilitate enquiries from all sections of the community.
Speed	The average time taken to investigate and adjudicate is 32 days. This is a very speedy service when compared to an average County Court case, which takes an average of around 80 weeks to be resolved.
Raising standards in the industry	The PCC argue that their presence and powers ensure high standards in the written media. This is because it pursues newspapers that have breached the industry's code of practice.
Independence from the industry	Although the PCC is funded by the newspaper and magazine industries, and although many industry personnel sit on the PCC, most of its representatives are not connected to the industry and are therefore not biased towards it.
Freedom of the press	The PCC is a self-regulatory body. This means that, in effect, through this agency the press regulates itself. This is seen as an advantage because government regulation of the press could restrict or undermine press freedom.

Right to privacy

In the United Kingdom there has been no specific law in relation to a free standing 'right to privacy'. However, there are numerous laws that protect your privacy. Since the implementation of the Human Rights Act (1998), individuals have significantly increased scope to use the law, therefore increasing their privacy. The Human Rights Act (1998) – Article 8, specifies how this law applies.

Human Rights Act (1998) – Article 8

(1) Everyone has the right for his private and family life, his home and his correspondence.

(2) There shall be no interference by a public authority with the exercise of this right except such as is in accordance with the law and is necessary in a democratic society in the interests of national security, public safety or the economic well-being of the country, for the prevention of disorder or crime, for the protection of health or morals, or for the protection of the rights and freedoms of others.

Article 8 means that the media cannot interfere in the private lives of the public and this includes individuals in the public eye such as actors, celebrities or politicians.

Activity: Privacy for all?

Some people argue that if you choose to go into public life, you are deciding to give up your privacy in return for fame. What are your thoughts on this?

Libel

Libel and slander are two forms of 'defamation'. A defamatory statement is one which injures the reputation of another person or organisation, effectively reducing their good name in the eyes of others.

- Libel is a defamatory statement which has a permanent nature, such as writing, printing, pictures, films and broadcasts made on the radio or TV.

- Slander is a temporary form of defamation, such as the spoken word.

Clearly, defamation has tremendous impact on the operation of both the broadcast and written media

– it means the media must be extremely careful how they portray people and what they say about them if they are to avoid a costly court case.

Case study: Dixon vs. the *Daily Mirror*

In 2009, the *Daily Mirror* reported that Tom Dixon, a serving police officer, had attacked his former fiancée and her new partner with a baton and CS spray. Mr Dixon made a formal complaint to the PCC, listing the inaccuracies of the story. Under direction from the PCC, the *Daily Mirror* removed the article and agreed that the story did indeed contain inaccuracies.

1 **Looking at this case, why do you think Mr Dixon decided to complain to the PCC?**

2 **If the PCC did not exist, what other options could he have had to put the record straight?**

3 **Write a summary of your thoughts and share them with your group.**

Human rights legislation

The Human Rights Act (HRA) (1998) is a very important piece of legislation. It sets out the rights that individuals can expect to enjoy in the UK. The HRA initially caused consternation among the press, particularly around two of the eighteen articles highlighted in the Act.

- **Article 8**: Everyone has the right to respect for his private and family life, his home and correspondence.

- **Article 10**: Everyone has the right to freedom of expression.

These two rights appear to be contradictory, and the press were concerned about the relationship between the two that would be established in **test cases** by the judicial system.

The HRA was adapted from the European Convention of Human Rights (UCHR). Across Europe, Article 10 had taken **precedence** over Article 8, giving the press a much strengthened position when the law came into effect in the UK. However, the provisions of the Act are not being applied equally across the courts. It has been argued that the higher courts are interpreting the legislation in the way that Europe intended, with freedom of expression taking precedence over the

right to privacy, but the lower courts are favouring individual privacy over freedom of expression. This highlights discrepancies in the way the law is applied – which is not a good situation for the press.

Key terms

Test case – a legal case that requires a judge to make a decision on a case, and which might have large-scale repercussions and lead to many other similar cases being brought to the courts.

Precedence – when a particular legal decision becomes binding on future similar cases.

Activity: Human Rights Act (1998)

Do Articles 8 and 10 of the Human Rights Act (1998) contradict each other?

If so, which should take precedence and why?

Discuss this in small groups then report back to the rest of the class.

Link

To understand how legal rules are created by precedent, see *Unit 22: Aspects of the legal system and the law making process* (pages 199–236).

Another aspect of the HRA with the potential to impact on the press is Article 12, which outlines issues regarding injunctions on information about to be published. An injunction is a ban on something. Article 12 makes it more difficult for a court to grant an injunction to prevent publication of a story. This supports the principle of freedom of expression and works in favour of the press.

Article 6

One part of the HRA which has been a disadvantage to the press is Article 6, which states that 'everyone is entitled to a fair trial'. By publishing stories about notorious crimes, or paying witnesses for their stories, the press can put the idea of the defendant's guilt in the minds of the public, even before a trial has taken place. The courts have recognised that this clearly compromises the defendant's right to a fair trial and have used Article 6 a number of times to restrict how the press report a case.

The HRA is generally a support to the press because it ensures their freedom of expression, but increasingly the press must be wary of breaching articles for fear of sanctions and censure by the PCC and the courts.

Costs and benefits of tight controls

One of the benefits of tight media regulation is that the public has a sense that the publications and programmes put out by the various media companies adhere to certain standards and, in the UK, can broadly be trusted to be accurate. Another benefit is that if a media story is incorrect, there are various agencies such as the PCC and Ofcom where complaints can be made, investigated and resolved. The costs of tight controls are that some stories cannot be reported in the media due to privacy or anonymity issues, even though the press may feel the public would want to know about them.

Censorship in other countries

Censorship can be viewed as the ability of individuals or groups in power to restrict freedom of expression, although a slightly wider definition is provided in the key term box. Censorship criminalises or suppresses the production of certain information and access to that information. Censorship is often explicitly defined in law, for example in the UK it is defined in the Obscene Publications Acts (1959 and 1964). The classification of films according to the ages of children who can view them is another type of censorship.

In other countries, censorship may rely on unspoken intimidation by government officials. This can leave people frightened to speak out on an issue for fear of losing their jobs or, in some countries, their lives. For example, Communist North Korea suppresses knowledge of how life is lived in other countries, particularly its non-Communist neighbour, South Korea. Political censorship means that people in countries such as Burma and Iran cannot demonstrate to demand the reforms they want without risking their lives.

Key term

Censorship – the examination of books, films, news, etc., that are about to be published and the suppression of any parts that are considered obscene, politically unacceptable or a threat to security.

Activity: Censorship

- What is your view of censorship?
- Is censorship a necessary or unnecessary step for a government to take?
- Is the 9 pm watershed a useful type of censorship?
- Are film classifications a valuable type of censorship?
- What other forms of censorship can you think of that affect you?

Create a table as a group that highlights the positive and negative aspects of censorship.

Table 24.3: The censorship debate – the arguments for and against censorship in the UK

For	Against
Censorship of violence may reduce levels of violence in society – people will not commit copycat crimes.	Censorship in any form is an attack on freedom of expression.
Protects society from offensive material.	Censorship rejects the notion that people should be able to decide for themselves what they see and read.
Sometimes the media needs to be censored to protect the public good, e.g. ensuring media coverage does not harm criminal or civil trials.	Censorship is conducted by the powerful against the powerless.
Censorship can be crucial in maintaining national security.	Censorship can be used by governments to prevent information becoming known which may harm their election prospects and public image.
Censorship can help respect the privacy of individuals.	An effective democracy relies on the free flow of information, discussion and debate. Censorship therefore harms democracy.
It can help some of the most vulnerable individuals in our society, such as children.	Censorship, in many cases, lacks scrutiny. It is merely the wishes of one group of individuals being imposed on others without checks and balances.

Activity: Censorship in China

China is a Communist society with very tight restrictions and controls on its own media agencies as well as the international agencies which operate within its borders. In 2006 Google offered China a version of its search engine, which had inbuilt censorship and blocked access to thousands of sites deemed unsuitable by the Chinese government. Google's offer was controversial, as some of the restricted documents included those describing human rights abuses occurring within China. In 2010 Google made the decision to stop censoring the results from Chinese searches and all users were redirected to its unrestricted Hong Kong site. The decision came after further restrictions on Web activity were put in place by China and the mail accounts of some Chinese Gmail users came under attack.

1 **Why would a country censor the information its citizens can access?**

2 **Why do you think Google made the initial decision to cooperate with China in 2006 and then pulled out of the country in 2010?**

3 **What kind of information would be deemed unsuitable in a country such as China?**

2.2 Self-regulation

The debate around media regulation hinges on whether the government should oversee regulation via legislation designed to restrict and monitor media conduct, or whether the media industry should have the power to regulate itself. The Communications Act (2003), which provided Ofcom with its powers, promotes the idea of self-regulation within the industry.

The thinking behind self-regulation is that by encouraging the press to draw up their own policies and standards, and handle complaints themselves, this offers increased flexibility and adaptability. Self-regulation is seen as more user-friendly for the industry than punitive-style regulations, which lack the ability to change quickly and respond to differing circumstances. In addition, it is argued that the media industry will be more likely to accept criticism and censure from a regulatory body that it is part of, rather than accepting criticism from the government.

Control of the Internet

The Internet is just another form of communication. There is some content on the Internet that could be deemed as illegal or offensive, such as inappropriate images and pornography. Although it is difficult to regulate these different forms of content on the Internet, we cannot simply ignore them. Criminal activity is also evident on the Internet, for example spam, scams, viruses, hacking, money laundering, identification and other forms of theft.

In the UK, illegal content is regulated by the Internet Watch Foundation (IWF), which encourages a self-regulatory approach. This organisation was founded in late 1996 by two trade bodies, the Internet Service Providers' Association (ISPA) and the London Internet Exchange (LINX), together with some large corporations such as BT and AOL. The IWF monitors activity on the Internet and uses its powers to prosecute and close down criminal organisations.

It is important that control mechanisms are in place to censor what information can be accessed and obtained on the Internet. For example, the Ministry of Defence (MoD) requests that certain limitations are placed on search queries, or that sites are censored to prevent a breach of national security. This is to prevent the locations and plans of military bases being used to organise terrorist attacks. Similarly, the plans of prisons are restricted so they cannot be used to assist in escape attempts.

Activity: Parental controls

1 Research the recent debates about controls to protect children from grooming by paedophiles.

2 What other threats are there to children using the Internet, and how can they be protected from such threats?

Freedom of the press

In any democratic society it is vital that the press are free to discuss current political issues away from the control of the government, who may apply bias or restrictions on what can be covered in a news story. Governments often have their own agenda in terms of what the media broadcast, and may prefer to restrict stories that criticise their policies in order to protect their position at the next election. This is hardly promoting a true sense of **democracy**.

Key terms

Democracy – a political system in which a government is either carried out by the people (direct democracy) or the power to govern is granted to elected representatives (Republicanism).

Deregulation – when the media is freed from the controls and constraints that might be imposed on them from an outside body, such as a regulator or the government.

Privatisation – when the media is privately owned as opposed to being owned by the government. For example, if the UK decided to sell the BBC to private investors.

It is also argued that self-regulation offers a much better service to the public who make complaints. Self-regulatory bodies, such as the Press Complaints Commission (PCC), are able to offer a fast, accessible and free service to anyone making a complaint.

Freedom of information

The Freedom of Information Act (2000) gives individuals or organisations the right to request information from any public authority, or by companies wholly owned by public authorities in England, Wales and Northern Ireland. However, organisations have a right to refuse if they think the information is available elsewhere. There is also a charge for the information, which may prevent people from accessing it.

Voluntary codes of practice

The media do adopt voluntary codes of practice, which are often conducted successfully. An example of this is the voluntary code of practice that protected Prince William and Prince Harry from media intrusion until they had completed their education. This included allowing the Princes to be free from harassment, checking that stories about them were correct prior to publication and not publishing photos which infringed their privacy.

However, some publications were prepared to push these guidelines to the limits. In 2000, *OK* magazine published photos of Prince William in the Chilean jungle where he was working while on a gap year. *OK* magazine argued that this was a public place and therefore their photographic coverage was entirely legitimate. Representatives for the Prince took the matter to the PCC who judged that the Prince was not in a location where the press would have normally been, and therefore his privacy had been invaded by the photographer.

Bias and propaganda

Propaganda is a specific type of communication aimed at influencing the opinions of others, rather than impartially providing information. Media bias can be obvious in books or broadcasts, when authors and presenters argue particular values in a written or verbal context. For example, bias can be conveyed in the media through the selection of stories, sequences and headlines. The use of propaganda is widespread in war situations, where it is very important that the public join together against a common enemy. For example, propaganda was used very successfully in Britain in both World Wars to exaggerate German and Nazi atrocities and play down British failures.

2.3 Ownership and revenue generation

Media empires

The media is dominated by a few giant global media corporations who own the majority of the Western media. The moves towards **deregulation** and **privatisation** in the USA and UK in the 1980s led to increased opportunities for media companies to buy up other media assets. This in turn resulted in the growth of transnational media companies. One of the main empires is News Corporation, owned by Rupert Murdoch, which includes such newspapers as *The Sun*, *The Times*, *News of the World* and *Sky* television.

Other giant global media corporations include:

- AOL Time Warner
- Viacom Inc.
- Walt Disney Company
- Bertelsmann
- Vivendi Universal
- General Electric
- Liberty Media
- AT&T
- Sony.

Did you know?

According to Forbes, Rupert Murdoch is worth an estimated $6.3 billion (£5.3 bn).

Activity: Influence of the media

Do you think that media owners exert influence over what the media publishes or chooses to report on? Discuss as a class then write down the key points, so you all have a 'hand out' copy.

Independence of the BBC

The British Broadcasting Corporation (BBC) is the largest broadcasting organisation in the world. It is funded by an annual television licence fee, which is charged to all UK households, companies and organisations using any type of equipment (including a computer) to record and/or receive live television broadcasts.

The BBC's main responsibility is to provide public service broadcasting within the UK, Channel Islands and Isle of Man. The BBC is an independent organisation that, in theory, should be able to produce and broadcast, within reason, whatever it deems newsworthy. Although state funded, in the sense that the government collects the licence fee, the BBC maintains complete independence from government influence. As the BBC has no advertising, it does not have to do what advertisers want either. This means it can focus on what the public wants and produce high-quality news, educational programming and entertainment without interference.

Commercial media companies argue that the BBC has an unfair advantage and does not have to compete in the media marketplace like other companies. However, supporters of the BBC see this as an advantage, as it doesn't have to cut costs and make poor-quality programmes, just to put profits into the hands of wealthy media owners.

Political bias

Political bias when held by a newspaper, TV channel or similar area of the media refers to pervasive or widespread support for a particular agenda or viewpoint. This contravenes the standards of journalism and is on a different scale to the individual views expressed by a journalist.

However, it can be argued that certain newspapers are on a political spectrum, following the left or right wing of political parties. These newspapers write for a specific audience or genre. For example, in the 2010 UK General Election *The Sun* newspaper declared itself Conservative, the *Daily Mirror* supported Labour and the *Guardian* supported the Liberal Democrats. You could argue from this that the stories written in those newspapers followed the political agenda of those parties rather than being independent.

Influence of advertisers

The impact of advertisers cannot be overstated. They have created tremendous wealth and revenue for newspapers and magazines. In the USA there are some media publications which make 70 per cent of their revenue from advertising and only 30 per cent from actual sales of the publication. In the UK the figure is closer to 50 per cent. This means that if a

---

Case study: The Hutton Inquiry

The BBC is a well-respected and influential member of the national and international media community. Although the government funds the BBC by charging all UK television viewers a licence fee, in theory the BBC is completely independent.

In September 2002 the UK government produced a dossier which argued Iraq could deploy weapons of mass destruction within 45 minutes. These claims strengthened the argument to go to war against Iraq.

In May 2003 the BBC's *Today* programme broadcast journalist Andrew Gilligan's report claimed that the dossier was in fact 'sexed up' and included information the intelligence service did not think was valid. The government denied the reports and heavily criticised the BBC for broadcasting the report. The government also named Andrew Gilligan's source of information as Dr David Kelly, a well-respected intelligence expert who worked for the government. Dr Kelly's name was made public on 10 July. By 17 July he had committed suicide.

The subsequent Hutton Inquiry into the incident blamed the BBC almost entirely. As a result Andrew Gilligan resigned, as did the Director General of the BBC Greg Dyke and BBC Chairman Gavyn Davies.

1 **The government appointed Lord Hutton to investigate the circumstances surrounding Dr Kelly's death. Can a government-appointed inquiry ever be independent?**

2 **What impact did the Hutton Inquiry have on the BBC?**

3 **Do you think the government applied pressure to the BBC? If so, can the BBC be considered independent?**

4 **Do you think it is fair that the BBC bears the brunt of the responsibility in the Hutton Inquiry?**

5 **What could the BBC do to make itself more independent from the government?**

publication upsets an advertiser, it could potentially lose millions. What could this publication do if a news story emerged that painted the products of a powerful advertiser in a bad light?

Did you know?

Depending on what is being advertised, it can cost anywhere between £250,000–£15,000,000 to create an advert. Additional costs then depend on what time it will be shown – peak time viewing can cost up to £2,500,000.

Case study: An unpopular truth

It has been announced that a local hospital unit carrying out child heart surgery is going to be closed down. The unpopular truth is that there are too few operations carried out at the unit for the surgeons to develop and maintain vital surgical skills in this highly-specialised area. It is felt that the success rate for the same operations would be higher if they were carried out at a larger, unit with highly-skilled surgeons, who regularly carry out these procedures, and have built up lots of expertise.

However, local newspapers headlines are encouraging people to fight to maintain their local services. The front page is full of stories of local people whose children had attended the unit.

1   **Which view do you think would sell more newspapers?**

2   **Can you find other examples of unpopular truths versus populism?**

Key term

Populism – supporting, or seeking to appeal to the concerns of ordinary people.

Ratings wars

Television channels strive to obtain the most viewers for the programmes that they show. The more viewers a programme receives, the more revenue the channel gains through advertisements. Ratings are important to any programme, as this form of feedback demonstrates how many viewers have watched it, and whether the programme should continue in future. The ratings for a programme also determine how much revenue can be charged for adverts. An advertiser will not pay to show an advert in the break of a programme that hardly anyone is watching, or pay to put an advert in a newspaper that no one reads; however, advertisers will pay premium prices to show their ads during popular programmes.

This in turn has led some commercial TV channels to produce reality TV programmes, such as Big Brother, which draw high numbers of viewers, but are not necessarily good quality TV. Some so-called family viewing programmes include sensational storylines that will attract more viewers. For the same reasons, tabloid newspapers tend to devote a lot more space to celebrity news than they do to articles about world events.

Quality of reporting

The media in some respects is in a difficult position. People want news that makes them feel positive, though some news by its very nature will be negative. This leaves the media with a choice. Do they tell the public the popular view and increase their sales, or do they tell the unpopular truth and risk alienating the public and reducing the number of people who buy their product? The case study opposite highlights what can happen when the media report unpopular truths.

Assessment activity 24.2

P3 **P4** **M2** **D1**   **:BTEC**

Working in a small group, design and produce a newspaper or magazine article which covers the issues of regulation, ownership and revenue generation within the media. You should be able to:

1   Identify the methods used in the regulation and self-regulation of the media in the UK. **P3**

2   Assess the independence of the media from owners, revenue generators and politicians. **P4**

3   Analyse the independence of the media from owners, revenue generators and politicians. **M2**

4   Evaluate the independence of the media from owners, revenue generators and politicians, and the media's ability to report objectively. **D1**

Grading tips

For **P3** you need to identify how the media is regulated, giving examples of both government regulation in the UK and beyond. You should include how the media self-regulate, e.g. when it chooses not to respect an individual's privacy.

For **P4** you need to assess the control exerted by owners, revenue generators, political or any other influences, and the effect this can have on public services.

To extend this assessment for **M2** and **D1** you will need to analyse the independence of the media from owners, advertisers and politicians. Discuss whether the media follows or leads public opinion (for example, in relation to issues such as the treatment of paedophiles or asylum seekers).

PLTS

By working as part of a team to produce your newspaper or magazine article, you will demonstrate your skills as a **team worker** and **effective participator**.

Functional skills

Producing a newspaper or magazine article will develop your functional **ICT** skills in developing, presenting and communicating information.

3.   How the public services are portrayed in the media

3.1 Positive and negative images of the public services

The public services are portrayed in a variety of ways by the media. The coverage can be both real, in that it highlights actual members of the public services performing the job that they are employed to do, or it can be a fictional portrayal, such as a TV drama, which may not be grounded in the live experience of many public service officers. The Police and the portrayal of crime dominates real and fictional representations of the public services.

A UK study found that tabloids report more crime stories than the broadsheets. *The Sun* dedicated 30.4 per cent of its coverage to crime news, compared to 5.1 per cent in the *Guardian*. What this highlights is that a substantial proportion of media time and energy is spent on the portrayal of public services. The number of crime dramas and public service related TV shows also form a large proportion of the UK's day-to-day TV viewing.

Negative images of the public services

The media views the public services in a variety of ways that can be viewed as negative.

Brutality

The media show incidents where public service workers, such as those in the Army and the Police, are brutal to ordinary citizens. An example of this was the alleged assault of a female protester at the G20 riots in 2009 by a Metropolitan Police officer. The officer was recorded striking the protester. An investigation by the IPPC cleared the officer of wrongdoing.

Corruption

The media will pursue suspected corruption in the public services and expose it for all to see. A good example of this is the MP's expenses scandal, when hundreds of MPs were found to be abusing their expenses system. Four of them are now facing criminal charges for their behaviour.

Police corruption is a relatively rare occurrence, but intense media coverage which sensationalises the few occurrences which do occur gives a false impression to the public and has a negative effect on police morale. See the case study on the West Midland Serious Crime Squad below for further discussion.

Racism

Racism has long been a charge levelled at the public services by the media, whether during the Brixton Riots in the early 1980s, the stopping and searching of black youths in the 1990s or the lack of recruitment of ethnic minority officers across all Police forces in England and Wales. However, it took the murder of a black teenager called Stephen Lawrence to put the subject firmly on the political and media agenda, when the Police Service was accused of **institutionalised racism** (see the case study on page 260).

Case study: West Midlands Serious Crime Squad

During the 1970s and 1980s the West Midlands Serious Crime Squad secured confessions to crimes from suspects by brutal and corrupt interview techniques. The allegations against them included making suspects write out false statements, putting plastic bags over the heads of suspects and suffocating them until they signed the confession. The squad was disbanded in 1989, and 30 of the convictions which were secured by the squad were found to be unsafe and were quashed by the Court of Appeal. These include such notable cases such as the Birmingham Six and the Bridgewater Four.

1 **Do you think increased pressure on Police officers to achieve crime fighting targets may lead to actions such as those described above? Explain your answer.**
2 **How would you propose to tackle police corruption?**
3 **Why does Police corruption make headline news?**
4 **Does media publicity on police corruption and miscarriages of justice create an inaccurate picture of Police conduct?**

Key term

Institutionalised racism – when people within a group or organisation share a collective view or approach that includes discriminating against those from a different race or ethnic background.

Blind obedience

The media may choose to portray the public services as lacking in discipline and judgement if they are blindly obedient when following orders.

Members of the public services are trained to follow commands given by higher-ranking members of their organisation. A positive example is when members of the Fire Service follow the commands of the leading fire officer during an incident.

Sometimes, however, people carry out orders that they would not normally, or that have tragic consequences. This is known as blind obedience because the person is 'shutting their eyes' to the potential consequences. The media sometimes use this term for the public services when they act without discipline and judgement when following orders.

Case study: Stephen Lawrence

Stephen was an 18-year-old A-Level student who was attacked and killed by a gang of white youths in April 1993. The Police investigation which followed failed to result in the conviction of any of Stephen's killers, and the Metropolitan Police Force was subsequently investigated. The Macpherson Report of 1999 into Stephen's killing concluded that the inadequacies of the murder investigation were the result of institutionalised racism within the force. For example, it was found that because Stephen was black the Metropolitan Police approached his murder investigation less vigorously than they would have another similar crime. Also, the Report concluded that the Metropolitan Police Force was reluctant to investigate Stephen's murderers fully because they were white.

The murder of Stephen Lawrence and the ensuing investigation and report made newspaper headlines throughout the mid to late 1990s. The media made great use of the findings of the Macpherson Report to highlight the failings of the Metropolitan Police Force in the Lawrence case, as well as highlighting various other racist allegations made against the Police.

The results of the media examination into this case have been largely positive, even though it was a negative portrayal of the Police themselves. The media coverage ensured that the inadequate and inappropriate investigation could not be swept under the carpet and that the recommendations from the Macpherson Report had to be seen to be acted upon. This encouraged and fostered change within the Police Service and put the issue of institutionalised racism firmly in the public domain.

However, media coverage of the murder of Stephen Lawrence did have a negative effect on Police morale, as although individual officers were named in the Macpherson Report, the force as a whole came under heavy political and media criticism. This affected many officers who had worked hard building up community and ethnic relations, and who felt as if the time and effort they had put in had been undone. Equally, the accusation of racism left Police officers uncertain of how to approach black individuals who they suspected might have committed a crime. Certainly the media attention on the issue at the time meant any genuine error might be reported in the press as a racist incident.

1 Why was the Police investigation of the murder of Stephen Lawrence flawed?
2 Why did the media cover this story in detail?
3 Do you think the media has helped improve the situation for reporting racist incidents to the Police?
4 What were the negative impacts of the media coverage of this case?
5 The original Macpherson report made 70 recommendations. Go to the Parliament publications website at www.publications. parliament.uk and search for 'Macpherson report 10 years' on to see how much had changed by 2009.

Activity: Blind obedience

Excuses given for blind obedience range from: just following orders, found it difficult to resist the commands given, or events happened too fast to be able to think clearly.

Examples of blind obedience from history include:

- Actions carried out by German soldiers during the holocaust and Nazi death camps in World War Two.
- Chinese troops firing on unarmed civilians in Tiananmen Square in 1989.

Can you think of any more recent examples of blind obedience in the UK or around the world?

Effects of negative images on public perception

The issue of compensation for Police officers who are injured in the line of duty is one that has received negative media coverage. Officers who attended the Hillsborough football stadium disaster claimed hundreds of thousands of pounds after they developed post-traumatic stress disorder (PTSD) in response to the events they had witnessed. The media were scathing in their response to the claims, noting that the families of the victims received 100 times less than one of the officers who claimed PTSD. The media opened the debate as to whether public service workers should have been entitled to any compensation at all since the activities which are likely to cause PTSD are an integral part of the job that they do. However, payments for PTSD are not the only financial issue relating to the

Police to appear in the papers. There have also been headlines surrounding pension fraud and malingering in order to claim sick pay.

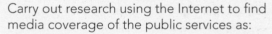

Activity: Police compensation

Why would the media choose to portray Police compensation so negatively?

Positive images of the public services

Members of the public services compromise their safety on a daily basis to protect our society from those who would seek to do it harm. However, the outstanding contribution of the vast majority of the public services towards social order, stability and personal often doesn't get reported. But on occasion the media does celebrate those public service workers who sacrifice their time, health and sometimes their lives to protect others.

Courage and self-sacrifice

The media tend to show the courage of ordinary public service workers when they are doing their jobs under extreme circumstances, for example the bravery shown by the troops in Afghanistan. There is also a lot of media support for the 'Help for Heroes' campaign.

The public services operate 24 hours a day, 7 days a week, 365 days a year performing acts of tremendous courage, bravery and self-sacrifice. Other examples of courage and self-sacrifice highlighted by the media include:

- the death of fire-fighter Rob Miller from Leicester Fire and Rescue Service who died in 2002 while searching a burning factory to see if anyone was trapped
- Fleur Lombard, a fire-fighter in Avon, who died in a supermarket blaze in 1998
- PC Andrew Jones of South Wales Police, who was fatally injured during a road collision in 2003 while chasing a burglar.

The list of public service officers who have given their lives for the protection and safety of others is long and distinguished. Although the press doesn't often comment on the day-to-day performance of the public services, when they do pay respect to remarkable acts

of bravery, such as those described, it helps to create admiration and respect for the public services among the general public.

Care

The media sometimes show the public services as caring for the general public and taking their needs into account. This is particularly true of educational and health services.

Discipline

The public services can be portrayed as a very disciplined group of people who do not respond to provocation and remain professional in the most challenging circumstances.

Adaptive or out of date?

The media can view the public services as adaptive and responsive to situations as they happen. Or conversely they can show them as out of date and unable to cope with the situations facing them.

Activity: Finding media images of the public services

Carry out research using the Internet to find media coverage of the public services as:

1 caring
2 disciplined
3 adaptive
4 out of date.

Service practice and morale

The positive and negative images of the public services as portrayed by the media can have the added impact of being able to affect service practice. The negative images of Police stop and search procedure being used primarily against black and Asian young men were a force for change in how stop and search is handled by the Police today. Stop and search also had a negative impact on the recruitment of ethnic minorities into the Police Service, which was another reason to amend how it was carried out.

Positive or negative stories about the public services in the media have a corresponding effect on the morale of service personnel: a negative story can reduce morale making the service less productive, and a positive story can have the opposite effect.

Assessment activity 24.3

In small groups of no more than four people, discuss the answers to the following:

1 Explain how positive and negative images affect public perceptions of the public services as well as service practice and morale. **P5**

2 Analyse how positive and negative images affect public perceptions of the public services. **M3**

3 Evaluate how positive and negative images affect public perceptions of the public services. **D2**

Grading tips

For **P5** you can use some case studies relating to positive and negative images of the public services, and how these affect public service personnel.

To achieve the pass and merit grades, this discussion will require you to explain and analyse the positive and negative images in the media that affect public perceptions of the public services.

(You will be doing more detailed work using case studies in Assessment activity 24.4.)

PLTS

By considering the positive and negative images in the media and how they affect the public services, you will demonstrate your skills as a **reflective learner**.

Functional skills

This discussion task will help you develop the speaking and listening portion of your functional skills in **English**.

3.2 How the public services use the media

In addition to being portrayed in the media, the public services are increasingly using the media to further their own ends. Some of the ways in which they use the media are described below.

Public health and information campaigns

The public services support government public safety campaigns. Good examples of this are:

- drink driving
- road safety for children
- crime prevention campaigns.

These come in the form of billboards, posters, newspaper advertisements and TV and radio commercials. Government figures for 2007 state that 9280 road accidents happened when a driver was over the legal limit for alcohol, and 2170 people were killed or seriously injured as a result. A large-scale publicity campaign can help the public be aware of the issues surrounding drink driving and the consequences of it.

Campaigns extend to children as well. Traffic is one of the largest killers of children under the age of 14. Government safety campaigns aim to make children more aware of these dangers when they encounter traffic. These campaigns are supported by Police officers who go into schools to promote the message behind the campaign.

It is not just the Police who advise on and support public safety campaigns. The Fire Service is heavily involved in promoting the government's fire safety campaigns on issues such as smoke alarms, kitchen fires, careless smoking, fire evacuation plans and hoax callers.

Appeals for information

The public services, particularly the Police, may call upon the media to help them appeal for information from the general public, for example on a crime recently committed. This may take the form of a press conference, a news story or a short article on a TV programme such as *Crimewatch*.

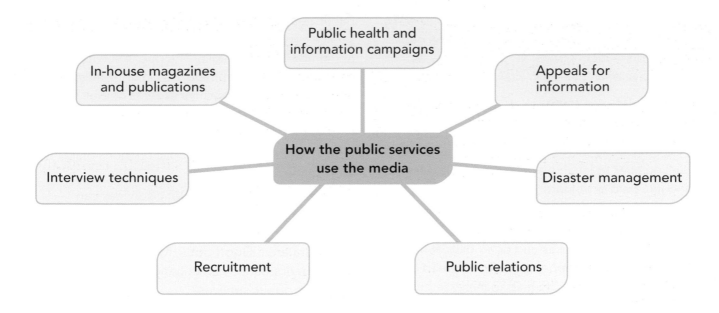

Figure 24.3: How the public services use the media

There are many occasions when the Police need to inform the public to be vigilant, perhaps after a sighting of a dangerous criminal or the abduction of a child. Equally, many crimes have witnesses who don't even know that they are witnesses until an appeal for information goes out.

Disaster management

The public services use the media extensively in a disaster management situation, for any or all of the following reasons:

- to inform the public to stay indoors in the event of a chemical or biological contamination
- to make a call for off-duty medical professionals to report to their hospitals
- to provide information on casualties and fatalities
- to warn the public to stay away from a disaster site
- to publicise helpline numbers for concerned individuals
- to reassure the public that a disaster is being dealt with quickly and efficiently
- to coordinate evacuation plans
- to call for specialised assistance such as counsellors or utility workers.

Censorship

The UK public services have to use censorship when releasing information to the media that might compromise their operations either at home or abroad. For example, the deployment of Prince Harry to Afghanistan was withheld from the media, both to protect him and his unit from insurgent attacks. The media broke the story regardless and Prince Harry was recalled home to the UK. The Police may use censorship during large-scale manhunts. For example, if they are closing in on a suspect they do not want him or her watching the news and finding out they have been located.

News blackouts are quite rare and they are used only when public service operations require it. Scotland Yard requested a news blackout when they interviewed Tony Blair for the second time regarding the cash for questions scandal in Parliament.

Interview techniques

Often in public services interviews, the recruitment team will use media examples to highlight actual events. The recruitment team will then want to evaluate the comments made by the recruits and compare them to how they should have actually dealt with the situation.

Public services personnel are sometimes interviewed by the media, or need to interview members of the public. This can be done more effectively if public services personnel have been trained in interview techniques.

Public relations (PR) and recruitment

All of the public services rely on civilian support to help them do their jobs. This may take the form of dialling 999, pulling over to let an emergency vehicle pass or working in a paid or voluntary capacity.

Services which come into contact with the public on a frequent basis need to be particularly aware of their public image. Press releases and open days at fire stations, for example, keep the public informed about the work the services do and help to increase public support for them.

Public relations can be harmed by many things such as service corruption, incompetence and poor treatment of members of the public. The public services use the media for damage limitation in circumstances like this and to promote the positive aspects of their work.

Public relations departments may also be responsible for producing in-house magazines. You can read more about the work of a public relations officer in Workspace on page 267.

A negative image of the public services can seriously harm recruitment and retention of staff within the services, so public relations is a really important area. Good publicity and attractive recruitment posters can enhance how the public views the public services.

4. Be able to review current affairs affecting public services

4.1 Case studies

The media often portrays the public services in a very different way to how they actually function in real-life situations. In TV crime dramas, the crime is always solved and the criminal is always caught and sentenced. In reality, the chances of catching a criminal for an offence are relatively low and a lot of public services work is very routine. However, this wouldn't make for a very entertaining programme, so the media manipulate the facts to make them more entertaining.

Case study: *CSI: Crime Scene Investigation*

In the popular crime drama *CSI: Crime Scene Investigation* we are treated to glamorous scientists who attend the scene of a crime looking as if they have stepped off a catwalk. The scientists have seemingly unlimited resources and lab time and are always able to use information gathered at the crime scene and equipment at the lab to deduce how the crime happened and who did it.

Real scene of crime officers do not recognise this picture of their work. Forensic specialists who attend crime scenes do so fully covered from head to toe in protective suits with hoods. They wear gloves and boot covers and may also require goggles. This is done so that the officers do not leave traces of their own DNA, such as their skin cells, hair or saliva, at the scene of the crime.

Once evidence is collected it can take some time to process, depending on the sample type, and it is often given to specialist labs to do the work. Results can take weeks or months to come back and may prove inconclusive when they do. However, showing all this would not make for the dynamic and exciting crime-fighting show enjoyed by millions.

1 Why don't the media show the reality of public service life?

2 How could you make a real life public service drama interesting?

3 Do you think this type of programme helps the work of the public services?

4.2 Fact

The media also have a duty to report on the factual aspects of the public services, including:

- news coverage of public order incidents such as the G20 riots
- coverage of wars and conflicts which British public services are involved in
- coverage of serious incidents involving the public services, such as the shooting of Jean Charles Menendez (see the Case study below).

The media also show factual entertainment programmes and documentaries about the lives and work of the public services, such as *Ross Kemp in Afghanistan* and *Traffic Cops*. This type of reporting gives a much more realistic portrayal of the public services and the actual work they do, although even these programmes can concentrate more on the exciting operational aspects of service life rather than the routine training and paperwork.

4.3 Fiction

The media also supply us with a great deal of fictional public service content in the form of books, television programmes, feature articles, films and stories. The fictional portrayals of the service can be very entertaining as they normally focus on the exciting aspects of the work. However, they give a very unrealistic impression of service life and this can lead to potential recruits having a very distorted view of what life in public services is like.

Activity: Fiction

List as many fictional portrayals of the public services as you can think of in the following categories:

- film
- TV
- books.

Compare your answers with the rest of the group.

Case study: The shooting of Jean Charles Menendez

Jean Charles Menedez, a 27-year-old Brazilian electrician, was shot dead on the London Underground by Police on 22 July 2005 after they mistook him for a terrorist.

The Police were on high alert after an attempted terrorist attack on trains and buses the day before. On the day of the fatal shooting, Mr Menendez left his flat and headed towards Stockwell tube station. Mr Menendez's flat had been under surveillance by Scotland Yard, as a suspected terrorist had been identified as living in the same building. The Police mistook Mr Menendez for the terrorist and followed him towards his destination. He was shot seven times in the head and once in the shoulder at close range as he sat on the train.

The media response after the killing was mixed, with some taking the line that the Police had a duty to protect citizens from terrorism, and others arguing that this was the murder of an innocent man and that the Police were brutal and incompetent.

1   What are the possible ways the media could present a real life factual event such as this?

2   Using what you have already learned about how the media can affect public perceptions, describe the techniques the media use to alter public perceptions of a story to favour either one side or the other.

3   Research the Menendez case in more detail using web-based news sources such as the *Guardian*, BBC News or *The Times*.

Assessment activity 24.4

Working in pairs, research and design an A3 poster which does the following:

1 Reviews at least two current case studies of media portrayal of the public services, including at least one factual and one fictional. **P6**

2 Analyses at least two current case studies of media portrayal of the public services, including at least one factual and one fictional. **M4**

The case studies can be TV programmes, films, video clips, newspaper articles, books or podcasts.

Grading tip

For **P6** you need to review the case studies, whereas for **M6** you must analyse them.

PLTS

By working as part of a team to produce a poster you will demonstrate your skills as a **team worker** and **effective participator**.

Functional skills

Producing a poster using a computer will develop your functional **ICT** skills.

Stephanie Wood
Public relations officer, local government office

I work as a public relations officer for the local government office. I work full time and my role is to manage the reputation of the organisation, as well as influence opinion and behaviour.

I have to use all forms of media and communication to build, maintain and manage the reputation of the organisation. Part of my role is to communicate key messages in order to establish and maintain goodwill and understanding between the organisation and the general public.

A typical day

The role is varied and tasks typically involve:

- planning, developing and implementing PR strategies
- liaising with colleagues and key spokespeople
- liaising with and answering enquiries from the media, individuals and other organisations, often via telephone and email
- researching, writing and distributing press releases to targeted media
- collating and analysing media coverage
- writing and editing in-house magazines, case studies, speeches, articles and annual reports.

The best thing about the job

The best thing about being a public relations officer is working with a range of different people on a daily basis. Two days are never the same, and I am always busy ensuring that the office maintains its positive reputation to the general public.

Think about it!

- What subjects have you covered in this unit that might give you the background to be a good public relations officer?
- What knowledge and skills do you think you need to develop further if you want to be a public relations officer in the future?

Just checking

1. What types of media are there?
2. What is a moral panic?
3. How does the Human Rights Act (1998) impact upon the media in the UK?
4. What is media self-regulation?
5. How does the media portray positive aspects of the public services?
6. How does the media portray negative aspects of the public services?
7. How do advertisers influence the media?

Assignment tips

Research and preparation

- This may sound very basic, but make sure you have read your assignment thoroughly and you understand exactly what you are being asked to do. Once you are clear about this then you can move on to your research. Doing your research well and using good sources of evidence is essential.

- Lots of learners rely too much on the Internet and not enough on other sources of information such as books, newspapers and journals. The Internet is not always a good source of information. It is very easy to use information from American or Australian websites without noticing – but your tutor will notice. Always double check the information you find, don't just accept it at face value. Good research and preparation is the key to getting those higher grades.

Primary research

- Primary research is a method of research where you go out and collect your information personally. Reporting first-hand findings will develop your understanding and help to improve your grades.

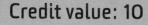

34 Environmental policies and practices

The impact of government activity, industry and commerce on the environment is an area of concern for citizens, governments and international bodies. This unit explores that impact and how the public sector is working towards sustainable development for the future.

It is generally agreed that demands placed on local, national and international resources and environmental systems, for example water, land, minerals and air, are unsustainable. An international definition of sustainable development is 'development which meets the needs of the present without compromising the ability of future generations to meet their own needs'. Globally we are failing both to meet the needs of the present (in terms of ensuring access to food, clean water and economic viability for all of the world's population) and to fully consider the needs of future generations.

This unit looks at some of the issues contributing to this situation. While studying this unit you will find out about the key environmental impacts that international, central and local government policies and initiatives aim to address. You will also find out about the guidelines and legislation intended to advise and support many government initiatives, and the role of the whole range of organisations involved in making and implementing policies to support sustainability.

You will then investigate the need for sustainable development, including the role of pressure groups in campaigning for it. Finally, you will consider the impact sustainable development is having on the provision of public services, including the national and international strategies and targets the public sector is striving to achieve.

Learning outcomes

After completing this unit you should:

1. know the impact of pollution and environmental damage
2. know the legal and regulatory framework which supports sustainability
3. understand the need for sustainable development.

Assessment and grading criteria

This table shows you what you must do in order to achieve a pass, merit or distinction grade, and where you can find activities in this book to help you.

To achieve a **pass** grade the evidence must show that you are able to:	To achieve a **merit** grade the evidence must show that, in addition to the pass criteria, you are able to:	To achieve a **distinction** grade the evidence must show that, in addition to the pass and merit criteria, you are able to:
P1 outline the impact of pollution and environmental damage on individuals and society in the UK **See Assessment activity 34.1 page 283**		
P2 identify domestic and international legislation and guidelines which support reduction of damage to the environment **See Assessment activity 34.2 page 297**	**M1** explain how the regulatory bodies support sustainability **See Assessment activity 34.2 page 297**	
P3 identify the role of the UK government departments and regulatory bodies in supporting sustainability **See Assessment activity 34.2 page 297**		
P4 outline the need for sustainable development **See Assessment activity 34.4 page 308**	**M2** analyse how pressure groups work to promote sustainability **See Assessment activity 34.4 page 308**	**D1** critically analyse UK public sector progress towards achieving strategies for sustainability **See Assessment activity 34.3 page 305**
P5 explain the role of pressure groups in promoting sustainability **See Assessment activity 34.4 page 308**		
P6 explain the impact of sustainable development on the UK public sector **See Assessment activity 34.3 page 305**	**M3** justify the targets set for the public sector to contribute to improving sustainability **See Assessment activity 34.3 page 305**	

How you will be assessed

This unit will be assessed by an internal assignment that will be designed and marked by the staff at your centre. The assignment is designed to allow you to show your understanding of the learning outcomes for environmental policies and practices. Assignments can be quite varied and can take the form of:

- projects
- role plays and scenarios
- presentations
- tutor observations
- written assignments

- case studies
- practical tasks
- leaflets
- posters.

Amran learns about the importance of protecting the environment

This unit has helped me to understand the difficult balance that exists between living in a wealthy society where I have lots of material possessions and ensuring our planet is still around and thriving in 100 years' time.

Before I studied this unit, I didn't really know about air pollution or environmental damage. Our group went to see a regeneration project near our college, on the river bank at Rochester in Kent. This was a former industrial site, which only a few years ago was covered in gravel, three gas holders and other industrial structures. With support from government grants the area is being transformed. First the pollution and rubbish had to be cleared from the site then new flood defences, a riverside park and houses were built. These included homes for elderly residents overlooking the river bank where wagtails and oystercatchers have repopulated the bay. The work is far from complete, but a total investment of £500 million is planned with 2000 new homes. Seeing all this was very exciting, but also quite daunting – it made me realise how much still needs to be done.

Having completed this unit, I'm much more aware of the importance of protecting our environment. This includes remembering to do the little things, such as not charging my mobile all night, turning lights off as I leave a room and not running water while I clean my teeth. I've also bought a stock of rechargeable batteries and generally I'm much more selective about what I buy – I check the packaging and how many air miles the product might have clocked up.

Past generations left industrial waste and pollution which my generation will need to deal with – I don't want to do the same for the next generation.

Over to you!

- **What do you know about the impact of environmental pollution and damage on your local community?**
- **How could you find out more?**
- **How can you make a personal contribution to sustainability?**

1. Know the impact of pollution and environmental damage

Think about the past 24 hours.

- What transport have you used?
- What energy have you used (for heat, light, entertainment)?
- What food have you eaten?
- What things have you bought? Were your purchases wrapped in plastic bags?

Your everyday actions can have a huge impact on the environment and the use of resources, many of which are non-renewable such as fossil fuels. As you read through this unit, think about how you could make a personal contribution to **sustainability**. You could get some ideas from the 'We Are What We Do' website (http://wearewhatwedo.org).

1.1 Pollution

Pollution is a word everyone is familiar with, but most people would struggle to explain what it means in full. Human activity always has an impact on the environment and often that impact is negative. Pollution takes many forms, for example industrial, chemical, heat and noise. We will look at these forms in more detail in this section.

Air pollution

Historically the main cause of **air pollution** in the UK was the burning of **fossil fuels** for both industrial and domestic use, creating high levels of sulphur dioxide. Sulphur dioxide is a colourless toxic gas caused by volcanoes, the burning of fossil fuels and industrial pollution. It can mix with water droplets in the air to form acid rain, resulting in environmental damage.

Acid rain often falls many miles from the source of pollution and can have a serious effect on soil, trees, buildings and water. As a result of acid rain, forests throughout the world are dying. In Scandinavia there are crystal clear dead lakes which contain no plant or animal life. In the UK freshwater fish are threatened and this could impact on animals too.

Key terms

Sustainability – meeting the current needs of society without compromising the ability of future generations to meet their own needs.

Pollution – the introduction into an environment of harmful substances, such as industrial waste, chemicals, heat and noise, as a result of human activities (either intentional or accidental). Pollution results in negative effects which may harm ecosystems, endanger the health of humans and other life, and impact on the enjoyment of legitimate uses of the environment.

Air pollution – anything that causes contamination of the air with harmful substances.

Fossil fuels – fuels formed by natural resources, such as decaying organic matter.

Did you know?

The burning of fossil fuels, such as petrol and diesel, creates a mixture of chemicals that includes **carbons**, **sulphates** and **nitrates**. These chemicals become suspended in the air in small particles known as particulates. Particulates that have a diameter of less than 10 micrometres (PM10s) and 2.5 micrometres (PM25s) can be absorbed into the bloodstream and have been linked by the World Health Organisation (WHO) to lung cancer, heart disease and breathing problems.

Key terms

Carbon – chemical found in all life on Earth. Different forms of carbon have different uses, for example hydrocarbons are found in crude oil and natural gas.

Sulphates – compounds of sulphuric acid. They are used in the manufacture of a whole range of products including medicines and building materials. They dissolve easily in water and contribute to acid rain.

Nitrates – chemicals used in the manufacture of a range of medicines. However, if they reach rivers and the sea they can pollute water causing illness in humans and animals and the death of fish and other marine life.

Another main source of air pollution is traffic fumes. In the UK, road vehicles are the third largest source of carbon emissions. These include:

- **Carbon monoxide** (CO) – a poisonous gas lighter than air with no smell or taste. Inhaling even relatively small amounts of the gas can result in severe injury and death.

- **Carbon dioxide** (CO_2) – a gas occurring naturally in small amounts in the Earth's atmosphere, but produced in large quantities by the burning of fossil fuels. An increase in the level of carbon dioxide in the atmosphere has contributed to global warming and climate change (see pages 274–5).

Traffic fumes are a complicated mixture of waste products created by vehicle engines. In addition to the carbons, they include a large number of pollutants such as:

- **Benzene** – a component of oil- and coal-based products. It is used when making a range of plastics, chemicals and pesticides and has been shown to cause cancer.

- **Lead** – a metal that has been used in the manufacture of products such as water pipes and paint. Lead dust and vapour can be inhaled or swallowed and can cause a range of symptoms including kidney damage and damage to an unborn child.

- **Formaldehyde** – another colourless cancer-causing chemical. It has a strong smell and is flammable. It is used in the production of household products like adhesive and in common building materials.

A recent EU study (*Europe's Social Reality: A 'stocktaking'*, 2008) concluded that air pollution reduces life expectancy across Europe by an average of nine months.

Did you know?

High levels of lead found in the blood of people living near Birmingham's M6 Spaghetti Junction (one of the busiest motorway intersections in Europe) in the 1970s contributed to the drive towards lead-free petrol in the UK.

Did you know?

The World Health Organisation (WHO) estimates that air pollution causes two million premature deaths worldwide each year. The majority of these deaths occur in developing countries that have poorer air quality. WHO also estimates that over 30,000 of those deaths occur in the UK and over 300,000 in Europe.

1.2 Environmental damage

Noise pollution

In addition to air pollution, traffic also causes noise pollution, or unwanted sound. Excess noise is at best an irritant and at worst can cause permanent damage to hearing and ongoing stress for those exposed to it. No one wants to live near motorways, railway lines and under the flight paths of aircraft. Workers in noisy environments are offered ear protectors to reduce any damage to hearing from excessive noise.

Environmental Protection UK identifies various causes of noise pollution including:

- noise in the street, for example car and burglar alarms sounding, noise from loudspeakers
- noise at night, for example from neighbour's parties, people leaving pubs, nightclubs, fireworks
- noise at work, including construction site and industrial noise
- noise from transport.

Did you know?

Current EU regulations mean the maximum volume personal music players can reach is 100 decibels – that's the same as a pneumatic drill heard from 4 metres away! Listening to an average 100-decibel sound for around two hours requires at least 16 hours' of rest for the ears to repair and avoid permanent damage. Deafness Research UK fears too many people are risking damage to their hearing by listening to their MP3 player too loudly and too long. EU scientists recommend 80 decibels is adopted as the new safe limit.

Visual intrusion

Visual intrusion describes the negative visual impact something has on the environment. For example, this could be:

- unsightly or poorly maintained buildings, gardens and open spaces
- overhead power lines
- brightly lit or excessively large business signs
- graffiti covering bus shelters, walls and buildings.

Light pollution caused by artificial lights used in developed societies causes 'sky glow' – an orange glow rising from towns. This artificial light overpowers the natural light from distant stars, which may have taken thousands of years to arrive at Earth. Not only does excess lighting cause pollution, it also wastes energy, much of it created from non-renewable sources.

Activity: Visual intrusion

Recent debate has focused on the use of wind turbines to generate electricity. While wind power is a renewable fuel source, the noise, visual impact and potential damage to bird populations caused by wind turbines has resulted in considerable opposition to wind farms.

1 **Research this topic further at www.clean-energy-ideas.com. List the advantages and disadvantages of wind turbines then research real cases where local communities have been active for or against their use.**

2 **Hold a class debate proposing either that wind turbines should be banned or that the future of green energy depends on a greater use of wind power.**

Global warming and climate change

Naturally occurring greenhouse gases, such as carbon dioxide, water vapour and **ozone**, trap heat in the Earth's atmosphere. This keeps the temperature of the Earth approximately 30 degrees Celsius warmer than it would have been. This warming of the Earth's atmosphere is called the greenhouse effect (see Figure 34.1).

Key term

Ozone – a gas found throughout the atmosphere, but mainly in a band between 15 km and 40 km above the Earth's surface. This ozone layer protects the Earth from harmful ultraviolet radiation and is vital for life on our planet. Ozone acts as a greenhouse gas at lower levels, helping trap heat, and so contributes to global warming.

However, human activities such as the use of fossil fuels and the resulting release of pollutants, dumping waste in landfill sites (see page 276) and intensive farming have caused levels of certain greenhouse

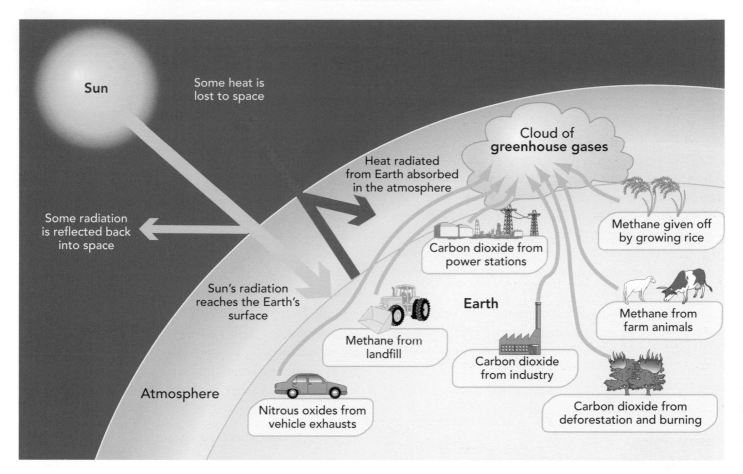

Figure 34.1: The greenhouse effect describes the warming of the Earth's atmosphere. Human activities are thought to have increased the levels of greenhouse gases in the atmosphere, resulting in climate change.

gases (mainly carbon dioxide and methane) to increase during the past two centuries. This has resulted in more of the sun's energy being retained in the Earth's atmosphere, and consequently average temperatures throughout the world are rising – a global increase of between 0.6 degrees and 1.0 degrees Celsius has been recorded over the past century. This process is known as global warming and has caused climate change (see page 279–80).

Depletion of natural resources

The depletion of natural resources, including minerals and oil, challenges us to:

- better protect and conserve the natural environment upon which humanity and all species of life on Earth depend
- reduce our dependence on non-renewable fuel sources such as crude oil and natural gas
- look for alternative renewable resources, for example generating energy using wind power, solar panel or hydroelectric schemes.

Did you know?

Cragside House in Northumberland was the first house in the world to be lit by hydroelectricity. In 1868, a hydraulic engine was installed to power the lights, laundry, kitchen and a lift.

In the UK, natural resources that have been depleted include fossil fuels (especially coal), oil reserves, fish stocks and forests. Wealthy, developed nations consume a disproportionate amount of the world's non-renewable resources, mostly through their use of fossil fuels to generate power (for example for cars, televisions and holidays abroad) and their high demand for consumer goods. Organisations such as the World Wildlife Fund (WWF) are therefore campaigning for a more **sustainable** approach.

Key term

Sustainable – able to continue over long periods of time.

They argue that we need to take care to consume the Earth's resources at a pace that allows the Earth to recover naturally, for example, to replace the forests that we cut down and give the fish stocks that we consume time to replenish. If we continue to consume the Earth's resources faster than they can recover, we will gradually deplete them to the detriment of all life on Earth.

Efforts must therefore be made to protect threatened resources. One example of this is the introduction of fishing limits (quotas) to protect cod in the North Sea when it was found that their populations had collapsed due to over-fishing. Reuse and recycling will also help to protect non-renewable resources and ensure they are available for future generations.

Some of the impacts of the depletion of natural resources are examined later in this unit, for example the reduction in rainforests is examined on page 298.

Did you know?

The WWF's *Living Planet Report* (available at www.wwf.org.uk) illustrates how humanity's demand on the Earth's natural resources currently exceeds the Earth's capacity for meeting that demand. Clearly this situation is unsustainable over the long term.

Use of landfill sites

Household waste has traditionally been dumped in landfill sites. Landfills are not designed to breakdown waste but to bury it – the environment is protected from waste pollution by containing the waste in waterproof plastic. While this approach prevents contamination, it effectively traps the waste in the ground, thereby creating land pollution for future generations to deal with. When old landfills have been excavated, 40-year-old newspapers have been found with easily readable print. By volume about a third of waste going to landfill is plastics, which takes hundreds of years to decompose.

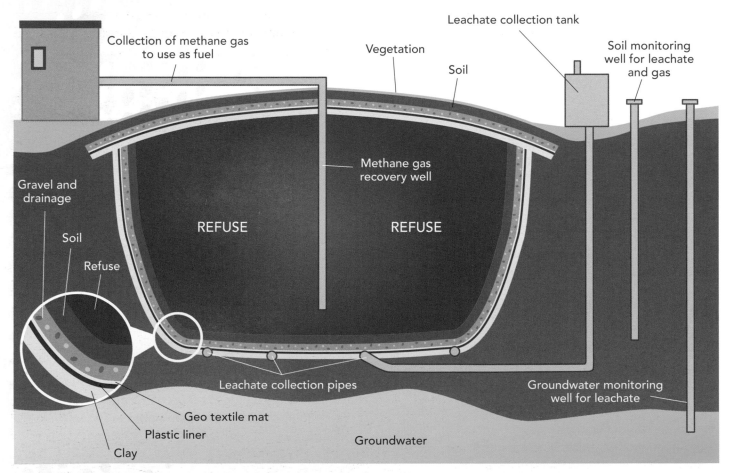

Figure 34.2: The structure of a landfill site. Landfill sites are carefully designed to bury waste in such a way that it does not contaminate the surrounding groundwater and air. When a landfill closes, the site, especially the groundwater, must be monitored and maintained for up to 30 years.

Waste currently going to landfill in the UK includes:

- 50 per cent of industrial and commercial waste

- 55 per cent of domestic waste

- 25 per cent of waste from demolition and construction.

The UK government is aiming to halve the amount of waste going to landfill by 2020.

Did you know?

The UK has the highest level of waste disposal via landfill in Europe, disposing of over 27 million tonnes of waste in landfill each year. In contrast, Germany (which has a population 25 per cent larger than the UK) sends only 10 million tonnes of rubbish to landfill annually.

Landfill has the potential to damage the environment in a number of ways.

- **Landfill gas** is produced by the landfill breaking down in the absence of oxygen (since its containment is airtight). The gas consists predominantly of methane and carbon dioxide, with small amounts of nitrogen and oxygen. This presents a hazard because it can explode and/or burn, and methane is also a greenhouse gas. The landfill gas must therefore be removed safely by a series of pipes within the landfill (see Figure 34.2).

- **Landfill leachate** is rainwater filtering through the landfill materials. Its toxicity depends on the materials in the site, but it often has high concentrations of chemicals including chlorine and pesticides. Leachate becomes dangerous when it drains away and mixes with groundwater (which is the main source of drinking water for over 40 per cent of the UK population). In the past, landfill leachate was allowed to slowly leak into the nearby environment, eventually mixing with the local groundwater system. Legislation now demands that landfill leachate is collected and treated to ensure minimal pollution of groundwater.

- **Air pollution** occurs as a result of wind-carried suspensions and unpleasant odours produced by the landfill site.

- If the waste is not contained properly, **soil contamination** can occur from chemicals discharged from the waste as it starts to decompose.

There are currently over 4000 landfill sites in the UK. It is estimated that collectively these sites release over 1.5 tonnes of the greenhouse gas methane every year as the waste decomposes.

1.3 Impacts of pollution and environmental damage

Impacts on individuals

The health and well-being of individuals exposed to pollutants will suffer. These impacts may be physical, for example illness following the ingestion of toxins, or emotional, for example stress experienced as a result of prolonged exposure to loud noise.

More than 12.2 million people in the UK suffer from allergy-related illnesses, including 5 million who suffer from asthma. Research has suggested a link between emissions from heavy good vehicles and the increase in allergies. Researchers in Germany found a 50 per cent increase in allergies among children regularly exposed to traffic pollution and strong links between how near children lived to busy roads and their probability of allergic symptoms.

The case study below describes the consequences of the ban on smoking in public places on the health of individuals in the UK.

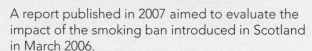

Case study: The smoking ban and health in the UK

A report published in 2007 aimed to evaluate the impact of the smoking ban introduced in Scotland in March 2006.

- Data from nine hospitals showed a 17 per cent drop in heart attacks year on year.
- Among non-smokers there was a 20 per cent reduction in hospital admissions from heart attacks.

A previous study undertaken one year after the smoking ban was introduced in 2005 in the Republic of Ireland found that:

- particulate matter in the air decreased in pubs by 80 per cent
- pub workers were breathing better (a decrease of up to 40 per cent of breathing problems)
- lung function in non-smokers improved.

1 **Why do you think bans on smoking in public places have been introduced throughout the UK?**

2 **What do you think are the advantages of such bans for the general public and workers in industries such as the pub and hotel trade?**

In the UK, workers in industries such as coal and lead mining, or those using **asbestos**, have experienced long-term negative effects on their health, as have workers exposed to excessive noise or chemicals in the workplace.

Key term

Asbestos – fibre made from magnesium silicate which has various industrial uses, including in fireproofing, electrical insulation and building materials. The inhalation of asbestos fibres has been linked to the development of cancers and lung disease. Since January 2005, the use and extraction, manufacture and processing of asbestos products has been banned in the European Union.

- Coal miners may absorb coal dust into their lungs. Prolonged exposure to coal dust damages the lungs and causes long-term ill health and early death.
- Workers involved in the production of asbestos and people exposed to asbestos in the work or home environment have also suffered lung damage. Inhaling asbestos fibres can cause asbestosis. Symptoms typically emerge up to twenty years after exposure and include reduced lung function and chest pains.
- Workers employed in very noisy environments (such as car manufacture) have suffered irreversible hearing loss (industrial deafness is a recognised industrial injury).
- Chemicals used in manufacture can have long-term health effects, for example the use of lead in paint manufacture (no longer permitted) exposed many workers to the potential of lead poisoning.

While financial compensation may be awarded for such injuries, the individual's quality of life and life expectancy are irreparably damaged.

Environmental pollution is not confined to one country or area of the world. For example, northern European nuclear-fuel reprocessing plants, such as the Sellafield plant in Cumbria, England, are one of the worst sources of nuclear waste and sea pollution. Traces of radioactive waste from northern Europe have been found in seas as far away as Greenland and India. Radioactive pollution contaminates fish stocks, which are later eaten by local people. This has the potential to result in stillbirths and birth defects.

Case study: Mercury poisoning in Minamata, Japan

Between 1932 and 1968, a factory in Minamata, Japan, discharged waste containing **mercury** into the sea. The mercury contaminated the fish and shellfish in the local bay, which were then eaten by the local population. From the mid-1950s, adults began to display signs of a strange disease of the nervous system characterised by clumsiness, difficulties walking, problems with hearing and swallowing, and uncontrollable shaking. Many of the victims died. 'Minamata disease', as these symptoms became known, was later shown to be the result of mercury poisoning. Tragically, a high number of children were born with congenital mercury poisoning, characterised by severe physical deformities such as gnarled limbs, deafness, blindness and brain damage. It is thought that 2265 people contracted the disease in the Minamata area.

1 **Research the impacts of mercury poisoning on sea and human life.**

2 **Research the uses of mercury in manufacturing industry.**

3 **Produce a leaflet which explains the need for responsible use of mercury in manufacturing.**

Key term

Mercury – a silver poisonous metallic liquid. It has various industrial uses, for example in thermometers, paints, batteries and pesticides. Use of mercury has dropped since the 1980s, when people began to understand its harmful effects on human health.

Did you know?

In October 2009 the United Nations (UN) took steps towards the implementation of a legally binding international treaty to prevent mercury pollution. It is hoped a treaty will be in place by 2013 to control the supply, trade and storage of surplus mercury.

Impacts on UK society

On flora and fauna

Many species of flora and fauna in the UK are currently under threat as a result of habitat loss, poor land management, pollution and climate change. Natural England, the UK government's advisor on the natural environment, reported in 2010 that as many as two animals and plants a year become extinct in England, and estimate that nearly 500 species have died out over the last 200 years. Currently almost 1000 additional species are threatened with extinction.

Examples of plant species now extinct in England include:

- *Mitten's beardless moss* – this was first recorded in Surrey and Sussex in the 1850s. A slower-growing species of moss, it was unable to adjust to changes in farming practice and is thought to have died out in the 1920s.

- *Irish Lady's-tresses* – a flowering plant growing on marshy meadows. It is thought to have perished as a result of fertilisers and herbicides used in farming.

Activity: Flora and fauna under threat

1 Why is it important to protect the UK's flora and fauna species?

2 Find out about work in the UK to conserve and protect UK plant species.

You may find the following websites useful:

- Plantlife (www.plantlife.org.uk)
- Natural England (www.naturalengland.net)
- Natural History Museum (www.nhm.ac.uk/nature-online/life/plants-fungi).

Climate change

In the autumn of 2009, typhoon Ketsana caused landslides and widespread flooding in the Philippines, leaving communities devastated. At the same time, in southern India, the worst floods ever recorded resulted in the River Krishna overflowing its banks, leaving millions homeless. 400 mm of rain had fallen in three days after a period of severe drought. Also in 2009, China experienced its worst drought in fifty years, with crops and livestock dying and over 4 million people facing a shortage of drinking water.

While it is impossible to prove that these extreme weather events are the direct result of climate change, there is compelling scientific evidence that climate change is affecting world weather patterns and has resulted in an increase in the number and intensity of floods, storms and heat waves (see, for example, the Case study on the Stern Review opposite).

Did you know?

A recent report concluded that by 2060 the Earth could warm by an average of 4°C unless urgent action is taken. In some parts of the world the impact could be even more severe, with temperatures rising by 10°C in parts of Africa and 15°C in the Arctic.

In the UK it is likely that climate change will result in:

- wetter and warmer winters
- an increase in average annual temperatures
- drier and hotter summers
- less snowfall
- increased risks of flash flooding and heavy rainfall.

In July 2007 many parts of the UK suffered severe flooding. The town of Tewkesbury, in Gloucestershire was completely cut off by the floodwaters with no road access for several days.

While climate change is generally considered to be an irreversible process, it is thought that by reducing the emissions that cause global warming we will slow climate change and the consequences for the environment will be less extreme.

Did you know?

Some scientists argue that the warming and cooling of the Earth is part of a natural cycle and not the result of human activity. However, even climate change sceptics acknowledge that we should do more to protect non-renewable sources of energy and reduce excessive consumption in the developed world.

Activity: Dealing with the consequences of climate change

1 Divide into small groups and select one of the severe weather events referred to above. Research it in more detail.

2 Discuss as a whole class what can be done to minimise the impact of extremes of weather (such as tsunamis and severe flooding) in the regions likely to be affected.

Environmental impact

Reuse of polluted land

There is a long history of industrial production in the UK, starting with the industrial revolution of the late-eighteenth century. Over the years many sites in the UK have become contaminated with chemicals from various industrial processes, including mining, agriculture and waste disposal. These contaminants, for example metals such as lead or mercury, or very acidic or alkaline substances, may break down harmlessly in the soil over the years or may pose a serious health risk to local populations. Figure 34.3 shows the ways in which local populations may be affected by contaminated land.

Case study: The Stern Review

The Stern Review was an independent review into global warming and climate change commissioned by the UK government in 2005, with the *Report on the Economics of Climate Change* published in 2006. This 700-page report explored the effects of global warming on the world economy. It considered the costs of ignoring climate change against the costs of doing something about it.

The Review concluded that climate change is an international problem that will impact on people's access to food production, water, health and the environment. It indicated that many millions could have to endure flooding, water shortages and starvation as the world warms. Poor countries will be most affected, even though they have contributed least to global warming.

The Report stated that:

- The Earth's climate is changing rapidly as a result of increases in greenhouse gas emissions caused by human activities.

- Higher temperatures cause soils and plants to absorb less carbon from the atmosphere.
- A likely outcome is that **permafrost** will thaw, releasing large quantities of the greenhouse gas methane.
- Global warming is likely to intensify the **water cycle**, increasing the risk of flooding and droughts.
- Warmer oceans and air are likely to create more storms, typhoons and hurricanes.
- If ice sheets in the Antarctic and Greenland melt irreversibly, the sea level could rise by up to 12 metres over a few centuries.

1 **Carry out research into the Stern Review. What does the Review suggest the impacts of climate change will be for the UK?**

2 **Produce a poster for your school or college highlighting five things learners could do to help reduce the impact of climate change.**

You can access the full Stern Review at www.hm-treasury.gov.uk/d/Executive_Summary.pdf.

Link

There is another case study on the recommendations of the Stern Review on page 303.

Key terms

Permafrost – ground that is permanently frozen.

Water cycle – the continuous movement of water on, above and below the surface of the Earth, as it evaporates into the air, condenses into clouds, and returns to Earth as rain, snow, sleet or hail.

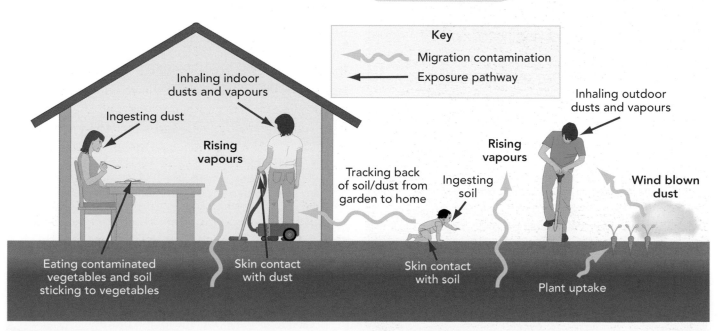

Figure 34.3: Pathways through which individuals may become polluted from contaminated land.

(*Source*: **adapted** from *An Introduction to Land, Contamination for Public Health Professionals*, Health Protection Agency, 2009, p.12)

Because of land shortage, development in the UK is currently focused on the restoration of land that was once used for industrial purposes, known as **brownfield land**. This land has to be made safe for the domestic and industrial developments that are needed to sustain and support the UK population. There is often a significant cost involved (both in finance and time), but it is considered a necessary cost that is being built into development planning.

Case study: Reclaiming contaminated land in the UK

Much of the land currently available for the building of houses in the UK was previously used for industry and development. Before being redeveloped for housing, this land must be cleared of residual pollutants. In recent years the UK government has sought to redevelop these brownfield sites in order to relieve pressure on **greenfield land** – currently it aims to build 60 per cent of new housing on reclaimed land.

Brownfield land may be derelict or disused and can only be redeveloped after the removal of hazardous substances such as chemicals and waste, which may be causing high levels of pollution, or after improving the structure of the land (for example where mining has taken place). Restoring this land can be an expensive process, but it also brings new life to previously derelict areas and helps to preserve the undeveloped countryside in the UK.

1 Should greenfield land be protected?
2 Should brownfield sites be redeveloped, even when the cost is more expensive than building on the countryside?

Pollution of water supplies

Water pollution threatens the ecology of rivers and oceans and food supplies for both marine life and humans. It can be caused by a variety of sources, as shown in Figure 34.4.

The potential pollution of water supplies must be considered and managed.

- River pollution may be caused by a number of factors including the use of pesticides and fertilisers in agriculture, which can be washed through the soil by rain to end up in rivers.
- Rubbish and waste can be carelessly thrown into rivers, creating pollution and becoming a hazard to fish and birds.
- Polluted water from manufacturing may contain chemicals that end up in rivers.
- Old tin, coal and lead mines pose a contamination risk.
- Water dripping through tunnels and mine shafts may pollute water supplies.

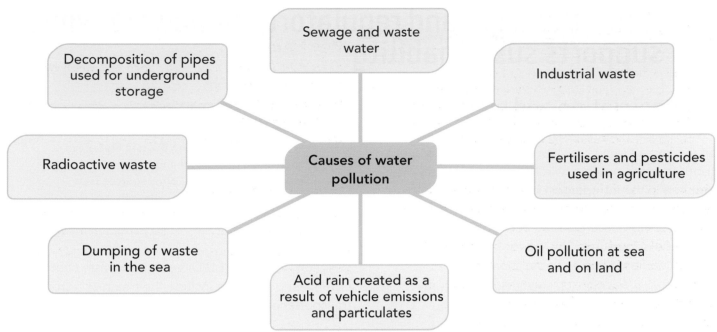

Figure 34.4: Causes of water pollution

European Union and UK government legislation and regulations aim to protect UK water supplies and there is some evidence that the levels of pollution are reducing.

Restoration and aftercare of land used for industrial purposes

Because of land shortage, development in the UK has to focus on the restoration of land that was once used for industrial purposes (see page 282). This includes land used for opencast and deep mine coal, quarries and landfill.

Where land is currently being used for activities such as mining, quarrying and landfill, aftercare and restoration of the land has to be planned into the development from the earliest stages.

PLTS

By outlining the impact of pollution and environmental damage on individuals and society in the UK, you will show that you are an **independent enquirer**.

Functional skills

By completing this assignment you will provide evidence for your functional **English** skills in **Reading and Writing**.

By word-processing your report for this assignment, you will evidence your functional **ICT** skills in **using ICT systems**.

Assessment activity 34.1   P1   BTEC

Human activity over the centuries has resulted in pollution and environmental damage throughout the UK. That damage has an impact on both individuals and on UK society.

Create a report that outlines the impact of pollution and environmental damage on individuals and society in the UK.

Grading tips

To achieve P1 you should make sure that you:

- discuss definitions of pollution, including air, noise, visual and land pollution, and give examples of each
- outline other types of environmental damage
- describe the impacts of global warming and climate change and the depletion of natural resources.

Your answer should outline the impacts both on individuals and UK society, including the impacts on flora and fauna and the environment, and the need for restoration and aftercare of sites used for industrial purposes.

You may wish to include examples of visits you have made to see the impact of environmental damage locally.

2. Know the legal and regulatory framework which supports sustainability

2.1 Legislation and guidelines

Over the last hundred years a growing awareness of the impact of human activity on the environment (both the national UK environment and globally) has resulted in the introduction of key legislation and regulation to ensure that human activity does not further compromise the local and global environment for future generations. We will look at some of that regulatory framework in this section.

Legislation in the UK has initially focused on the disposal of waste, starting with the Control of

Remember!

Remember when researching this unit that regulation and legislation changes, so you should use the Internet and other sources such as newspapers to keep up-to-date with the latest developments.

Pollution Act (1974). EU Directives on waste control have extended this to include the treatment, storage, transportation and recycling of waste.

Hazardous Waste Regulations (2005), List of Wastes (England) Regulations (2005) and List of Wastes (Wales) Regulations (2005)

Control of Pollution Act (1974)

Household Waste Recycling Act (2003)

UK laws

The Asbestos (Licensing) Regulations (1983) and the Control of Asbestos at Work Regulations (1987)

Waste Strategy 2000

Environmental Protection Act (1990)

Sustainability legislation

End of Life Vehicles (ELV) Directive (1997)

EU Directive on the Landfill of Waste (1999)

EU Directives

Waste Electrical and Electronic Equipment Directive (WEEE Directive) (2003)

Figure 34.5: European and UK legislation which supports sustainability

Did you know?

EU legislation falls into two types:

- Directives set specific goals for action but it is the decision of the EU member state how to achieve that goal.
- Regulations become law in all member states the moment they come into force.

UK legislation

Control of Pollution Act (1974)

This Act provided a comprehensive approach to waste control and pollution. It also extended existing controls on discharging polluting matter into controlled waters without a licence. The spreading of sewage sludge on agricultural land was exempt from the licensing system and agricultural waste was largely excluded from the controlled waste regime.

The Asbestos (Licensing) Regulations (1983) and the Control of Asbestos at Work Regulations (1987)

These Acts regulated work involving asbestos use (in insulation coating and fire protection). By the terms of these Acts:

- operators had to be licensed by the Health and Safety Executive (HSE)

- employees were to be given information, instruction and training to prevent their exposure to asbestos in the workplace

- control measures, including the provision and use of personal protective equipment, were introduced.

Did you know?

The use of asbestos has been banned by EU regulations since 1999.

Environmental Protection Act (1990)

This Act aimed to protect the quality of the environment. It remains a key piece of environmental legislation, controlling many aspects of how the environment is protected and regulated on a day-to-day basis. It is enforced by the local authority's Environmental Health Department. The Act:

- defined waste
- outlined the roles and functions of the waste collection and disposal authorities
- defined the role of the **Environment Agency**

Key term

Environment Agency – UK government agency that aims to protect and improve the environment and promote sustainable development.

- established criminal offences in relation to waste, the waste management licensing system and the statutory duty of care in relation to waste.

Waste offences include (among other things):

- knowingly permitting controlled waste to be deposited in water or on land

- knowingly allowing controlled waste to be kept, treated or disposed of without a licence

- the disposal or treatment of controlled waste in a manner likely to harm human health or pollute the environment.

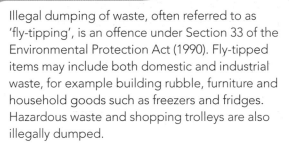

Did you know?

Illegal dumping of waste, often referred to as 'fly-tipping', is an offence under Section 33 of the Environmental Protection Act (1990). Fly-tipped items may include both domestic and industrial waste, for example building rubble, furniture and household goods such as freezers and fridges. Hazardous waste and shopping trolleys are also illegally dumped.

If you are caught fly-tipping you can be prosecuted. Conviction could result in a fine of up to £50,000 and a maximum prison sentence of 5 years.

To crack down on fly-tipping, local authorities use CCTV and hidden cameras. Local authorities also name and shame convicted illegal dumpers.

Waste Strategy 2000

This strategy set out the UK government's policy for sustainable waste management. It introduced a number of recycling targets, including:

- reducing the amount of industrial and commercial waste sent to landfill by 85 per cent (of 1998 figure) by 2005

- recycling or composting at least 33 per cent of household waste by 2015.

Since then the strategy has been reviewed annually and an annual progress report produced. In October 2009 the UK government declared their commitment to becoming a 'zero waste' economy. By 2020 the government wants the UK to generate power from a quarter of its household waste and recycle a further 50 per cent, leaving only a quarter to end up as landfill.

Case study: Recycle or be fined

The Local Government Association (LGA), which represents 400 local authorities, has asked the government for powers to reduce charges for householders who sort and recycle their rubbish. Councils face fines of £150 per tonne for landfill waste and the LGA fears these costs will need to be passed onto council tax payers.

1 Discuss the options open to local authorities, government and individuals to reduce landfill and encourage recycling.

2 Do you think it is fair to reduce council tax for those who recycle and increase charges for those who do not?

3 What might the impact be on elderly and disabled council tax payers?

Household Waste Recycling Act (2003)

This Act requires all waste collection authorities in England to collect a minimum of two types of recyclable waste from all households in their area. Types of recyclable waste are listed as:

- batteries
- glass
- garden waste
- wood
- varnish
- paint
- food waste
- paper
- plastic
- metals
- shoes
- textiles
- electrical or electronic waste (known as e-waste).

The Act aimed to increase recycling by households above the then current figure of 15 per cent. Local authorities must comply with the Act by the end of December 2010, but by late 2009, 90 per cent of households in England receive collections of at least two of these recyclable materials. In this way the Act has made a real contribution to increasing household waste recycling in the UK, although there is still some way to go.

Did you know?

In 1997, only 7 per cent of England's household waste was recycled. Today the figure is closer to 27 per cent, although performance varies considerably from one local authority to the next. (Source: DEFRA, 2010.)

Hazardous Waste Regulations (2005), List of Wastes (England) Regulations (2005) and List of Wastes (Wales) Regulations (2005)

These became UK law in July 2005. They set out procedures that must be followed when carrying, disposing of or receiving hazardous waste. This includes the requirement that consignment notes track the waste 'from cradle to grave'. The Regulations also require producers of hazardous waste to register their premises with the UK Environment Agency.

EU directives on waste

The European Union's legislation on waste consists of three main aspects:

1 An overall framework for the management of waste which sets out the key principles and definitions.

2 Laws on specific waste, such as batteries and oil, including measures to reduce hazards and increase recycling.

3 Laws on treatment operations, such as incineration (burning) and landfill, which establish standards for waste facilities to abide by.

There are a significant number of EU directives affecting waste management. The main EU directives address the disposal of industrial and household waste (using landfill sites), since this has been shown to be a significant contributor to pollution.

Did you know?

Full details of the EU directives on waste can be found at www.wasteonline.org.uk/resources/InformationSheets/Legislation.htm.

EU Directive on the Landfill of Waste (1999)

This legislation (Directive 1999/31/EC) is designed to prevent or reduce the negative effects of landfill waste on the environment, in particular on surface water, groundwater, soil, air and human health. It applies to all landfill sites and had to be implemented in member states by July 2001. The original Directive has been extended several times and is under constant review.

Directive 1999/31/EC identifies three categories of landfill waste, as shown in Table 34.1.

Table 34.1: Different categories of waste as defined in the EU Directive on the Landfill of Waste (1999/31/EC)

Category of landfill waste	Description
Hazardous	Waste which is harmful to human health, or to the environment, either immediately or over an extended period of time. Included in this category are asbestos, strong acids, pesticides, used mobile phone batteries, engine oils and hospital and clinical waste.
Non-hazardous	Waste that does not pose a risk to human health or the environment, such as general household waste.
Inert	Waste that will not dissolve, burn or otherwise physically or chemically react, biodegrade or adversely affect other matter with which it comes into contact in a way likely to give rise to environmental pollution or harm to human health.

The Directive states that waste must be treated before being accepted into a landfill site. The purpose of treatment is to ensure that:

- recyclable waste is removed, so avoiding it unnecessarily going to landfill
- the volume of waste is minimised
- any potential hazards are removed
- the waste is easier to handle.

As part of these measures, local authorities (who have the responsibility for the collection of household and business waste in their geographic areas) are encouraging all of us to sort through our waste before disposal in order to identify and separate out any waste that can be recycled. Figure 34.6 indicates how this might be done.

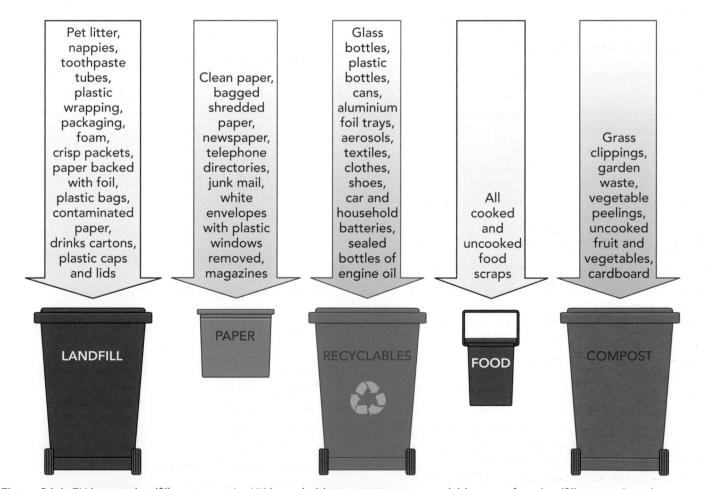

Figure 34.6: EU laws on landfill waste require UK households to separate out recyclable waste from landfill waste, though practices for waste disposal can vary from one local authority to the next

Some waste, such as liquid waste, explosives, flammable waste, electrical waste, vehicle waste and used tyres, is not allowed to be disposed of in landfill sites.

The EU Directive also established a system of operating permits for landfill sites. Member states must now licence and monitor landfill sites against various criteria, including:

* the types and total quantity of waste to be deposited
* the capacity of the disposal site
* the proposed methods for pollution prevention
* the plan for closure and aftercare procedures.

Waste Electrical and Electronic Equipment Directive (WEEE Directive) (2003)

EU legislation restricting the use of hazardous substances in electrical and electronic equipment and promoting the collection and recycling of such equipment came into force in February 2003. The legislation provides for collection schemes to be set up so that consumers can return used electrical waste free of charge, thereby increasing reuse and recycling. The WEEE Directive also requires mercury, lead, chromium, cadmium and flame retardants to be replaced by safer alternatives.

The WEEE Directive became UK law in 2007.

Did you know?

Two-thirds of electrical waste in the European Union goes to landfill sites or is exported outside the EU, posing a potential risk to health and the environment. Only one-third of electrical waste is appropriately treated.

End of Life Vehicles (ELV) Directive (1997)

This EU Directive aimed to reduce waste from vehicles (both cars and vans) being scrapped.

* It established tighter environmental controls on sites where vehicles are treated.
* It introduced targets for recycling, recovery and reuse, limiting the use of hazardous substances in both replacement vehicle parts and new vehicles.
* Disposal of vehicles became free of charge to owners from 2007, with producers of vehicles being liable to pay all or most of the disposal from that date.

The UK implemented the ELV Directive (1997) through its End of Life Vehicles (ELV) Regulations of 2003 and 2005. Currently in the UK, vehicle producers are required to provide owners of their brands of vehicles with facilities for their disposal. A public register has been set up to state how far producers of vehicles have met the 85 per cent target for recovery, recycling and reuse of their brands of vehicles.

UK Sustainable Development Commission (SDC)

The SDC is the UK government's independent adviser on sustainability. It functions as an executive non-departmental body (Executive NDPB), which means the SDC is not part of a government department and carries out its work without interference from government. Originally established in 2000, the role of the SDC was subsequently extended as a result of the government's 2005 *Securing the Future* strategy (see opposite).

The SDC's responsibilities include:

* reviewing the extent to which the government is meeting its targets on sustainable development
* increasing public awareness of the importance of sustainable development
* reporting on various environmental issues, such as nuclear power
* drawing on expert opinion to advise government ministers on environmental issues.

Its work covers various policy areas including climate change, energy, health, housing, local and regional government, and transport.

Link

See page 296–7 for more about the Sustainable Development Commission.

Did you know?

You can find out more about the SDC and their work by going to their website: www.defra.gov.uk/sustainable/government/index.htm.

2.2 UK government initiatives to support sustainability

UK Sustainable Development Strategy

The UK government launched its original strategy for sustainable development in 1994. This was reviewed in 1999 and again in 2005, when *Securing the Future* was published. *Securing the Future* emphasises the need for delivery at local, regional and government levels. It also highlights the international aims of sustainable development from the 2002 Johannesburg World Summit on Sustainable Development.

Did you know?

You can read the document *Securing the Future* by going to www.defra.gov.uk/sustainable/government/publications/index.htm.

Securing the Future is overseen by the Department for Environment, Food and Rural Affairs (DEFRA), but all parts of UK government share responsibility for making sustainable development a reality. To this end, targets are set throughout the public sector related to promoting sustainability and improving energy efficiency and waste reduction.

Link

You can find out more about *Securing the Future* on pages 302–3 of this unit.

UK central government initiatives

Energy efficiency grants

The UK government funds grants of up to £3500 per household for those entitled to certain benefits (for example income support, council tax benefit and pension credit) to improve their home's energy efficiency and heating. In England this fund is known as Warm Front. Those who receive the money can use it for a range of insulation and heating improvements, including loft insulation, draught-proofing, cavity wall insulation and installing a new boiler.

Did you know?

The Warm Front scheme is known as Warm Homes in Ireland, the Energy Assistance Package in Scotland and the Home Energy Efficiency Scheme in Wales.

Carbon Emission Reduction Target (CERT)

The current three-year Carbon Emission Reduction Target (CERT), which runs from March 2008 to April 2011, requires domestic energy suppliers operating in the UK with a customer base of over 50,000 customers to achieve certain targets for improving home energy efficiency. By offering their customers significant reductions in the cost of installing energy efficiency measures, it is hoped that energy suppliers will contribute towards savings in carbon dioxide (CO_2) emissions. CERT requires suppliers to focus *at least* 40 per cent of their activity on providing energy-saving measures to a 'Priority Group' of vulnerable and low-income households, for example those receiving benefits and pensioners.

Did you know?

Many local authorities also offer grants for council tax payers to install energy efficiency measures in their houses.

Activity: Energy efficiency grants and CERT

With public services currently facing budget cuts, discuss whether public funds should be used to support energy efficiency initiatives and CERT.

Public education

Both central and local government have set up a number of schemes to improve public awareness of environmental factors, for example the impact of climate change, the consequences of dumping waste and the benefits of reusing and recycling.

In 2007, the UK government launched the *Act on CO₂* campaign (see http://actonco2.direct.gov.uk/home.html). Research carried out by the government had shown that while people understood what climate change is, they did not realise what they could do in their lives to help combat global warming. *Act on CO₂* is designed to provide practical advice on how people living in the UK can reduce their carbon footprint. For example, recent *Act on CO₂* campaigns include:

- Drive 5 miles less a week
- Remember: reduce, reuse, recycle
- Save water
- Save money, save energy.

Target setting for public services

In 2002 the Department for the Environment, Food and Rural Affairs (DEFRA) issued the government's framework for sustainable development on the public sector. All parts of the public sector – including central, regional and local government and the wider public sector – are responsible for delivering the UK sustainable development strategy. To achieve this, action plans have been introduced in order to achieve certain targets; examples are given below and in the case study.

- In the National Health Service (NHS), in order to demonstrate carbon reduction, targets have been set on building energy use, waste and water, and travel and transport.
- The Building Schools for the Future (BSF) programme, launched by the Department for Education and Skills (DfES) in 2004, aimed to rebuild or remodel every secondary school in England. One of its main commitments was carbon reduction in schools, with facilities that enable learners to monitor the amount of energy consumption, recycled materials used for construction, and rainwater used to flush toilets.

Key terms

Audit – to examine financial accounts or business practices to check they are correct.

Biodiversity – variation among living organisms. This includes diversity within species, between species and of ecosystems.

SSSI – Site of Special Scientific Interest; environmentally protected areas within the UK.

Habitat – the place where an organism lives.

Case study: Sustainable development and environmental policy in HM Prison Service

HM Prison Service (HMPS) has a programme to enhance its energy efficiency and reduce its environmental impact, developed in line with government targets. To this end, HMPS introduced a sustainable development strategy and policy in 2003, to be overseen by a representative of the Sustainable Development Working Group.

Successes include the setting up and **audit** of waste management units at all prisons, leading to reduced waste and cost savings. In light of this, some establishments have received internationally recognised environmental management system certification.

A national **Biodiversity** Action Plan (BAP) has also been introduced, supported by a staff awareness campaign. HMPS manages the second biggest government estate (after the Ministry of Defence). There are several sites with designations as **SSSIs** which must be managed with care to preserve the rich species at each site. Surveys have revealed that a number of important species can be found, including bats, dormice and otters.

As well as species protection, HMPS has identified a range of **habitats** on its estate, ranging from ancient woodland to salt marsh, unimproved grasslands to rivers and lakes. Partnerships have been developed with organisations such as the Ancient Tree Forum and Environment Agency for protecting streams, rivers, lakes and other valuable habitats. A partnership was set up in 2002 with English Nature, the Royal Society for the Protection of Birds (RSPB), the Wildlife Trusts and the British Trust for Conservation Volunteers to support HMPS.

A sustainable development report is published annually as are newsletters, posters and leaflets. Yearly conferences are also held. HMPS is also undertaking reviews of sustainable development for major construction projects.

1   Why is it important that public services such as prisons are involved in sustainable development?

2   How can the Prison Service justify expenditure on environmental projects at a time of cut back in public expenditure?

Recycling schemes

The UK Sustainable Development Strategy sets targets for recycling. It also encourages individuals, communities and public sector organisations to actively seek to recycle wherever possible.

Central and local government websites provide details of what can be recycled and the services that exist (both kerbside collections and recycling sites). For example, the Waste and Resources Action Programme (WRAP) is a government-funded body which provides support and advice to local authorities on recycling (see www.wrap.org.uk).

Local government initiatives

Securing the Future (2005) requires all UK local authorities to build sustainability into all their activities. To this end, every local authority must publish a Sustainable Community Strategy on their website.

Local authorities are required by both UK and EU legislation to contribute to reducing waste. Each local authority must work towards waste disposal in their area being revenue neutral or even income generating. Local authorities must work with private and voluntary organisations in their area and must provide kerbside collections of recyclable materials.

Activity: Local government initiatives

Carry out research on your local authority website into:

- the recycling services provided by your local authority
- the waste management strategies and initiatives your local authority is involved with
- your local authority's sustainable community strategy.

2.3 International initiatives

Kyoto Protocol

The Kyoto Protocol was adopted in Japan in 1997 and came into force in 2005. It is an international agreement of the UN Framework Convention on Climate Change. Its main feature is to set binding targets for the European Union and 37 industrialised countries to reduce greenhouse gas emissions over the five-year period 2008 to 2012. The greenhouse gases targeted by the Kyoto treaty are:

- carbon dioxide (CO_2)
- methane (CO_4)
- hydrofluorocarbons (HFCs)
- perfluorocarbons (PFCs)
- sulphur hexafluoride (SF_6).

Because it is recognised that for the past 150 years developed countries have been responsible for the majority of emissions, the Protocol places a higher duty on developed countries under the principle of 'common but differentiated responsibilities.'

Under the Protocol, each country is responsible for meeting targets largely through national measures. In addition there are three market-based mechanisms.

1 **The Clean Development Mechanism (CDM)**

   An industrialised country that has signed the Kyoto treaty can sponsor an emission-reduction project in a developing country. This allows the industrialised country to earn certified emission reduction (CER) credits, which it can then use to count towards meeting its own Kyoto targets. An example of a CDM project is a rural electrification project using solar panels or the installation of more energy-efficient boilers in the developing country.

2 **Emissions trading**

   This allows (usually developing) countries with spare emission units to sell their excess capacity to countries that are over their targets (usually the industrialised nations). (Emission units are a way of measuring the carbon usage or footprint of various activities.) In this way, the Kyoto Protocol created a new commodity of emission reductions or removals. Carbon is now tracked and traded like other commodities. This has become known as the carbon market.

3 **Joint implementation**

   This allows developed countries to host carbon-reducing projects funded by a second developed country. The arrangement sees the credits generated go to the investor country, while the emission allowances of the country hosting the project are reduced by the same quantity.

Copenhagen Conference

The Kyoto Protocol was revised at the Copenhagen Conference in December 2009, when 115 world leaders signed the Copenhagen Accord. This agreement accepts the scientific case for climate change and aims to restrict global temperature increases to no more than 2 degrees Celsius. However, there was failure to achieve an international commitment to the reduction of greenhouse gas emissions in order to achieve this goal. It was generally accepted that the outcome of the conference was a small step towards world sustainability, and many world leaders voiced disappointment that more had not been achieved.

EU policies

Did you know?

Full details of current EU sustainability policies (which are summarised below) can be found at http://ec.europa.eu/environment/policy_en.htm.

Climate change

The EU played a key role in the development of both the 1992 United Nations Framework Convention on Climate Change (UNFCCC) and its Kyoto Protocol.

Since the 1990s the EU has been taking steps to reduce its greenhouse gas emissions. In 2000 it launched the European Climate Change Programme (ECCP), which led to the endorsement of a range of measures and policies including the EU Emissions Trading System. Data and predictions suggest that the 15 countries that were EU members at the time Kyoto was ratified will reach their emission reduction targets. In 2007 'Limiting Global Climate Change to 2 degrees Celsius: The way ahead for 2020 and beyond' was adopted by EU leaders. This commits the EU to reducing greenhouse gas emissions to 30 per cent of 1990 levels by 2020.

Industry and technology

To encourage European industry to adopt policies which are environmentally sound, the EU has introduced a range of initiatives.

- The biannual European Awards for the Environment recognise firms who have implemented successful environmental management programmes, designed innovative products or worked on pioneering projects with developing countries.

- The *Directive on the control of major-accident hazards involving dangerous substances* is aimed at reducing the risk of industrial accidents.
- The Integrated Product Policy (IPP) seeks to minimise environmental degradation during product manufacture, use and disposal. It looks at ways of encouraging use of greener services and products.

Land use

The EU is densely populated, averaging 117.5 people per square kilometre. EU policy aims to protect natural landscapes and habitats and to reduce the impact of road traffic, thereby helping to manage congestion, air pollution and greenhouse gases.

- The *Directive on Environment Impact Assessment (EIA) for projects* and the *Directive on Strategic Environmental Assessment (SEA) for plans and programmes* make sure any major environmental impacts are identified, assessed and considered when member states take decisions regarding land use.
- To improve the use of the EU's coastal areas, an Integrated Coastal Zone Management (ICZM) was introduced, as was a major EU-wide project regarding coastal erosion.

Biodiversity

There is a political commitment to halt biodiversity loss within the EU by 2010, the main cause of which is habitat loss caused by farming, forestry and changes in land use. To this end, the EU has established over 26,000 protected areas, known as the Natura 2000 network, covering an area of 850,000 km^2 (over 20 per cent of EU total territory).

Noise

In 1996 the EU developed a framework for noise policy. The main purpose was to provide a common basis across EU countries for tackling and reducing noise pollution. This was followed by EU legislation relating to sources of noise, such as aircraft, motor vehicles and railway rolling stock. This sets clear milestones by which member states must have implemented noise reduction measures.

Sustainable development

The EU Sustainable Development Strategy (SDS) came into being in 2006 following an extensive review process which started in 2001. It aims to develop

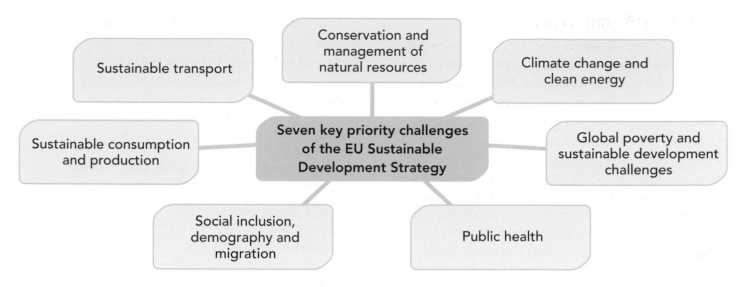

Figure 34.7: The seven key priority challenges up until 2010 of the EU Sustainable Development Strategy

more sustainable consumption and production within the EU, while also bringing about a greater integration of policies and working practices with nations outside the EU.

The EU Sustainable Development Strategy sets goals and actions for seven priorities up until 2010; these are shown in Figure 34.7. The EU recognises the importance of research, commitment from member states and public education in achieving these goals.

Waste

The EU's waste management strategy is based on three principles:

1. *Waste prevention* – reducing the amount of waste created by more efficient production and reuse of resources, such as the reduction in product packaging.

2. *Recycling and reuse* – some EU countries already recycle more than half of packaging waste.

3. *Improving monitoring and final disposal* – waste that cannot be reused or recycled should ideally be incinerated (and used to generate power) rather than sent to landfill.

Case study: Getting involved with EU Water Framework Directive initiatives

As a result of the EU Water Framework Directive (WFD, see page 294), the UK has set up a number of initiatives to ensure that UK rivers and coastal waters will comply with the targets on water quality by 2015.

One such initiative is the Speke and Garston Coastal Reserve, part of the Mersey Waterfront Regional Park. The plan was to create a wildlife haven on previously derelict land. The area had seen many years of neglect and decline. Regeneration was planned to encourage local people to take a pride in their area and to encourage businesses to invest in the area, which is close to Liverpool John Lennon airport. The site is very important as it is home to birds such as the dunlin and the shelduck.

Young people from South Liverpool were invited to share their ideas and views on the Speke Garston Coastal Reserve. In addition, a Young People's Panel was set up by Mersey Waterfront, to involve local teenagers in the plans for the development of the coastal reserve. Their views were noted and used to support funding applications and new landscape designs for the project.

1. **Research WFD initiatives taking place near where you live at the following websites:**

   - www.defra.gov.uk/environment/quality/water/index.htm

   - www.wfduk.org/.

2. **Why are such initiatives important?**

Water

The EU Water Framework Directive (2000) provides for the management of all inland surface waters (for example rivers and lakes), groundwater, transitional waters (those areas where sea water and freshwater meet) and coastal waters in order to:

- prevent and reduce pollution
- promote sustainable water use
- reduce the impact of flooding and droughts
- protect aquatic species and their habitats.

The Directive also aims to classify all water as being of either high or good quality by 2015.

2.4 Role of Environment Agency

The overarching role of the Environment Agency (EA) is to protect and improve the environment and to promote sustainable development. It is an **executive non-departmental public body** responsible directly to government. The Environment Agency advises government and business on how to deliver real improvements for the environment by putting environmental issues at the heart of decision making and providing low-carbon solutions. The strategy of the Environment Agency for 2010 to 2015 is to:

- put individuals and their communities at the centre of its work
- act to reduce climate change and its impact

- improve and protect land, water and air quality
- work with the government, public and private sectors to use resources efficiently.

The Environment Agency's many roles are shown in Figure 34.8.

Key term

Executive non-departmental public body (NDPB) – agency working on behalf of government to deliver a particular public service. The agency carries out its own work free from government intervention, operating with its own staff and budget.

Dealing with environmental issues

Examples of the Agency's specific activities include:

- producing flooding maps which highlight areas in the UK at risk of flooding, and providing advice to those living in flood areas
- working with industry to protect human health and the environment
- as a regulator, monitoring the work of potentially hazardous business operations, issuing licences to organisations undertaking these activities and regulating their activity
- helping industry and commerce use resources efficiently
- issuing angling and boating licences

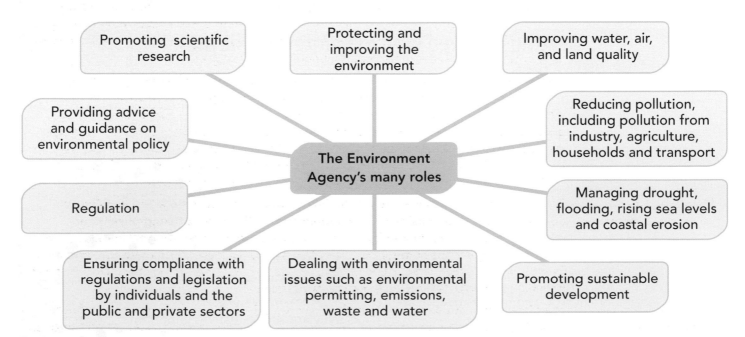

Figure 34.8: The different roles of the Environment Agency

- protecting wildlife (the agency is involved with around 400 projects each year to improve habitats of species under threat)
- issuing permits for groundwater activities, mining waste and installations, radioactive substances, waste, and disposal of batteries
- restoring lakes and rivers.

Ensuring compliance with regulations and legislation

The Environment Agency takes law enforcement and prosecution actions, including issuing fines, against those who do not act responsibly towards the environment. The EA can:

- issue enforcement and prohibition notices

- suspend or alter environmental licences
- issue injunctions (to prevent illegal activity)
- carry out remedial works (and recovery of costs from those breaching regulations).

However, before going to court the Agency encourages businesses and individuals to ensure their working practices support environmental protection. Sometimes enforcement and prosecution becomes necessary to ensure breaches in the conditions of licensed activities are dealt with or unlicensed activities halted. If a company or individual has committed a criminal offence, the EA can prosecute, administer a caution or issue a warning.

The Environment Agency has various techniques it uses in its role as regulator, as outlined in Table 34.2.

Table 34.2: The Environment Agency's role as regulator and law enforcer

Type of regulation	How it works
Direct regulation	This is the Agency's main method of regulation. Environmental permits are issued to manufacturing and business which clearly state the level of pollutants that can be released to air, land or water. In this way environmental emissions are restricted. The organisation to which the permit is granted must comply with its terms (or risk a heavy fine). Environmental permits are typically issued for: • 'complex process' industries such as chemical works and power stations • sewage treatment works • waste management sites, such as landfill sites and incinerators • industries that use radioactive materials.
Environmental taxes	Taxation is one method of discouraging organisations from polluting the environment – two examples are the Landfill Tax and Climate Change Levy. In this way the Agency can ensure that polluters pay for damaging the environment. Conversely, a reduction in or stopping of taxation is a positive financial incentive to encourage environmentally responsible behaviour. Taxation is most effective where the organisation is able to switch to alternative, readily available, less polluting practices or goods.
Trading schemes	These are a low-cost solution by which organisations trade their allowances for waste, emissions or resources while collectively remaining within regulatory limits (i.e. the overall cap is the sum of the initial allocations). The UK already has a trading scheme for greenhouse gas emissions. The Environment Agency's role in trading schemes is to advise the government on whether the scheme can work; it may also take charge of implementing the scheme. Schemes for trading oxides of nitrogen (NOx) and sulfur dioxide from power stations and biodegradable municipal waste are currently being proposed.
Negotiated and voluntary agreements	Sometimes organisations approach the Environment Agency to negotiate a voluntary environmental target outside of legal requirements. These can often achieve better outcomes than those required by law, although the organisation's original impetus may be to avoid legislation or regulation. Recently the EU achieved a voluntary agreement with the motor industry regarding emission targets, and in the UK the chemical industry is committed to voluntarily reduce the use of pesticides.
Provision of advice and guidance	To help avoid pollution occurring in the first place, the Environment Agency sets out to educate people through advice via their website, direct contact with business and through information and awareness campaigns.

2.5 Role of Defra

The Department for Environment, Food and Rural Affairs (Defra) is a central government department responsible for ensuring that:

- the UK agricultural sector thrives and people in the UK have a healthy, secure and sustainable supply of food
- the natural environment is healthy and any risks to the environment are managed
- the UK economy is resource-efficient, low carbon and sustainable.

Defra is responsible for ensuring food security and enabling farmers to produce sustainably, efficiently and with care for the land. It maintains high animal welfare standards, managing the identification and movement, health and welfare of farm animals. It also oversees the administration of £3 billion each year from the European Union to support UK agriculture.

Defra is also responsible for managing water quality in the UK. To this end it enforces various EU Directives, including those designed to:

- prevent pollution in bathing waters
- protect fresh fish populations
- improve and protect shellfish life and the quality of shellfish for eating

- ensure the safe treatment and disposal of sewage
- prevent pollution of water including reducing nitrates, oil pollution and the contamination of groundwater.

Defra is also responsible for setting policy, regulations, legislation and guidance for environmental issues including flooding, marine and coastal access, air quality, noise, use of chemicals, genetic modification, waste and recycling and climate change.

Case study: The Darwin initiative

The Darwin Initiative was first announced in 1992 at the Rio Earth Summit. It helps countries that are rich in biodiversity but financially poor to meet their objectives under one or more of the three major international biodiversity conventions – the Convention on Biological Diversity (CBD); the Convention on International Trade in Endangered Species of Wild Flora and Fauna (CITES); and the Convention on the Conservation of Migratory Species of Wild Animals (CMS). Assistance is provided in the form of funding and access to UK expert guidance on biodiversity.

To date the Darwin Initiative has funded 672 projects and has brought 213 UK organisations into partnership with 861 organisations in host countries. Over £73 million has been spent supporting these projects in 148 different countries.

The Advisory Committee recommends which applications should be funded. It is made up of academics, government advisors, scientific experts and key figures from the private sector. Defra is responsible for providing the Secretariat for the Darwin Initiative.

1. **Research the Darwin Initiative at http://darwin.defra.gov.uk.**
2. **Why do you think the UK government set up the Initiative?**
3. **How important are initiatives like this for global sustainability?**

2.6 Role of Sustainable Development Commission

The Sustainable Development Commission (SDC) was established as a result of the government's 2005 *Securing the Future* strategy.

The SDC acts as an independent watchdog, monitoring government progress towards its targets on sustainable development. It also offers support, advice and appraisal on how to put issues of sustainability at the heart of government policy in the UK. It produces reports on economic, environmental and social issues, such as nuclear power.

Since February 2009, the SDC has been an executive non-departmental body (Executive NDPB) with its own legal identity. This means the SDC is not part of a government department and carries out its work without interference from government. The SDC's Commissioners are recruited as public appointments by the Prime Minister with the agreement of the devolved national parliaments.

The work of the SDC covers ten policy areas:

- climate change
- consumption
- economics
- education
- energy
- engagement
- health
- housing
- local and regional government
- transport.

Link

See page 288 of this unit to find out more about the role of the Sustainable Development Commission.

Assessment activity 34.2

Produce an article for the school/college newsletter which covers the following criteria:

1   Identify domestic and international legislation and guidelines which support reduction of damage to the environment. **P2**

2   Identify the role of the UK government departments and regulatory bodies in supporting sustainability. **P3**

3   Explain how the legislation and guidelines to support sustainability are supported by regulatory bodies. **M1**

Grading tips

- To achieve **P2** you will need to give examples of legislation and guidelines supporting sustainability, such as the EU Landfill Directive. You should also identify UK local and central government initiatives, giving examples to illustrate your response. Finally, you should describe key international initiatives, including the Kyoto Protocol and EU policies.

- To achieve **P3** you must include reference to the roles of the Environment Agency, Defra and the Sustainable Development Commission in supporting sustainability.

- For **M1** you should think about how regulatory bodies employ both positive encouragement to abide by sustainability guidance and potential sanctions for non-compliance.

PLTS

By explaining how the regulatory bodies support sustainability, you will show that you are a **reflective learner**.

By explaining how regulatory bodies employ both positive encouragement to abide by sustainability guidance and potential sanctions for non-compliance, you will demonstrate your abilities as a **creative thinker**.

Functional skills

If you word-process your article, this assignment may help you to develop your functional skills in **ICT**.

3. Understand the need for sustainable development

3.1 Concepts of sustainability

Development to meet present and future needs

Governments in the UK, the EU and internationally have woken up to the necessity for development to encompass both the needs of the present generation and those of the future. Sustainable development implies that the needs of both current and future generations can be balanced. However, we all experience conflicting needs in our lives; for example, we all need clean air but we also want access to motorised transport to take us to college or the shops. In the same way, individuals and companies seek to profit from the clearing of rainforest areas although this results in the loss of animal and plant species. Indeed, over half the deforestation which has occurred in Africa is the result of poor famers practising subsistence agriculture, so ensuring that they and their families do not starve.

- What happens when one country's desire for electricity produces acid rain that damages the rivers and lakes in another country?

- What is the outcome when the need of individual families for firewood conflicts with the need to conserve top soil and prevent erosion?

- How do we decide which needs are met? How do we balance these conflicting needs?

Sustainable development suggests that the ability to meet the needs of the future depends on how well we balance economic, social, and environmental objectives when making decisions today.

Sustainable consumption and production

Evidence shows that the **carbon footprint** of food production and consumption can vary greatly (see Table 34.3). Meat is the most energy-intensive to produce because it uses large quantities of water (a 150g hamburger takes 2400 litres of water to produce). Animals give off methane which contributes to global warming. Other contributors to the carbon footprint of food are transport and fertilisers, processing and packaging and keeping food chilled or frozen.

Did you know?

- 43 of the 100 bestselling products in UK supermarkets contain palm oil. Palm oil has contributed to the rainforest clearance in South-East Asia.

- 15 million hectares of tropical rainforest (an area larger than England) are lost every year through deforestation.

- Farmers in Brazil can make $300 per hectare by clearing rainforest and growing soya beans.

- Rainforests will have disappeared within the next 50 years unless the world takes action.

- Deforestation releases more carbon dioxide into the Earth's atmosphere than all the ships, cars and planes combined.

- Over 50 per cent of the world's animal and plant species are found in rainforests.

Key term

Carbon footprint – the amount of greenhouse gases produced in our day-to-day lives through the burning of fossil fuels for energy used in transport, heating and power.

Table 34.3: The carbon footprint of UK foods

Food	Kilogram of CO_2 for every kilogram of food produced
Lamb	17.0
Beef	16.0
Potatoes	0.5
Pork and chicken	6.0
Bread	0.9
Tomatoes	9.0
Chocolate bar	2.0
Pure fruit smoothies	8.4
Fizzy drinks	5.0

It is estimated that industrialised countries produce 25 per cent of their carbon dioxide emissions from the food they consume. In Sweden food labels now list the carbon dioxide emissions associated with that produce, from fast food burgers to pasta and vegetables. Guidance recommends carrots as being preferable to tomatoes and cucumbers (as they are grown in heated greenhouses). Increasing fish consumption is not recommended (to save Europe's depleted stocks), but Swedish consumers have been advised to replace red meat with beans or chicken. If the guidance is followed, Sweden could cut its carbon dioxide emissions from food production by up to 50 per cent.

Changing product and service design, production, use and recycling

Increased awareness of the environmental impact of different methods of production has caused many companies (and their customers) to modify their approach. One key issue that has been recently highlighted is packaging. Today UK consumers are increasingly looking to reduce packaging and buy products in packaging that can be recycled or refilled, or to purchase products that are concentrated (thereby requiring less packaging).

Germany produces 30 million tons of waste each year. The Green Dot system means that shops and manufacturers have to pay for excess packaging – the more packaging there is, the higher the tax. The result of this tax has been producers have used less metal, less paper and thinner glass in their packaging, which has in turn reduced the amount of packaging waste in Germany by one million tonnes a year. The Green

Manufacturers of electrical items and batteries are required to dispose of these safely, so must consider the materials used in manufacture carefully.

Dot system also means that customers can dispose of their excess packaging at the store before taking their purchases home.

Designing for the environment requires businesses to:

- assess the environmental impact of their product
- select materials with low environmental impact, such as recycled and recovered materials and those from renewable sources
- avoid hazardous or toxic materials
- select clean, lean manufacturing processes (i.e. those which cause minimal pollution and are based on energy efficient production; these are often linked to the Japanese 'kaban' system that minimises waste on the production line)
- produce with energy and water efficiency in mind
- design for minimum waste.

3.2 Impact of climate change

Reducing greenhouse gas emissions

As individuals living in the UK, we add to greenhouse gas emissions every day through our various activities. The main greenhouse gas responsible for climate change is carbon dioxide (CO_2), which is produced through the burning of fossil fuels for energy (for example, for heat, light, transport and power). By making small changes in our daily lives we can work to reduce this carbon footprint.

Activity: Carbon-friendly alternatives

Consider the table below.

Activity	Carbon-friendly alternative
Tumble-drying laundry	Hanging laundry outside to dry
Buying food imported from abroad	Buying local produce or growing your own food
Holidaying abroad	Holidaying in the UK
Drinking bottled water	Drinking tap water
Buying new clothes and furniture	Mending and repairing existing clothes and furniture

1 Explain how each of the alternatives listed in the table above would reduce greenhouse gas emissions.

2 Add five more examples to the chart. You may find the following websites useful:
- www.carbonfootprint.com
- http://actonco2.direct.gov.uk.

Preparing for climate change impact

It is thought that climate change will result in less predictable weather patterns in the UK, with more frequent droughts, storms and flooding. To help prepare for these impacts of climate change, the UK government is suggesting practical measures we can all take. These include:

- improved insulation of buildings to ensure heat loss is minimised; this will keep homes warmer in the winter months and cooler in the summer months

- saving water, for example by collecting rain water to use in the garden and not running the tap when cleaning teeth; by showering instead of having baths

- not paving over gardens for parking – this helps to prevent flooding because the soil soaks up rainwater

- keeping houses cool in the summer months by creating green spaces on roofs (plants absorb the sun's heat and provide shade).

Did you know?

More ideas about what you can do as an individual to help prepare for climate change can be found at www.direct.gov.uk/en/Environmentandgreenerliving.

3.3 Use of natural resources

Natural resources that sustain life

Water, air and unpolluted soil are essential to sustain human, animal and plant life. Human activity releases a number of substances into the atmosphere, many of which have a detrimental effect on the environment. Pollutants can accumulate in the water, air and soil.

- The main air pollutants come from burning fossil fuels, combustion engines and cigarette smoke. They include carbons, nitrates, sulphurs, particulates and benzene. These pollutants not only affect the air we breathe (and thus our respiratory and cardiovascular systems) but also return to the ground as acid rain, polluting the soil and rivers.

- Water becomes polluted from chemicals, oxygen-depleting wastes, plant nutrients and radioactive materials. Infectious agents such as parasitic worms and bacteria can get into the water from human and animal waste.

- The main sources of soil pollution are chemical waste (by-products of manufacture and farming or the products of landfill).

To sustain life on the planet in the long term, it is vital to ensure that pollution is managed and the effects of previous pollution identified and dealt with.

Did you know?

Concern about the impact of chemical pollutants, both on the food we eat and in terms of longer term soil pollution, is part of the rationale for the growth of the organic farming movement.

3.4 Building sustainable communities

The concept of building sustainable communities is based on the need to:

- look after land (both rural and urban) and the local environment
- develop in an energy-efficient way
- work in partnership with local communities and organisations.

The UK government launched *Sustainable Communities: Building for the future* in 2003. It set out a long-term plan to ensure sustainability in both rural and urban communities and to address regional imbalances in housing supply and demand. The aim is for development that meets the social, economic and environmental needs of both current and future generations. Some of the key issues raised were the need to protect the countryside, stop the wasteful use of land and reuse previously developed land.

Code for Sustainable Homes

The UK government's Code for Sustainable Homes was introduced in England in 2007. It is intended as an environmental impact rating system to guide industry in the design and construction of energy-efficient

What are the advantages and disadvantages of sustainable housing?

and sustainable housing. Standards have been set to improve energy efficiency in the planning, designing and building of both new and refurbished buildings. The Code also set the target for all new homes to be zero carbon by 2016. In addition, the refurbishment of existing housing has a big role to play in meeting long-term carbon reduction goals.

Case study: Energy efficient buildings in Aberdeen

In 1999 Aberdeen City Council (ACC) adopted an Affordable Warmth Strategy. Since then, a large part of their housing stock (over 26,000 properties) has been improved, with better insulation and heating systems. The key objectives of this work were a reduction in carbon emissions, sustainability and affordability.

Energy efficiency for the 59 multi-storey properties proved hard to tackle. To solve this problem ACC decided to pilot a Combined Heat and Power (CHP) project at Stockethill. This involved the use of a central boiler to heat a number of homes through a network of underground insulated pipes. The use of a central boiler brings benefits such as competitive fuel purchasing and the ability to use alternative energy supplies, including renewable energy.

Prior to the installation, tenants were paying between £7.80 and £15.00 a week for their water and heating and an average of £181 for electricity per year. After the introduction of CHP, tenants paid £4.75 per week for heat and water. Those choosing

to buy their electricity from the Aberdeen Heat and Power company paid £159 per year. Total fuel costs per household fell to £387 per year, or £7.44 per week, against previous costs of £18.48 per week.

1   **Research the ACC project at the following websites:**
    - www.aberdeencity.gov.uk (type 'City turned on to cheap efficient power' in the sites search engine)
    - www.energysavingtrust.org.uk (from the Home page, select the 'Business and public sector' tab then 'Information Centre'. Click on 'Publications and Case Studies' and in the Keywords search type 'Aberdeen City Council').

2   **What do you think are the advantages of this type of project?**

3   **What are the issues and problems local authorities and tenants might face in setting up this type of project?**

Developing green, open spaces

The distribution and quantity of open and green spaces in urban areas will be of increasing importance with global warming. The practice of individuals paving over their gardens to make drives for their cars is one example of how reducing open ground has contributed to flooding. Rainwater that would have been absorbed by the ground now flows off paved-over drives and has to be carried away by overloaded drainage systems. Legislation now requires that permeable materials must be used if gardens are to be made into drives and planning permission obtained.

An even distribution of various sized open and green spaces will help the future achievement of Natural England's Access to Natural Green Space in Towns targets, ensuring everyone has access to wildlife and green spaces within 300 metres of their homes.

3.5 Strategies for sustainable development

United Nation's Framework Convention on Climate Change (UNFCCC)

The UNFCCC was set up with the goal of stabilising the amount of greenhouse gases in the atmosphere so as to prevent dangerous climate change from human activity. The first convention was held in 1992 in Rio de Janeiro (and has since become known as the Rio Earth Summit), with 154 countries signing the agreement. Since then, 192 countries including the USA have ratified (approved) the convention.

Agenda 21

Agenda 21 is a comprehensive action plan to be followed by all UN members on a local, national and global level. It covers every area in which human activity impacts on the environment. It has been adopted by over 178 governments and its full implementation was reaffirmed at the Johannesburg World Summit on Sustainable Development (WSSD) in 2002.

Agenda 21 covers:

- economic and social issues such as poverty, the need to change consumption and the need to promote sustainability
- the management and conservation of resources including protecting biodiversity, fighting deforestation and controlling pollution
- the implementation of sustainability including education, technology transfer and science.

Link

UK and EU strategies for sustainability have been discussed earlier in this unit, on pages 286–8 and pages 289–93.

UK government strategies

Securing the Future (2005)

The UK government launched its original strategy for sustainable development in 1994. This was reviewed in 1999 and again in 2005, when *Securing the Future* was published.

Securing the Future aimed to provide clear direction and purpose in tackling the key issues of sustainability by working to achieve social, economic and environmental goals in unison. The strategy acknowledged the importance of working collectively across all UK government departments to implement the policy and lead by example. It also highlighted the need to work to change public attitudes and habits, for example the public perception that individual efforts were insignificant in tackling the 'global' issue of sustainability, by working with community groups and schools to spread its 'positive' message.

Since 2006, when the findings of the Stern Review (see page 281 and the case study opposite) were published, the UK government has accepted the findings and has used the report's recommendations to inform UK policies.

Sustainable consumption and production
- Achieving more with less by looking at how goods and services are produced.
- Reducing the inefficient use of resources.
- Breaking the link between economic growth and environmental degradation.

Climate change and energy
- Changing the ways in which the UK generates and uses energy.
- Reducing activities that release greenhouse gases.
- Preparing for the inevitable effects of climate change.

Priority areas for shared UK action on sustainability

Sustainable communities
- Giving local communities more power and say in the decisions that affect them.
- Tackling poverty and environmental degradation.

Natural resource protection and environmental enhancement
- Understanding environmental limits. Implementing recovery where it is needed.
- Ensuring a decent environment for everyone.

Figure 34.9: The priority areas for shared UK action identified in *Securing the Future* (2005)

Case study: Recommendations of the Stern Review

The 2006 Report on the Economics of Climate Change (the findings of the Stern Review) argued that climate change is a global problem demanding an immediate international response. The Report added that there is still time to reduce the worst impacts of climate change if humanity takes immediate action. Indeed, the Review found that the advantages of early and robust action far outweigh any economic costs, and lack of action could lead to a 5 per cent loss of global **GDP** each year.

The Stern Review proposed various key actions to reduce the greenhouse gas emissions that cause global warming. These include:

- expanding emissions trading schemes globally
- technology cooperation, including support for research into new low-carbon technologies
- action to reduce deforestation
- adaptation so that the poorest nations can integrate climate change policies into their development and the wealthiest countries increase support and overseas aid.

Do you think the recommendations of the Stern Review are sufficient to counter climate change?

Link

The case study on page 281 gives some of the main findings of the Stern Review.

Key term

GDP – gross domestic product. A country's overall economic output in terms of the value of goods and services made within that country in one year.

Did you know?

The Stern Review has been globally influential, informing the Copenhagen Climate Conference of 2009 (see page 290) and the Stern Symposium, held in Washington DC in March 2009. The Stern Symposium aimed to place a global perspective on the United States' climate change action plan, and was attended by chief executives of large US companies, academics and politicians.

UK local authorities Sustainable Community Strategies

As part of the implementation of *Securing the Future* (2005), UK local authorities are expected to build sustainability into all their activities. To this end, each local authority will have a published Sustainable Community Strategy which will be accessible on their website, as will all public sector organisations (for example the Prison Service strategy described in the case study on page 290).

Activity: Researching your local authority's SCS

Research the Sustainable Community Strategy for your local authority.

- How useful do you think it is?
- What do you think are the benefits of such a strategy?
- What might be the problems in implementing it?

3.6 Impact on public sector

Government policies

To achieve the international commitment for targets on reducing emissions and improving sustainability made by the UK government, it is vital that the UK public sector makes a substantial contribution.

Indeed, *Securing the Future* (2005) places emphasis on the role of public sector organisations in assisting the achievement of the strategy.

- Planning regulations now require public sector organisations to consider green buildings and technologies when undertaking development.
- Public sector organisations have also been set targets to reduce waste, water consumption and emissions from road travel.

Did you know?

The public sector in the UK employed 6,039,000 people at the end of June 2009 (*Source:* www.statistics.gov.uk.)

One area where the public sector is already showing impressive achievements is in ICT, as the case study below shows.

UK-wide targets for 80 per cent emissions reductions by 2050

The UK government set targets for 80 per cent emissions reductions by 2050 when the Climate Change Act (2008) was passed. This Act also established the Committee on Climate Change (CCC) as the independent body with responsibility for advising Parliament on progress made in reducing greenhouse gas emissions.

Case study: UK government green ICT policy – cutting its carbon footprint by 12,000 tonnes

It was estimated that the public sector's use of ICT is responsible for up to 20 per cent of carbon emissions generated by government bodies (460,000 tonnes annually). In 2008, 110 public sector organisations signed up to the government's Green ICT strategy. Its aim was to make public sector ICT carbon neutral within four years.

By September 2009 the UK government claimed it had saved £7 million through its green ICT policy and cut its carbon footprint the equivalent of taking 5000 cars off the road. Savings had been achieved by encouraging double-sided printing, switching off PCs at night and replacing computers less often.

Some notable successes included:

- The Crown Prosecution Service (CPS) saved £2.35 million by replacing computers and printers

every five years rather than every three, thus ensuring less hardware waste.

- The Department for International Development donated a thousand old laptops to charity for re-use in developing countries.
- The Home Office saved £2.4 million annually by removing unused ICT equipment which had been left on standby, thereby saving wasted power.
- The Department of Work and Pensions (DWP) saved 200 million sheets of paper by changing to double-sided printing.

1 **What do you think of the measures described?**

2 **What are the issues and problems for public sector organisations seeking to reduce their carbon footprint?**

Assessment activity 34.3

In this assignment you will need to review the targets set for public sector organisations in the UK and critically analyse the progress made.

1   Explain the impact of sustainable development on the UK public sector. **P6**

2   Justify the targets set for the public sector to contribute to improving sustainability. **M3**

3   Critically analyse UK public sector progress towards achieving strategies for sustainability. **D1**

Grading tips

- One way to approach **P6** is to research two or three specific organisations and use your findings to help illustrate your explanation.

- To achieve **M3**, you will need to identify what the targets are and then put forward an argument to support their worth. You will need to consider whether, at a time of overall constraint in public sector expenditure, the introduction of sustainability targets is justifiable. What costs, if any, would there be from not meeting those targets?

- For **D1** you will need to review some of the targets set in documents like *Securing the Future* (2005) and look for data to show whether the UK public sector is on target to achieve them. You should also consider whether the targets set in UK and EU strategies are sufficient to ensure that sustainability can be achieved.

PLTS

By explaining how the regulatory bodies support sustainability, you will show that you are a **reflective learner**.

When justifying and reviewing the setting of public sector targets, you will demonstrate your ability to be a **creative thinker**.

Functional skills

This assignment may help you to develop your functional skills in **English** and in **ICT** (if you word-process your answer).

3.7 Role of pressure groups

Most people in the UK (and indeed in the EU and internationally) now accept the need for sustainable development and to review the behaviour of individuals, industry, commerce and governments in achieving this. This acceptance has been brought about in part by the work and campaigning of a number of pressure groups. These groups work in a variety of ways to raise public awareness and place pressure on governments for change.

We will look at a few of these pressure groups in this section. However, when carrying out research for your assessment activities you will need to look at a broad range of groups whose activities link to the sustainability issues that engage you.

Raising public awareness

There are a large number of groups involved with campaigning for sustainability. These pressure groups campaign on a range of issues, many specific to endangered environments or species.

One example is the Energy Saving Trust, an independent UK organisation funded by government and industry, which promotes action to reduce man-made climate change. The organisation offers free information and advice to people in the UK on how to conserve water, reduce waste, be more energy efficient and make sustainable travel choices. It also provides help to individuals related to their personal circumstances, for example by directing individuals to sources of grants for insulation of their homes. Another element of its work is an Energy Saving Week, held each October to encourage households to stop wasting energy.

Influencing government policy

Part of the work of pressure groups is to write to and petition government ministers on key issues and for change. For example, Friends of the Earth is a UK-based pressure group that lobbies politicians and companies with an aim to change their attitudes to sustainability. Founded in 1971, it has successfully raised awareness on a whole range of environmental issues, including the launch of doorstep collections for recycling and encouraging drink manufacturers to reuse glass bottles. It is often called on to advise the UK government on policy issues.

In the UK, all mainstream political parties have now embraced (to some extent, at least) a green, sustainable agenda – and certainly the work of pressure groups such as Friends of the Earth has helped to achieve this.

Did you know?

Research by MORI in 2009 found that 10 per cent of UK voters felt the environment would be a key issue on which they would vote in future – up from 3 per cent at the time of the 2001 election.

Involvement in mainstream politics

The Values Party, founded in New Zealand in 1972, is considered the first national environmental political party. It contested the 1972 general election, with policies then considered radical, including zero economic and population growth. By 1975 it had won 5.3 per cent of the public vote in New Zealand.

Before the founding of the Values Party, there was little focus by political parties on environmental issues. Political lobbying was seen as the remit of pressure groups such as Greenpeace. Mainstream politicians generally failed to take such campaigns seriously. Indeed, in 1985 the French government authorised the sinking of the Greenpeace ship *Rainbow Warrior* in Auckland, New Zealand, with the aim of preventing the ship interfering in a nuclear test in Moruroa. A photographer was killed when the ship sank.

The Green Party in the UK and Europe

- The UK Green Party was founded in 1973. In the 2008 local elections the Greens received more votes in Norwich South than any other party, at 33 per cent. In the European Elections of 2009 the Green Party polled 8.7 per cent of the vote and two MEPs were elected. In the 2010 UK general election, Caroline Lucas was elected MP for Brighton Pavilion, becoming the first Green Party MP in the House of Commons.

- The German Green Party (Die Grünen) has been most successful electorally, comprising 49 MPs and being the third biggest political party in Germany.

- The Swedish Green Party (Miljöpartiet) polled 17 per cent in the 1995 EU elections.

- The Green Party in both Finland and Italy contribute to national government, holding the post of Minister for the Environment in both countries.

Campaigns and events

Early campaigns and events focused on issues such as animal protection and nuclear testing (such as the Greenpeace initiative mentioned above). However, as science has provided greater evidence of the potential impact of environmental issues (such as the use of fossil fuels and deforestation), a huge range of campaigns has grown up. Many of these are still organised and funded via charitable and third sector (non-government and non-profit-making) organisations, but an increasing number are sponsored by governments at international, European, national and local levels.

Case study: Love Food Hate Waste

In 2008 the pressure group Love Food Hate Waste found that shop-bought lunches cost UK employees over £5 billion a year, and at the same time almost the same value of lunch foods stored in our fridges are later thrown away. This means that over 2 million tonnes of food which could be used in packed lunches goes to landfill each year.

The Love Food Hate Waste campaign encouraged people to make a packed lunch instead of buying a shop-bought lunch. They argued that this could save each of us £120 every year and help to reduce the amount of food waste going to landfill.

1 **Find out about the work of Love Food Hate Waste by going to their website (www.lovefoodhatewaste.com).**

2 **Are you inspired to make changes in your life by this pressure group? Explain your answer.**

Local, national and international pressure group activity

There are various examples of pressure groups operating at the local, national and international levels to raise the awareness of individuals and organisations regarding sustainability issues.

- Freecycle is an international organisation with over 6 million members. Its purpose is to support members in reusing and recycling goods, so keeping them out of landfill. You can find out more by going to its UK website (www.uk.freecycle.org).

- Greenpeace is an international organisation which campaigns for a number of issues such as protecting oceans and forests, preventing climate change and promoting renewable energy. It focuses on international solutions to global problems, organising public campaigns and working with policy-makers and industry to bring about change. You can find out more by going to its UK website (www.greenpeace.org.uk).

Many local organisations also work to support sustainability by encouraging individuals and organisations to reduce waste, recycle and reuse. Links to your local organisations can often be found through your local authority website under waste and recycling.

Protests at Kingsnorth Climate Camp in March 2009.

Assessment activity 34.4

1 Create a PowerPoint presentation which outlines the need for sustainable development. **P4**

2 Create a leaflet which:

- explains the role of pressure groups in promoting sustainability **P5**
- analyses how pressure groups work to promote sustainability. **M2**

Grading tips

- To achieve **P4** you will need to define what sustainability means and the consequences of not embracing sustainable development, both for the UK and for the global economy.

- One approach to achieving **P5** would be to use a pressure group that is also a political party and a pressure group that focuses on campaigning activity and describe their roles both now and over the past 50 years (as the need to change to sustainable policies has gradually moved from minority to mainstream thinking). Use these examples to illustrate your answer. You will need to think about raising awareness of the public, corporations and government, pressure group campaigns and events, and other pressure group activities.

- To achieve **M2** you will need to develop your ideas from **P5** by analysing the way pressure groups have worked and how successful (or otherwise) they have been in raising awareness, influencing government policy and gaining representation in mainstream politics.

PLTS

By researching pressure groups and analysing their role in supporting sustainability, you will give evidence that you are a **reflective learner**.

Functional skills

Creating a PowerPoint presentation will help you develop your functional skills in **ICT**.

Jo Adesina
Environment Officer

I work closely with colleagues in the Environment Agency and organisations from both the public and private sectors, such as personnel from waste and water industries and agriculture. My key role is to ensure that the organisations I deal with comply with legislation. Although compliance is important, the role is much more focused on educating (both organisations and their staff) and carrying out testing and other checks when on site.

A typical day

Every day is really different. I spend a lot of time visiting sites and organisations. For example, one day last week I started by visiting a waste disposal site to check regulations were being followed. That was followed by a visit to a site where we are dealing with an investigation into an oil spillage pollution incident.

The next day I checked out a landfill site then visited a new company that provides information on waste minimisation and pollution prevention. Then it was back to the office to review reports, write letters and deal with phone messages and queries. This included preparing case files for an enforcement action against a company for failing to obey regulations.

I really like being out and about and meeting people. In this role good communication skills and a flexible approach are vital. I also need to make sure I keep up to date, as UK and EU legislation changes often and the advice I give has to be correct. I also attend regular training. My basic training covered the technical aspects of the job, but I've also been trained in techniques for carrying out investigations, including visits to sites, collecting evidence and preparing court cases.

When I'm out on site, I have to wear PPE (personal protective equipment). This includes a high visibility jacket and hard hat. Clearly on some of the sites I visit they have heavy vehicles moving about, so I have to be both protected and visible! When we are investigating a potential pollution incident we need equipment for accessing the polluted area, taking samples and keeping the samples safe while we take them back for testing.

The best things about the job

I love working outdoors and I'm passionate about protecting the environment, so the job meets both those needs! It's also very rewarding when the advice and support I give to a company helps them to safeguard the environment. On the other hand I get really angry when I see dead fish in a river polluted by chemical dumping or things like batteries and old tyres in a landfill.

Think about it!

- Why is it important that the work of Environment Officers involves liaison with a range of both public and private sector organisations?
- Why is education and prevention seen as more effective than enforcement action?

Just checking

1. Find definitions for each of the terms listed below:
   a) Air pollution
   b) Noise pollution
   c) Environmental impact
   d) Habitat
   e) Global warming
   f) Greenhouse effect
2. Briefly explain what the Kyoto Protocol aims to achieve.
3. Suggest three reasons why sustainable development is important.
4. Summarise the key points of Agenda 21.
5. The Stern Review has been very influential on government thinking both in the UK and internationally. What were the report's main recommendations?
6. Explain the roles undertaken by the Environment Agency in enforcing legislation and regulation.
7. How can the Code for Sustainable Homes contribute to sustainable development?
8. Give three examples of the impact of pollution and chemicals on human health.
9. Explain how the work DEFRA undertakes contribute to sustainability.
10. Describe the work of one pressure group involved in 'green' issues in your local community

edexcel

Assignment tips

- Plan your work. Before you start writing any assignment, decide how you will research the topics and how you will present your answer. You may find a mind map or spider diagram helps you with this.

- Make your own glossary of key words and definitions as you go along, so that you have your own quick reference guide always to hand.

- Keep a timeline of the key events. You could organise this into international, EU and UK dates and milestones.

- Always use reliable websites and textbooks for your research. All public service organisations have websites which have lots of useful information. For example, http://ec.europa.eu/environment/policy_en.htm would be an excellent starting point for finding out about the role of the EU and sustainability.

- Keep a detailed note of all the references you use (for example, include the date you accessed a website and the page numbers of reference books). This will help you when writing your bibliography.

Glossary

Accountable – required or expected to justify actions or decisions.

Acquitted – found not guilty of a crime.

Acrophonically – using a word as the name of the alphabetical symbol representing the initial sound of that word.

Advocate – the person who speaks on your behalf in court and presents your case. This can be a solicitor in Magistrates' Court but it is usually a barrister in Crown Court and the superior courts.

Aftercare – the short- or long-term care of victims of major incidents.

Aims – why you are going on the expedition.

Air pollution – anything that causes contamination of the air with harmful substances.

Airway – a plastic tube inserted in an unconscious person's throat via their mouth to ensure a clear airway during resuscitation.

Analogue technology – analogue is the process of taking an audio or video signal (often the human voice) and translating it into eletronic pulses. It is relatively inexpensive, but here are limits to the amount of data it can carry.

Anti-Semitic – characterised by hostility or prejudice towards Jewish people.

Arbiter – the person who is the independent third party during an arbitration, such as a judge.

Arbitration – when an impartial third party tries to assist the plaintiff and the defendant to come to a mutually acceptable outcome rather than pursuing the case any further.

Asbestos – fibre made from magnesium silicate which has various industrial uses, including fireproofing, electrical insulation and building materials. The inhalation of asbestos fibres has been linked to the development of cancers and lung disease. Since January 2005, the use and extraction, manufacture and processing of asbestos products has been banned in the European Union.

Audit – to examine financial accounts or business practices to check they are correct.

Avoidance behaviours – techniques that people use to avoid or evade conflict, communication and responsibility.

Bail – after being charged with an offence, bail is being granted liberty under certain conditions until the next stage in your case.

Barrister – a lawyer who acts as an advocate in court by speaking on their client's behalf and presenting their case to the court.

Bearing – a measurement of direction between two points. Bearing is usually given either a direction such as 'The hikers proceeded on a north-easterly bearing' or as a number based on the degrees of a compass, e.g. 'The ship travelled on a bearing of 36 degrees'.

Behaviourism – the study of human behaviour.

Bench – an area where a court has jurisdiction.

Biodiversity – variation among living organisms. This includes diversity within species, between species and of ecosystems.

Breach – to break or violate a law, agreement or other regulation. Also, failing to fulfil a duty or obligation.

Bronze Command – (also known as Operational command) located at the scene and involves the rescue operation by the emergency services and other agencies.

Brownfield land – previously developed land, which may or may not be contaminated.

Calibrated – marked into smaller divisions, such as millimetres or degrees.

Carbon – a chemical found in all life on Earth. Different forms of carbon have different uses; for example, hydrocarbons are found in crude oil and natural gas.

Category 1 responders – the organisations that are at the centre of planning and responding to an emergency. Category 1 responders are the emergency services (Police, Fire and Ambulance), local authorities and the Health Protection Agency.

Category 2 responders – these include the Highways Agency and the utility companies (gas, water and electricity).

Censorship – the examination of books, films, news, etc., that are about to be published and the suppression of any parts that are considered obscene, politically unacceptable or a threat to security.

Circuit judge – sits in either County Court or Crown Court and is based on one of the six court circuits in England and Wales.

Civil court – a law court which deals with the private affairs of citizens such as marriage and property ownership.

Cognitive – relating to the mental processes by which a person can know, become aware of and make decisions about their self and their environment.

Conditioned response – behaviour an organism has learned to carry out in response to a conditioned stimulus.

Conditioned stimulus – an environmental factor that an organism can be taught to respond to in a certain way.

Confederate – someone who takes part in a study but is not a genuine participant. Confederates are given instructions by the researcher to play a specific role.

Control measures – the preventative measures you put into place to try and make sure that the hazard doesn't cause a high risk. For example, a control measure on a busy road is a zebra crossing; control measures when abseiling are a safety harness and a helmet.

Controlled drug – any substance whose availability and use is restricted by law. Controlled drugs are organised into categories depending on their usefulness as a medicine and their potential for misuse (dependency).

Core competencies – basic or key skills.

Coroner's Court (inquest) – an enquiry into sudden, unnatural and suspicious deaths.

Court of the first instance – the court that has primary jurisdiction over a case. It is the court where the offence will first be tried.

Curfew – a set deadline by which young people have to return to a certain place such as their home. An order that children under a certain age must not be out on the streets after a certain time in the evening, usually between 6 pm and 9 pm depending on the age of the child.

Custody – the exercise of power to deprive a person of his or her liberty.

Debrief – to question participants in detail after an incident.

Defendant – the person or organisation that is accused or being sued.

Degrade – break down, decompose.

Democracy – a political system in which a government is either carried out by the people (direct democracy) or the power to govern is granted to elected representatives (republicanism).

Deregulation – when the media is freed from the controls and constraints that might be imposed on them from an outside body, such as a regulator or the government.

Detained – held in custody.

Digital technology – breaks the signal into binary code (a series of '1's and '0's) and sends it to the device at the other end (phone, modem, etc), which reassembles the code into the original signal. Because digital technology corrects any errors that occur during transfer, there is less distortion than with analogue, and digital can also carry much more data.

Disaster – great or sudden misfortune.

Dispensation – exemption from a rule or usual requirement.

DNA – deoxyribonucleic acid. Genetic coding, found in the body's cells.

Double jeopardy – the rule which prevents defendants being tried twice for the same crime. It is expected to be scrapped in murder cases after a major inquiry published by the Law Commission.

Duty of care – responsibility to ensure the safety of self and others.

Duty solicitor – a solicitor whose services are available to a person suspected or charged with a criminal offence for free.

Dynamic security – the Prison Service describes dynamic security as the process of looking for patterns in intelligence, close monitoring of gang members, sharing of information, building close relationships with external agencies and partnerships to share intelligence, along with tackling the drug and violence issues.

Emergency plan – a detailed outline of the procedures to be followed in the event of an emergency.

Emergency planning – preparing for foreseen and unforeseen emergency incidents.

Empirical – knowledge gained from observation and experiment.

Environment Agency – UK government agency that aims to protect and improve the environment and promote sustainable development.

Epidemic – the spread of disease throughout a community. It is normally contained within that area.

Exempt – free from the same obligations as others.

Expedition – any journey that has a clear and defined purpose.

External audit – audit undertaken by a government department, inspectorate or organisation working on the government's behalf. External audits are usually published.

Extradite – when the government of one country sends a citizen accused of a crime to stand trial for that crime in another country. For example, the Lockerbie bomber was sent from Libya to face trial in the UK.

Fixed penalty notice – a set penalty issued on the spot by the Police, usually an amount of money.

Forensic examination – a detailed examination of a crime scene, or of material gathered from a crime scene, using scientific techniques. The results of this investigation may be presented as evidence in a court case.

Formative review – the process of reviewing the effectiveness of an action while the action is ongoing. An example would be gathering feedback from your expedition team members during your planning and execution so that the expedition can be improved on a continuous basis.

Fossil fuels – fuels formed by natural resources, such as decaying organic matter.

Fraud – an act of deception intended for personal gain or to cause loss to another person.

Free will – the ability to choose one's actions free of external constraints.

General audit – this may be undertaken internally or by an external body. It would include benchmarking performance against other public and private sector organisations.

Gold Command – (also known as strategic command) where the plans, or strategies, are drawn up by the senior officers to attempt to bring a successful conclusion to an emergency. This command is located away from the scene of the incident – usually at Police headquarters.

Greenfield land – undeveloped land, including countryside and green belt areas.

Habitat – the place where an organism lives.

Hazards – anything that may cause harm, such as chemicals, working at height, river crossings or fire.

Highways Agency – branch of the Department of Transport responsible for managing traffic and dealing with congestion and traffic problems on the motorways and other main roads in England.

HM Coroner – the person who holds inquests into deaths that are thought to be of a violent or accidental nature.

Holistic – the view that you cannot understand something by looking at its component parts in isolation, but only by looking at the fully functioning organism or system as a whole.

Human trafficking – the movement of people across borders, usually by force or deception, in order to exploit them for financial gain.

Indictable offence – a serious criminal offence which must be tried in Crown Court.

Inferior judges – circuit judges, district judges and other judicial officers.

Institutionalised racism – when people within a group or organisation share a collective view or approach that includes discriminating against those from a different race or ethnic background.

Internal audit – audit undertaken by personnel employed by or working on behalf of the public service organisation. It is not usually published for the general public.

Judicial immunity – when judges are protected from the legal consequences of their decisions.

Judiciary – the collective name for the judges who work in courts and decide on legal cases.

Jurisdiction – a court's authority to hear and decide on a case.

Jury tampering – when a jury's decision about a defendant's guilt or innocence might have been influenced by financial bribes or intimidation.

Kettling – the penning in of protesters to a confined area and not allowing them to leave for significant periods of time.

Lay magistrate – 'lay' in the context of magistrates means 'ordinary'. Lay magistrates are ordinary people who volunteer and are trained for the role.

Layering – having enough clothing so that you can mix and match items and add or remove clothing, depending on the weather conditions.

Legislation – law which has been created and enacted by a governing body, such as the government.

Local Resilience Forum – a meeting of the emergency services and other invited agencies who are brought together to discuss emergency planning issues so that the community is prepared and ready to return to normal in the event of a major incident. (To be resilient means to quickly bounce back to normal after a shock or upheaval.)

Logistics – the detailed coordination of a large and complex operation.

Major incident – an event or situation which threatens serious damage to human welfare in a place in the UK, the environment of a place in the UK, or war or terrorism which threatens serious damage to the security of the UK.

Malicious – intending to do harm.

Manslaughter – killing committed without the intent. Manslaughter is considered a less serious crime than murder, which is killing another with intent.

Matrix system – a system of digital instructions and directions on motorways that inform motorists of hazards and diversions.

McKenzie friend – a member of the chaplaincy, a probation officer, a tutor or a fellow prisoner.

Measuring wheel – a special wheel-shaped device which allows you to measure long distances on the ground by pushing it along.

Mediator – a person who acts to help solve disputes between others.

Mercury – a silver poisonous metallic liquid. It has various industrial uses, for example in thermometers, paints, batteries and pesticides. Use of mercury has dropped since the 1980s, when people began to understand its harmful effects on human health.

Microblogging – a form of blogging which uses much smaller pieces of content. It may be just a sentence, an image or a video fragment. Twitter is a form of microblogging.

Mitigate – to reduce or lessen.

Mnenomic – a pattern of letters or words that aids memory.

Modulating electromagnetic waves – radio transmitters cannot all send out the exact same message on the same carrier wave. If they did, all you would hear on your radio would be a garbled, mixed-up version of all the transmissions. So that each wave doesn't overlap with others, it is modulated, or changed, to make it unique from other signals. This is why you can pick out specific stations on your AM/FM radio.

Moral panic – the public expression of concern that results from media coverage of an event.

MP3 players – devices that use audio compression technology originally developed in the 1990s to decrease the size of music files, without compromising quality.

Navigable – to navigate. In Low's Gully, the team thought the expedition looked straightforward to navigate – therefore they thought it was navigable.

Negative reinforcement – when the rate of a learned behaviour decreases following the application of a conditioned stimulus.

Negligent – lack of proper care or attention.

Network – groups of equipment, individuals and agencies acting together to increase efficiency and effectiveness through shared information and resources.

Neurology – the scientific study of the nervous system.

Nitrates – chemicals used in the manufacture of a range of medicines. However, if they reach rivers and the sea they can pollute water causing illness in humans and animals and the death of fish and other marine life.

Objectives – what you are hoping to get out of the expedition by the end.

OECD countries – those nations which have joined the Organisation for Economic Co-operation and Development.

Ozone – a gas found throughout the atmosphere, but mainly in a band between 15 km and 40 km above the Earth's surface. This ozone layer protects the Earth from harmful ultraviolet radiation and is vital for life on our planet. Ozone acts as a greenhouse gas at lower levels, helping trap heat, and so contributes to global warming.

Pandemic – the outbreak and spread of an infectious disease over a large geographic area.

Permafrost – ground that is permanently frozen.

Phobia – intense fear of something.

Physical security – ensuring the physical prison environment is secure by the use of entry gates, walls, bars, locks and CCTV (closed circuit television).

Physiology – the scientific study of the body's physical, biochemical and mechanical systems.

Plaintiff – the person or organisation claiming to be a victim.

Plea before venue – the process by which it is decided in which court a criminal case will be heard.

Podcast – a series of audio or video media files that are released periodically and can be downloaded. The files can then be stored on a computer, iPod or other device, ready to be used offline.

Pollution – the introduction into an environment of harmful substances, such as industrial waste, chemicals, heat and noise, as a result of human activities (either intentional or accidental). Pollution results in negative effects which may harm ecosystems, endanger the health of humans and other life, and impact on the enjoyment of legitimate uses of the environment.

Populism – supporting, or seeking to appeal to the concerns of ordinary people.

Positive regard – the sense of acceptance or approval one person has for another.

Positive reinforcement – when the rate of a learned behaviour increases following the application of a conditioned stimulus.

Precedence – when a particular legal decision becomes binding on future similar cases.

Prevention of conflict – identifying a problem that might be occurring early enough for it to be resolved quickly and easily.

Primary Care Trust – a statutory body that provides healthcare by bringing together medical personnel and resources to improve the health of the people they serve.

Prison adjudicators – deal with offences and charges against prisoners.

Privatisation – when the media is privately-owned as opposed to being owned by the government. For example, if the UK decided to sell the BBC to private investors.

Procedural security – the identification, establishment, enforcement and audit of security policies.

Prosecute – take legal proceedings against someone for breaking the law.

Prosecution – when legal proceedings are established against a person or organisation.

Prosocial behaviour – actions intended to benefit others and not for personal gain.

Psychodynamic – psyche means mind, and psychodynamic theory views the mind as exerting a powerful influence on human behaviour in terms of an individual's motivation and drives.

Psychological – relating to mental states and emotions rather than the physical body.

Public enquiry – an open investigation held in front of a public audience by a government body in the UK or Ireland. Interested members of the public and organisations may make written submissions as evidence, as well listen to evidence given by other parties.

R v Howell – in criminal law, cases are written as R v Smith or R v Jones. The R stands for Rex if a king is on the throne and Regina if a queen is on the throne. The v stands for versus, and then the surname of the person who is accused of the crime, such as Smith or Jones, is given.

Reasonable suspicion – Police officers must have reasonable grounds to suspect you have been, currently are, or will be involved in a criminal act.

Remand – If you are placed on remand it means you are imprisoned until your trial.

Repressed – information or experiences that are buried deep in the mind such that the individual concerned is not aware of their existence.

Resuscitation – action taken to revive a person who is not breathing

Right of audience – for potential High Court judges, this is the legal right to act as a lawyer in the High Court. For potential circuit judges it is the right to appear in court as an advocate.

Risk – the chance that someone might be harmed from a hazard.

Risk assessment – an evaluation of the seriousness of the hazard or threat, the likelihood of harm occurring and the measures needed to reduce the hazard or threat.

Roamer – a small ruler on the side of a compass, calibrated for measuring distances.

Satellite uplink – a communication system that creates a link between a transmitter on Earth and a satellite in space. The satellite can then transmit the information to another location.

Scientific methodology – a rational method of investigation based on recording observable and measurable evidence. Scientists seek to record data about the environment and in this way test theories and draw conclusions.

Self-actualisation – the achievement of a person's potential in life.

Served – when a person involved in a court case is provided with documents or requests to appear at court.

Silver Command – (also known as tactical command) the link between Gold and Operational command. It is closer to the scene, usually in an outer cordon.

Social influence – when a person's thoughts or actions are affected by other people.

Solicitor – lawyer who deals with a whole range of legal matters.

SSSI – Site of Special Scientific Interest; environmentally protected areas within the UK.

Strike off – when a professional organisation such as The Law Society can remove a solicitor from an approved list of practitioners. It effectively removes the solicitor's right to practice law.

Submissive behaviours – techniques that people use to defer to the opinions of other people who are seen as having more power. It is a means by which people avoid taking responsibility.

Sue – to institute legal proceedings against a person or institution, typically for redress (financial compensation).

Sulphates – compounds of sulphuric acid. They are used in the manufacture of a whole range of products including medicines and building materials. They dissolve easily in water and contribute to acid rain.

Summary jurisdiction – responsibility for less serious criminal matters.

Summative review – the process of reviewing an action and making judgements about its effectiveness when the action is complete. An example of this would be gathering feedback from the expedition participants at the end of the expedition.

Summons – a formal request to attend court.

Superior judges – judges who operate in the superior courts, such as the Court of Appeal or the High Court.

Sustainability – meeting the current needs of society without compromising the ability of future generations to meet their own needs.

Sustainable – able to continue over long periods of time.

Tabloid – a newspaper which is designed to provide a very broad overview of news and may focus on particular stories which are scandalous or entertaining rather than particularly newsworthy. A broadsheet provides more in depth coverage of the news focusing more on issues such as politics or the environment rather than entertainment.

Teambuilding – strategy whereby teams work together in a different setting, for example while undertaking an outdoor sports activity, in order for them to understand how other team members work best.

Terrain – the territory you are travelling over, such as a hill, mountain or path. It can also refer to the conditions underfoot. For example, if the terrain is rough there may be lots of loose rocks around; if the terrain is boggy then it will be wet and muddy.

Test case – a legal case that requires a judge to make a decision on a case, and which might have large scale repercussions and lead to many other similar cases being brought to the courts.

Threat – something that is likely to cause harm.

Tort law – the branch of law that covers civil wrongs, such as trespass or product liability.

Traverse – to travel or cross terrain.

Triable either way offences – offences that can be tried in either the Magistrates' Court or the Crown Court.

Triage – assessing the condition of casualties and attending to the most serious first.

Trust – a legal arrangement where one party transfers the ownership of assets to another party who manages the assets for the benefits of others. It is sometimes used in place of a will.

Unconditioned response – a behaviour we perform automatically, such as scratching an itch.

Under caution – an interview where you are informed of your rights. Information provided while under caution can be used in court as evidence.

Vetting – process of checking prospective jury members to ensure they meet the eligibility criteria.

Vindicate – clear of blame or suspicion.

Volumetric control – the amount of property a prisoner is allowed in their cell is measure by volume. Property must fit within those set guidelines.

Warrant – a legal document signed by a judge instructing the Police to carry out a particular action, for example carrying out an arrest or searching a suspect's property.

Water cycle – the continuous movement of water on, above and below the surface of the Earth, as it evaporates into the air, condenses into clouds, and returns to Earth as rain, snow, sleet or hail.

Wicking – the movement of moisture away from the body to the outside of a fabric, which helps keep you warmer and dryer. Not all materials wick so it makes sense to choose expedition or sports clothes that do.

Wild camping – camping in the countryside, not at a campsite. This needs to be done carefully so that you do not cause problems for livestock or farmers.

Writ – a document starting an action in the High Court. It tells the defendant who the plaintiff is and why they are making a claim.

Index